NORMAN'S PLAN
OF
NEW ORLEANS & ENVIRONS
1854
B. M. NORMAN, PUBLISHER
JEFFERSON CITY
FIRST DISTRICT
SECOND DISTRICT
THIRD DISTRICT
FOURTH DISTRICT
1st Ward
2d Ward
3d Ward
4th Ward
5th Ward
6th Ward
7th Ward
8th Ward
9th Ward
10th Ward
MISSISSIPPI RIVER

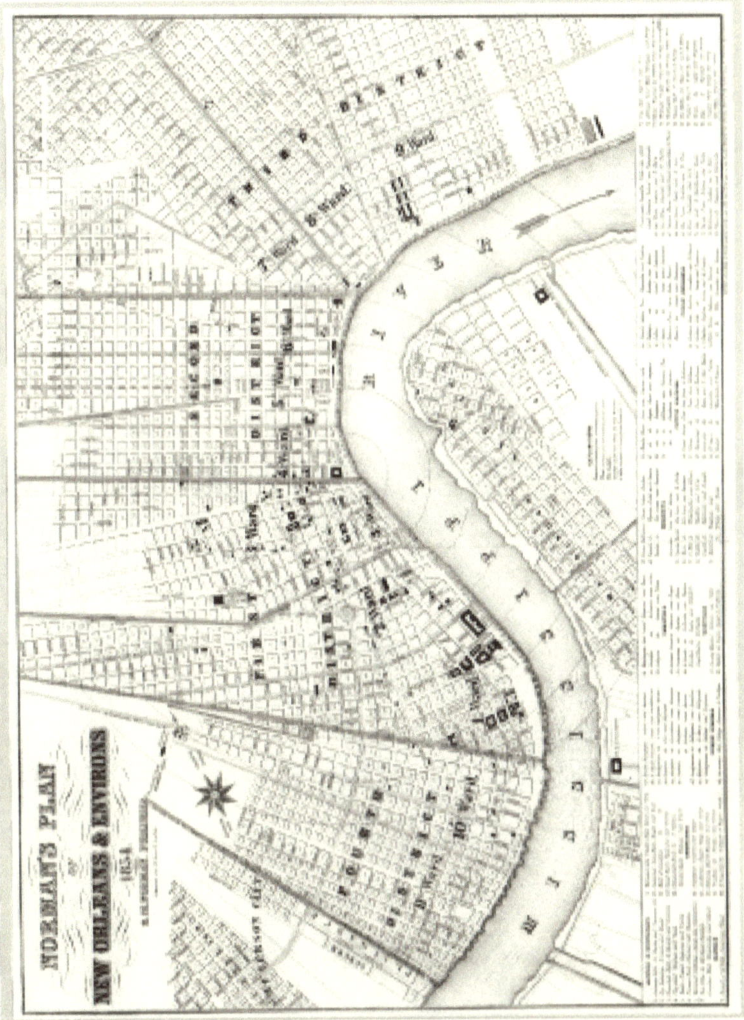

PRAISE FOR *DRAUSIN AND JOSEPHINE*

"With exquisitely rendered detail, John Wulsin brings to life the story of Drausin and Josephine whose journey meanders and flows like the Mississippi River itself. It is a saga of ancestry and possibility, sultry as a bayou, as tangled and exotic as Spanish moss. For anyone interested in teasing out America's roots, this is a must-read."

- Terry Gamble, author of *The Eulogist*, *Good Family*, and *The Water Dancers*

"John Wulsin has composed a vibrant, multi-generational novel. Meticulously researched, lyrically written, *Drausin and Josephine: We Too Shall Pass* navigates from New Orleans to Cincinnati. This jambalaya of a story brims with musicality, authenticity, and most satisfying savor."

- David Sloan, author of *Stages of Imagination*, *Earth School*, and *The Irresistible In-Between*

"In this finely wrought and engaging debut novel, John Wulsin's great gift is his eloquent comprehension of humanity caught both in the currents of history and the passing of time, ever-changing while staying the same. In scope and depth of compassion, *Drausin and Josephine: We Too Shall Pass* invites comparison with the works of James McBride and Isabel Wilkerson."

- Bruce Coffin, author of *The Long Light of Those Days* and *Among Familiar Shadows*

"This teeming, cosmopolitan first novel, *Drausin and Josephine: We Too Shall Pass*, ribbons through both space and time."

- Sarah Bird, author of *Daughter of a Daughter of a Queen*, *Last Dance on the Starlight Pier*, and *The Flamenco Academy*

"John Wulsin has the gift. His sentences sing with erudite perfection, and his characters seem to enter the page cradling years of old souls inside them. It is a joy, a discovery of personalities and places to read about the saga of a family traveling north to Cincinnati to escape racism by passing from Black to White."

— Dede Reed, author of *Velvet Spring* and *The Turkish Girl*

DRAUSIN

AND

JOSEPHINE

WE TOO SHALL PASS

JOHN H. WULSIN JR.

atmosphere press

I dedicate this book to all members of families who have
ever felt lost, wondering what their story actually is.

And to Barthelemy and Adelaïde.

However early a lie sets out,
even if truth sets out in the evening,
truth will catch up with lie.

—WOLOF PROVERB

CONTENTS

PART 3

THE PATTERNS OF OAK BRANCHES
INFORM THE ACORN AND ENSUING
GENERATIONS OF TREES.

FAMILY TREE—BACAS

Jean-Baptiste Manuel Bacas (1739-1817)
— Marie Louise Catherine Landrony (1756-1796)

Arnaldo Bacas (1778-c.1783)

Barthelemy Bacas (1780-1858)
— Adelaide Pouponne Beaulieu (1783-1855)

Joseph Valmont (1807-1862)
— Anne Louise Essayleme

Adhemar, Maria, Henry, Paul

Luisa (1809) — ?

Jean-Baptiste (1812-1885) — Rose Selina Saulay

Richard

Drauzin Valsin Bacas (1813-1863)
— Josephine Young (1818-1898)

Barthelemy Bacas (b&d. 1838)

Aline Adelaide Bacas (Wulsin) (1839-94)

Drauzin Bacas (Wulsin) (1842-1910)

Lucien Bacas (Wulsin) (1845-1912)

Eugene Bacas (Wulsin) (1847-1864)

Laure Bacas (Wulsin) (1849-1902)

Clarence Wulsin (1853-1897)

Lillie Alice Eve Wulsin (1856-1928)

Mary Josephine Wulsin (1858-1866)

Ademar H. Wulsin (1861-1862)

FAMILY TREE—BACAS

(10 children, of whom seven survive into adulthood,
Josephine started age 20, 1838-61=23 years)

 Adelaide Emilia (1817-?) — Andre Heno

 Marie Josephine Felicie Bacas (1820-1908)
 — Hurter Paul Livermore

 Leon (1821-?)

 Felix Bacas (1823-1824)

 Elizabeth Coelina (1826-?)
 —Pierre Fredrick Le Rond

Marie Luisa (1783-1809)
— Dominique Cossé, dit Chevalier (1762...)

 Marie Josephine Cossee — Firmin Berthelot

 Dominique Cossée (1807-1819)

 Jean-Baptiste Cossée — Adele Dubois

 Barthelemy Cossée (1807-1818)

 Luisa Cossée

Leon (1785) — Marie Celeste Tregre

 Jean-Baptiste (b&d. 1809)

 Marie-Euphremie (1811-1812)

 Anatole (1814)

FAMILY TREE—TASSY

Lt. Joseph Tassy (?-1794) — Marie-Francoise Lalande

Josephine Tassy (1790-1868) — Samuel Charles Young II

Samuel Charles Young IV (1812—1869)

Joseph Samuel Young (1816-1817)

Philippe Young (1816?-?) — Adèle

**Josephine Tassy Young (1818-1898)
—Drauzin Valsin Bacas (1813-1863)**

Barthelemy Bacas (b&d. 1838)

Aline Adelaïde Bacas (**Wulsin**) (1839-94)
m. Michael V. Daly()

Drauzin Bacas (**Wulsin**) (1842-1910)
m. Julia Carson

Margaret Wulsin

Lucien Bacas (**Wulsin**) (1845-1912)
— Katherine Roelker

Lucien Wulsin II (1888-1964)

Frederick Roelker Wulsin (1891-1960?)

FAMILY TREE—TASSY

Eugene Bacas (**Wulsin**) (1847-1864)

Laure Bacas (**Wulsin**) (1849-1902)

Clarence Wulsin (1853-1897) — Cecilia...

Robert Wulsin

Cecilia Wulsin

Lillie Alice Eve Wulsin (1856-1928)

Mary Josephine Wulsin (1858-1866)

Ademar H. Wulsin (1861-1862)

Josephine Tassy (1790-1868) — Simeon Mathé (?-1835?)

Louis [Francois?] Mathé

Melinda Macerte Mathé — ...Dawson

Simeon Brou Mathé — Florida Marie Reggio

Raphael Simeon Mathé — Dorrestine Reggio

PART I

CHAPTER I:
UNION, 1836

Though it was January, the camellias were blooming in New Orleans outside the Church of St. Rose de Lima, blushing pink even in the dusk. That early Monday evening, January 20, 1836, forty-five-year-old Josephine Tassy Mathé, who had finally been allowed to marry just three years earlier, wore black to her daughter's wedding. She raised her widow's veil in the late light as she entered the church up Bayou Road on the arm of her second-born son, Philippe Young. Last dusk allowed reds, yellows, and blues of the window-panes to faintly stain the shade growing above candlelight.

Increasingly disappointed during her ten years with Philippe's father, Samuel Charles Young II, Josephine Tassy had become equally fulfilled and blessed during her ten years with Simeon Mathé. She missed Simeon like a wound, yet she glowed with both the actuality of their union and the public distinction granted their marriage. The Crescent City experienced her now as the Veuve Mathé—Widow Mathé—respectably. And Josephine Tassy Mathé's heart was full of joy for her daughter, Josephine Tassy Young.

As she took her seat in a pew near the altar, Veuve Mathé smiled and nodded at Adelaïde Pouponne Beaulieu, seated across the aisle with her Barthelemy Bacas. In her sympathy for Adelaïde, Josephine couldn't help thinking it would be truer for Bacas's *s* to hiss rather than remain silent.

Adelaïde, fifty-three years old, returned the nod, noting Josephine Tassy's silk dress, though a somber red-tinged black, like a glowing coal, was beautifully cut, reflecting her natural elegance. Adelaïde, her own dress a muted cedar, was thrilled for her and Barthelemy's son, Drauzin Valsin Bacas. Did this mother of nine wish that she and her beloved Barthelemy could have enjoyed their own wedding in Cathedral St. Louis? Yes, certainly. Had the law allowed. But both her loyal love of Barthelemy, as difficult as he could be, and the bounty of their surviving eight children were riches far beyond what she had ever dared imagine in her enslaved youth. Adelaïde chuckled inwardly at the thought of her long-departed Muslim Wolof grandmother, born in Senegal, seeing her here inside the Catholic church.

Drauzin, twenty-three, entered from the side of the nave to stand near the altar, elegant in his dove-grey morning coat, with his best man, brother Jean-Baptiste. They watched their eldest brother seat his wife and three-year-old son before continuing his usher duties. The bridesmaids shimmered lavender in the evening candlelight in their silk gowns, each holding posies of white gardenias. standing by Jean-Baptiste and Drauzin. Then the young ringbearer ushered in the two flower girls, each in their lavender dresses. The organ started playing the processional; the congregation rose to its feet.

As patriarch Barthelemy Bacas watched Samuel Charles Young IV "father" his sister the bride down the aisle, his scarred, calloused hand squeezed Adelaïde's; he was also content with this new union. Considering who his son Drauzin was, this lovely, quiet, yet strong Josephine seemed a fortunate fit, clearly Drauzin's choice.

The Veuve Josephine Tassy Mathé was equally proud and fulfilled, beholding her two-fold brood, her Youngs up front, her five-year-old Mathé at her side. Josephine felt her beloved, recently departed Simeon merging with her and their youngest leaning back on her now, soon to settle into her lap. Across the aisle, Adelaïde was sensing her first born, who had died his first year, at her breast and shoulder. These two mothers of many each felt her own long-departed mother as well, like moon-glow.

Bride Josephine proceeded, bounteous bouquet of scent-exuding gardenias, white roses, and lilies preceding her, shimmering gold-white satin gown cut across just below the shoulders, gigot sleeves billowing voluminously from shoulder to elbow while her waist tapered narrowly. A white satin train, attached at the shoulders and belted at the high waist, flowed behind her floor-length gown; the whole gesture of her lovely neck rising from her open shoulders suggested a white flower opening sumptuously, generously, as she glided on her brother's arm toward her handsomest man.

When they arrived at the altar, brother Samuel raised his sister's white veil, kissed her cheek, and joined the band of brothers at the groom's side. Josephine's hair, parted in the middle, cascaded shining black corkscrew curls down either side, and a band of white lace haloed her one pearl hung in the middle of her forehead like a drop of dew. Josephine, glowing like moon become sun, handed her bouquet to her maid-of-honor and stepped forward beside Drauzin. She stole a glance at her beloved, handsome face shining, standing firm and resolute. She felt his left hand reach for her right one; he gave a gentle squeeze.

Back a few rows on Josephine's side sat a short but forceful young man, soldier-straight, lip crinkled, left eye twitching, jaw set under its first black mustache. His right fist clenched. Back a few more rows sat a stately lady, resplendent in emerald-green gown and golden shoes, her abundant hair artfully arranged by her own skilled hands. Beside her, the city's handsomest man and finest fencer sat regally in his finest charcoal-grey frock coat and leggings, his hat beside him.

"Welcome to the sacrament of the holy marriage of Drauzin and Josephine," intoned the priest with a pleasing combination of ageless reverence and youthful enthusiasm. Dusk had long gone; the glow was all candlelight, tinged with frankincense. All the faces reflected and enhanced the candlelight. The altar was the heart of it all. The city listened through the hallowed walls.

When Drauzin Valsin Bacas and Josephine Young completed their vows to each other, the priest looked to the heavens and raised his arms, concluding, "In nomine Patris et Filli et Spiritus Sanctus, amen." In the name of the Father and the Son, and of the Holy Spirit, amen. Bride and groom exchanged rings—double interlocking bands of gold with "J Y + D V B 20 Jan, 1836" inside each. They kissed and turned, holding hands, to face the congregation. Before they stepped down the aisle they beamed at family and friends, who radiated back at them. Drauzin's smiling uncle Nonc Fulsain Bacas, their parents and siblings, nieces and nephews, old, young, and in between.

The one exception, soldier-stiff, stared icily. But his silent disapproval was of no matter. As Drauzin and Josephine emerged, arm in arm, they basked both in the candled glow of the grand church of St. Rose de Lima and in the bounteous blessings from their people.

Neither had a clue how strongly they would later need such sustenance.

CHAPTER 2:

TASSY, 1791

The Josephines' family liked to say they reached way back to royalty, which they did after a fashion. It might be truer to say they reached into royalty.

The story is, one of her ancestors, Francois Felix de Tasty, had been the personal surgeon of King Louis XIV of France. He was so successful that, upon retirement, his son Charles-Francois Felix inherited the responsibility, also successfully, until one day a crisis threatened the monarchy. Charles-Francois Felix successfully removed an anal fistula from King Louis XIV, thereby saving the life of the Sun King, a feat celebrated in two ways. Drawings of the royal fistula circulated widely among Louis's circles. And consequently Charles-Francois Felix de Tasty was ennobled in 1690. His blood became blue and he prospered.

A century later the French Revolution declared "Liberté, Egalité, Fraternité" to be rights for all men. In New Orleans, Marie-Françoise Lalande, a quarter-Negro free woman of color, a "quadroon," had been born the grandchild of a Mali-born slave. Marie's mother was considered "mulatto," half white, half black, a term derived from "mule," the neuter offspring of a horse and a donkey. Marie gave Canadian émigré Guillaume-Michel Perreault a son, Firmin. Marie-Françoise's own white grandfather had also originally hailed from Quebec. When forty-years-older Perreault died in 1790, his will freed all his slaves and left several properties to Marie-Françoise Lalande, who kept his son and took his name, Perreault.

Also in 1790, a Joseph Tassy, age thirty-three, served in New Orleans as witness in a legal suit between two slavers (frigate owners). Joseph, a blue-blooded armateur, equipper of sailing vessels, a lieutenant auxiliaire, was a privateer slaver himself, plying the triangle of trade between Bordeaux, Ivory Coast, and the Caribbean. Lieutenant Joseph Tassy fell in love with Marie-Françoise Lalande Perreault. Although the Tassy surname appears already in Saint-Domingue in the latter eighteenth century, it does not appear in New Orleans until 1790. Perhaps Joseph Tassy, or a relative, had fathered children already in Saint-Domingue.

In February 1791, Marie-Françoise gave birth to Josephine Tassy, considered "octoroon." Spanish-owned Louisiana's law did not permit white Joseph and colored Marie-Françoise to marry.

Josephine's family had a portrait of a bewigged, unquestionably white, and very plump Admiral Francois Tassy, perhaps father or uncle to Joseph; he seems to have navigated the stormy waters of the French Revolution cannily, perhaps staying largely out to sea, where he may have eventually drowned. In 1792, a twenty-seven-year-old priest from New Rochelle, also named Tassy, was attacked in Marseilles, hacked in the shoulder, and killed. His mutilated, bloody body was dragged through the streets and hung up in two different places before being finally arranged high on a square opposite the church. New Rochelle was at that time a port busy with the trade of furs, sugar, and "black gold," meaning slaves.

Lieutenant Joseph Tassy was summoned by France's new government to report to his birthplace, Marseilles. Against advice, he returned, trusting. On January 26, 1794, he was condemned to death by the Revolutionary Tribunal of Marseilles for allegedly aiding the English. The guillotine fell on Lieutenant Joseph Tassy. How blue was the new blood on those cobblestones? Joseph's daughter Josephine Tassy was three.

Marie-Françoise Lalande not only survived the execution of her beloved Lieutenant Tassy, but—quite the business woman—Mme. Lalande Perreault actually thrived. She had her men and her children; What she lost in men she invested in land and slaves. She brought up her children with awareness of some heritage from the old world, combined with practical savvy to make their ways in the new.

Generally, Maman Marie-Françoise would burn juniper berries in her house to purify the air and dispel mosquitoes. She had basilique, sweet basil, around and inside the house for good luck. She planted the long, thin-leaved papa plant and the fat, round-leaved mama plant in the ground at the same time, so good luck would bless the household all year round. She fed her babies tea made from mud-dauber nests to strengthen them. The little ones slept on mattresses of cypress moss to strengthen them. When Josephine was teething, her mother tied a dried swamp lily around her neck; she would rub her children's teeth with crawfish to help the teeth cut more easily.

By the time Josephine was five, she had already weathered the usual hurricanes and two major epidemics of yellow fever. During such epidemics, men fired off cannons at night to help dispel the presumably deadly night airs. Windows were closed tight at sundown. While yellow fever besieged the city, when Josephine was two and then five, the children each wore a camphor bag around their necks. And Marie-Françoise made for the three children boots of yellow paper covered with tallow, snuff, and mustard. For fever and chills she alternated peach-tree-leaf tea and red-pepper tea. Although Marie-Francoise suffered the loss of at least three men, her children survived heartily.

On St. Joseph's Day, March 19, Josephine's maman made three different types of St. Joseph's bread, shaped as crucifix, heart, and flower, as well as stuffed artichokes, stuffed crabs, stuffed peppers, stuffed celery, stuffed eggs, and stuffed tomatoes. Dessert included pies and pineapples. On Maundy Thursday, before Good Friday, Marie-Francoise cooked nine varieties of greens in the home, "Gumbo z'herbes," for good luck. Everyone knew that any egg laid that day never spoiled. Some said an egg laid and buried on Good Friday would be good a year later. The children tried a couple of years, but never remembered a year later where they had buried the egg. On Good Friday, the Tassy family would visit nine churches on foot, in silence, to bring good fortune.

Josephine enjoyed her half-brothers, Firmin and Apollinaire, playing, wrestling, singing, making up games galore about all their animal friends. When the children had open sores, Maman beat mullein leaves and applied the pulp in a compress. When they sprained ankles or wrists, she either wound the sprains with snakeskin or applied a piece of mud-dauber nest mixed with vinegar. "O, non, chou-chou, never kill our wasps," she told them again and again over the years. "Their nests mend us."

When Josephine developed a ruby-red sty in her grey eye, Marie-Françoise told her to put a rose in a water glass, and then place it outside where the dew would fall on it. Before sunrise, Josephine wiped her eyes with the dewy rose. She took the rose inside and used it three times each day for three days.

When Josephine was ill, Marie-Françoise would dress her in white or blue, a garment of cord, woven cotton or hemp strands, dedicating her to the Virgin Mary. Sometimes little Josephine wore the cord for months—even years.

When Josephine had a headache, Maman tied a string with nine knots around her neck and wrapped her head in banana leaves. When it was likely that one of the children was suffering from playing in the sun too long, usually a pain in the back of the head, she would bathe the forehead three times a day in a pan of bayou water. When the sun sank, Maman would throw the water toward the bayou.

She taught her children how to settle the water from the bayou by crushing peach seeds in the bottom of a pail, drawing all the dirt to the bottom, leaving the top water purified. Young Josephine especially loved to help the slave Dolores settle the bayou water, watching the clear slowly surface from the silt.

Josephine and her brothers knew mermaids swam in the bayou. But when Dolores warned the children of the loup-garou, Marie-Françoise did not shush her. "Loup-garou will fret yo, yes! yo better be good. Somebody want to do bad work, dey rub demselves wit voodoun grease an' comes out—big red eyes, pointed nose—hair all over, long pointed nails—just like wolves is.

"De only way to chase a loup-garou away from you is frogs; dey's scared o' frog. Sometimes bats go down chimney, stan' by yo bed, suck yo blood, and soon yo a loup-garou—soon youse dancin' at deir balls on Bayou Goula, mens and womens togedder, a lost soul. Hang a new sifter outside yo house. Dey got to stop an' count every hole in 'at sifter; den you catch 'em and sprinkle 'em wit salt. Dat sets 'em on fire an' dey steps outta dem shaggy old skins and runs away—Some loup-garous change into mule and work deir own land." Did Josephine ever notice a sifter on a nail outside the kitchen door? Yes, most kitchen doors in New Orleans featured one, it seemed.

Marie-Françoise Lalande Perrault brought up her daughter Josephine Tassy, like many other free daughters of color in New Orleans, to be prepared in case a wealthy white Creole or American gentleman might care for her and her children, at least in the first stages of adulthood, and, with luck, always. She enrolled Josephine in the color annex of the Ursuline Convent School, where she learned to sing a pretty song, which she loved, make Alençon lace, and sew a fine seam, both of which she disliked. Although not much for reading, she enjoyed the company of others, polished her manners, became cultured in dancing, music, and song, and became also as comfortable in the usually healthy fermenting of gumbo ya-ya (gossip) as she felt comfortable in the company of Mother Mary and the many saints.

With her honey-golden skin, full lips, aquiline nose, surprising grey eyes, flowing black hair, burgeoning bust, and lithe grace in her movements, Josephine felt confident in her beauty, and gradually more aware of her reorienting effect on men. The manscape altered when Demoiselle Tassy passed by. Josephine was protected by her mother and brothers as she became a lovely young woman.

Naturally playful and casually coquettish, she nevertheless showed early signs of a growing sense of self. Unlike some of her friends, Josephine was not preoccupied with positioning herself to be hooked like a prize fish, to be landed in a fancy boat. She was more interested in piloting her own craft.

Yes, she enjoyed dancing regularly at the nearby Tivoli Gardens. Josephine knew she would soon have to cover her tresses in a tignon, the only head-cloth both required by law and permitted for all free women of color, so the white women would not be outshone in beauty in all ways. For now, Josephine especially enjoyed swirling her long, dark waves above her swishing Pompadour taffeta gowns. Not velvet, non, for an unmarried girl. Particularly in yellow, purple, or scarlet, each of which she made herself, she drew all eyes to her.

Yet Josephine, at age seventeen, had had one night a strange, mysteriously powerful, though simple dream. In it, mainly, a chant repeated, drum-driven.

Boom popo de ohoh, what do we know?
Boom popo de ohoh, what do we know?
What do we do with each person we choose?

Such a question, such a call, had an effect—not of making her at the time more interested in whom she was dancing with, but rather, of causing her to view most of her partners more like waters that simply enabled her to move, to swim in the music.

Josephine approached her mother about beginning to do business. Marie-Françoise, having long recognized a kindred spirit, gave her daughter piastres for her own first slave purchase. Maman recommended the legal services of their good neighbor, Samuel Charles Young II, well esteemed in the city.

Josephine knocked on the appointed day at the twenty-fourth house on the right on Bayou Road. Black Betty opened the door and ushered her into her master's office, as the widower's three surviving children scattered out into the backyard. M. Samuel Young rose in his canary yellow vest and short-tailed coat, graciously taking the hand of his client, Demoiselle Tassy, and leading her to a cushioned, upright leather chair. Between white brow and ruddy cheeks framed with silvering side-burns, his blue eyes sparkled.

"Mlle. Tassy, enchanté, je vous assure."

"Si, M. Young, mercie for helping me with this, my first purchase."

The next knock brought Mme. Gonzales, owner of the slaves for sale, into the room. When M. Young established that both parties were intent on proceeding with the transaction, he recommended that they step out front to the porch to confirm that the slaves were to Josephine's approval.

Josephine saw at the far end of the porch Catherine, one year older than Josephine, almost as tall, black, strong, naturally upright. For a long moment they looked each other in the eyes, Josephine's grey, Catherine's black; then Catherine's lowered. In her arms a seven-month mulatto-rouge baby nursed as Catherine slightly swayed. Josephine could tell the child's father was probably Indian, Ouimas. The baby looked healthy, shining, content in his labors.

Back in the office, Samuel Young spread the papers for the two parties to review and sign. And so, on September 28, 1808, Josephine Tassy paid Mme. Gonzales 600 piastres for each slave. After M. Young ushered Mme. Gonzales out the door, he turned to Josephine. "Mlle. Tassy, félicitations. You have done well. Should you ever have need of my services in the future, it would be a pleasure for me to serve you." He bowed.

Josephine Tassy led her slave, Catherine, holding her baby, back up the street toward her house; she felt substantial, proud, as though captaining her own fleet. She felt confident in the ways M. Young had handled the whole transaction. And, crossing her own fatherless threshold, she became aware she was glowing. Yes, proud to purchase her first slave. But she was only half aware she glowed far more due to something she had not known in her own home: the presence of a mature man.

CHAPTER 3:

BACAS—THE LOUISIANA PURCHASE, 1800

The Bacas family, many knew, had shown up in New Orleans sometime in the 1770s. Jean-Baptiste Manuel Bacas, born in Genoa, had started an inn on the northwest side of town. In time he moved down to the Vieux Quartier—the French Quarter—and bought a house at 116 Rue St. Louis, right above the intersection with Bourbon St. He married Marie Louise Catherine Landrony, who hailed from Arkansas Post. They had three children: Marie Luysa, Barthelemy, and Leon. Jean-Baptiste built cabinets, apprenticing his sons.

Jean-Baptiste Bacas purchased a teenage slave, Adelaïde Beaulieu, to help his daughter Marie Luysa when she married Dominique Cossé dit Chevalier in the St. Louis Cathedral of New Orleans in 1800. The birdlike bride, charmed, glowing, unknowing, soon bore three sons, one plus twins, in the Bacas family home on 116 Rue St. Louis. Marie Luysa took great comfort in the help and even companionship of same-age Adelaïde, strong, high-cheeked, coppery-bronze. Marie Luysa and her sons called Adelaïde "Pouponne," a standard term for the nurse of a baby or children.

Adelaïde came from the Chauvin Beaulieu clan downriver, a "Grif" mix of French, Senegalese Wolof, and Chaouchas Indian, Cajun in the blend. Her mother had been such a blend as well, and many fellow slaves assumed Adelaïde's father to have been Master Beaulieu. However, her actual father had been a French Canadian coureur de bois, literally a woods-runner, evicted by the British from Isle St. Jean, arriving in Louisiana in 1767.

In Louisiana, Adelaïde's father plied his wares paddling his pirogue, a dug-out cypress, through the bayous, trapping and trading in furs, alligators, fish, and supplies, a southern cousin of the coureurs de bois who worked the waterways of the northern woods of Canada, up where the mightiest of the water world were sturgeon instead of gators. Adelaïde's industrious older sister Pauline steadily saved money as a seamstress, and finally became able to buy her own freedom from Master Beaulieu.

Marie Luysa's brother Barthelemy was a combination of dark and light, tall, broad-shouldered, with dark hair and growing side-burns, yet fair-skinned. Barthelemy took up space, with the growing power of a man of few words. Tending to brood, he felt lightened by glowing Adelaïde Pouponne.

At that time, one-third of the African Americans in New Orleans, and one-fifth of the whole city, were HLC, hommes libres de couleur, or FPC, free people of color. In 1806, new laws prohibited slaves from purchasing their own freedom, and from receiving a master's inheritance in mixed-race common law marriages.

Adelaïde's sister Pauline had fortunately purchased her own freedom just before that gate of possibility closed. In fearful reaction to the recent success of the slave rebellion in Haiti, the local authorities forbade any Haitian free people of color from entering New Orleans at all, like trying to keep disease from entering port.

However, successful Pauline Beaulieu, now FLC, femme libre de couleur, was still allowed to purchase from Jean-Baptiste Manuel Bacas the freedom of her sister. Adelaïde

Pouponne Beaulieu, age twenty-three, was free to leave 116 Rue St. Louis to discover her own destiny.

Adelaïde, in beige cotton dress and orange tignon, bid a warm adieu to Michi Jean-Baptiste and his three children: to weeping Marie Luysa, wife of gracious M. Dominique dit Chevalier, whom Adelaïde had always liked but never trusted; to young M. Leon, whom she always trusted; and to M. Barthelemy, to whom she had surrendered herself. Barthelemy stood tall, silent. She felt his eyes hold her, but she was not sure how. He withdrew into the shadows before she finished departing.

Beyond the Bacas threshold of 116 Rue St. Louis, Adelaïde, on her own for the first time in her life, wandered the bright streets, ambling aimlessly, savoring the anywheres her feet were choosing. She felt the papers in her pocket, declaring her manumission. The paper felt firm; she wondered how strong the words were worth. She had heard stories enough of papers burning and shackles clanking closed. Adelaïde dared to whistle. She found no resistance.

At Place d'Armes she watched palm trees feather-finger breezes; she snatched a short banana from a festoon-leafed tree. She pirouetted. Then, she simply sat at a café, nibbling a beignet plantain and sipping choco-chaud; she wondered what other kinds of beignet her free father may have enjoyed in his early life up in Canadian Acadia. By late afternoon she arrived at sister Pauline's home on Rue Claude, where Barthelemy had had his slave Alfonce deliver her modest belongings.

"Sister Pauline's home." Will someone ever say, "Adelaïde Pouponne's home?" How has my dear Pauline done this herself, and then done it again, for me? I have always only been locked in another's house. First I discover wings on my feet instead of chains. Now I walk freely, when I choose, into Pauline's home. Fancy that.

Pauline touched foreheads with her sister, holding her

firmly by the shoulders. Leaning back to behold her anew, she spoke the Wolof words, "Def ca ban gay man (Do it while you can)." Adelaïde responded, "Def ca ban gay man," smiling. Then both repeated it simultaneously, laughing aloud. Pauline wrapped Adelaïde in her arms, long. Adelaïde hugged Pauline as though she were the tree of life. The sisters realized each was weeping, smiling through tears. Pauline said, "That was the key Gramerre gave Maman to give us, always the key—Def ca ban gay man. You are one strong woman, ma chère Pouponne Adelaïde. Who knows what you will do now, Adelaïde Beaulieu, sans Pouponne?" Adelaïde laughed at the notion. The sisters celebrated with a modest champagne. After each sip, Adelaïde sighed.

During the night, Adelaïde listened. She felt the upper half of her heart light. She felt the lower half heavy. The next day, the sisters went to market together and splurged at Pauline's insistence. They bought whatever might delight Adelaïde—a simple, long-sleeved, white pleated cotton dress, sky-blue ribbon belting below the bust, and a straw "bonnet," orange ribbon flowering to the side. Then the sisters enjoyed café and a mille feuilles pastry, such lightness in the sweet-creamed phyllo layers. Simply feeling allowed to delight felt to both sisters like new breathing, as though each now had two lungs instead of just one.

They shared stories of their lives since Adelaïde had been sold to Bacas. Adelaïde said, "Night an day I tended Maria Luisa an her boys. They all call me Pouponne; they seemed content with my care."

"And..."

"And?"

"And ... her brothers?"

Adelaïde looked at Pauline. "Why, they're decent, gentlemen I would say."

Pauline kept her gaze on her sister. "Adelaïde ..."

"Well, the older one, Barthelemy, we got ... close."

"An, what does that mean now?" "I don' know. I don' know. And you, Pauline, and you?

"Me, well, little sister mine, most important thing is, as you know, my needlework kept me from the fields, those same fields where cuttin' cane aged Maman 'bout a decade a year. 'Til she died. Masser Beaulieu long rented out me 'n my needle to plantations around. He let me keep 10 cents to the dollar, which I saved and saved. Until finally, "

Adelaïde interwove, "Every slave's dream,"

"Yes, every slave's dream, finally I bought my freedom, myself. Def ca ban gay man."

Pauline smiled, and Adelaïde nodded. "Thank heavens, and thank you forever," kissing Pauline on both cheeks. "And you ... any man?"

"Non, non ma soeur, no man at me. I have too many needles, hah! Thank heavens!"

During the second night, Adelaïde listened. The third morning, Pauline looked at her sister. A new gravity, a new focus. "Oh, dieu de dieu! Non! C'est pas possible! Adelaïde, you can't be thinking—he'll, he'll own you. Adelaïde, you know he may be a brute, that one."

"Not with me, chère Pauline. I realize now that I have surrendered to Barthelemy not just my body but also my soul. You'd be surprised how he gentles me. One is always the sheep of one and the lion of another. I have found my own lion. With me, he's mostly sheep."

"Adelaïde! You're by damn givin' up the gift of a lifetime, the gift I by damn needle-slaved to give you."

"Non, Pauline, stop. Stop! All my life you h've been my elder, my leader, my protector, even my mother. Now, ma chère soeur, is indeed my time, my time. Def ca ban gay man. I have to do it now, while I can. Life with Barthelemy is world enough for me. Here—you be guardian of my papers, in case I ever need them. I expect not to. You have given me an ultimate gift, my liberty, the liberty I now actually have, to offer even greater gifts, my love and myself. If, that is, he will have me."

Pauline had never imagined that the fruit of all her labors for her sister would be so surrendered, so swiftly. Yet in the calm of Adelaïde's eyes, the firm jaw, even the regular rhythm of her breast, Pauline saw no retreat, no defeat, and no loss of freedom. She beheld standing before her not a slave, but a queen, a stately queen. "I see, chère soeur; better I throw wood on the fire God lights than try to put it out. You clearly burn for Barthelemy. I bought your freedom. I give you my blessings—but that Bacas bastard had better do right by you."

"He will."

"Adelaïde, ma soeur, please wait at least until you know you *really* know."

"Pauline, for you, my liberateur," with a kiss and a long embrace, "I will try to wait until I know I really know."

One afternoon weeks later, Barthelemy was working in his wood shop in the courtyard at 116 St. Louis. He felt he was being watched. In the late light, washing the sweet-scented pittosporum shrubs, he looked up—Adelaïde's bronze skin shone almost gold in a flowing white dress he'd never seen.

Barthelemy straightened. "Adelaïde? Adelaïde." he whispered. His eyes teared.

He stepped forth into the courtyard glow. Her tan canvas valise lay on the ground behind her. She looked open as a flower, yet with a will to re-root. He stepped close to her. Her arms relaxed, and she gazed up at him. He wrapped her silently, slowly, in his long arms, her heart soothing his to a healthier beat. When he lowered his arms, he saw her hazel eyes were as wet as his.

"Are you sure?" Barthelemy asked. Adelaïde nodded.

"I had to let you go, you know."

Adelaïde nodded again. "I know. I—choose—you."

"Thank heavens, ma chère Adelaïde." Barthelemy took a deep breath. "I, I have been looking up the road, what's ahead, and all I see, all I feel, without you, chère Adelaïde, is ice. With you, I see my way light, flourish."

"And I, I have been delighting in my days, freer than a bee. I play and dally. I savor, I wander. And in my nights, I hear an echo, hollow, of a beat which is not mine. I do not feel my own heart beat. The beat I feel, I hear, is your heart, Barthelemy. I realize my heart is now your heart. I have given my heart to you. I left my heart with you. My heart is not out there in the endless streets. My heart is here with you, at 116 St. Louis.

"I will not abuse you, my heart."

"I know. I know true."

He kissed her lips, like velvet, like oak; then he picked up not her valise but her, and carried her not to the slave quarters there in the courtyard, but up to his own room on the third floor. The valise he brought up later.

That brief sequence of impromptu exchanges constituted, in essence, their vows, the private ceremony of marriage of Barthelemy Bacas and Adelaïde Beaulieu, no public one being allowed by law. Barthelemy's widower father, Jean-Baptiste, enumerated the social, legal, and financial consequences of such a union, extending a finger for each. Barthelemy's repeated response: "Yes, I know—" Sensing the uncharacteristically quiet depth of his son's resolve, Jean-Baptiste gave his blessings to the union. His fatherly instinct told him Adelaïde Pouponne had a better chance than anyone he knew of planing smooth some rough knots of this son's soul.

The following year, Pouponne herself began to wax like the moon. Adelaïde Beaulieu and Barthelemy Bacas had their first child, Joseph Valmont Bacas. A boy, a joy; with their Joseph the next generation of the Bacas clan began. The next year,

Barthelemy's younger brother Leon married Marie-Celeste Tègre out west in St. John the Baptist Parish, where they chose to settle.

A new law required all free people of color to be registered as HLC. Adelaïde Pouponne Beaulieu, mate of Barthelemy Bacas, dutifully and proudly registered as FLC, Femme Libre de Couleur, a free woman of color.

In 1809, the three sisters-in-law, Marie Luysa Cossé, Adelaïde Pouponne Beaulieu (although not officially an in-law), and Marie-Celeste Bacas, waxed together like triple moons. In April, in spite of all efforts of both high-carrying Adelaïde and low-carrying Marie-Celeste, Marie Luysa Bacas Cossé hemorrhaged in labor so severely that she did not survive the birth of her daughter, Marie Josephine.

Dominique Cossé dit Chevalier, in spite of his previous attentions to other birds, fell on the bed, gasping, tear-drenching his cooling wife. "Non, non, mon oiseau, non, non, mon oiseau," he cried, endangering his delicate new daughter. Adelaïde Pouponne, who had positioned the baby to absorb as much as possible of the still-lingering warmth of her mother's body, swooped little Marie Josephine off the bed.

Adelaïde and Marie-Celeste had always thought of Dominique Cossé as a young man with le coeur comme un artichaud—a heart like an artichoke, a leaf for each woman. Yet, resisting Adelaïde Pouponne's urgings to step away, Dominique shifted onto his back in his brocade vest and red foularde, right arm holding Marie Luysa to him. He directed Adelaïde Pouponne to place little Marie Josephine into the crook of his left arm, where he sheltered her with a surprisingly delicate touch, turning from one to the other in a slowing rhythm of grief-groan and almost silent dawn-sigh. Adelaïde knew that in his grief he was again treating her like a slave; yet, more importantly perhaps, she now knew this artichoke at least had roots.

On May 2, Jean-Baptiste Bacas was born to Marie-Celeste

and Leon Bacas, and died. All Bacases were already wearing black.

Adelaïde Pouponne herself gave birth on May 11; it was clear to both her and Barthelemy that their girl would be named Luysa Bacas. In the wake of one dead mother and one dead son, Adelaïde and Barthelemy felt graced, blessed, to bear their own Luysa. Adelaïde Pouponne Beaulieu tended to both babies, Marie Josephine and Luysa, like a second set of twins, after deceased mother Marie Luisa's own older Cosse boy-twins.

New Papa Barthelemy had long had a partnership with two American traders he referred to by their surnames, Valmont and Wilson, in many Caribbean ventures. From Wilson he bought twelve-year-old Ernestine, mulatto, for two hundred piastres to help with the Cossé boy twins and the girl "twins" especially, as well as with his and Adelaïde's own little Joseph Valmont Bacas, named after Barthelemy's partner Valmont himself. Brother Leon's Marie-Celeste successfully gave birth to Marie-Euphremie Euphrosine Bacas in 1811, although the fragile infant expired in fever months later. Adelaïde Beaulieu gave birth again, to Jean-Baptiste Valcour Bacas in 1812 and, a year later, to Drauzin Valsin Bacas on September 6.

Baby Drusino was christened in the old octagonal baptistry of St. Louis Cathedral, even though his mother and father could not, of course, be married there. His godfather was Hector Beaulieu, brother of Pauline and Adelaïde, and "resident of St. Domingue." Hector himself had long proven his worth to his master as a "coureur de bois," or fur trader, like Adelaïde's free father. Hector had found his first degree of freedom while still a slave, navigating the bayous to trade furs, hides, and fish with Indians, other plantations, and bayou outposts for goods and money for his master. He paddled with the art and craft of a Mic-mac or a Chippewa and enjoyed aller à la passe, hunting snipe and woodcocks, among les prairies molles, the swamps and trapping grounds.

Hector, like his sister Pauline, had succeeded in purchasing his own freedom from slavery. He had sailed almost immediately for Haiti to enjoy the slaveless brave new world. There he heard, saw, and smelled ten blacks butcher three mulattos right down the street. He realized that continuing tensions between blacks and mulattos in Haiti made life for him more dangerous there than on the Beaulieu plantation. He then sailed to Havana with many disillusioned others. Finally, Hector returned to New Orleans in the Cuban expulsion of the "Francezas" just before the New Orleans doors closed to entering FMC over age fifteen. Eventually, Hector Beaulieu found work with Barthelemy's cousin, little Drusino's namesake, Drauzin Valsin Bacas, at the apothecary shop on Rue Chartres.

In January 1815, cousins Drauzin and Barthelemy Bacas, along with other citizens of New Orleans, joined General Andrew Jackson's thousand soldiers to fight as carabinières alongside Jean Lafitte's glamorous, grungy pirates. Jackson's patchwork army defeated the much larger force of well-seasoned British regulars one foggy morning on the battlefield of Chalmette, downriver aways toward St. Bernard Parish. Adelaïde's brother, Hector Beaulieu, ran the apothecary shop himself during the battles, supplying the American army's hospital with well-needed bandages and medicines.

In spite of increasing American control, "Louis" was still somehow the name of life down here. The Bacas family on Rue St. Louis. The heart of the city—St. Louis Cathedral. Lake St. Louis. The new state of—Louisiana. The whole Louisiana Purchase—salvaged.

CHAPTER 4:
JEAN-BAPTISTE
MANUEL BACAS, 1817

The first funeral little Drusino could ever recall was his grandfather's. The four-year-old of course did not know that his father Barthelemy Bacas, while Granpère was still warm, had sent his slave Nelson to the printer with the announcement of the death. "Yes, Michie," obeyed Nelson before immediately posting black-framed notices on occasional trees up and down Rue St. Louis and for several blocks around. Meanwhile, Barthelemy sent Alfonce to certain men, mainly family. "Yes, Michie," replied Alfonse, before delivering personal invitations to the funeral service of Jean-Baptiste Manuel Bacas at 116 Rue St. Louis at four o'clock the next day, le 11 fevrier 1817.

As soon as the slaves departed, Leon Bacas, short, fairer of face, came eagerly up to his older brother Barthelemy, standing tall and dark-browed, with cheek-chop whiskers accenting his long earlobes and chisel-chin. "Cher frère, what can I take care of? Food? Drink? Notary?"

"Leon, mon vieux, non, I have it all in hand. Adelaïde has the food. You just focus on packing your family." Leon took one step back, shrinking; he looked his brother in the eye, nodded, and turned to the task that had been dictated his priority. The family's croque-mort, undertaker, and his crew

were already treating the body of Jean-Baptiste Manuel Bacas
with cloves and peppermint.

Today, as elegant as anyone in town at any time of day, that croque-mort, the undertaker, stood back at the side in formal, grey-
striped trousers, double-breasted overcoat, black high-heeled
shoes, and tall silk hat, blacker than his molasses brown face
and hands. All wore black. The brothers Barthelemy and Leon
together greeted visitors as they came to pay their respects.

When their deceased sister Marie Luysa's widower husband,
Dominique Cossé dit Chevalier, appeared, suave gautée shielding his dashing chin, the two brothers stiffened and looked at
each other, wondering whether to let him in. Dominique's fifteen-year-old son, Jean-Baptiste Cossé, also stiffened back in
a corner. When Dominique's twelve-year-old twins, however,
shouted, "Pa-pa," running toward him, the two Bacas hosts nodded at each other and greeted their black-sheep brother-in-law
as civil as winter. Their cousin, the elder Drauzin Valsin Bacas,
an apothecary's assistant, stood slightly back to the side, olive-
skinned, with a drooping mustache, greeting many as well. The
Chevalier filled and emptied his glass fast.

When Père Antoine, the beloved priest from Cathedral
St. Louis, nodded to him, Barthelemy strode to the center
of the living room salon, with its high ceilings and almost
floor-to-ceiling windows, candles lit around the room, and
orchids, white camellias, branches of cherry blossoms, and
sweet-scented winter honeysuckle. Barthelemy welcomed and
thanked all for coming "to honor your friend and our father,
Jean-Baptiste Manuel Bacas. Born in Genoa, he became a successful merchant, settling for a time in St. Domingue in the
Caribbean before moving to New Orleans, where he initially
ran an inn on the German Coast upriver. He married Marie
Louise Catherine Landrony of Arkansas Post and bought this

fine home at 116 Rue St. Louis in 1779, continuing to prosper in trade. Jean-Baptiste Manuel had served in the local militia, becoming a captain."

Here Barthelemy paused, nodding to his cousin Drauzin Valsin Bacas, silently acknowledging what everyone already knew well: their own service with General Andrew Jackson and the pirate Jean Lafitte, defending New Orleans against the British in 1815. "Jean-Baptiste Manuel Bacas presided over the growing family as his sons," nodding to brother Leon, "became successful cabinetmakers. A fulfilling story in a new world, for a long life of seventy-eight years."

A small man of substance, Jean-Baptiste's body looked smaller still in the coffin before the closing. The brothers and others carried the coffin out of the living room, pivoting in the front hall alongside the staircase, then moved out the front door and down the three steps carefully, sliding it onto the black-lacquered hearse-carriage awaiting beneath leaden skies. The undertaker climbed up to take the reins of the stately white horse. The steel wheel rims syncopated the percussion of the horseshoes on the ballast stones cobbling the streets. Barthelemy and Leon led the somber men of the family behind the priest the four blocks up Rue St. Louis to St. Louis Cemetery No. 1, where the coffin was lowered into the marble, aboveground funeral box long ago ordered by ailing Jean-Baptiste.

Nonc Drauzin, as the children called their father's cousin, moved as a quiet presence among the four little musketeers, Dominique's Jean-Baptiste, his twins Ti-Barthelemy and Ti-Dominique Cossé, and Barthelemy's eldest, ten-year-old Joseph Valmont Bacas, all so far behaving like young men. As Père Antoine performed the sacrament of the funeral rites, the sky started to drip. Afterward, Barthelemy and Leon shook hands with le croque-mort, "A la prochaine fois." Till next time.

Back home, upstairs, the ladies and girls had relaxed a little after the funeral procession had departed for the cemetery. Barthelemy's Adelaïde Pouponne Beaulieu presided, tending to her own three-week-old Adelaïde Emilia. Naturally regal, with broad brow, cinnamon skin, shining black hair, high cheekbones, hazel eyes, and forward chin, Adelaïde surrounded all with her attention, calming. The two eight-year-old girls swirled back and forth in their black dresses between the Adelaïdes, mother and daughter, and Leon's five-month-old Marie-Anne, held occasionally by Leon's fair wife, Marie-Celeste, otherwise by Ernestine, the slave. Both mothers were clad in black as well.

Adelaïde Pouponne handed baby Emilia to Ernestine and went down to be sure Marcelite and the courtyard kitchen crew were properly preparing dinner for the men below as well as for the female family on the second floor. She returned upstairs before the men returned from the cemetery, tending to the various children, including Barthelemy's four- and five-year-old boys and Leon's three-year-old, all playing under the staircase.

At one point, Adelaïde heard her daughter Luysa say to her motherless cousin Marie Josephine, "I heard the dog howl." Marie Josephine replied, "And I heard the cricket chirp; I knew the death would be soon." Young Marie Josephine responded to Adelaïde, "Si, Maman Pouponne," just as often as Luysa Bacas called Adelaïde "Maman."

The men returned in drizzling dusk, as oil lamps were being lit along the streets. At the door they shook off the oiled-silk umbrellas they had opened at the cemetery. Coal fires burned in the fireplaces of both the living room and the adjoining dining room. Alfonce and Ernestine had set the cochon de lait, the suckling pig, in the center, with a crawfish bisque at each place, to be followed by a mighty gumbo of crab, shrimp, chicken, and sausage, thickened with sleeves of okra. Café noir always ready. Wines soon flowing. Bière douce, ground here in the courtyard from pineapple peelings, brown sugar, cloves, and rice. Root beer for the children.

Through the high windows upstairs, Adelaïde and her sister-in-law Marie-Celeste gazed out strangely, almost in a trance, through the iron-lace balcony. Downstairs, the fireplaces flickered, dancing reflections on the wet cobblestones, amid numerous candlelights glowing, growing in the darkening drizzle. The two listened; tones lowered in the dining room below. Their eyes met. Marie-Celeste smiled, biting her lip.

"Adelaïde, twelve years ago, you were Pouponne, doing all Bacases' bidding beautifully. A year later, freed, you chose to return to Barthelemy. Now, chère soeur, you preside, Queen of Rue St. Louis. What a wonder." Adelaïde nodded affectionately. "I am indeed blessed," she said, placing her hand on Marie-Celeste's shoulder, "I am grateful for how you know me. And I am sad that you, my sweet soul-sister, must soon depart."

"I have though to say, dear Adelaïde, sometimes I fear for you. Leon has little room here, overshadowed by his older brother. And you, and you?"

"T'en fais pas, no worry, chère soeur. I thrive, I thrive."

Down below, all males stood in the dining room before the feast. Nonc Drauzin put a hand on his young nephew Joseph. Brother Leon stepped back. All followed suit, turning toward tall, hulking Barthelemy.

Barthelemy strode forth and stood behind the armchair of the former patriarch, Jean-Baptiste Manuel Bacas. He looked at the men and friends of the Bacas family, nodded, and said, "Que Dieu vous bénisse," May God bless you. The others took their new places, brother Leon at his right, cousin Drauzin at his left, the priest Père Antoine, the tutor Basil Crockère, brother-in-law Dominique Cossé, his three sons, and young Joseph, who watched and listened, silent.

Barthelemy raised his glass. "A la memoire de Jean-Baptiste Manuel Bacas, qui a commencé tous pour nous tous, en ce nouveau monde de Nouvelle Orleans. Et à notre mère, Marie Louise Catherine Landrony." To the memory of Jean-Baptiste Manuel Bacas, who started all for all of us, in this new world of New Orleans. And to our mother, Marie Louise Catherine

Landrony. Barthelemy, the new patriarch, sat. Then the rest of those assembled sat.

Gradually, feast-cheer bubbled. Girls giggled above, men laughed below. At one point Adelaïde stood behind her seated sister-in-law, lilylike Marie-Celeste, hands resting on her shoulders.

"It has been good," said Adelaïde.

"It has been good," responded Marie-Celeste, bringing her hands up, holding Adelaïde's. Adelaïde would miss Marie-Celeste and her family, soon heading back west to her family in Edgard, Côte des Allemandes. And Marie-Celeste would miss Adelaïde and her family, though she would not miss her brother-in-law, Barthelemy. Yet it had been good.

The three little boys—Barthelemy's Petit Jean-Baptiste and Drusino, and Leon's Anatole—reappeared for some dessert. "We been playing with Arnaldo. M'we bring him some pigulasto?"

"Mais si, chous-chous." And back the boys went under the third-floor staircase with their invisible fourth playmate. Adelaïde met Marie-Celeste's glance. Arnaldo, the older brother of Barthelemy and Leon, had died decades ago, at about the age of their sons.

Down below, the men had enjoyed their desserts of frosted layer cakes, fruit cake, and neat cones of pigulasto, a pastry of dough and molasses. They now savored cigars and Hennessy Cognac VOP. Dominique Cossé dit Chevalier swayed to the hall and returned with his mandolin.

After his first three notes, Adelaïde, up above, handed baby Emilia to Ernestine to be put to sleep. Then she and Marie-Celeste, who kept slightly restless Anne-Marie in her arms, led the procession downstairs as ladies and children joined the men in the two rooms—really one with the adjoining doors open. Leon fetched his clarinet. Barthelemy even pulled out his cello. The young boys clambered around Joseph and the twins, who drummed gently on their chairs.

Soon music flowed like wine. At times children danced. Adelaïde took both hands of Marie-Celeste, squeezing gently. Then, clearly wearying, she made her way to sit by Barthelemy.

Basil Crockère, the handsome tutor, said, "Ah, mon Bartolomeo, mon Leon, votre pere m'a fait confiance au commencement, votre pere." Your father entrusted me from the start. Then he played an exquisite French tune by Chevalier St. George on the flute.

Nonc Dominique dit Chevalier whipped out a monocle and put it in place. "Le monocle de ton oncle," he said to the children, who chuckled and groaned with delight, repeating it to each other countless times; it would become a family phrase among the children. He began his tale: "Je me rapelle, I recall, when our cher M. Jean-Baptiste Bacas was sitting right here, where he lay this afternoon. I stood before him, my pompadour prepared just perfectly, at the hardest moment of my life.

"'Cher Monsieur Bacas,' I began, 'it is with the greatest of respect and humility that I, votre servant, Monsieur Dominique Cossé dit Chevalier, do dare presume to request that you graciously deign to consider the possibility of granting me the providential, even eternal, blessing of your benign, sage, even magnanimous permission to be granted the delicate hand of your beautiful daughter nonpareil, Marie Luysa, in the sacred institution of marriage.'

"I shifted my silver-headed cane to my left hand, raised my right, and began a series of flourishing S's in, I may say, an elegant bow, also nonpareil. Silence. Still silence. I could hear only M. Bacas puffing his cigar. As my back started to ache, and I slowly straightened, I became aware that my shirt was all wet, only with sweat, on this unusually dry day." Some smiles, mild chuckles.

"M. Jean-Baptiste Bacas's eyes penetrated right through my eyes, like a veritable bayonet, I tell you, right down my throat, right down to my heart and my lungs, right down into my stomach and my ready-to-burst loins"—some deeper guffaws from the men—"right down into my shaking knees"—some ladies laughing—"into my shiny leather boots, which were trying hard to hold onto the floor.

"'You—' he said between puffs, then—nothing, nothing. Now I am afraid my pants will soon become wet too, and not from sweat."

The boys shouted, "Non, non!"

"I want to explode like a balloon to relieve myself." The boys guffawed while the girls tried to restrain their smiles. "I feel nauseous, almost to vomit. Still, nothing, nothing, just, 'You—' hanging in the air, like a veritable sword. I start to feel a mosquito bite right below my navel."

"Oh, mon Dieu, oh, mon vieux," said Adelaïde and Marie-Celeste, chuckling almost in chorus.

"I then realize I am about to sneeze, which could explode everything." Some of the children shrieked, imagining double messes. "I start to dance slightly, tightly, squeezing my knees to each other, trying to squeeze my nose inside. I see that chandelier, with its oak-leaf molding, starting to spin in a tight circle as I hold on harder and harder to my silver-headed cane, cutting my palms with my fingernails."

"'—had better marry my daughter.'"

"'Eh, pardon, Monsieur?'"

"'You—had better.'"

"'Quoi? Oh, oh, mon Dieu. Oui, Monsieur, certainement, oui, Monsieur Bacas, merci Monsieur Bacas, mille fois, Monsieur Bacas!' I want to hug him, there as stern as an old oak, but of course I do not. I back out of the front door; I almost stumble down those three steps, forgetting my hat, having to go find a latrine down the street as fast as does not look too ridiculous. Oui, je me rapelle, moi. Notre Monsieur Jean-Baptiste Manuel Bacas."

The whole gathering was laughing, some wiping their eyes, children only gradually settling down. Little Drusino and Petit Jean-Baptiste started to reenact the scene out in the front hall. As the gathering subsided, Nonc Dominique dit Chevalier ever so gently plucked his mandolin, soon crooning in his tenor a song of loss, moistening most eyes for very different reasons.

Oh, ooh, oh, ooayoo,
Ma Luysa, buhring me a little wauhter, ooh.

Dominique had warmed the family gathering with his self-demeaning story. But his song to his long-dead wife Luysa, on the one hand touched the family tender, while on the other hand it pained them, reminding the adults of both his neglect of her and his gambling away most of her dowry.

Barthelemy, new master of the house, rescued the unraveling mood, singing in his basso profundo a gentle hymn to his queen:

Deläide, mo la Reine, Deläide, my Queen,
Chimin-la trop longque pou aller.
Chimin-la monte dans les hauts;
Tout piti que mo ye.
M'alle monte la-haut dans Courant.
Bonsoir, mo la reine—
C'est moi Bartel qui rive.

Deläide, my Queen, Deläide, my Queen,
This road is too long to travel,
This road climbs into the heights;
As small as I am
(some chuckled lightly here, the singer being so big)
I will get there, by the stream.
Good night, my Queen—
It is I, Bartel, who arrive.

Barthelemy's beloved Adelaïde responded with a different tune:

When you come to my house,
You must come through the field;
It just suit me.
If you can't bring corn, bring meat and meal;
Because it just suit me.
If you can't bring flour, bring dago cheese
Because it just suit me.

Each time Adelaïde sang the refrain, "Because it just suit me," she was looking at Barthelemy, her hand on his knee, in a combination of straightforward declaration and of humor, permeated with loving gratitude for the continuing devotions of the now-new master of the house. And with each refrain he nodded, smiling.

Petit Jean-Baptiste roused the children to sing one of their favorites:

The rooster and the chicken had a fight,
The chicken knocked the rooster out of sight,
The rooster told the chicken, "That's alright,
I'll meet you in the gumbo tonight, tonight,
I'll meet you in the gumbo tonight."

On the last line, the children shouted all the louder, startling young Anne-Marie, whose eyes had closed in Marie-Celeste's arms. She started to cry gently. Marie-Celeste sang an old Creole lullaby to Anne-Marie:

Fe dodo Minette
Trois Piti cochons du laite
Fe dodo mo piti bebe

Jiske lake de quinze ans—
Quand quinze ans aura passe
Minette va se marier.

Go to sleep, Minette
Three little suckling pigs
Go to sleep, my little baby
Until the age of fifteen years—
Minette will then marry.

Eventually, at a signal from Adelaïde, the children said
goodnight to the adults, and Marcelite and Ernestine put the
young ones to bed upstairs, Barthelemy's on the second floor
and Leon's on the third. However, ten-year-old Joseph lin-
gered with the older boys, soaking in the musk, music, smoke,
and perfume of the men and the women in his life.

Later, Adelaïde sang:

Tou to milattresses laye
Ape passe pou blanc
Avec to blanc layes
Ye alle dans l'Opera Français
Mais ye fout ye deyer.

All you mulatresses there
Are passing for white
With your white men
You go to the French Opera
But they throw you out.

Adelaïde sang knowingly, looking lovingly at each of her
family members. The adults knew she would never enter the
Opera Français. Most smiled receptively, nodding in understanding. Young Joseph noticed varying glances among them.
Barthelemy went blank. Nonc Dominique shook his head.

Nonc Leon nodded sympathetically. Tante Marie-Celeste's eyes moistened. At the end, Nonc Drauzin gave a slight bow to Adelaïde.

During the whole evening, Adelaïde and Marie-Celeste had been reading the tones, colors, moods, and moments, periodically glance-checking with each other. The tides of the Bacas family were turning. The fortunes? Time would tell. Adelaïde knew her blustery Barthelemy was a different man from his restrained father, Jean-Baptiste Manuel. Marie-Celeste, sad to leave Adelaïde, was nevertheless glad to be returning to her own home after these weeks, glad to be rescuing her Leon from the shadow of his big brother Barthelemy, and a little concerned to leave Adelaïde "alone" at 116 St. Louis.

At a nod from Adelaïde, Barthelemy stood, cleared his voice, and raised his glass. "Thank you, chère famille and friends. May we offer a final toast to the father of our tribe, Jean-Baptiste Manuel Bacas. May his soul rest in peace."

The adults looked around at each other, mostly smiling, nodding.

As some started to depart, ten-year-old Joseph ran to his Nonc Drauzin at the front door, gave him a great hug around his waist, and was kissed in return on each cheek. From the side of the door, he heard Nonc Drauzin almost whisper to Barthelemy while stepping out into the pouring rain, "Genoa?"

Little Joseph, confused, looked up to see Nonc Drauzin's eyebrows raised, eyes wide open. Then he saw his father's eyes narrow and his jaw clench as Barthelemy growled, "Genoa!"

The next day, after meeting with the attorney about their father's Will, Barthelemy and Leon took their brother-in-law Dominique Cossé down across the street to Pierre Maspero's café. Barthelemy read to him a section of their father's Will.

"I, Jean-Baptiste Manuel Bacas, declare my son-in-law,

Dominique Cossé, to be 'Chevalier Paratonnere,' Sir Lightning Rod, who, having squandered my daughter's, his deceased wife's, inheritance, will neither see his children anymore, nor have any access to their remaining inheritance."

Dominique bit his lip; his eyes teared; the brothers rose.

At the house, Monsieur "dit Chevalier" embraced each of his four children and then walked out of 116 Rue St. Louis, never to cross that threshold again. In the ensuing years, no Bacases ever found confirmation of Cossé's actual "Chevalier" status. The only clue was a book on chivalric heraldry Dominique had bought at an estate sale in 1799, the year before marrying Marie Luysa Bacas.

Leon resumed packing his family for their departure. At one point Barthelemy put his hand on his shoulder. "I am sorry, my brother," he said. "With Marie Luysa's four, and our four, and us still expanding—"

Leon looked up at his older brother. "Ça va, mon vieux. It was clear at my wedding years ago: this Bacas must go. We are fine in Edgard on the Côte Allemand. This Bacas household has room for only one brother."

CHAPTER 5:

BAYOU ST. JEAN, 1817

After Samuel Charles Young II, the Pennsylvania-born law-yer, had helped his unusually lovely young neighbor, Josephine Tassy, age seventeen, with the legal transaction of her first pur-chase of slaves, the then-thirty-seven-year-old widower even-tually served as alderman for the Eighth Ward of New Orleans from 1812 to 1815. Josephine Tassy had soon had him as her own alderman—twenty years elder, in fact. By early 1812, when twelve-year-old Samuel Charles Young III died of consumption, the name of Josephine's first baby, born January 28, made her relationship with the widower clear. In Samuel Charles Young IV, Josephine Tassy now had her own brand-new Young.

That same year her country gave birth to the world's first steamboat, "New Orleans," which Josephine and her baby boy saw gently rocking in her berth at the town dock. Lawyer Samuel Young II helped Faubourg Trêmé, including much of Bayou Rd., become legally incorporated as a neighborhood, especially for free people of color. On April 30 Louisiana became the eighteenth state of the Union, still an uncom-fortable abstraction to many of the long-time residents of recently Spanish and French New Orleans. And that same year the second war against the young nation's previous masters, the bad old Brits, began.

Late the afternoon of June 24, 1817, Josephine Tassy, mother by now of three Young boys, had Catherine prepare the horse-trap. Samuel had recently returned from the House of Representatives in Washington, DC, where he was pursuing a grant of public land for both a charity hospital and a college of New Orleans. And he was already off again helping a client, Toutant-Beauregard, at the Contreras Plantation down in St. Bernard Parish.

Josephine headed up Rue Bayou all the way to Bayou St. Jean, leaving her horse and cabriolet in a sheltered opening. *Bayou St. Jean. Bayou St. Jean.* Josephine always loved saying it, loved hearing it. *It sounds the way the bayou itself so dreamily flows, even like the melody of who I am,* she thought.

She imagined Choctaw and Ouimas Indians on their hunting and trade migrations paddling from salty Lake St. Louis, now called Ponchartrain, all the way down the Bayou, then portaging the two-mile trail along the Esplanade ridge to the acute bend in the Mississippi River, now capped by the Vieux Quartier, the French Quarter, at the crescent in the river. She liked the old trail's good old names: Rue Bay St. Jean, Avenue Bayou St. Jean, Bayou Avenue, Bayou Rue and now sometimes Bayou Rd. But her own name for it she most loved the music of—Rue Bayou St. Jean.

Josephine made her way by foot along a familiar, slightly overgrown trail in the descending dusk. Doves called long and low. Hummingbirds darted in straight lines for final feedings among bromeliads, hibiscus, and scarlet trumpet vines. Occasional white egrets stalked the shores. A large, black-bodied bird with a honey-brown neck perched on a fallen tree, turning its head up and down stream, "gulping" continuously. Giant cypress trees dripped in the drizzle. Lovely pink oleander blossoms belied their poison. She heard low thrumming and saw a glow growing from a torchlit clearing among the cypress, near the shore of the still bayou. Soon, orange flames danced in the black eyes of alligators, live logs floating.

Gradually, more people appeared around the unlit bonfire. Doctor John Montanee, in red loincloth and blue face tattoos, sat on a throne wrought of cypress branches. On a higher throne, her yellow skin wrapped in red handkerchiefs, presided Saloppée, Voodoun Queen: a blue and scarlet tignon crowned her, scarlet shawled her shoulders, a blue cord ringed her waist. Her arms dripped beads, bracelets, and rings. By her feet stood a tall teenage girl in white, with flowing black hair and a regal nose. One woman came up to Queen Saloppée, expressing her request.

Then, in turn, Josephine stepped forth. "S'il vous plait, chère Reine honorée, Saloppée, si possible, laisse moi la prochaine fois sois donnée une fille, une petite fille." If it may please you, dear honored queen, Saloppée, allow me next time to be given a daughter, a little girl. "Si Marie Reine de Ciel me permet, Saloppée, honorée. Liba, aide moi, Dani, aide moi." If Marie, Queen of Heaven, should permit me—St. Peter, St. Michael, help me.

Queen Saloppée summoned a helper-woman, then sent her into the shadows.

Josephine felt more received by the eyes of the girl in white, who, with her caramel skin, seemed almost a mirror-image of Josephine, her younger self, though Josephine's own wavy black tresses were wrapped beneath her golden tignon. The helper-woman returned with a deep red pomegranate, which Saloppée told Josephine to place beneath her bed with cloves. The Voodoun Queen seemed as hard as yellow poplar.

As though it had cool-burned away the low-swimming clouds, the full moon, yolk-orange, appeared in the east, seemed to pause, then rose slowly, washing the clearing, offering shadows new, shortening in the bayou, blue.

Saloppée welcomed all to the gathering. "Bienvenu. Dis midsummer night we celebratin' La Fête de St. Jean-Baptiste;

Jean-Baptiste, wattah-baptizuh fo' de fire-man; Jean-Baptiste, wild man ob locust 'n' honey, unwordy to tie de sandals ob de Comin One; Jean-Baptiste, head on a pladder, so we can fine de higher fire, like dese cypress trees on dis Bayou St. Jean."

Thrumming became drumming as Doctor John led a handful of men, intensifying their beat, till they stopped, all silent. Into the space men brought a barred cage, onto the top of which Saloppée stepped. Inside the cage—the god Vodu, the large holy grass snake within, the zombie, who knows the past, who sees into the present, and who gleans the future.

"Oh, Damballah-wedo, serpent-god, ohh! Light de fire!" Saloppée cried. She started to writhe and spasm, head and arms almost jerking from her neck. She started to chant-sing; the people echoed, line by line:

Eh! Eh! Bomba, hen! Hen!
Canga bafio te!
Canga moune de le!
Canga do ki la!
Canga li!

Eh! Eh! Bomba, hen! Hen!
Tie up the abusers!
Tie up the whites!
Tie up the action spirit!
Tie them up!

Doctor John reached up to Saloppée's shivering arm and started to shudder, as another took his other arm, then someone else, a chain growing, one mighty centipede dancing around the rising bonfire. Occasionally a woman fell onto the ground, writhing, shrilling, almost unnoticed as the chain closed the gap, like a healing snake. *Eh! Eh! Bomba, hen! Hen!* Like a healing snake.

The girl in white hung back by Josephine, watching all,

not ready herself. When Queen Saloppée released the human chain, dancers spun off like sparks. When a glistening black man reached toward Josephine, she realized it was time to recede, having made her mission. She and the girl in white nodded to each other. The girl kissed her own fingers, then aimed her hand straight as a lance at the pomegranate Josephine happened to be holding at her navel. Josephine merged into the shadows of the bayou. A swamp owl who-who-ed through cypress-dappled moonlight.

CHAPTER 6:

DRAUZIN VALSIN BACAS, 1818–30

In the slowly expanding world of Drusino, now "petit" or "Ti-" Drauzin Bacas, his father, Barthelemy, was the Sun King. Ever since Barthelemy had moved down to the second-floor master bedroom and up to the head of the table after his father's death, he determined almost everything with unquestioned authority, dominating the dining room and any room he entered, except perhaps his and Adelaïde's bedroom. Although his father was their sun, Ti-Drauzin often imagined Père's face obscured in storm clouds. Ti-Drauzin's mother, Adelaïde, was the moon, actually determining the rhythms and the flows of their lives.

When the seven Bacas and Cossé children played salle à manger, or dining room, under the cypress tree in the court-yard, twin Barthelemy Cossé would take his place emphatically at the head of the table, standing, standing, standing. The girls, Luysa Bacas and Marie Josephine Cossé, would take turns as either Maman-Pouponne at the other end, or as slave Ernestine serving. Twin Dominique Cossé would play his own long-absent father, humming absent-mindedly. Joseph Valmont liked to play Alfonce, slave-serving. And the younger boys, Ti-Jean Batiste and Ti-Drauzin, played themselves, waiting, waiting, hopping from foot to foot, until finally "Barthelemy" sat down emphatically, as did the others en suite.

Then, after an unbearably long silence, one of the boys would pretend to forget and make a peep, and "Barthelemy's" hand would bang the table furiously as all twitched and pretended to catch jumping plates and falling glasses. Ti-Jean-Baptiste would start to weep pathetically, so squeakily that everyone would burst out laughing.

Then "Barthelemy" would thunder and bang again. All would quiet. "Maman-Pouponne" would signal "Ernestine" with her eyes, would soothe muffled Ti-Jean-Baptiste with her hand under the table, and "Barthelemy," master of the house, would have regained control of the mutinous ship.

After miming eating in utter silence, "Maman-Pouponne" would eye "Ernestine" for dessert, and then they could all finally burst into loud, joyous songs. A few years later, when the children became aware that father Barthelemy was serving on the City Council, they transformed the scene from the dining room table to the Council meeting table, imagining the same culmination, his banging fist enforcing silence on the rest of the Council of New Orleans.

When Luysa and Marie Josephine squabbled with each other, or picked on the younger boys, and Marcelite or even Maman Adelaïde Pouponne herself would scold them, the accused youngsters would always say, "Oh, mais non, c'était Coco Robichaux qui me l'a fait—who made me do it—" And the children knew, but would never say, the silent part of that story— that the naughty girl Coco Robichaux had been snatched by a loup-garou, a werewolf.

Each New Year's Eve after he learned to write, Ti-Drauzin and his older siblings would write an important note along these lines:

My dear Père, my dear Maman,
I wish you a Happy and Prosperous New Year.
I will be a good little boy.
I will not tease my little sister anymore.
I will love you with all my heart.
—Drauzin

And Adelaïde, called "Pouponne" by the three Cossé boys, "Maman-Pouponne" by their sister Marie Josephine, who never knew her actual birth-mother, and "Maman" by the Bacas children, accompanied each child's new robe de jour de l'an, day robe, and chapeau de jour de l'an, day hat, with a note:

These four little verses tell you good morning,
These four little verses give you my love,
These four little verses give you my gift,
These four little verses ask you for mine.

Sometimes, Ti-Drauzin, his brothers, and cousins would accompany Alfonce, running alongside the wagon down five blocks to the Mississippi to fill barrels with river water. They loved playing on the shore, finding pieces of driftwood, a gooey boot, even an iron spike sticking half up out of the mud. They watched big-gulleted pelicans perched on the pier swoop to the water, scoop slivering silver to guzzle down their long, upstretched necks.

In the spring the river could be high, not so far from the waterside walking boards. In winter, the water could be way down and out, opening up gravelly sandbars they sometimes dared wade out to when Alfonce was not looking. Usually, the boys managed to find a few crabs, Cajun dwarf crawfish, a burrowing devil crawfish, and even occasionally a four-inch Ohio River shrimp, dead or alive. Sometimes Joseph sold crawfish to a street hawker for a few reales. Drauzin traded one with another boy, who offered an iron ring he'd found in the mud.

Returning to 116 St. Louis, they would help fill the ollas, large clay jars around the house and courtyard, with the muddy river water. When he was five, Ti-Drauzin put into a bowl an Ohio shrimp he'd found and fed it for three days before Joseph finally told him it had been dead all along. When the boys brought crawfish, Ernestine got the girls singing an old song the Negro children in her bayou country used to sing to tease Cajun children.

Poor crawfish ain't got no show,
Frenchmen catch 'em and make gumbo.
Go all 'round de Frenchmen's beds,
Don't fine nothin' but crawfish heads.

Slaves Marcelite and Ernestine loved to tease Luisa and Josephine. "You ready to drink de Mississippi mud-waters straight, hen, jeunes filles?" Everyone in New Orleans knew the waters of the Mississippi made women fertile. The girls would squirm away, half-disgusted, half-mystified.

Then Ernestine would drop a lump of yellow alum into each olla, and the children would stir for awhile. Ti-Drauzin especially loved to stir, entranced, first with his big wooden spoon whirling around clockwise, stronger and stronger, till he had a clear whirlpool, almost down to the bottom, then reversing his spoon, slowly starting counterclockwise, shaping his maelstrom into a beautiful spiral, then reversing, and so on. The first task was to mix the alum into the river water, which took steady vigor. Then ever-gentler stirring allowed the mighty river's silt to settle, leaving the upper water gradually "clarified" for their own home use. Marcelite taught Ernestine and the children to sing:

Drawin' a bucket of water
For my oldest daughter.

> Give me the racket and the silver spoon
> And let my pillar come over, come over.

Gradually, as their singing became more energetic, the girls and Joseph and JB, as they increasingly called Ti-Jean-Baptiste, would jump up while Ti-Drauzin would continue stirring. The two girls would join hands while Joseph and JB would join hands over and across theirs during the verse. Then they would all slide their arms down to the waist, shouting,

> Bunch o'rags!
> Bunch o'rags!
> Bunch o'rags!
> Bunch o'rags!

Sometimes Marcelite told stories to Ernestine that the children found fascinating. Her aunt Dolores had chased away the evil spirit of a storm with an axe. Once, Marcelite told of a witch who had entered a good woman's house. "—She tole witch to go into other room. So ole witch gone out and lef' her skin alayin' on floor. Woman jump outta bed an' sprinkle it wit' salt an' pepper. Ole witch come back, put on her skin, start ahollerin', jumpin' up an' down, like acrazy, 'I can't stan' it! I can't stan' it! Sompin' bitin' me.' Ole witch holler, 'Skin, don't you know me?' tree times, but salt an' pepper keep bitin'. Woman took de broomstick, shooed ole witch out, and den she disappear in de air, jus' lak dat."

Luysa and Josephine especially felt spooked, holding each other, even wailing a little. Marcelite reassured them, saying, "If you feels a place witch-creepy, you say, 'Holy Fadder, don' let dis ting bodder me.' He ain't gonna let it hurt you."

Sometimes Marcelite and Ernestine would be doing the laundry in the courtyard, scrubbing the clothes hard, wringing them out, and they would start singing a song from the cane plantations.

White folks want de niggers to work an' sweat,
Wans dem to cut de cane till dey is wringin' wet.
We poor niggers git nothin' atall,
White boss cusses an' gits it all.

Cut high, cut low,
Swing fast, swing slow.

Bend yo' back, tote it to de lift,
White boss hollers if yo' ain't swift.
De Lawd take keer of us when we is dead,
But in de canefield de white boss cracks yo' on de head.

The children would line up in a row, swinging their pretend machetes in beat; then, when "de white boss cracks yo' on de head," they took turns who would fall down, a limp rag on the ground, while the others kept swinging, singing. Only after some years did Joseph realize that Marcelite and Ernestine only sang this song when Père Barthelemy was not working in his woodshop in the courtyard—when de white boss was away.

Ti-Drauzin was the lightest-skinned of the siblings, with the thinnest lips. Adelaïde, concerned he was anemic, regularly had him drink a glass of water a rusty nail had soaked in. Since he leaned toward sickly, she'd have him swallow tallow to loosen a chest cold. Barthelemy always had tallow in his shop to keep saw-blades and planes from rusting, and to loosen screws in hardwood.

For boils or an inflammation Adelaïde made a poultice of shredded wild potato. Each spring the whole family drank sarsaparilla tea to purify the blood. When the boys scraped or cut themselves, and occasionally when Barthelemy in the woodshop cut himself, Adelaïde would apply cobwebs to staunch the bleeding. On the other hand, when someone just felt listless or slack, she placed leeches on the nape of their neck, to draw out bad blood.

The Bacas courtyard was not fancy; it was a working courtyard. In addition to the stable for the two horses, the cabriolet, and the wagon, it included latrines, laundry, summer kitchen, the slaves' quarters on the second floor above it, vegetable garden, chicken coop, and most importantly, Barthelemy's workshop.

All the boys spent hours in there, especially Joseph, watching their father work with Alfonce and Nelson, helping when they could, making little swords, bows and arrows, pirogues, ships. The Bacas boys were absorbing the craft through both osmosis and Père's gruff, clear, once-for-each-task-for-each-child instruction. After Père's "once," Joseph would often patiently help JB or Ti-Drauzin with their still-confused steps in a task, sometimes slyly guided by Alfonce or Nelson when Barthelemy was sufficiently preoccupied. Mainly, Père was the model, the template, according to which each son eventually became at least a journeyman woodsmith, cabinetmaker, or even éboniste.

Ti-Drauzin loved the various woods stacked on wall racks: oak, the hardest except for ironwood up north and mesquite out west; elm; sycamore; maple; dark walnut; willow for bending; ash for straight-strength; pine and cedar air-clearing and moth-proofing, and the best in water; then surprisingly strong spruce; cypress; palm; ebony; locust; linden, best for carving; and even bamboo. Each type of wood had a different smell and texture, and was best for a specific purpose, according to its hardness or softness, its color, its grain, and its durability.

Tools adorned another wall. A whole range of hand-saws— rip to cross-cut, big-toothed to fine, two-man for logs to coping saw for intricate scroll-work. Hammers ranged from light to heavy, from small jeweler, round-nubbed, through claw hammers, to heavy hand-sledge and canvas-covered, wood-headed mallets. Nails and screws galore were all in increasing sizes, in labeled wooden box slots in broad drawers. Beautiful hand-drills beckoned, with their polished walnut hand-knob at the tip. Cherry-handled chisels of all widths were sharpened daily. Beautiful planes for shaving smooth edges and surfaces had blades adjustable to appropriate heights.

Various cheap sandpapers weren't as effective as shark-skin. Later, by the late 1830s, a new English product, glass-paper, would make its way into the shops of the Bacases and other fine cabinetmakers of the city. The glass-frit's sharp edges were a much more effective abrasive than the easily smoothing sand glued to hide or rough papers.

Pedal-driven lathes turned bowls, table legs, and more. A pedal-driven band saw for certain cuts. Such foot-work enabled hand-work.

Sometimes, Ti-Drauzin would close his eyes and listen to the rhythms of the hammers on the chisels, the whirring pedal-driven saws or drills, the planing, the filing, the sand-ing. *I wonder how the craft of the original Creation sounded, and Cain's descendants—Jabal, Jubal, and Tubalcain, building the first cities.*

And care, care. Always sweeping before starting, during the work, after the work, always sweeping up sawdust and leftover wood. Careful measuring three times always, before any cutting. Careful measuring of angles, of upright plumb, of horizontal level, after anything is put together. Always clean-ing, oiling, sharpening the tools. And always, a crucial part of the diligent mastery that the boys learned early on: the tools must always be returned to their proper places, never left about. Opening windows to let sawdust clear. Barthelemy, cutting or sanding, usually had his blue or brown foulard over his mouth and nose.

Barthelemy's father had originally added to his trading ven-tures the beginnings of cabinetry- making in his workshop. Back in those days, the task of finishing veneers and varnish-ing, the gluing of thin layers of flitches (fine woods) in patterns, was confined to the special, sawdust-free shops of ébonistes, who had originally specialized using ebony. Barthelemy had apprenticed as a boy with an éboniste over on Rue Bienville.

After the French Revolution abolished the long-lingering medieval guilds, restriction evaporated, shops merged, and Barthelemy himself became known as a master éboniste in his own cabinetry shop, particularly enjoying crafting veneers in contrasting patterns of dark mahogany and paler woods. While the boys were still young, the slave Alfonce helped when needed, since Cecile, Barthelemy's prime shop slave, had run away years earlier. He had been hit one time too many in Barthelemy's bursts of exasperation.

Onto one wall Barthelemy had nailed a section of one of his early projects, an octagonal table with eight different woods, initially a stunning, complex treasure, which within a year had split apart unevenly as each wood seasoned, dried, and contracted at different rates and degrees—a constant reminder of the folly of youthful haste.

Ti-Drauzin always remembered watching Joseph aid his father, designing and then crafting the intricate cypress mill-work on the fireplace mantels and the ceiling moldings in the Bacas' living and dining rooms. Only in his early teens would Drauzin become aware of the citywide regard for the competence, fineness, and mastery of his father's skills as carpenter, cabinetmaker, joiner, and éboniste.

Proud that their father and uncle had fought with the pirates Lafitte and General Andrew Jackson against the British in the Battle of New Orleans, the Bacas children loved to play pirates in the courtyard. Pretend Jean and Pierre Lafitte respectfully protected a beautiful woman, allegedly royal, as pirate-mate; the childrens' tables were ships captured. In their scenarios, passengers were ransomed, contraband slaves resold, treasures kept, and goods sold cheap on the black markets of New Orleans.

Although Père Barthelemy had little to say on the matter, the children loved to get Nonc Drauzin talking when he came over to help Barthelemy in the shop. About the battle of New Orleans, Nonc Drauzin told them that the crucial idea to use cotton bales as a redoubt on the treeless Chalmette battlefield had actually come from a slave, though usually attributed to General Jackson's brilliance.

But the Bacas children were especially interested, of course, in the pirates themselves. "One night," continued Nonc Drauzin, "during a long watch-duty, one of Lafitte's lieutenants told me that Jean Lafitte and his pirates in the bayous of Barataria remained so powerful because of guardian phantoms." Yes, guardian phantoms—bad land spirits. Of these bad kinds of land spirit, revealed Nonc Drauzin, there were seven: bulls, lions, dogs, babies, snakes, persons, and pearls.

"Now, water spirits are good," Nonc Drauzin continued. "Now, that Gaston le Cocq, he's a treasure hunter. That Ton Pimpton, he don't dig; he's spirit comptroller—'you gotta be careful an' you gotta be clean,' he told me. 'You got to suffer too—'

"Lafitte would take five, six men to bury treasure. He'd tell all but one who would be the guardian of the treasure. They'd bury all the silver, gold, jewels. 'Now: who will guard?' asks Lafitte. One pirate says, 'I will.' The others (not Lafitte) kill him and toss him in alongside. He becomes guardian spirit of the treasure."

Sometimes the children wondered if the shop slave Cecile had joined Lafitte's men. "Betchya he's on some island, that Cecile, guardian spirit of this treasure or that," said Joseph, which gave them all chills.

In later years, as the boys roamed the city more, they'd often find themselves five or six blocks east at the blacksmith shop of the pirate king's brother, Pierre Lafitte. The boys loved to watch not only the fires of the forge, the sparks and bangs of the orange-glowing iron being hammered, but also the comings and goings of high folk and low, from the governor's mansion to the bayous of Barataria.

Just two blocks down Rue St. Louis from home, at the corner with Chartres St., was Pierre Maspero's slave exchange coffeehouse. The boys looked inside at the long, beaten, oiled tables, the low, sooted beams clanging with hanging copper pots and pans. They imagined Jean Lafitte huddled there in a corner with General Andrew Jackson, old Hickory, as ill as he was, making plans for how to meet and defeat the British, and what the ensuing pardons and possible privileges would be for Lafitte's pirates in a successful aftermath.

Everyone knew that across the street, former Mayor Girod had offered to shelter in his home, Emperor Napoleon, in case he might escape from the notorious island prison on St. Helena. When the Emperor crossed over into historical immortality in his prison cell at age fifty-one in May 1821, all New Orleans knew the Emperor would never enter the Crescent City after all.

On autumn nights Ti-Drauzin savored drifting to sleep to the music of the small orchestra wafting over the rooftops and treetops from the Court of Two Sisters, during the frequent quadroon balls there, just down from Bourbon St. In the daytime the boys would periodically venture in there to look again at the wide-spreading willow tree under which Jean Lafitte was said to have dispatched three men in succession in their final duels, in one night.

One Sunday, the older children returned home after mass at Cathedral St. Louis, changed clothes, and ventured back out to the streets, following the heartbeat of the city up, over, and across Rampart St. to Congo Square, just outside the Vieux Quartier. There, some men sat on large Konga drums. Others played the four-stringed banze as slaves danced—without chains, without whips, without orders—in rhythms galore, shifting, subtle, complex, whole textures of movement and feeling absorbed by dancers, musicians, and all present, listening and being played by the music itself. What an education for these young bodies and souls. Drauzin saw Ernestine was dancing while Marcelite stood off to the side. He saw them see him see them.

That night at supper, when the children were allowed finally to speak at dessert, Drauzin told his parents of seeing Marcelite and Ernestine at the dancing, Ernestine moving, Marcelite still. "The drums rocked the city," he said.

Adelaïde looked at Drauzin, weirdly wondering if some Wolof ancestor were speaking through him. He was particularly intrigued with the banze, later to evolve from its Senegalese origins into the banjo.

Drauzin loved listening to any music. Joseph often played the violin at night, with their father on cello, although Jean-Baptiste, as he grew, showed a finer sensitivity on violin. Luysa and Marie Josephine loved playing four-in-hand on the piano, especially Schubert, when one of them, or anyone else, might be feeling sad. Their tutor, Basil Raphael Crockère, had introduced the children to Schubert's exciting, contemporary music.

Gradually, Drauzin found more and more ways to weave in among anyone's playing, harmoniously, enhancingly, on flute, clarinet, guitar, any music giving him pleasure. On his own he often recreated tunes the next day on a mandolin. Of the various children, he was the most flexibly adept, and perhaps the most soothed, entranced, making music.

CHAPTER 7:
JOSEPHINE YOUNG, 1818–32

Mlle. Josephine Tassy had given birth to three sons with Samuel Charles Young II: Samuel Charles Young IV, Philippe Augustus Young, and Joseph Samuel Young. And she had bought and sold seven slaves by the time her wish was granted with the birth of a girl, Josephine Young, in the midst of a yellow fever epidemic on August 11, 1818. For the gift of daughter Josephine, Maman Josephine always felt more grateful to the girl in white than to the Voodoun Queen herself, Saloppée, that night back on the Bayou St. Jean. Little Josephine's older brother Joseph Samuel survived the yellow fever too but, severely weakened, died the next year. In addition to buying and selling slaves, Maman Josephine, bereft though she was, was buying real estate.

Meanwhile it became clear that her striking beauty was nevertheless not sufficient to keep Samuel Young II from fathering children with Black Betty as well, so much so that Samuel granted Black Betty her freedom in 1822. His cheeks and nose ever more ruddy from excess of fruit of the vine, his silvering hair ever more leaden and askew, his buttons ever more unbuttoned, Samuel Young was elected alderman no more. In fact, fewer and fewer clients knocked on his door.

Josephine was already free, not needing to divorce him since they hadn't been allowed to marry in the first place; she forced upon Samuel his freedom from her. In daughter

Josephine Young's earliest years, her father Samuel was so fast receding from her life that she learned little of his father tongue, English. At times, mother Josephine Tassy would say to her children, as explanation, "Your father simply became ever more unbuttoned."

Up to this point in her life, Josephine Tassy had experienced in some ways the typical patterns of a placée, a placed one, in which young lovely octoroon Josephine had been taken in by older wealthy white Samuel, in this case American, who had enjoyed her beauty, her youth, her flesh, their relationship, and her mothering of their several children for more than a decade. Together they had reached the often inevitable juncture of parting ways. The norm was that white *he*, since their colored offspring were not allowed to inherit, would nevertheless continue to provide for colored *she* and their offspring, including their lodging in the neighborhoods of Trêmé or Maurigny.

Here, Josephine Tassy departed from part of the pattern. For by 1822, Josephine Tassy and two other men, three free persons of color, owned the whole block on Bayou Rd. between North Claiborne Ave. and North Roman Rd., a total of two arpents—a unit of land of nearly an acre per arpent. The norm was also that now Samuel Young would marry a proper white woman, which in his case had already happened twice, too far back in his past. And the norm was that octoroon Josephine Tassy would now become available to a man of color.

Down at 45 Bayou Rd. lived Rozette Toutant Brou, unmarried Creole mother of eight. Her father had been Toutant Beauregard; on Ursuline Ave., one street west of Bayou Rd., Rozette's Mathé daughter, Hortense, was busy building a family of twelve with

Firmin Perreault, Josephine Tassy's half-brother.

Rozette's Mathé son, Simeon, was handsome, with a well-kept beard and mustache, a steady, rich voice, and a gentle manner. Also a careful carpenter. Although Simeon was long familiar to Josephine as Hortense's reliable, enjoyable brother, with whom she had had both real estate and slave dealings, Josephine found herself suddenly looking into the eyes of an equal, a brother of sorts, yes, but an alluring, mischievous, independent man who asked little and gave like a tree. Fatherless Josephine Tassy had by now had more than enough "father" in Samuel Young II. When she looked at Simeon Mathé anew, she knew that she, finally her own woman, had found her own man.

One day, Maman Josephine Tassy was brushing the walnut-brown hair of seven-year-old daughter Josephine Young, who, having always thought her mother to be the most beautiful woman in the world, was only beginning to realize, observing other women more carefully, that she actually *was* the most beautiful in her world. "Maman, am I lighter than you, who is lighter than Granmère?"

"Yes, chou-chou, you are indeed lighter."

"Why?"

O, mon Dieu, Josephine thought to herself. *Here it comes. I've been dreading this. My boys never asked. But my Josephine, myself. Wouldn't you know? How do I respond now? Mercy.* "O, chou-chou, you really want to know?" Nod. "—Well, your great-great-grandmother, from Mali in Africa, was black as night in day. With a white man from Quebec, she had your great-grandmother, making her mulatto, half-white, half-black. With a white man, she had my mother, Marie-Françoise Lalande, making her quadroon, quarter-black. When she fell in love with French Lieutenant Joseph Tassy, also white, she had me, your mother, making me technically quinteron, though most people just think of me as octoroon or metis. You see, mulatto—one half; quadroon—one quarter; octoroon —one eighth. I, Josephine Tassy, am one-eighth black."

"Then what am I?"

"Well, I fell in love with your father, Samuel Young, also white, making your full Young brothers and you, Josephine Young, what some would call sextaroon, or technically hexadecaron—one-sixteenth black."

"Aww, ça n' vas pas, Maman, sextaroon? Hexadecaron? Hexadecaron. I am hexadecaron!? That's stupid. One-sixteenth black? But that makes no sense; I'm all colored!"

"Yes, but you are quite light—and some would also call you Mustée, or Mamalouque."

"What? I am Mustée, Mamalouque, sextaroon, and hexadecaron?" She repeated that several times, starting to giggle, which grew. Josephine had felt reluctant with each response of hers, almost like pulling tissue from her flesh. And yet, soon mother and daughter were both giggling at the absurdity. "And my children?"

"Well, if you marry white, you'd have—one-thirty-second, which would be—septaroon, Mustefino, or Sang-melé."

"Oh no, septaroon, Mustefino, Sang-melé!" They shouted out together.

"And if I married a black, black man?"

"They'd be black septaroon instead of white septaroon."

"And, either way, they'd have—" asked Ti-Josephine.

"One-sixty-fourth—Sambo, Griffe."

"Sambo! Griffe!" Both shouted it out as Maman shook the hairbrush, stridently stamping her right foot forward on each stressed syllable, imitated, of course, by Ti-Josephine, "Sambo, Griffe! Sambo, Griffe!" Maman's too-strident stamping slightly scared Ti-Josephine, snapping her out of her nervous giggle-fit.

"Mama, this doesn't feel funny any more."

"Si, ma Josie chère, I haven't felt it funny at all."

"I feel all chopped up into little pieces on a cutting board. Can we stop?"

"Of course, my sweet, of course," wrapping Ti-Josephine around, doing her best to re-enwomb, to reintegrate her too little daughter.

"Maman, I wish I hadn't asked you."

"Me too. I wish I had not answered you so. And I'm putting all your little pieces back together, each with a petit baiser." And Maman kissed each piece. Ti-Josephine squirmed, delighting back together.

"The only thing that matters, my dear Josie," stroking her long hair, "is that we are all lots of colors.

"You don't understand it, and I, your own mother, don't understand. But, ma chère chou-chou, in our world here, these ridiculous matters somehow still matter, I am so sorry to say. Ca me fait de la peine. It pains me, it pains me." She brushed her exhausted daughter's vibrant, wavy dark hair.

After another while of subsiding quiet, young Josephine spoke. "But what actual color am I?"

"Oh, ma chère Ti-Josephine, who knows? You are light. It so depends, on the time of day, on the time of year, on what you're wearing, on whom you're standing near. It so depends. Are you white, pale, high yaller, or yellow? Gold, brass, butterscotch, caramel, buckskin, tan, tawny, cinnamon, or copper? Rouge, red, red mahogany? Olive, nut-brown, plain mahogany? Grey, walnut, coal-black, the deepest blue-black, raven-black, purple-black? What color are you?

"A saying goes, 'Yaller folks all mulatto, quadroon near white as Missus.' Maybe quadroon Granmère Marie-Françoise Lalande is usually pale 'yaller,' like light Dijon mustard? Maybe your octoroon Maman Josephine Tassy is often a pale amber, in some lights even 'white'? And you, ma chère petite moi, maybe you, ma chère Ti-Josephine Young, have skin the color of pearl, or slightly musky dawn, with your green, green eyes. Maybe."

"And you with your grey, grey eyes, ma chère Maman."

"Si, Chérie, your green, green, my grey, grey eyes, si."

"Maybe your grey eyes your gris-gris, Maman,"

"Si, Chérie," laughing, with a kiss, "and your green eyes your gris-gris, your Voodoun good luck charm, ma petite Josephine, toi, ma petite moi."

At age thirty-four, Josephine Tassy gave birth to her fifth child, her first son by Simeon Mathé, Louis Francois, followed within a year by her second daughter, Matilde Melicerte Mathé. Josephine Young was growing up with little of her father Samuel, with the companionship of her older Young brothers, Samuel IV and Philippe, and now, after a seven-year hiatus in transition, her new Mathé half-siblings.

One pleasure for young Josephine in the new family constellation occurred whenever the Toutant Beauregard family would come up from Plaquemines Parish to visit Granmère Rozette, bringing along a second cousin just her age, Pierre Gustave Toutant Beauregard, whom Josephine affectionately called GT. Small, with buckskin complexion, he busied them building forts, which he charged her to decorate.

When Josephine Young was eleven years old, her mother gave some of the eastern edge of her property to the city of New Orleans so the large street Esplanade could be built along the Esplanade Ridge, largely paralleling Bayou Rd., leaving it quieter. As with most of her neighbors, Josephine Tassy's gift was freely given, the contract "requiring only for compensation the building of banquettes in Curb Stone and the repair of fences."

When Josephine turned twelve, the state of Louisiana passed a law forbidding slaves to learn to read or write. It was too late on Bayou Rd.; Maman Josephine had taught both Catherine, now forty, and her twenty-two-year-old son, Giles, how to read. But no new reading for new slaves. Young

Josephine found herself, more often than before, visiting her father Samuel's house, specifically the French section of his library, which was in increasing disarray. She would sometimes spend hours putting it back in order before bringing home her new reading. She wished she could put her father back in order, too.

When Maman Josephine had her seventh child, Brou Simon Mathé, her second son by Simeon Mathé, the wise state of Louisiana passed the Statute of 1831, clarifying and reaffirming that while white mothers and fathers may legitimize their natural children, and while free people of color may legitimize their colored offspring of lawfully contracted marriage, whites and coloreds may not do so together. Young Josephine and her Young brothers would clearly remain illegitimate in the eyes of the law. But Maman Josephine and Père Simeon saw a new avenue—one that would, however, be dramatically delayed.

First, slow-blooming Josephine Young finally experienced her first blood-sign that she was becoming a woman. Her mother brewed for her tisane de feuilles de lauriers, the laurel leaves helping both cramps and stomachaches. Inwardly modest to the core, young Josephine was emotionally far behind her slow-to-awaken body. Catherine enjoyed checking Josephine's heels for any sign of yellow tinge. Ever since young Josephine had asked Catherine the first time, and her response had been, "Checkin' fo' signs yo' gonna be spinster," an overt glance from Catherine at Josephine's heels was enough to flush blush into those same almost peach-blossom cheeks. Catherine enjoyed the predictability of the process.

Young Josephine, checking privately in a mirror, could see no yellow tinge, yet she realized once again that her own skin was indeed usually lighter than her mother's amber, which was lighter than her Granmère's mustard "yaller," a progressive paling. Just what color was her own skin? She could not say. Maybe some combination of dusk and dawn? Her dark hair flowed, wavy, with natural hints of red.

But daughter Josephine's own dramatic internal developments were quickly eclipsed; before much of the year had passed, the whole city was seized by yellow fever, starting down by the river and "flooding" north. Although he may have died anyway, long-weakened 61-year-old Samuel Charles Young II was the first of the intermixed clan to succumb to yellow fever, which was reinforced by the charging cavalry of cholera. Samuel Young, the formerly respected alderman, had had the ear of Napoleon's emissary way back in 1803, assuring him that the western states would someday become independent. Now Samuel died alone, intestate.

Mr. S. C. Young II left nothing for his white Young children but debt and one fiddle, four pistols, two hundred books (a large number in those days), and a bust of Napoleon. The three older Young children from the previous mother left the house and everything except the four pistols. Samuel Young IV, Philippe, and sister Josephine brought to Maman's house the fiddle and the books, leaving the bust of Napoleon for any remaining vultures.

Bronze John, as the fever was called by some, returned to New Orleans with a vengeance. Remembering how her mother had gotten her through two childhood epidemics of yellow fever, Josephine Tassy tied a bag of camphor around the necks of each of her children. She succeeded in wrapping the feet of her three Mathé children in boots of yellow paper covered with tallow, snuff, and mustard. But there she failed, of course, with her three older Young children.

When Granmère Marie-Francoise Lalande succumbed to acute chills, fever, and aches in late October, the two Josephines made her drink cup after cup of tea, alternating between red pepper and peach-tree leaf. Deeply concerned as the days and nights passed, Maman Josephine was urged by Simeon to go visit the Widow Paris on St. Ann St. in case she might help. When the Josephines knocked, the door opened to Maman Josephine's double surprise, and to her daughter's ignorant awe.

Standing in front of them was the womanly version of the lovely teenage girl in white at Saloppée's midsummer ceremony on Bayou St. Jean back before baby Josephine had been born, even conceived. Maman Josephine had always thought that girl in white had somehow helped Josephine's next child to be a girl. Now the woman before them had fully caught up to her regal nose, an epitome of harmonious poise. Remembering that she had felt then as though she were looking in a mirror at herself, Josephine could tell the Widow Paris was recognizing her as well.

Josephine said to their host, "Yes, la voila, my daughter Josephine here was indeed born next. I have always wanted to thank you." The young widow modestly shook her head while taking Maman Josephine's right hand and young Josephine's left hand together in her own hands, enjoying looking into mother Josephine's grey eyes and daughter Josephine's green eyes.

"Mon Dieu, Madame," continued Josephine, "I had no idea that the Widow Paris is you! May I tell my daughter a story I have heard about you?"

"Yes, of course, as long as it is essentially true."

"Josephine, when this beautiful woman before us was just a few years older than you, chou-chou, she told the visiting Duc d'Orleans that he would one day become king of France, which did indeed, to everyone else's surprise, including his own, come to pass. She goes to mass every morning, before artfully ministering to the hair of ladies of New Orleans, often helping certain Creoles through dye, straightening, or wigs to hide any hints of café au lait heritage. In addition, she has helped many people, rich and poor, with many kinds of problems." The Widow Paris stood patiently.

"And the story I really want to tell you says that one day she was walking down Bourbon Street. Ahead of her, along the curbside banquette with her entourage, walked none other than Saloppée, her former teacher, the Voodoun Queen of New Orleans. The Widow Paris called forward, commanding, 'Saloppée. The time has come. Step back.' Saloppée stopped, stood still, silent. As she turned her head slowly back, her face almost dissolved like a falling cloth. Saloppée threatened curses upon the Widow Paris; Marie LaVeau insisted.

"Then Saloppée could tell. She stepped aside, hissing, her yellow parchment skin shriveling. The strength was now with Marie LaVeau, the new Voodoun Queen of New Orleans, who proceeded, followed by that same entourage."

Young Josephine was now as stunned as her mother had been when the door had first opened. The Widow Paris was none other than the already legendary Marie LaVeau! Sly Simeon. Marie, smiling, nodded, acknowledging the truth of Josephine's story. "How can I help you?" When Josephine explained her concern about her mother's illness, versions of which Marie LaVeau would hear hundreds in the coming month, she had two responses.

"One suggestion: In two inches of water in a tub, stand an axe head on its nose in the water. Balance three black horse-hairs and a white one on the edge of the axe. Sprinkle a small amount of red pepper on the horsehairs and push the tub under her bed, not disturbing the contents. Scatter a handful of cornmeal in the form of a cross in front of the patient's bed and wet the cross with rum made from molasses. Then repeat:

"Heru mande, heru mande, heru mande.
"Tigli li papa.
"Do se dan godo.
"Ah tingonai ye!

"My second suggestion: To your bags of camphor on the children, add a picture of St. Joseph. I also suggest, Chère, to pray to Mère Marie and to Dani, St. Michel, to help shrieve your mother's soul, to prepare her for her journey."

Marie LaVeau kissed the forehead of both mother and dauther, and Maman Josephine left for the Voodoun Queen a basket of brown, white, and blue-green eggs.

The Josephines followed Marie LaVeau's instructions, placing the tub under Granmère's bed. Within two days the fever, chills, and vomiting in fact subsided. Relief permeated the family until young Josephine noticed that Granmère's skin was yellowing (clearly no sign of spinster). Soon, vomiting resumed, this time with blood. Maman Josephine knew the liver and other organs were under attack. Within three more days, Marie-Francoise Lalande, mother of eight, departed on her journey to the afterlife. Her son, Firmin Perreault, father of ten, followed, as did her other son, Apollinaire, and Firmin's own son, Firmin Mathé Perreault.

Josephine Tassy, dumb with grief, knew at least that her family was not unique. Five thousand deaths were recorded in ten days. In twelve days, a sixth of the population of New Orleans was buried. Dead-carts carried corpses like bales on the levee.

Welcome to womanhood, Josephine Young, she thought.

CHAPTER 8:

MARCELITE, 1829

One evening, Barthelemy was sitting in the courtyard in the dusk, smoking a white clay pipe. Adelaïde had been helped by Marcelite and Ernestine to put to bed les cacahouettes, the peanuts, the younger batch of Bacases. Nine-year-old Marie Josephine and eight-year-old Leon were upstairs babbling to each other in bed, and Marcelite was still singing three-year-old Elizabeth Coelina to sleep. Young Adelaïde Emilia was now twelve.

As the family kept expanding, Barthelemy had purchased the house next door, 114 St. Louis St., linked by the street-to-courtyard narrow passageway. By now the Cossé boys had all moved on, Dominique finding their father afar, the others not. Josephine Cossé, now twenty, chose to remain with her cousin-twin Luysa. Joseph, age twenty-two; JB (Jean-Baptiste), seventeen; and Drauzin, now sixteen, were sleeping in the new house, joining the family at 116 St. Louis St. for meals and the natural flow of home life.

Drauzin, this night, was playing on his twelve-string Genoa mandolin under a sycamore in the corner of the courtyard. He sought sounds for the scents from the crepe myrtles, their fragile red blooms above the waxy branches, and especially the wafting white and the yellow jasmines, turning the modest, utilitarian courtyard by day into Alhambra by evening.

After Marcelite had tucked in little Elizabeth, reappearing

on her way back from the latrine, Adelaïde invited her to take a seat in the deepening dusk. Drauzin felt Marcelite was a cascade of roundnesses, her head, her cheeks, her shoulders, her chest, her waist, her thighs, embodying her ambiance.

Adelaïde looked at her slave and asked, "How old are you now, Marcelite?"

Pause. "I'm not sure, mebbe thirty-five, Mme. Barthelemy."

"Tell me about your mother."

Pause. "Not much to say. Don' know where she be. Las' I know, she had fi'teen chillun, each by a differen' man. Each time she had a chile, she'd get sold again. Allus havin' to fine a new man."

"Oh, Marcelite—do you know anything 'bout your daddy?"

More pause. "I can' picture him. Jules his name. Jules. Massa Valsin, out St. Jean Baptiste Parish, lock him in a tight standin' box, nails all stickin' in de sides. Don' know why. Affer two day and nights, he 'uz ant-bit, fly-bit, ripped all over, an los' an eye. One slave, a Drauzin, same name 's your boy, tol' me dat one year later Jules jus' up'n' disappeart. Nobody know. Soul-catchers searchin' up norf. Nobody know."

"Oh, Marcelite, my dear Marcelite."

Back under the sycamore, Drauzin's mandolin silenced.

Two days later, in midafternoon, Adelaïde called Marcelite over to the desk in the corner of the living room. Drauzin stood nearby.

"Oui, Madame?"

"Marcelite, I know your birth was special, despite being born a slave." Marcelite listened blankly, not daring to understand, although she certainly knew her Madame had been born the same. "You have helped me mother my own children. I will always be deeply grateful."

Marcelite nodded and bowed slightly. Adelaïde continued,

"I, now forty-six, will have no more. You, thirty-five, could still have yours."

Marcelite winced, gritted her teeth, and shook her head. Adelaïde, looking into Marcelite's tightened eyes, picked up a piece of paper. Never having learned to read or write, even while her children were well tutored by Basil Crockère, Adelaïde had asked Drauzin to familiarize himself with the document, which she now asked him to read aloud to Marcelite:

"State: Louisiana; city: New Orleans; parish: Orleans.

"Abstract: Adelaïde Beaulieu, age forty-six, a free woman of color, presents that she is the 'legitimate owner' of a thirty-five-year-old female mulatto slave named Marcelite, whom she intends to manumit. She vouches that Marcelite has 'always behaved like a dutiful servant' and has 'never been guilty of any thing which might legally prevent her from being affranchised.' Adelaïde Beaulieu therefore asks that the sheriff 'be authorized' to post up the notices 'as the law directs.'"

Marcelite looked first at Drauzin, then fiercely at Adelaïde, checking for a ruse. Adelaïde showed her "signature"—a mark at the bottom of the page.

"Ma-nu-mit," Marcelite uttered slowly, sound by sound.

"Yes." Adelaïde, beaming to burst, weeping, repeated, "Yes, Marcelite, manumit. I—free—you. You are free to go, Marcelite."

Marcelite, cheeks wetting, took deep breaths, groaned, "Oh, Lawd," and stepped into the warm arms of Adelaïde Pouponne Beaulieu. Adelaïde whispered into her ear, "Any friend who gives you a fish, you better to get him to teach you to fish. Bless you."

Marcelite then hugged Drauzin and pinched his cheek with joy, leaving him grinning. "Oh, pas possible! Pas possible!" She left the living room for her quarters out back.

The next day Marcelite bid farewell amid song, cheers, and tears from les cacahuettes. Ernestine held herself tight, dour, apart. When the front door closed after Marcelite, Adelaïde collapsed onto an ottoman in the living room, groaning almost like a donkey, sounds her family had never heard from her before. Her children gathered around her. She looked into their faces, sighing, "Oh, mes enfants, oh, mes enfants." Barthelemy lowered his oak-tree neck and kissed her gently atop her head.

CHAPTER 9:
MARKET, 1833

That evening in the courtyard before Marcelite's manumission, while Josephine Young was growing toward her womanhood on Bayou Rd., Drauzin Bacas, plucking his mandolin at 116 St. Louis St., had overheard two facts during the conversation between his mother and Marcelite. Those two facts silenced his mandolin. They had not let go. He could hardly free himself from them, festering like two wounds. The name of the slave who had told Marcelite of her father Jules's escape had been Drauzin. And the name of Jules's torturer, the master, had been Valsin.

Surprisingly, Drauzin Valsin Bacas's Bacas clan had survived the simultaneous yellow fever and cholera plagues of 1832 intact. In fact, Drauzin's older brother, Joseph Valmont Bacas, had married Anne Louise Essayleme earlier that year; they were settling into their new life together on the second floor of 114 Rue St. Louis well before the plagues hit.

Drauzin had started to suffer a kind of compulsion he hardly understood. Many nights he experienced a recurring nightmare. An over-muscled man twisted, eyes clenched, mouth cut open in a grimace like a tipped cup, screeching as his right arm brought down a whip. Under the whip, an unusually small man looked up, eyes wide, mouth in mirroring wide grimace, silent, neck ringed with five-inch spikes, shackled hands upreaching, beseeching. The more Valsin whipped, the more he shrank. The more Drauzin was whipped, the more he grew, sometimes breaking the shackles. Sometimes, Drauzin began then to whip Valsin, and the nightmare resumed, the two figures interchanging in size and position.

By day Drauzin Valsin Bacas sometimes felt forced, even invisibly ushered, down Rue St. Louis. So it was one May day that this young man, now twenty, stepped onto the street, dressed as always when not working in his father's shop: plain black cravat-band round his neck; white shirt with wide, turn-over collar; vest; wide-lapelled, double-breasted frock coat; and round-capped, wide-brimmed straw hat. He had washed his stained, calloused hands, cleaning the nails of sawdust and oil-grime. Drauzin's slender fingers belonged, he saw so clearly, on keys, strings, and flute holes, rather than wielding hammer, chisel, and plane.

Although he wished he could leave his frock coat behind in the midday heat, he wore it as armor, his badge of respectability, his ticket for mostly free movement. In case of emergency, however, he made sure to have his proof-of-freedom papers in his coat pocket, another recent requirement of all hommes libres de couleur, HLC, by that American, English-speaking government. Otherwise you could easily get muscled into a barracoon and sold to slash sugarcane the rest of your short-lived days.

Drauzin never took the streetcars starred for Negroes only. He knew he walked with the bearing of a free man. Yet one never knew, these days. Yes, he had overheard white Creoles say to each other, "Mount a mulatto on a horse and he'll deny his mother was a Negress." Drauzin was not denying his chère Maman, but he grew daily more aware that his liberty hung on a slendering thread.

Yet again he had left Père Barthelemy thundering in the shop at discovering another midday disappearance. "That damn son doesn't know how to stick to his tools." Nevertheless, Drauzin felt called to what he'd hardly taken notice of as a boy, having simply accepted it as part of his life's background. Several blocks south he came to perhaps the fanciest hotel in town, Hotel St. Louis, dominating the whole block between Chartres (called Charter by more and more Americans in New Orleans) and Decatur. The hotel looked to Drauzin like the prow of a huge ship, its wrought-iron balconies evoking decks.

With confident aplomb born by now of familiarity, Drauzin entered the grand doors held open by a mulatto slave in regal red attire. As he approached the Rotunda, he changed pace, as always, almost choosing each step, in slow motion. He felt as though he were entering the Roman Pantheon, where, under the dome of the heavens, each of the twelve deities had stood in its own portal.

However, in place of twelve deities stood three different auctioneers. The temple was become market. Drauzin knew Christ was due to overthrow the podiums with the sword of his wrath. But until He actually arrived, Drauzin kept coming. The sellers, D. M. Wilson, Theophilus Freeman, and J. A. Beard, each took a third of the circumference of the Rotunda, preparing their respective merchandise. The merchandise stood center stage at each of the three stations. The buyers, mostly men, an occasional woman, mostly white, some mixed, from many states, sauntered from station to station, inspecting the merchandise. The buyers' personal slaves, not for sale today, lounged in the middle of the Rotunda, visiting with each other. Off to the side, preparing his desk for later official transactions, perched the notary Jacquemines.

Drauzin focused sometimes on the slaves for sale, sometimes on the buyers, and occasionally on the sellers. He remembered, two years earlier, having become fascinated by a tall, lanky gentleman in blue trousers and straw hat, an apparent spectator. The young man's eyes were keen as a hawk's, while his white face was open, like the surface of a still pond. Drauzin had found, mysteriously, that his face seemed to reflect what the slaves for sale might be experiencing inwardly, whereas most of the spectators and buyers simply reflected the outer scene.

Drauzin had seen enough of these charades by now that he could usually tell which slaves were actually older, their hair having been blacked with boot polish by the trader. In the back rooms he'd watched sellers pinching lips and cheeks of both men and women, often quite painfully, to spring blood of apparent vigor and health into their countenances. If one slumped, the seller would thwap him or her on the back with his short-whip to make them stand straight. Back in the year of Marcelite's manumission, 1829, the city had passed an ordinance forbidding slave pens, of which there were about twenty, within the Vieux Quartier, increasingly known in increasingly Anglo New Orleans as the French Quarter.

Drauzin had listened, smelled, and watched through knot-holes in the high wooden fences at the major slave pen on Chartres and Esplanade, just beyond Barracks St., the old city walls. He remembered the fresh poster out front that read, "A gang of likely young Negroes—Field Hands, Mechanics, House Servants, Washers, Ironers, Nurses, etc. Fifty from one plantation, sold low under full guarantee." Typically about a hundred and fifty men, women, and children huddled in the house-lot-sized pen, steeped in a stench of piss, shit, and old sweat, offset only by the odor of bacon, fried galore to fatten fast the merchandise for market.

By night the enslaved group was essentially jailed; by day they were cleaned, put in "new," impressive clothes, exercised to help health, and generally prepared for market. These pens supplied traders all over the city, about two hundred of them. It is true to say that all the force, all the gravity of slave transactions in the whole country funneled into and ended up, like the mighty, muddy Mississippi, down in New Orleans. These slave pens were the delta of the nation's slave trade. One could also say that the highest form, the epitome of this lowest kind of transaction—this buying living human bodies as property—occurred in the Rotunda of Hotel St. Louis.

The inspections continued before the actual auctioneering began. One prospective buyer pulled open the lips of a man to see how healthy the gums and teeth were, then pulled back the lids of the eyes. At a nod from another buyer, the seller Freeman commanded, "Dance!" and the man sprang into contredanse steps in as lively a manner as possible, with a smile pasted on. One buyer felt the arm muscles and back of a man, another the breasts, hips, and legs of a woman. One male slave was told to pick a woman up over his head and spin her high. Another buyer took a male slave into the back room to check out the man's cock and rocks for breeding; then he took a woman in back to check out her everything for pleasure and breeding.

At noon the bidding began at all three stations, the auctioneers ebbing and flowing in their breathless patter, catering, cajoling, inviting, teasing, poking the prices as high as possible up to the final hammer. Drauzin understood by now that the auctioneers, sellers, and some of the buyers knew that before summer set in, the traders would try to clear out their pens, selling at lower and lower prices to avoid property-destroying diseases. One mother and daughter were sold for three hundred twenty-five piastres. One strong young buck sold for eight hundred. One heavyset black woman for four hundred fifty.

Drauzin's eye caught a storm across the rotunda. Standing next to a short, handsome, olive-skinned young man in simple grey was a young woman in yellow, lighter-skinned than her companion, but much darker in mind. The friend placidly focused on a strong black man being shown by D. M. Wilson, the unctuous seller in a green shadbelly coat. Prices were rising for the black buck until a buyer ripped his shirt down, showing on his muscled back a web of scars like termite tunnels. Troublemaker. Prices back down.

Next, a lighter-skinned fourteen-year-old, Charlotte Rankin. The woman just sold, tears in her eyes, begged her new master to buy her daughter too. But he, a kind-looking gentleman in a frayed overcoat, said there was no way he could afford to. The mother broke to her daughter, grabbing her fiercely, both weeping on each other, mother begging someone out there to buy them both together. Wilson tried parting them, to little avail, stepped back, watched buyers grow impatient, and finally whipped the mother, first on the arms, then the neck, forcing her back as her wailing keened.

A fat, cheek-flapping man stepped forward and took the girl to the back room with Wilson, who returned shortly, holding up his right hand facing the audience, middle-finger raised, announcing, "Virgin indeed! Virgin indeed!" The fat man wiped his hand with his handkerchief. Prices rose fast, eclipsing the fat-man, till... *hammer-bang*. Charlotte Rankin, deemed a fancy girl, sold for twelve hundred. A skinny, pocked, leering fellow walked away with his prize. Mother moaned; daughter screamed. The auctioneer proceeded to the next item of merchandise.

Drauzin's head twitched; he realized he would have bought mother and daughter together if he had the money. To set them free? Suddenly, for the first time ever, Drauzin wondered if his own mother, Adelaïde Pouponne Beaulieu, had been treated like Charlotte Rankin when Granpère had bought her to help Tante Luysa. Drauzin felt dizzy, then bit his cheek bloody at the thought.

He remembered Ernestine saying D. M. Wilson had sold her to Barthelemy back in 1812. Drauzin had learned only recently that Wilson and Joseph Valmont had been trading partners with Papa Barthelemy Bacas way back, doing Caribbean business in rum, sugar, and—slaves. Barthelemy had so valued their partnership that he had, in fact, named his firstborn son after Joseph Valmont. Then Valmont and Wilson had somehow swindled him, leaving Barthelemy forever embittered against Americans. Young Joseph Valmont Bacas had grown up, after the swindle, never hearing the name of the man for whom he'd been named.

Drauzin moved closer to Wilson's station, observing his thick salt-and-pepper hair, sharp like a hedgehog, no neck, chunk-shouldered. His eyebrows dark-clouded the ice-blue eyes on reddened whites. His skin was motley like old paper, red-veined from too much rum. A bulbous, purplish nose overshadowed a wart with tufts of red, black, and white hairs erupting out of his left cheek. His lips were knife-thin. When Wilson wasn't doing the animated work of his trade, the left side of his mouth fell slack, leaving the right side in a natural sneer.

Drauzin shuddered and held his breath. He remembered that Evangeline had also referred to the trader as Dawson Wilson. For a time-stopping interlude, which would never quite disappear, Drauzin thought that he himself, Drauzin Valsin, had been named for this beast, Beelzebub's bruiser, Dawson Wilson. Was he beholding himself in this namesake? He felt bile in his blood. Drauzin the slave. Valsin the torturer. Dawson Wilson, the swindling, finger-fucking slavetrader. *Who am I? What kind of monster am I, patched together of such pieces?* Then reason rescued him, as he remembered of course that he'd been named for his father's cousin, dear Nonc Drauzin Valsin Bacas, now called Fulsain. Drauzin started to breathe again, as though close to having been possessed.

As his own storm released him, Drauzin realized that in that stormy young woman across the way, as lovely as she appeared in her tulip-yellow, bare-shouldered, gigot-sleeved dress, he could hardly discern particular features. He couldn't tell if she were going to faint, vomit, or charge Wilson and attack him. From his own quasi-nausea, he could tell she felt poisoned. She suddenly pivoted, almost burning a hole in

Drauzin as her eyes for a moment caught his; then she charged out of the Rotunda, half-kicking the glass door at the entry. Her departure only slowly dawned on her companion who, seeing her nowhere, trailed out to find her.

Wilson now was presenting two children, a boy and a girl, ages ten and twelve, who looked as white as the mayor's own children. Drauzin realized that about a third of the sales he had witnessed over recent years were of children younger than thirteen. Drauzin Valsin Bacas felt as he had once as a boy, playing too many hours shirtless in the Mississippi mud— sun-poisoned. Slave-sale-poisoned, Drauzin veered back in an overheated haze to the Bacas workshop.

CHAPTER 10:

MARRIAGE, 1833

Josephine Young returned from her cabriolet ride with Pierre Gustave Toutant Beauregard, whom she still called GT in family circles. The ride into town had been enjoyable, mostly tales of his first year in the military Academy of West Point in New York State way up the Hudson River. As longtime childhood cousins, it was appropriate for them to explore this city together when GT was in town. However, since, strictly speaking, Josephine was the half-sister of GT's Mathé cousins, he was becoming aware of his childhood companion as other than simply a cousin, a shift of which Josephine remained hardly aware.

The stop at the Rotunda had clearly been a mistake. His attempts at apology, explanation, or dismissal had as much effect as a chigger on an ox. Silence ended up as the path of least resistance. Back home on Bayou Rd., Maman Josephine, melon-swelling with child, did her best to host a genial tea with the uncomfortable cousins before GT returned to his own family at 45 Bayou Rd.

Afterward, Josephine looked at her mother silently, long, strong. For a moment she tried to imagine her mother at age fifteen. Smoothed, thinned. Girl-woman. Capable broodmare? She felt nausea in her blood.

Finally, Maman asked Josephine what the matter was. Josephine asked, "Maman, whom have you sold?" At first

Maman did not understand. Then, by the intensity of her daughter's ensuing silence and burning look, she grasped the nature of the question.

"First, I bought Catherine and Giles, whom we still have."

"*Sold*, Maman, *sold*."

"Well, first sold must have been Marie."

"How old?"

"Must have been—about fourteen."

"To whom?"

"Oh, a man named Albert."

"Why?"

"*Why?* Why, to make money."

"How much?"

"Six hundred fifty piastres."

Long pause. "Who else?"

"Who else, must have been Rose."

"How old?"

"Probably fifteen."

"How old?"

"Fifteen. Fifteen."

"To whom?"

"To a gentleman named Antoine Lamarlere."

"Gentleman? Why?"

"Why, to make money."

"Why, Maman, why? Why?"

Pause. "To make more money."

"How much?"

"Seven hundred fifty."

"Who else?"

"Please, Josie, ça suffit."

"Who else?"

"Sally."

"How old?"

"Nineteen."

"To whom?

"Deblanc."

"Deblanc!? He's one of the worst! From down in Atakapas?"

"Yes."

"How much?"

"One thousand."

"How much?"

"One thousand."

"One thousand, for Sally. One thousand for Sally. How much for me, I wonder? Why don't you sell me? How much am I worth, now that I'm fifteen? More? Less? Shall we stick in the finger to see if I'm virgin still? More? Less? You going to sell me, Maman? Shall I be a fancy girl? Sell me, Mam-mon. Sell me! Mam-mon, Maman, Mam-mon! Sell me!"

"Oh, my Josephine, oh, ma chère Josephine, forgive me, forgive me, please forgive me," said her mother. She wept as her daughter left, slamming the door—quite uncharacteristic, although Josephine Young had done it almost twice now in one day.

"No less, no more, no more, my dear, dear, wholly Josephine, no more, je te jure—I swear to you—my priceless Josephine." By now the elder Josephine was whispering to the empty room.

There are no records of any more slave transactions by Josephine Tassy.

In fact, Josephine Tassy herself soon ceased to exist, on paper at least. After an icy week with her silent daughter, substantially pregnant Josephine Tassy married her beloved Simeon Mathé in Cathedral St. Louis on May 20, 1833. The white citizens of New Orleans may have been petitioning against admittance of foreign Negroes that spring. But the Catholic Church and the priest, dear old, bowed Père Antoine, publicly endorsed and officially blessed the union of Simeon and Josephine. No more, no mere jumping over the broom together, à la typical slave "marriages."

When the bride looked into Simeon's eyes and said, full-heartedly, "I do," and Simeon said, "I do," her elder daughter felt her mother was finally receiving her due. Heart-hardened Josephine Young was entranced by her mother's bounteous beauty. Carrying her eighth child, Josephine Tassy Mathé was finally allowed to be recognized, honored, and indeed blessed in her role as both mother and wife.

Her daughter Josephine, part of the detritus of the long-dissolved "union" between Samuel Young and her mother, was deeply touched and mighty proud. This was no marriage à la main gauche, left-handed marriage, mistress material à la plaçage. This was marriage à la main drôite, a proper, public, sanctified, right-handed marriage. And yes, both Josephines could feel the difference.

Quite simply, the younger melted into long-running tears of joy and gratitude, tinged with remorse at her week of ice-treating her mother, in whom she had detected shifts on several levels. Forgiveness-freed, young Josephine's heart danced, even sang. Samuel Charles Young IV, Philippe Augustus Young, eight-year-old Louis Francois Mathé, seven-year-old Matilde Melicerte Mathé, and even two-year-old Brou Simon Mathé shared wholeheartedly in the celebration of the modest but mighty marriage.

In July, Madame Josephine Tassy Mathé gave birth to Simon Raphael Mathé, in whom she took special joy in the wake of the recent deaths of her mother, brother, nephew, and first "husband." Maman joyed in her new baby being the fruit of the union of her actual, publicly sanctified marriage. Perhaps little surprise that this eighth child would some day manage an important part of the family story.

CHAPTER II:

BAYOU ST. JEAN, 1833

Unlike Josephine Tassy, who chose to change her name, the elder Drauzin Valsin Bacas was forced to change his. Josephine joyfully added Mathé as a surname upon the happy occasion of her marriage to Simeon. Elder Drauzin had unhappily changed his name to Fulsain due to pirates.

Way back in December 1814, in Maspero's Cafe, Jean Lafitte had not hesitated, grinning charmingly, his butter knife swirling like a rapier, to point out to General Andrew Jackson the similarity of his own name, Lafitte, to Lafayette. While the General thought the comparison presumptuous, he could not help being respectingly amused by the wily pirate. Fever-plagued as General Jackson was, his motley army of a thousand soldiers plus some Tennessee and Kentucky squirrel hunters, fifty-two Choctaw warriors, and the citizen militia of New Orleans needed some kind of Lafayette, in addition to his own sickened version of George Washington, if they were to accomplish a major upset against the British behemoth, the finely uniformed red lobsters.

Warmed by the whiskey in their coffee, the two men agreed to a deal: In exchange for a pardon for all of Lafitte's men, Lafitte would supply Jackson's army with additional manpower of seasoned fighters and, crucially, a substantial supply of weapons including seventy-five hundred pistol flints, which the army desperately needed. Jackson appreciated the approval of Governor William Claiborne, who certainly recognized that Lafitte's offer was crucial to their slim possibility of success.

And it was. That foggy morning at Chalmette, Lafitte himself had courageously crept up close enough to the British front line to be able to return and tell the artillery exactly how far to aim their cannons to start demolishing the polished, shiny redcoat regiments before they could see any targets themselves. And Lafitte's own naval artillery specialists, led by Dominique Youx, had been crucial, even brilliant, in that cannon accuracy on land. Mission accomplished, on both sides of the deal.

However, predictably, it was not long after the successful battle and war that local American officials, displeased at the continuing presence and activity of Lafitte's heroic, law-bending pirates, reverted to familiar old intolerance. Within several years, at new Governor Jacques Villeré's instigation, Lafitte's men became once again personae non grata and were booted out of the bayous of Barataria. Industries and agents that had supported them in New Orleans were also sniffed out and treated harshly.

Jean and Pierre Lafitte, who had enjoyed their brief stint of local respectability, led their men and entourages west along the coast, setting up a new base on Galveston Island for their activities.

Ramon Depardieu, the proprietor of the apothecary shop on Rue Chartres, had continued to provide medical supplies for the Baratarians; so he left with Hector Beaulieu, Adelaïde's brother, to join Lafitte on Galveston. Drauzin Valsin Bacas, the assistant apothecary, paid a severe fine, avoiding prison. The shop was closed. Disgraced and disgruntled, Drauzin Valsin Bacas changed his name to Fulsain Bacas and moved north to Rue Bayou to craft a new life with the family trade of carpentry and cabinetry.

⚜

Now, in 1833, Fulsain's former namesake, twenty-year-old Drauzin Valsin Bacas, was loading up the wagon in the courtyard of 116 St. Louis. At times Barthelemy's shop, when not too busy, would help Fulsain fill orders. During a recent lull Drauzin, JB, and Joseph had made a dozen walnut ladder-backed chairs for Fulsain. The lathes had been busy. The brothers were carefully arranging the chairs, wrapped in burlap, tying them firmly yet gently with hemp rope, so Drauzin could take them to Fulsain's shop on 209 Bayou Rd. for staining and delivery.

Fulsain, hair certainly greying over his olive skin, bulking somewhat, even more full-cheeked, welcomed Drauzin ever kindly, helping him unload the chairs outside his shop. As Drauzin was unloading his fifth chair, he stopped, glancing across some yards. There, in a simple lavender dress, carrying eggs from the chicken coop, was the young woman who had stormed out of the Rotunda. As she stepped inside with her delicate bounty, he could not tell if she had noticed him.

After Drauzin helped his Nonc Drauzin—Fulsain to the general public—apply the first coat of walnut stain to all the chairs, he gladly accepted his uncle's offer to take the cabriolet up to Bayou St. Jean and enjoy Fulsain's pirogue on the water for the rest of the day.

Although Drauzin knew early afternoon fishing would not be prime, he loved simply paddling through the silent waters skimmed over with duckweed, among yellow and white water lilies, puffed up like pastries on their flat green leaves. He lowered a long line to troll for crayfish. He passed a family of turtles sunning on a mostly submerged cypress log. He did cast in some shade along the shore. He recalled Nonc Fulsain showing him how to hunt a "water-turkey"—anhinga—by scaring it to go underwater where it drowns, the body rising. He was glad it was too early for the gallinippers, the world's largest mosquitoes, to be out devouring. He did love the big brown bats who devoured *them*, and the slow rhythms of swamp owls later at dusk, calling "who-youuu, who-youuu," like sentries identifying.

Drauzin loved the light clitter-clatter of palm leaves in the slight breeze now. At one point, as he heard a squirrel chit-chitting high in a willow, he noticed in the shadows a brownish spotted and barred cat, not much larger than a housecat, patiently watching the squirrel. Like a mini-leopard, it had to be a margay. Drauzin had never heard of one this far north. Then a surprising color caught his eye ahead, along the shore through a cross-hatch of branch and leaf. Lavender.

Feathering his paddle without lifting it from the water, he silently maneuvered his pirogue to glide along the shore. Soon lavender started rising; then it crescendoed before his eyes, which, above his own delighted grin, for a moment looked directly into the astonished, astonishingly green eyes of the lovely and (Drauzin dared to think) perhaps also delighted young woman of both the Hotel St. Louis Rotunda and Bayou Rd.

She, of course, was experiencing her own double surprise. First, at a person appearing at all out of the many-greened stillness, and so close to her, breaking, entering her own day-dreaming. She could hardly see his features because behind and around his head, slightly blinding her, was a fan glint-ing light. The sun was, in fact, from her angle, right behind his head. And second, she recognized that young man from the Rotunda, whom she had hardly remembered until she had indeed noticed him this morning outside Fulsain Bacas's shop.

"Enchanté, Mademoiselle."

"You!" she exclaimed, stepping back slightly.

"May I?" He gestured toward the shore on which she stood. She half-nodded, puzzled, still trying to catch up with hap-penings. With a final swirl of his paddle, Drauzin guided the pirogue even closer alongside the soft, low bank. He placed the paddle across the gunnels, bracing his weight as evenly as possible as he rose slowly, stretching his right leg gingerly onto the land, balancing as he shifted shoreward, keeping his craft close with his left foot until he had almost all his weight on terra firma. Then he stepped out of the pirogue and tied its bowline to a young tree. "Drauzin Valsin Bacas," he said, bowing modestly and smiling.

After a pause, observing him up close, she curtsied slightly. "Josephine Young." She turned from him. "You were—there."

"There" sounded to Drauzin like a whiplash, a surprise amid the lavender. He recalled her fury as she had stormed out of the rotunda.

"You buy? Or sell?" Her words hit hard.

Oh, Lordy, of course. How many times had he heeded the weird siren call he never understood, pulling him back again and again to the Body Bazaar, the Soul Shop, the Spirit Sellers? Scores? Slave to slavers. Of course. It must reek from his pores.

"I? Buy? Sell? Why, a mandolin most likely, I suppose."

After seeing him earlier this morning, she had recalled among the crowd at the Rotunda a different quality in his interest in the proceedings. She of course did not know that what she had noticed in that strikingly handsome young man was similar to what he himself had noticed two years earlier in the man with the blue pants: an inward interest. Above a broad brow, Drauzin's dark hair, combed flat, danced out in curls above his ears. Above a clear chin his lips were thin but not severe. His brown eyes intent. She surprised herself to be trusting this stranger greeting her.

He saw before him a likely girl; not a classic composition of stereotypical beauty, but lovely with her slightly full lips, her slightly full nose, her green eyes glistening in her dawning complexion, dark hair shining reds in the sunlight. Her countenance was, for him, a fresh definition of beauty. Surprisingly, considering her dramatic departure from the Rotunda, he sensed in her a calm like a tree, a depth like waters.

"Josie?" came from further along the shore, and in a moment a strong young man appeared, dark haired, his skin even fairer than Josephine's, with similar green eyes, shouldering a fishing pole and a hefty, long-whiskered catfish. He stopped for a moment, clearly surprised to see a man, saw she seemed fine, looked him over, and stepped forth to introduce himself. "Samuel Young."

"Drauzin Bacas."

"Ah, yes, Fulsain's nephew. Pleased to meet you." A quick glance at Josephine. "We must go. We'll probably see you again."

Were those green, green doors of hers actually windowing me? Drausin wondered. *Who got the better catch on the Bayou today? That would be I.*

CHAPTER 12:

THE HANDSOMEST MAN, 1834

The expanding Mathé family had the benefit of the increasing presence of the handsomest, best-dressed man in town. Simeon's friend, the multitalented carpenter Basil Raphael Crockère, became the legal "under-tutor" of the Mathé children, which benefited Josephine's Young children to whatever degree they wished, as well as through inevitable osmosis.

Born in plaçage of white plantation owner and quadroon mother, Basil Crockère had been educated in Paris, earning a degree in mathematics. A fencing master, he had white students galore at his fencing academy in Exchange Alley. Although no white man would duel him, the lore was that he had sent a score beneath the loam on foreign shores. He was valued most in the region for building stately, multidimensional staircases in antebellum mansions. He had both a legal wife and a mistress. Creole society tolerated two women per man, not more. He struggled against the limitations of his color. Basil's son Joseph was a shoemaker, a profession of respect in the Creole community.

Passing time with Simeon and Josephine some summer evenings, Basil Crockère noticed that young Josephine, despite her quiet ways, enjoyed sitting on the front steps, offering gentlemen callers sweet crackers, lemonade, bier creole, and grenadine, which she enjoyed making from pomegranates.

One morning in bed, still half asleep, Drauzin Bacas became aware of a strange thought drifting in his morning mind like a pirogue on a bayou. "I have to go to her; I'm like a thief, reaching like a fork." That afternoon, he appeared at her front steps for grenadine.

Young Josephine noticed that whenever her mother would drop a knife, it was likely Drauzin would show up that day. He enjoyed spending time with Josephine on the Bayou St. Jean, usually accompanied by brother Philippe or Samuel Young. Drauzin and Josephine never returned to the Rotunda.

Occasionally they enjoyed dancing at nearby Tivoli Gardens. When Drauzin, handsome in sage-green, long-tailed coat and dove-colored trousers, danced with Josephine, lovely in her dull-rose dimity gown, he often thought of two words: "quiet light." Whereas her mother Josephine was compelling to look at, magnetic, drawing all to her, "his" Josephine was more looking than looked at, more beholder than beheld. Drauzin thought of Mme. Mathé sometimes as a dramatic combination of Venus and Mars, with some Athena. His Josephine he experienced more and more like Artemis, the moon, content to reflect the light of others.

Josephine liked dancing with Drauzin, not that he danced her off her feet. He was always in rhythm, though. In fact, she gradually realized that his touch was so light that he seemed to lead, not her directly, not in front of her, but somehow all around her, even allowing the music itself to lead through him.

Some feast days Drauzin would join Josephine's family as they enjoyed the hustle-bustle around Tivoli Gardens. The drama and pageantry of the bullfights, fated to climax in the black bull's final fall. The farcical chaos of the greased pig chase; sand on hands disqualified a player. The impossibility of climbing the greased pole—how to rise highest? Stilt-walkers dancing, like Ibis courting, or gods presiding. Silver-dollar pitching—

closest to the line wins. Cockfights. Then a poor gander would be plucked and greased so agile horsemen could weave and scramble to try to pull off the head. Modern jousters aimed to catch rings on spears from the back of their horse. And finally the straight-speed horse races. On these feast days, Drausin realized, the daily struggles of the street were altered, humorized for an interlude.

Occasionally Drauzin and Josephine arranged to meet at Congo Square after Sunday mass. Even though by now slaves had long been forbidden to purchase their own freedom, many from all around continued to bring their goods to market on Sundays: food, weavings, carvings, tools, and so on. Most of these slaves were unaware that Congo Square in New Orleans was, since 1817, the only public place in the whole country where slaves were officially allowed to congregate, sell, and dance in public. Four, five, maybe six hundred slaves gathered. Callas, rice fried cakes, were a popular item to nibble on during the day; gumbos galore were available to dip from, each slightly different.

This particular Sunday, Drauzin met Josephine and her brother, Samuel Young. Various musicians played all kinds of instruments, African and European, including bamboula drums, banzes, gourds, quillpipes made of reeds strung together like pan flutes, beautiful wood-barred marimbas, violins, tambourines, and triangles. A throng of dancers stirred at the beginning of the Creole folksong "Toucoutou."

Thirty to forty women gathered in the center, wrapped in varieties of belle-belle, silk, gauze, muslin, and percale dresses ornamented with fringes, ribbons, bells, shells, and balls. They began, after a prelude of drums was amplified by tambourines, triangles, and marimbas, to sing the first two verses, as other instruments joined in and around the beat, never dwarfing the voices:

Ah! Toucoutou, y conin vous,
Vous te in Morico.

They repeated muscularly the second line, "Vous te in Morico!"
Then a strong gang of men joined the women, almost
naked, wrapped in some Indian cloth and sash, many with a
tail of panther, fox, coon, or skunk, as well as bells jingling on
their ankles, bits of tinkling metal or tin rattles, evoking copper gris-gris from Sudan, and even—Drauzin wondered—possibly shredded or shed shackles. Together the men and women
made long, strong, exaggerated gestures, "scrubbing" all over
themselves, then each other,

Na pas savon qui tace blanc
Pou blanchi vous la peau, Pou blanchi vous la peau.

Ah! Toucoutou, we all know you,

 you are a blackamoor.
There's no soap strong enough
to whiten your dark skin.

Then, for the second stanza, four men and women stepped
to the front together, crossing their arms, raising their noses,
crossing their legs together, first left over right, then right
over left, as though they were sitting, and shifting.
At times Samuel imitated some of the dancers' explosive,
graceful moments. Drauzin and Josephine remained more outwardly restrained; while keenly attentive to the dancers, they
were as aware of each other, dancing in the blood.

Endans theatre, quan va prenne loge,
Comme tout blanc comme y fot,
After the second line, the other dancers, in mixed groups
of four, imitated the box-seaters and spread out, pretending to

enter a box seat. During the final two lines of the stanza, the original "box-seaters" all leaped up straight, then threw their right arms out like spears at all the imitating "box-seaters," shaking their heads and spears as the others scampered off to the periphery with their tails between their legs.

Ye va fe vous jist deloge,
Na pa passe tantot.

In the theater, when you take a box,
Like all the nice white folks,
They will just put you out,
You will never stay inside.

For the final stanza, the same dancers who had originally been in the theater box started doing a stylized caricature of a waltz, although syncopated by the Senegalese Wolof drum rhythms. The other groups appeared at the end of the verse, trying to dance the same. The "whites" then shook their spear-arms at them, who first started to dissolve, then started exploding in their own angry versions of the waltz, riffing on the rhythms, as the "whites" began moving more and more like the rest of the dancers, but awkwardly, clumsily, making all those watching laugh and laugh.

Quan blanc leyes va donin bal
Vous pli capab'aller.
Comment va fe, vaillante diabale,
Vous qui l'aimant danser?

When the white folks go to a ball
You will never be able to go.
What will you do, you pretty devil,
You who like to dance?

During the rest of the afternoon, hundreds of slaves danced for hours. Drauzin, Josephine, and Samuel noticed various clusters in different parts of Congo Square: black, thick-lipped, broad-nosed Kongolese, often drummers; aquiline-featured Wolof from Senegal, often playing stringed instruments; dancers from Mali, Gambia, Guinea, Niger; Creole—Louisiana-born of all hues; and others shipped down from all over the southern United States, as far as Virginia and the Carolinas. Drauzin thought of the variety of woods in his father's shop. He and Josephine wondered into which group each of them would best fit.

"Moi, Senegal," said Drauzin.

"Moi, Mali," said Josephine.

The three each found their favorite gumbos, enjoying a bowl with rice. Josephine chose a Creole gumbo with shellfish, tomatoes, and some ham in a thickener of filé, ground sassafras. Drauzin preferred a Cajun gumbo, with shellfish and andouille sausage, in a thickener of both okra and dark roux, hog lard and flour, cooked until a few shades from burning. They shared a slice of pain patate, sweet potato baked onto a cake with black pepper and spices. The vendors fanned their wares with chasse mouches, fly whips made of colorful papers.

Then, a single, slow drumbeat called everyone's attention. A single woman sang a haunting melody as a single man danced.

Mo te ain negresse,
Pli belle que Metresse.
Mo te vole belle-belle
Dans L'armoire Mamzelle.

I was a Negress,
More beautiful than my mistress.
I used to steal pretty things
From Mamzelle's armoir.

Danse Calinda, Bou-doum, Bou-doum,
Danse Calinda, Bou-doum, Bou-doum!

The second time through, other men, all bare to the waist, wielded sticks, each balancing a bottle of water on his head, engaging in mock battle to the rhythms of the song. The third time through, other women joined in the singing. Any time a bottle dropped, that man left the field. When the winner was proclaimed, all the women joined him dancing one time through. Then the other men returned, and the dancing proceeded through the stanza, again and again, improvising, elaborating, rhythms altering, expanding, tightening, most dancers falling down on the Bou-doum, Bou-doum, until suddenly, somehow, and everyone knew when—silence.

Danse Calinda and the afternoon were over.

They walked back toward the Youngs' cabriolet, enthralled by the artistry they had witnessed on many levels. Glowing, they felt they'd been immersed in the fountain of youth Ponce De León had sought long ago. Then Drauzin stopped by a notice freshly posted on a golden-leaved tree.

"Negress named Rosalie, between 50 & 60 years of age, having iron collar with three branches, does not remember master's name, but he lives in Faubourg Lacourse. Owner please claim said negress and pay costs. N Trepagnier, Sheriff."

Drauzin had seen such a collar before, one branch behind the head, two on either side, sometimes with bells hanging. Certain sterner masters in the region punished a first escape attempt with six lashes and six to twelve months wearing an iron collar. Imagine, twenty-four hours a day. Fifty to sixty years old. On a sugarcane plantation especially, that was old. Rosalie must have felt desperate to have escaped again. Drauzin, Josephine, and Samuel wondered where she might have headed, how, and why. What blacksmith could she find to crack off the collar? And what would her master do when she was returned this time? Axe off half a foot? Right around the corner from the fountain of youth, the three had found the tree of knowledge of evil.

Had the three of them each wanted to dance with the slaves in Congo Square? Yes, in fact, at times almost irresistibly. Yet an invisible golden wire had prevented them from jumping or falling into those waters.

On the other hand, late one recent afternoon, while walking along Rue St. Louis past the many gaming halls, Drauzin and Josephine had slowed down at Antoine's, the brand-new, elegant restaurant. Through the windows they saw the fine settings for the best, the wealthiest, the whitest. Stopping, they had looked at each other, each wondering about entering to take a table. They smiled, honoring the invisible iron wire preventing them from taking their place with both Creole and American white society. They knew they had to move along, or apply for a job there. *But could we have entered in the late light and been seated?*

Josephine, daughter and granddaughter of white men, knew that in certain lights, Drauzin's skin looked alabaster to her. Drauzin, as far as he knew, was likewise the son and grandson of white men. They were both familiar with the adage, "Money whitens; poverty darkens." Fancy up the clothes a notch or two, and who knows? A little candlelight, and presto, white Creoles instead of gens de couleur? They also knew the unspoken assumption, almost a law, among Creoles of color: "Thou shalt not marry darker." Although Drauzin and Josephine were still far from a direct conversation about marriage, they nevertheless both felt and knew that that law had nothing to do with the quiet, growing comfort they found in each other.

Boom. Boom. Boom. Cannon from Place d'Armes sounded the curfew—all slaves were meant to be in, all men of color too, unless they had proof of business. No point inviting undue attention from the City Guard. Brother Samuel urged Josephine home in the cabriolet, trotting their bay. Drauzin walked home by Rue St. Louis at a brisk pace, under shadow-casting oil lamps hanging high on walls.

And then—M. Pierre Toutant Beauregard would periodically return from West Point or St. Bernard Parish and take over. Drauzin would recede. He accepted it. He understood. It was a family pattern, a long-time childhood habit. But it was hard. Beauregard was aware that in his absence Bacas had been spending time with Josephine, but he gave it no mind. The young soldier had quickly sized up Drauzin Bacas, dismissing as weakness precisely the quality Josephine valued in Drauzin's dancing. Whenever GT, as Josephine called him, returned to St. Bernard Parish, Drauzin and Josephine resumed their patterns together.

On the day of St. Michel, known in Voodoun circles as Dani, Drauzin Valsin Bacas summoned the courage to send Alfonce from 116 St. Louis St. to deliver by hand the following letter to M. Simeon Brou Mathé, 325 Bayou Rd.

Monsieur, September 29, 1834

> *I had hoped to have the pleasure of seeing your demoiselle.*
> *I could not help but love her.*
> *Since my intentions are—if I am the suitable one according to you—to seek the honor to be her husband.*
> *That is why, Monsieur, I take the liberty to address myself to you on the hope of obtaining your consent in order that I may freely frequent your house. Persuaded that it is much better that the parents know the conduct of the young man who*

*wants to visit, if you would like references about me, please write
to Mssrs. Valmont Matisse, B. Crockère and their wives. If this is
not enough, I can give you gentlemen who have seen me born.*

I am, Monsieur, in awaiting your response,
Your truly humble and obedient servant,
D. Bacas

The next morning, Claire, a slave of M. and Mme. Mathé,
delivered to 116 Rue St. Louis a note for Drauzin Bacas.

*Monsieur, you will no longer have the pleasure of seeing our
demoiselle. You are not welcome to visit. You and she are not
meant to be.*

Avec Certitude,
Je reste,
S. Mathé.

In early October, Drauzin sent Alfonce to deliver by hand the
following letter to Josephine Young herself, 325 Bayou Rd.

Mademoiselle, October 5, 1834
*I hope you will forgive he who loves you for the liberty he
takes in writing you. Guided by the honor and the love I have
for you, I have hardly hesitated to make known my intentions
to your parents. Refused by them, I would like to know if you,
as they say, will deprive me of your presence. Don't exaggerate
to keep me from knowing if you don't want me. I will go away.*
*If, on the other hand, you love me, I will come to you by
sunset, and in that way you will still be my fiancée.*
*Oh my friend (or lover), if you only knew how sick I have
been since he refused me. The fever has been high for three days.*

But your picture, your image, has followed me into the darkness without one faithful friend to console me. May God permit these words He knows are dear to fall over you like a shadow.

I am waiting for your response,
D.

P.S. You will excuse my presumption if that is how you hear this, my humble letter.

Josephine Mathé's heart wept for her daughter in those days. But she had given her own heart to Simeon Mathé, publicly in Cathedral St. Louis. When Simeon had told Basil Crockère that young Bacas had sent him a letter, Bazile had smiled. Simeon had grumbled, "He mentioned you as a reference."

Basil smiled. "That young Drauzin Valsin Bacas is one good soul."

"Yes, he may be good, but he doesn't row his own boat; he's content to float."

"What I do to help your children become is what I did to help those Bacases become," said Basil. "That Drauzin, unlike his father, is a gentle soul who can speak French as fine as Paris. And oh, what music he makes!"

But both Josephine and Basil knew that everyone knew, at least in the Toutant/Beauregard/Mathé clan, that Josephine Young had long been fated for M. Pierre Toutant Beauregard.

Maman Josephine, blessed as she was in her marriage with Simeon, deferred to his authority. She chafed nevertheless at how men piloted women like boats on the river of New Orleans.

One afternoon, young Josephine was sitting on the back porch, feeling trapped. Basil Crockère came out, glanced down, and sat by her. She leaned her head, face teary, on his shoulder. "Oh, cher Basil, what am I to do? What am I to do?"

He took her hand. "My dear girl, is it so bad? Your GT is handsome." She nodded, then shook her head gently. "Your other, is he your handsomest?" She smiled, nodding certainly.

Then one of the most handsome, influential people in the Creole community thought of his longtime friend, one of the most influential people in all New Orleans, and he whispered two words into Josephine's ear: "Marie LaVeau."

CHAPTER 13:

CUPID'S VOUDOUN, 1835

On Rue St. Ann, the slave Saffron ushered Josephine Young into the receiving room of Marie LaVeau. Josephine could see why some spoke of similarities between this tall, stately, strikingly beautiful mother of twelve and her own stately, beautiful mother of eight. Marie LaVeau looked into Josephine's eyes. She recognized her fondly, intrigued to see the woman version of the daughter whose conception she had apparently succeeded in helping that night long ago on the Bayou St. Jean, on the Eve of St. Jean Baptiste.

Saying that Basil Crockère had sent her, Josephine told of her plight: her stepcousin P. G. T. Beauregard's assumption—her stepfather Simeon Mathé's insistence—and her sweetheart, Drauzin Bacas. Marie LaVeau asked her to describe their first meeting. Josephine mentioned her surprise just two years ago on Bayou St. Jean, the young stranger's head in the fan of glints of light.

Marie smiled and nodded emphatically. "Well, well, Josephine Young! You, Chérie, have seen the gilded splinters; you have seen the gilded splinters. That means—you have his heart. You just want to secure it. And you can, my dear Josephine.

"Create your own poudre de perlainpainpain—pixie dust. Yes. On a windy day, gather seventeen floating seeds from a thistle. Remove the down from the seeds. Rub the seeds over the honey sac of a bee, caught on a clover blossom leaning in the northerly direction. Mix those seeds with three white beans buried for three days under a mound of table salt. Then add the bean-seed mix to a portion of salt measured in a black thimble. Rub this powder in your lover's clothes, and he'll be yours, sooner or later, for all time. As for the other one—I try never to hurt a soul."

Josephine shook her head and pulled back her shoulders, shocked at such a thought. But Marie LaVeau had people come to her with all kinds of wishes.

"Meanwhile, take a hair of your desired one and sleep with it under your pillow. Carry a piece of the weed called John the Conqueror in your pocket. That's your gris-gris—your amulet. Above all, dear Josephine, trust your heart." Marie held both of Josephine's hands, then made the sign of the cross over Josephine's heart. "Trust your heart and its ways."

Over ensuing weeks, watching patiently, Josephine managed finally to succeed in making her poudre de perlainpainpain, feeling, of course, slightly foolish—and yet, one day she noticed that Drauzin, working over at Fulsain's shop, had left his coat on the fence. Josephine slipped discreetly over to it, sprinkled the powder around the coat, put a bit in each pocket, and dusted some on the inside of the coat so it would go into his shirts as well. Fortunately it was virtually scentless. Josephine grinned, feeling like a sneaky girl, which of course she was, with a most noble, most secret mission.

Drauzin recovered from his fever without hearing Josephine's hoped-for response. Adelaïde put a hand on her son's shoulder and asked what he was suffering. Seeing that she could see, he told her of Simeon Mathé's letter refusing his request to court Josephine.

"Are you bleeding?"

Pause. "Yes."

"Mon cher Drusino, you do not bleed if you are stabbed."

Reading his mother's consoling hazel eyes, he gleaned she was differentiating: better to be cut than stabbed, better to bleed out from the surface than to bleed deep within.

Feeling strengthened, he embraced her. "Si, Maman, certainement."

Drauzin consoled himself. He bought a piano, a wooden chordophone without a cast-iron frame on the sounding board. He loved to play; he began to offer lessons to local children and soon adults as well. When some families wanted a piano of their own, he would find one, buy it for them, and make a profit in the process. Drauzin gradually grew some savings, which added to his modest income from Barthelemy's cabinetry shop.

One Sunday weeks later, Josephine went to mass at Cathedral St. Louis. Coordinating her exit with Drauzin's, she managed to whisper in his ear, "Mo coeur tâcher dans to chaîne comme boskoyo dans cypière"—My heart is linked in your chain like cyprus knees. He was so affected by her cinnamon scent and her breath in his ear, and by what she said, that he did not notice Josephine plucking a hair from a curl behind his ear. She brisked by, wearing the lavender of their first meeting on Bayou St. Jean. He slowed to a stop, entranced in after-scent, after-voice, after-image, cypress knees exuding clouds of cinnamon. Drauzin could now hope again.

November 1835 was damp. Simeon Mathé, for whom Josephine Young was generally grateful in spite of his adamant refusal of Drauzin's request, began to cough. His cough deepened over weeks, and eventually Simeon could not get out of bed. Fever and chills intensified. His breathing shallowed and grew more raspy. The coughs began to feel as though they were emptying not just his lungs but his whole body, leaving him wracked and exhausted. Eventually the coughs blooded his lips. Pneumonia, exacerbated by decades of wood dust from his work, consumed him, catalyzing acute asthma as well. Toward the end of the year, forty-two-year-old Simeon Mathé, the beloved, official, publicly sanctified husband of Josephine Tassy Mathé, failed to take his last feeble breath.

Without the barrier of Simeon's withheld approval, and with her mother's previously withheld blessing, Josephine Young was free to marry her beloved Drauzin Bacas. With the sorrow of her stepfather's passing came the elation of planning her wedding. Grief and joy, strands in one braid. Could Marie LaVeau interweave both into her wedding hair?

Drauzin too mourned the passing of a person he knew to be his Josephine's most concerned father figure, a man of strong moral fiber, although he'd lacked the imagination to recognize the fire of Josephine's and Drauzin's love.

On January 20, 1836, Josephine Tassy Mathé sat in the church pew and wished that her husband could be there to celebrate her daughter's wedding. She had felt increasingly fulfilled and blessed during her ten years with Simeon Mathé. The pain of missing him still felt like an open wound, yet she took comfort from both the actuality of their union and the public distinction granted it. She felt great satisfaction in the respectability of being acknowledged as Veuve Mathé, and even greater joy for her Josephine Young as her radiant daughter prepared to marry Drauzin.

Veuve Josephine Tassy Mathé nodded at Adelaïde Pouponne Beaulieu, who smiled back, clearly joyful at the nuptials of their children. Adelaïde shifted her gaze to the dusk-glowing stained-glass windows and mused upon her enduring loyalty to Barthelemy. Difficult as he could be, he had been willing to be her partner in life. Though their offspring would never be materially rich, they were her riches—riches far beyond what Adelaïde Beaulieu had ever dared imagine in her enslaved youth. She chuckled inwardly at the thought of her long-departed Muslim Wolof grandmother, born in Senegal, seeing her here in the Catholic church.

Drauzin entered from the side of the nave to stand elegant in his dove-grey morning coat near the altar with his best man, brother Jean-Baptiste. He felt somewhat faint as he considered the significance of this day. *I stand in this position where my white father Barthelemy could not, because my brown mother Adelaïde could not walk the aisle to marry him in a church, according to our laws. Thank heavens my mother is brown, so I can await my brown beloved at the other end of this aisle.* He straightened his shoulders and looked around the room, appreciating the bright faces watching from the pews, a floral meadow. He and Jean-Baptiste saw their eldest brother Joseph seat his wife, Anne Louise Essayleme, and their young son before continuing his usher duties.

The bridesmaids stood shimmering in the evening candlelight in their lavender silk gowns, each holding posies of white gardenias.

Josephine's older brother, Philippe Young, had joined Drauzin's brothers, Joseph and Leon, standing by Jean-Baptiste and Drauzin. Then the young ringbearer ushered in the two flower girls, each in their little lavender dresses.

Josephine appeared in the entrance, white-veiled, on the arm of her brother, Samuel Charles Young IV. Her eyes took in the scene, glistening. *Oh, Papa, if only you were here*, she thought. *Not just tonight but for all those years.* Then she blinked her eyes and took a deep breath. *Bronze John took him off in the plague several years ago, but today my dear Samuel IV is here in my father's place.* She squeezed her brother's firm arm.

The shining brow of her beloved beaconed from the far end of the aisle. Josephine gazed at Drauzin and thought, *For me, right now, this aisle is the Milky Way.*

The organ started playing the processional, Drauzin's choice—Pachelbel's Canon in D. The congregation rose to its feet.

As Barthelemy watched Samuel "father" his own sister, the bride, down the aisle, he thought, *And so it goes.* He was content with this new union; considering who his son Drauzin was, this lovely, quiet, yet strong Josephine seemed a fortunate fit, clearly Drauzin's choice. The patriarch felt a pang in his chest; for a moment he wondered if his heart was giving out. He placed his calloused, scarred hand over his heart even as he realized that he most felt regret—regret that their lives in New Orleans' 1830s were so vexing, so complicated. And regret that he wasn't able to honor his children the way they deserved. *But this is the way it is,* he thought, and moved his hand to his knee. Adelaïde placed her own upon his, warming.

The Veuve Josephine Tassy Mathé was equally proud and fulfilled, beholding her two-fold brood, Youngs up front, five-year-old Brou Simon Mathé at her side. Josephine felt her beloved, recently departed Simeon Mathé strangely overlapping with her littler Simon Raphael, leaning back on her now, soon to settle into her lap. Across the aisle, Adelaïde Pouponne was feeling her Felix, who had died his first year, at her breast and shoulder. These two mothers of many each felt her own long-gone mother as well, like moon-glow.

Bride Josephine proceeded, feeling led by both Pachelbel and her Drauzin. In turn, Drauzin, bedazzled, beheld his future arriving. During the ceremony he maintained his composure outwardly while singing inwardly. Yet Drauzin found himself bewildered. For a moment he felt, beholding Josephine, *I am looking not at, not in, but inside my own mirror.*

And Josephine, looking into Drauzin, thought, *My whole being is realigning.*

A few rows back on Josephine's side, Pierre Gustave Toutant Beauregard sat soldier-straight, lip crinkled, left eye twitching, and jaw set under his first black mustache. He kept clenching and unclenching his fist, replanning. *Who will I marry now?* He was disgusted at how things had turned out with Josephine; everyone knew they were long intended for each other! He snorted, and then, feeling eyes turn to him, pretended it was a cough. A few rows back, the stately lady in emerald green, Marie LaVeau, Voodoun Queen of New Orleans, and Bazile Crockère, the city's handsomest man and finest fencer, eyed each other, amused. They recognized P. G. T. Beauregard's contemptuous outburst for what it was. Marie LaVeau was pleased, however, with her arrangement of the bride's hair, black curls cascading beneath the white halo of lace, all framing the single pearl pendant on her brow.

Vows concluded, ceremony at end, the young married couple faced the congregation. *I, quiet I, feel like the light of the world,* thought Josephine. Beside her, Drauzin wondered, *Am I the keeper of the flame, or is she my keeper?*

M. et Mme. Drauzin Valsin Bacas walked hand in hand toward the congregation, oblivious of the icy stare from PGT and soaking up the sun from Marie, Basil, Nonc Fulsain Bacas, and everyone else, who beamed blessings upon the newlyweds.

As they traversed their Milky Way, they basked both in the beauty of the grand church of St. Rose de Lima and in their bounteous blessings, not knowing how strongly they would later need such sustenance.

CHAPTER 14:
DRAUZIN AND JOSEPHINE, 1836–46

Josephine Tassy Mathé's eldest daughter began her married life in her mother's home, 325 Bayou Rd., as was common Creole custom. Veuve Mathé had splurged, secretly ordering a classic ciel-de-lit fashioned by the renowned M. Dufau. Pale blue silk spread heaven above the bed, on which, instead of traditional chubby cupids frolicking, the mother of the bride had commissioned M. Dufau to portray Apollo, god of music, with his lyre, chasing Daphne who, as she turned into a laurel tree, reached her arms to receive him. Cream-colored dentelle valenciennes, fine lace, trimmed the edge.

Fortunately, M. Dufau finished the scene in the heavens weeks before the wedding. Unfortunately, at a New Year's Eve soirée hosted by M. Dufau for friends at his club, they had been pleased to receive a keg of rum at a good price. Fortunately, the first round was enjoyed; unfortunately, the second became impossibly foul-tasting. M. Dufau finally split open the keg with an axe to find the rum-pickled corpse of a small, bearded man. Of course, over the weeks the boys in the streets could not stop repeating their new chant, "One man pickled in Dufau's rum. One man ru-eened Dufau's rum."

Although M. Dufau was never held responsible for the death, that evening did cause the death of both his membership in the club and the finest making of ciel-de-lits in New Orleans.

But the brothers Young had hidden Josephine's ciel-de-lit in one of Fulsain Bacas's sheds before the debacle, so it was indeed a delightful surprise when bride and groom returned after the reception to Bayou Rd. for their first night together under Daphne and Apollo.

Also according to Creole custom, Drauzin and Josephine were not allowed to leave their room for five days. Catherine brought their food and tended to their needs. Josephine was not allowed on the streets for two weeks. During the third week of their marriage, the bride and groom moved with Josephine's trunks, certain personal furniture, and the ciel-de-lit from their honeymoon suite on Bayou Rd. down to their new home, sharing the third floor of 114 Rue St. Louis with Drauzin's closest brother, JB. Slave Ernestine helped them settle in. Maman Adelaïde Pouponne Beaulieu welcomed Josephine, sympathetic to Drauzin's mate, remembering her own navigating of the new, not always so clear bayous of the Bacas family ways. The pass-through between the two houses insulated the younger generation somewhat from the domineering ways of the patriarch.

Sometimes, as Drauzin and Josephine enjoyed their early-marriage frolics, he would sing to her under Daphne and Apollo,

Oh-o-oh, Mah Lady,
Oh-o-oh, Mah Lady,
Oh-o-oh, Mah Lady Jo-o-oe!

She would be darling Daphne, turning into laurel, reaching for him; he would be divine Apollo, reaching desperately for her, singing, "Oh-o-oh Mah Lady Jo-o-oe!" and they would collapse laughing in each other's arms. Both pictured the source of their song, the old local kindling man going into neighbors' yards to cut their wood into kindling, singing his sawing song through his smoking pipe under his greasy cap.

Then the two modest newlyweds would cover each other's mouths, shushing in embarrassment that Jean-Baptiste in the room next door or Joseph and Louise down below might have heard them, which, of course, they had.

With some savings from carpentry, music lessons, and piano buying and selling, enhanced by Josephine's dowry, Drauzin managed to purchase a piece of property, 323 Claiborne St. near Bienville, for rental income. He gradually bought more instruments for himself, including a silver flute, both tenor and soprano clarinets, and a guitar, all of which he loved playing. Soon he was able to offer beginner's lessons in them as well.

One evening after supper, out in the courtyard, Drauzin, impromptu, told the whole Bacas clan the story of Pan and Apollo, and their musical contest before the gods. Drauzin took turns playing each of the gods, first Apollo on Joseph's violin, his own guitar, or mandolin, and then Pan on flute or clarinet, starting with simple, familiar pieces, then improvising in evermore challenging musical complications, until finally Apollo finished with a flourish on the violin, and the gods deemed him the victor.

At one point along the way, Josephine stepped over to a wall, returning with strands of passion vine, weaving a "laurel" crown and presenting it to mighty patriarch Barthelemy and gracious matriarch Adelaïde, who willingly rose at the right moment as towering Zeus and presiding Hera to crown proud Apollo, after which Pan then stomp-scampered off in fury.

At that point, to even Drauzin's surprise, brother JB jumped forward and grabbed a clarinet, announcing that he, Dionysus/ Bacchus, as the father of Pan, knew his son should have won. He proceeded to play the clarinet excruciatingly, evoking howls of pained laughter. Drauzin, who had reappeared as Apollo in his laurel crown, played a sequence of emphatic chords on the mandolin and declaimed majestically, arm pointing fiercely out the alley exit, like God the Father banishing Adam and Eve from the Garden of Eden, "Bacchus/Bacas, va-t-en—get out! Bacas va-t-en!" Everyone laughing joined in the chant, "Bacchus/Bacas, va-t-en, Bacas va-t-en!" as JB-Bacchus/Bacas slunk away, his back curved like a dog with his tail between his legs. Ernestine, Alfonce, Nelson, and the other slaves loved discreetly listening to Bacas family music, especially when Drauzin was playing. Now they broke into cheers, applauding the tour de force performance with everyone else.

Not surprisingly, it was not long before Lady Jo-o-oe knew she was enceinte, with child, and not much longer before she began to show. However, all were surprised when she began to give birth suddenly one night in June, her seventh month, to a little boy, just more than a handful, whom she agreed with Drauzin to name Barthelemy. The patriarch was honored. The boy struggled, even to nurse.

By September, in a fever, Barthelemy Bacas the Younger expired. Josephine was devastated. Drauzin felt their room a tomb, the boy's little chirpings, squeakings, and mufflings echoing for months. Josephine, supported well by Adelaïde, Joseph's Louise, slave Ernestine, and especially her own mother, Josephine Mathé, strove to become more careful in her ways.

Adelaïde Pouponne Beaulieu and Veuve Mathé, each stately as African queens, enjoyed and respected each other. They sometimes joked, wondering whether Adelaïde's Senegalese Wolof ancestors had first captured and sold into slavery Josephine's Mali Bambara ancestors, or the other way around. Obviously both, whether Wolof or Bambara, had been sold like cattle at some point.

If Josephine Young Bacas now found a spider in the room,

she certainly did not kill it; doing so would bring more bad luck. A cricket singing in the house would bring luck all year. A cricket did indeed sing in the room, and this time, having "failed" her first time, Josephine respected a period of confinement in her later months. She allowed no one to comb hair in the room then; she allowed no one to sweep under the bed during her confinement. On Christmas Eve, 1839, she received a gift, not without significant labor. Ernestine deftly unwrapped the chord from around the neck, then raised up a hefty girl, whom Drauzin and Josephine named Aline Adelaïde Bacas. The matriarch was touched. Aline Adelaïde Bacas thrived, hearty, bobbing like a cork in the early waters of her life.

New Orleans thrived too; by 1840 it was the third largest city in the thriving United States. The Bacas clan continued to expand. Jean-Baptiste Valcour Bacas married, in St. Louis Cathedral, Rose Celina Saulay from Orleans Parish, together joining brother Drauzin, Josephine, and Aline on the third floor of 114 St. Louis.

The year 1841 saw a change close at hand. In April, Barthelemy made a gift to his beloved Adelaïde. Barthelemy Bacas officially manumitted the slave Ernestine, officially age thirty-nine, though probably actually forty-three. Adelaïde had always remembered the look on Ernestine's face twelve years earlier when Marcelite had departed from the Bacas family at 116 St. Louis as a free woman. Since she had arrived at age twelve, Ernestine had grown into her role, fairly filling the shoes of Marcelite for the family. She bore much of Marcelite, perhaps even more of Adelaïde, and of course of her own mother, wherever she might be. It gave Adelaïde, above all, a deep joy to "kiss the bird as she flies."

This time the whole family gathered in the courtyard, placed Ernestine in the center of a circle, and, swaying gently, sang to her one of her favorites, which Adelaïde often sang, and which they had all come to love.

Kum ba ya. Ya.
Kum ba ya. Ya.
Kum ba ya. Ya.
Ah, Ah, Kum ba ya.

Come by here, my Lord, Come by here.
Come by here, my Lord, Come by here.
Come by here, my Lord, Come by here.
Oh, Lord, come by here.

Alfonce, Nelson, and the other slaves, at a nod from Adelaïde, joined the circle of singing in a concentric ring; Adelaïde merged them into the original circle. At the center, Ernestine swayed and sang too, spinning slowly counterclockwise, sometimes looking at each in the circle, sometimes, eyes closed, listening to each, like a camel drinking her fill, before leaving the confines of the oasis.

There were double-kiss embraces from everyone. For Drauzin's youngest sibling, Elizabeth Coelina, now fifteen, and Joseph's Louis Adhemar, now eight, Ernestine had been their only Mammy in memory. Ernestine and they would miss each other almost like blood. When their skin had become dry under too much sun, feeling ashy, it was Ernestine who always had the pomegranate oil or shea butter ready to restore the sheen.

Ernestine knew her horizons were widening, almost unimaginably. She thought she might do people's hair. She had a knack for the range from straight to wavy to tightly curly. She could also become a seamstress. She not only followed patterns well, but she also created patterns and had an eye for combining surprising colors and materials. She also was always the one whom children and adults went to for wounds and illnesses. Maybe she would find work in a hospital. As well as she had been treated by Barthelemy, Adelaïde, and the whole family, compared to the plights of many slaves, Ernestine now, for the first time in her life, had choices. There was a limit to the range of them, but they were choices.

On the other hand, as she was stepping forth from the protection of the courtyard of 116 St. Louis, Ernestine knew as well that her expanding horizons of liberty might contract at any moment to the iron manacle. With her new strength, she felt a new fragility. Like Spanish cattle wild on the savannahs, she could be caught for a plantation any time. She knew many such stories. As she herself was freed, Ernestine knew that in New Orleans the invisible manacles for all people of color continued to tighten.

Adelaïde knew what Alfonce, Nelson, Betsy, Rose and the other remaining slaves were wondering. Drauzin and Josephine watched them as well. Drauzin and JB were also watching their mother keenly, wondering if she would succumb to those frightening donkey brayings they remembered after Marcelite's departure. But no, this time, a large sigh. More joys since then had done their part in healing certain wounds deep within Adelaïde Pouponne Beaulieu, FWC.

Josephine loved rocking her precious Aline Adelaïde to sleep with a favorite lullaby of many mothers and mammies in New Orleans, adapting it to this particular Christmas gift, repeating again and again, weaving a cocoon of song around petite Aline:

> Fais dodo Alinette,
> Trois piti cochons du laite,
> Fe dodo mo piti bebe,
> Jiske lage de quinse ans—

Quand quinze ans aura passés
Alinette va se marier.

Go to sleep, Alinette,
Three little suckling pigs,
Go to sleep, my little baby,
Until the age of fifteen years—
When fifteen years shall have passed
Alinette will marry.

Josephine would not cut Aline's hair until after one full year, and then only during a full moon.

When Josephine and Drauzin received another winter gift on January 10, 1842, Josephine found herself drawn to a different lullaby, with which three-year-old Aline became familiar, while always feeling "Fais Dodo, Alinette" to be her sleep-song. "Crab Dans Calalou" became the home harbor for baby Drauzin Valsin Bacas, the new Ti-Drauzin.

Fe dodo, mo fils, crab dans calalou,
Papa, li couri la riviere,
Maman, li couri peche crab.

Go to sleep, my son, crab is in the shell
Papa has gone to the river,
Mamma has gone to catch crab.

And Josephine would add a verse for Aline:

Fe Dodo, ma fille, crab dans calalou.

Sleep, my daughter, crab is in the shell.

Joseph Bacas and Louise, blessed with their own boy Louis Adhemar back in 1833, had grown sad as no one came to join him over the ensuing years. Although Josephine had encouraged her, of course, to visit Marie LaVeau, Louise had felt too spooked by the notion. Finally, almost desperate, Louise asked Josephine to accompany her. The visit went well. Louise was utterly unspooked by this unusually beautiful soul, by whom she felt blessed with deeply sympathetic understanding.

Louise began to drink a cup of Mississippi water a day, unclarified. She renewed her prayers to St. Marie, mother of God, three times a day. And, at Marie LaVeau's suggestion, each night, as she drifted toward sleep, she imagined herself as a beaming lighthouse, guiding a journeying soul, whoever he or she may be, in to the harbor of her home. And lo and behold, Henry Valmont Bacas arrived on the second floor the same year as Ti-Drauzin on the third floor.

With no Ernestine, Josephine was feeling so overwhelmed that she and Drauzin were shocked to find themselves considering a possibility that they both rejected for months. Eventually though, urgent necessities convinced them to take a step which they promised themselves was only interim, a bridge. They bought a slave. Claire.

They consoled themselves slightly that Josephine's brother Philippe Young had treated her well, that they were separating her from none of her family, and in fact Josephine already knew her well. Claire was bright—and brightening. Drauzin and Josephine hated taking this step, yet they felt they had to, and they promised each other that when the crucial interlude passed, they would free Claire.

In 1844 Maria Bacas joined her brothers Henry and Louis Adhemar in the family of Joseph Bacas. The following year she was fast followed by Albert Paul; Maman Louise's lighthouse was suddenly attracting armadas to fill their long-lonely harbour.

Papa Drauzin and quite enceinte Josephine took little Aline,

Ti-Drauzin, and helper Claire to visit Josephine's Perrault cousins' plantation. Unexpectedly, Drauzin's and Josephine's third child decided to arrive three weeks early, on January 19, down south in Plaquemines Parish, a glowing coal they named Lucien. Drauzin's brother Jean-Baptiste Bacas and Rose Celina Saulay welcomed their own Richard Thomas Bacas in 1846. The two houses of Bacas on Rue St. Louis were fairly bursting.

CHAPTER 15:
DOWN…1837–43

There was, Adelaïde Pouponne Beaulieu thought, a kind of norm of storms that everyone became used to as part of the Bacas family. Her usual copper calm curved increasingly into a comma between her eyebrows.

The year after Drauzin and Josephine's wedding, the grimness had notably intensified. The whole country was suffering financial panic thanks to President Martin van "Ruin." England's Depression the previous year, in 1836, had lowered cotton prices. A new tariff had lowered the value of American sugar. "Already," said Adelaïde's beloved Barthelemy, "One hundred thirty-six plantations have collapsed amid numerous bankruptcies. Less money means less confidence, which means fewer orders, certainly for new furniture, and even for fixing old furniture. It does not matter that the quality of Baca's craftmanship is esteemed citywide." Even Alfonce was rarely needed in the woodshop anymore.

Barthelemy and his four sons, Joseph, Jean-Baptiste, Drauzin, and Leon, were idle too often. Joseph—round-faced, broad-shouldered, the big-hearted doer—had taken to building carts and wagons, for which he figured there'd always be need. JB, slender, with both face and mind like a hawk, read keenly, devouring history and natural science.

Drauzin, broad brow presiding over his well-proportioned face, was reflective, always listening. He was also a reader, most recently of Alexandre Dumas's *The Three Musketeers* and his just-published story *The Count of Monte Christo*. But Drauzin, above all, found this slack time in the woodshop an opportunity for playing more music, though fewer families could afford lessons, much less pianos.

His savvy wife Josephine, ever her mother's daughter, had suggested they take some of her dowry and his savings from earlier carpentry, music lessons, and piano buying and selling, and in fact do the crazy thing of purchasing more property, available increasingly cheaply because of the Depression. Drauzin, having already purchased an investment property at 323 Claiborne St. soon after their wedding, now, together with Josephine, managed to buy a shotgun house at a good price on North Roman St., the next block up from Derbigny St. The affectionate notion regarding such New Orleans houses was that you could shoot a shotgun through the front door and straight out the back door.

Leon, lean, a fiery, restless teen, explored the Vieux Quartier's night-time, sleeping too much of the day. Maman Adelaïde, for her part, grew all she could in the vegetable garden. She shifted from wax to tallow candles in the household.

Dinner times at 116 Rue St. Louis became trials. One night grim silences hung at the table like glass. Only the patriarch dared shatter that glass. First, Barthelemy's fists clenched by his plate at the head of the table. Then they banged the table like hefty drumsticks. The first bash twitched Drauzin's head. He covered his ears for the rest, teeth clenched. Barthelemy shouted thunder. Joseph's four-year-old, Louis Adhemar, peeking in at the door, had recently discovered a "weather vane," a vertical blue vein that started to bulge down Granpère Barthelemy's leathery forehead, like a snake eating a mouse, when storms were a comin'. This one had clearly arrived. Louis Adhemar scampered to shelter in the out-sheds of the family compound until the threatening weather passed. Drauzin fancied his father to be not a carpenter but a blacksmith, striking fire from iron. Drauzin could see that his mother, while not the target of this god's wrath, was struck by it nevertheless, like all her family. The four sons felt trapped at the table, frozen in irons. Drauzin felt he and his brothers were like horses being beaten, flinching, gathering forces 'til they might dare kick out. Although the rages were never aimed at Barthelemy's beloved Adelaïde, they took a toll on all, including, of course, Barthelemy himself. Adelaïde attended most to the one hurting most, the tyrant himself.

After the Depression subsided, in 1843, Barthelemy decided to add a new business, Croque-Mort, with Raoul Bonnot, his father's undertaker, as his model. M. Bonnot's son, well aware that the Bacases had provided them generously with business over generations, was generous in return with practical advice, pleased in fact to have M. Bacas's interest, rare in his unsavory work. The Bacas men converted a shed, bought tubs for washing, grew herbs for preparing the bodies, and acquired fancy duds as their uniforms. They built a light, four-wheeled wagon as a hearse, fashioning lathe-turned poles along the sides, covering all in the fine shine of ebony lacquer. The men applied boot-black anew at each funeral.

There was more than enough business in town, but no Bacases took to undertaking as a profession. Joseph didn't like the fancy attire. Drauzin didn't like having to cater to clients' clans. Leon didn't like death. JB disliked the business but was fascinated with the corpses. In fact, Barthelemy had to prevent this curious son from dissecting some of the bodies. As for Barthelemy, he disliked being at others' beck and call, especially given the demanding unpredictability of the grim reaper himself. One year of cold, usually old bodies was enough. No more undertaking was undertaken.

CHAPTER 16:

...AND OUT, 1846

By 1846, the economy was generally prospering again. And prosperity likes furniture. The Bacas men were back to busy in the woodshop. The household was bursting; seven little ones crawled and ran around, sometimes climbing the legs of the mighty grandfather like bear cubs on an old oak. Sometimes that was fine, but more often it was all Granpère could do not to kick them off.

The Bacas teapot was brought to a boil for a variety of reasons. Though not unusual in New Orleans at the time, all the Bacas boys turned men, still living at home after all these years, made for volatility. And sometimes Barthelemy was short-tempered from being wracked with pains in his back, wrists, knees, and ankles, all aggravated by increasing gout; the cabinetry craftsman was therefore less able to hoist, maneuver, and lever as he had done so masterfully for decades.

One evening, Adelaïde Pouponne Beaulieu—Maman, Granmère—now sixty-three years old, was savoring her own long-stemmed clay pipe under the mimosa tree in the courtyard dusk, a practice she had been enjoying since her childbearing years had ended. She took stock of their Barthelemy Bacas tribe, as she had ten years earlier at young Drauzin's wedding. Three of their four surviving sons had married, with seven grandchildren between them, multiplying. She half-consciously started adding up and—"Cho! Co!"—was a bit shocked to come up with eighteen. Her eyebrows rose.

While the sons had been multiplying, four of the five daughters had been subtracting themselves from the household, leaving Adelaïde longing for each. Even after these subtractions, the arithmetic of the household added up to eighteen. A wonderful surprise to realize. Her copper countenance glowed.

Adelaïde remembered walking away from 116 Rue St. Louis long ago, alone, during her first day of freedom, her whole adult life before her, open, an empty field. Who could have imagined? Now, she could hardly fit everyone into this overflowing home—plus Alfonce, Nelson, Claire, and the five other slaves. Mon Dieu! Twenty-six. Her queenly jaw, always the foundation of her composed beauty, tightened a moment. She, Adelaïde Beaulieu, purchased in her teens as a slave, a Pouponne to help mother others, had lo and behold built her own family, indeed her own clan, full and free—a picture she had never dared imagine as a child.

However, as joyful a cornucopia as her life was for Adelaïde Pouponne Beaulieu, she was concerned for her mate of forty-one years. Barthelemy Bacas, now sixty-six, master carpenter, master measurer and counter, never thought of counting family. He just knew it was often too much. It wasn't unusual for her mountain of a man to reach his limits. She well understood why the fine woodworking slave Cecile had long ago run away from the shop. She had often wondered how Cecile fared. Her occasional inquiries over the years at Congo Square had only yielded one clue. Some heard he'd stowed away on the ship Phoenix, bound for Cartagena.

⚜

For many reasons, it did not surprise Adelaïde to learn that her four sons had arranged a visit to Barthelemy's cousin, Nonc Drauzin Bacas, known now as Fulsain Bacas. Young Drauzin and Josephine would frequently visit her mother up on Bayou Rd. During his nephew's visits up the street, Nonc Fulsain, hearing about life at 116 St. Louis, would sometimes make allusions that young Drauzin eventually pursued further. What he discovered led Drauzin to arrange the meeting of the four Bacas brothers plus Fulsain at 209 Bayou Rd., sans Père Barthelemy.

"Mes chères neveux," Nonc Fulsain had begun in his warm, embracing voice. Both the quality of his voice and the affection in his eyes offered the brothers a calmer shelter than they'd known under their father. "You probably know that your father's mother, your grandmère Marie Louise Catherine Landrony, whom you never knew, came from Arkansas Post. You may not know that the symbol of Arkansas Post is a 'manteau à trois villages,' a painting on an early eighteenth-century buffalo robe of three villages, picturing the common practice there of French, Spanish, and Quapaw Indian intermarriage."

The brothers had absorbed the news and nodded, acknowledging likely implications. "However, more importantly, you probably also do not know—"

When they finished their powwow with Nonc Fulsain, all four brothers had been equally shocked at the thoroughness of their collective ignorance.

One morning not long after, Adelaïde watched her four sons, coffee cups in hand, stride across the courtyard toward the woodshop where their father awaited them. Drauzin followed his two older brothers, as always, and Leon, not surprisingly, brought up the rear. Adelaïde considered Drauzin more the surround, the periphery of the brothers' foursome. When would he find his own stride? Now blue smoke again climbed her copper brow, enhancing her red-gold tignon as she sat and savored another puff of her long-stemmed clay pipe in her wicker armchair beneath the mimosa tree.

Adelaïde's Barthelemy had greeted the day grumpy, grousing about "wasting work time for a 'meeting,' with my own sons no less, all apprenticed to me, here. I've made them all decent journeymen, and they still live in the family compound, here, even the older three with wives and children. Bacas men? Ha! Bacas boys."

Those older three had warned their wives to keep the children out of the courtyard today. After a couple of hours' work, the Bacas cabinetmakers had cleared a table.

Now, as the brothers were making their way from the kitchen back across the courtyard to the shop, Maman Adelaïde tightened her tawny shawl around her shoulders, puffed her pipe, and pondered. *Having been my master's slave, having experienced the affections of his son, I savored my freedom at twenty-three when dear sister Pauline purchased mine. Then I chose, like a turtle returning to the beach of its birth—I, a free woman—chose to return to Barthelemy, the birth for me of love. Simply, my freedom allowed me to recognize that I cherish his love. Now, nine children later, I still cherish his love, as difficult as he can be with others.*

Adelaïde discerned a distinctive shift in the gaits of her sons. Colts becoming stallions? Drauzin too? She recognized that they were no longer approaching their master.

Inside the shop, Barthelemy, grizzled and hulking, cast a large shadow from one end of the cleared-off, still sawdusty work table. He glanced at his sons, resenting their work interruption. To his right sat first-born Joseph, his troubled eyes wanting to warm his father. Next to him, youngest son Leon eyed his father like a stranger, for danger. To Barthelemy's left, second son Jean-Baptiste revealed little yet seemed to read every gesture like an experienced gambler. And Drauzin seemed serene, more listening than looking. Barthelemy Bacas sensed something here of wolves, but dismissed the pack members on either side of him rather as overgrown cubs hanging around the den too long.

Joseph began, "Papa, we, your sons, have good work and a good home here. You have taught us well. Our Bacas furniture is respected throughout our town. We are grateful. Our families grow. We think about our futures after you and Maman have gone. We worry and we wonder."

"Worry? Wonder? What is there to wonder? Your only worry is to work. I've given you the tools for that. What you do with them is your only worry. And that is that. And you know, and you understand. That is that," Barthelemy repeated. "Now, let's get back to work." His overcast eyebrows, storm-clouds roiling, resolved themselves back in line.

Jean-Baptiste, calm, asked, "What do you mean, 'That is that'?"

"Oh, mon Dieu, JB, you know very well. The laws of our land allow no inheritance to pass to the children of a white man and a woman of color. That's that."

"With all that we, your sons, have helped you build up and generate, increasing your wealth, spreading your good name, we and our sisters are to receive nothing at all?" said Jean-Baptiste.

"Does that seem right or fair to you, Père?"

"No, it does not," said Barthelemy. He smacked a hand on the table for emphasis. "But that's how it is. That's that. Your mother and I have lived with that fact all our lives together. When we chose each other, we chose that."

"Can you imagine how the law could decide such an unfair policy?"

"I think the whites decided such a law was necessary to protect their white world."

"The whites?"

"The whites."

Jean-Baptiste sat back, allowing a long pause, before nodding at Joseph. It looked to Barthelemy like the end of the meeting, but it didn't feel that way.

"Papa," began Joseph, "do you remember saying goodbye to Nonc Drauzin that drizzly evening of Granpère's funeral, back almost thirty years ago?"

"Why certainly, I suppose. Of course I said goodbye to him. What of it?"

"Do you remember what he said to you?"

"I don't know, probably 'Bon soir, merci bien.'"

"I do know," said Joseph. "I was right there at the door step, ten-year-old little me. It puzzled me for weeks. Then it completely floated from my mind. Yet the other day, when we were visiting with Nonc Drauzin, I suddenly remembered again. He whispered a question in your ear, Papa, one word: 'Genoa?'"

Barthelemy froze for a moment, only now remembering.

"'Genoa?'" Joseph repeated. Then he asked, "Why was that a question, Papa?"

"I don' know, I don' know." But something deep within Barthelemy was tightening, dimly intuiting the direction of the wolves' attack.

Jean-Baptiste took over. "We are all glad and grateful that you and Maman chose each other."

Barthelemy nodded, piercing JB with his eye, wondering what fang might lurk behind such a smile of a statement, which JB and his brothers did, however, mean sincerely and with the greatest respect.

"Our Granpère, Jean-Baptiste Manuel Bacas, was born in Genoa, n'est-ce pas?" Jean-Baptiste continued.

"Si!" growled Barthelemy.

"Around 1739?"

"Si."

"And he came to New Orleans and married Marie Louise Catherine Landrony, your mother?"

"Si."

"And your father, Jean-Baptiste Manuel Bacas, died

February 10, 1817, age seventy-eight?"

"Si, idiot!"

The four brothers Bacas were now on the edges of their chairs, eying their father, yes, like wolves eying a bear, watching for the way to the heart of the man.

Jean-Baptiste continued. "Do you know, cher Père, that a gentleman arrived in New Orleans in the 1770s from Saint-Domingue? His name was Juan Bautista Bacusa."

Barthelemy sat still, silent. He looked at JB as though he might rake this son's throat with his claws, daring him to continue. JB dared.

"He had been born in Gonaïves, Saint-Domingue, in what year—ah, 1738." All stilled. Like a skilled chess player, JB had just moved his bishop into position. "At first in New Orleans Juan Bautista lived at 7 Levee North—" now JB moved his queen into position. "Then he married a young woman named—Luisa—Catarina —Landrony, Luisa Catarina Landrony, n'est-ce pas, Père?"

Barthelemy's jaw clenched, a vise with nothing to crush.

"And Juan Bautista Bacusa bought—116 St. Louis, 12 Agosto, 1779, n'est-ce pas? And then, in this very casa, aqui, Juan Bautista and Luisa Catarina had a son, Bartolome, n'est-ce pas, Père?"

Barthelemy turned his head some, glancing up at a corner of the shop, fixing on a spider-web thick with sawdust and flies, one squirming slightly. But Barthelemy was actually seeing something much further back in time.

After a brief silence, Barthelemy made his countermove. "So, Jean-Baptiste Bacas, my Papa, spent some years in Saint-Domingue first, before coming to Spanish New Orleans. Simple. Understandable confusion explaining the coincidences. What's the point of all this?"

JB looked at his brothers, each confident in his navigating the battlefield of the chessboard. Drauzin nod-nudged him to continue.

"Granpère served in the local military?"

Barthelemy nodded.

"Even rising to Captain?"

Barthelemy nodded, sipping uselessly at his empty coffee cup. Setting up the check, Jean-Baptiste proceeded.

"Do you know, Père, that Juan Bautista Bacusa joined the Spanish military of New Orleans in the early 1790s?"

Nod.

"By 1793, he was a sublieutenant—" Tentative nod. "—in the New Orleans Negro Militia."

Barthelemy—stock-still.

Check, Jean-Baptiste inwardly called. "Juan Bautista Bacusa became Captain, commanding the Battalion of—Quadroons."

Barthelemy's eyes raced crazily to random parts of the shop.

"Juan Bautista Bacusa is listed as dying on February 10, 1817, age seventy-eight." *Checkmate*, JB inwardly declared.

Barthelemy's shoulders slumped. He looked down for the longest time. The brothers sat in the silence of new truth.

Eventually, from the deflated batch of sacks in the chair, came a subdued voice, "It's true—My father tried—late nineties—it worked."

More silence. The brothers looked at each other, surprised to have arrived. A collective sigh.

Joseph, "Paa-paa,—you can set it right, who you are! You and Maman can marry! We, your children, can inherit! Paa-paa!"

More silence.

Barthelemy looked at each of his sons. His ashen face darkened. Then rose a rumbling from deep within.

"I—will—be—white."

Now, again looming large, he was seeing only red.

"Père, please," said Leon.

"Père, we can all go through this together!" said Drauzin.

"Père, you... you can set this all true... and right," said Jean-Baptiste.

"Pa-pa, pleeease," pleaded Joseph.

"You—" Barthelemy snarled at his firstborn. "I *never* should have named you after that sniveling American trader traitor." Joseph Valmont Bacas cringed. All Barthelemy was hearing now was his own growing thunder.

"I—am—" he erupted, "white!" He banged his fist down—the law.

Leon, furious at his father bruting his brother, was yet more furious at his father betraying his own origins and his own children. Leon rose, out-roaring him. "Sa-leau! Le père le pire!"

Barthelemy stood, growled, grabbed his walnut chair, raised it high above his head, and cursed at his sons, "Vous—bâtardes!"

The other brothers Bacas rose and stood with Leon at the end of the table, shoulder to shoulder, readying. Leon said icily, "Non, c'est *toi* le bâtarde." Barthelemy eyed him, then each son in turn. "Va-t-en! Fous le camp, tous!" he shouted, crashing the chair down onto the table, which held as the chair smashed into pieces, one of which Leon caught flash-fast. Barthelemy collapsed onto the table, groaning in the wreck of his own furniture, one finger dangling at an angle.

Soaring doves left silence. The table was intact, yet something larger than the chair had shattered. The sons stood immobile, like a bas-relief. As always, the master, though groaning, had the last word. Drauzin saw eldest Joseph as the table, inwardly taking the brunt of the blow. Leon, frozen fire. Drauzin leaned his shoulder into Leon's, steadying him. And JB, who so deftly guided Barthelemy through the chess match to truth—no board left to play on. The silence shackled the sons. The moment was still the master's.

Joseph, shoulders sloping, slow-turned toward the door. Jean-Baptiste looked blankly at his other brothers and nodded, starting his turn. Leon was already turning.

Drauzin thought, *This is not how this should end.* He reached deep beneath his usual role in the brothers four, then did the hardest thing he'd done in his life. He came up hard-humming, broke the silence, and whisper-sang,

> White folks want de niggers to work an' sweat,
> Wants dem to cut de cane till dey is wringin' wet.

Drauzin could feel his brothers, emptied, breathe in big. They joined him, increasing forte:

> We poor niggers gets nothin' atall,
> White boss cusses and gits it all.
> Cut high, cut low,
> Swing fast, swing slow.
> Stronger, louder,
> Bend yo' back, tote it to the lift.
> White boss hollers if yo' ain't swift.
> De Lawd take keer of us when we is dead,
> But in de canefield de white boss—

The brothers looked at each other, nodded, and at "cracks" smacked their hands on the table, a simple echo of gestures they'd improvised as boys in the courtyard, now echoing Barthelemy bashing the chair:

> —cracks yo' on de head.
> In de canefield de white boss cracks yo' on de head.

Barthelemy flinched on the "cracks"-smacks, speared Drauzin with icicle eyes, and slumped into another chair, still groaning.

The three brothers Bacas now followed Drauzin, pivoting out the door. Slowing across the courtyard, Drauzin started what he remembered loving as a little boy at Granpère's funeral gathering:

The rooster and the chicken had a fight,

His brothers joined:

The chicken knocked the rooster out of sight,
The rooster told the chicken, That's alright,
I'll meet you in the gumbo tonight, tonight,
I'll meet you in the gumbo tonight.

On the last two lines they fairly roared. Drauzin, though trembling, felt stronger than he ever remembered.

Adelaïde had listened, of course, to the weather rumblings across the courtyard throughout the meeting of the Bacas men. She could hear various voices, some soft, one harsh, JB's often leading the way, until the volcano began to erupt, matched by Leon's blast, then Barthelemy's roar, and finally the crash of what must have been at least a broken chair. She hoped nothing more.

Adelaïde Beaulieu's heart swelled for her sons. Her brow furrowed. She noticed dark splatters on her yellow dress. She realized her right forefinger had been drawing blood in her left palm. Her pipe lay in pieces on the ground. She leaned down to pick up the pieces, then let them settle instead in the soil beneath the mimosa tree.

Something about the sight of her four sons crossing the courtyard seemed strangely wrong. Then she realized: *They were walking without shadows.* When she remembered it was roughly midday, she knew how strangely right the sight. *Joseph always led with his heart, JB with his smarts, now Drauzin with his art.* Adelaïde could tell the Bacas family dynamic had shifted forever.

She recalled her mother's tales of being ravaged by her

master, then beaten by the master's wife. Her mother had been squeezed in the vise of both her master's violent attraction and her mistress's humiliation, ravaged as the object of his lust, beaten as the object of her fury. Adelaïde now marveled at the accuracy of her own intuition when she was just twenty-three—perhaps against all odds—that however bad a brute her beloved Barthelemy might be, he nevertheless would never hurt her, his chosen mate. And he, her chosen mate, had not.

But Barthelemy had hurt his sons, terribly. Her heart was breaking for all their children, especially these newly stronger sons. She also grieved for her broken husband, the lonely love of her life, who chose to remain white.

Adelaïde turned toward the shop, wondering what wreckage she might find.

The brothers Bacas knew they were unlikely ever to spend a night together again under the same roof. By the end of the week, all four had moved elsewhere. Drauzin and Josephine took Aline Adelaïde, Ti-Drauzin, Lucien, slave Claire, and their ciel-de-lit to 325 Bayou Rd. to join Granmère Mathé and Philippe Young, his Jamaican wife Adèle, and their two children.

"Maman," Drauzin had insisted to Adelaïde Pouponne, "come with us."

"Non, mon cher Drusino," Adelaïde had responded. "My love is my fortress. I have always been safe with him." Drauzin wished he knew that to be true, though he could not remember Barthelemy's wrath targeting her.

Joseph and JB each found lodging for their families. And youngest brother Leon? Who knew? One rumor said he'd gone to sea, signing on with a merchantman to Cartagena. Another held that he'd disappeared into the back alleys of the Vieux Quartier, fathering a child with a black woman. A more elaborate version of that plot was that Leon hit the streets with a vengeance, sampling the range of the fashionable nymphs of the pave, dealing in stolen goods and culling shipwrecks, some "manmade." And the last rag of rumor was that Leon had escaped a prison ship. After that, nothing.

When Drauzin's sister Elizabeth Coelina Bacas married M. Pierre Frederick LeRond, her three older brothers sat together three rows behind her parents in the church. Josephine stayed home on Bayou Rd. with infant Eugene, born March 16, 1847. When Drauzin returned home from the wedding, he found a flurry in the yard. Baby Lucien, sleeping on his back beneath a pecan tree, had awakened, and a pecan had fallen into his right eye, leaving him crying furiously, of course. Granmère Josephine regularly applied a compress of honey and yarrow. Although the eye healed in time, Lucien would never see much through it.

Adelaïde and Barthelemy returned to 116 St. Louis St, now inhabited by a family of two.

CHAPTER 17:
EXODUS, 1848

Newly banished Drauzin Valsin Bacas was welcomed by his original namesake, now Fulsain, for any work he might wish to do in his cousin's woodshop. Little Lucien especially loved to linger, dawdle, play, and make things there. He loved the different smells, colors, and textures of each of the many kinds of woods stacked neatly in their proper places. Sometimes he fancied that in the woods he was smelling the colors of the rainbow. He was entranced by the shapes and patterns of the tools hanging on the walls. The sawing, drilling, sanding, hammering—for little Lucien, Fulsain's woodshed was a concert hall, housing a poly-sense symphony.

Papa Drauzin loved passing hours in the pirogue on the Bayou St. Jean, alone, rarely with Josephine in her multimothering years, then increasingly and delightfully, with some combination of Aline, Ti-Drauzin, and soon Lucien. Aline, almost eight, was starting to take up the paddle, pulling quite strongly when needed. Sometimes, when Drauzin paddled long among the ducks and muskrats, even all the way up the bayou to its mouth at Lac Ponchartrain, he liked to sing old coureur de bois songs that Maman Adelaïde had loved as a child, that her Acadian father used to sing, plying his Cajun ways through these southern bayous. One was a particular favorite of Aline, Ti-Drauzin, and gradually Lucien:

Parmi les voyageurs––la charge sur le dos,
En disant: camarades, Ah! grand Dieu, qu'il fait chaud!
Que la chaleur est grande! Il faut nous rafraichir.
A la fin du voyage, on prendra du plaisir.

Among the voyageurs––packs on our backs,
We say, Comrades, oh, great Lord, it's hot!
Mighty hot! We need to refresh ourselves.
At the end of this journey, we'll have our fun.

One day, Drauzin realized with a start that his grandfather, Adelaïde's father, must have learned this song up north on Isle St. Jean, now called Prince Edward Island by the British, and here he was singing it to his own children down south on Bayou St. Jean.

Paddling, drifting, Drauzin could forget, even about the riverbanks; he didn't know if time slowed down, as it surely seemed, or if it somehow even turned inside out. His pirogue sometimes felt so light it could float on dew. Young Lucien loved to rest his head on one arm on the gunnel, letting his other arm hang, fingers drifting in and on the water, as though he were drawing, even writing, as he saw Aline and his parents do on paper. And the shores drifted by.

Sometimes Lucien spotted two eyes on a floating log among the water lilies, watching him. Lucien sometimes closed his good left eye, opened, closed, opened, closed, "watching" sparklings of light on the water, like little lights dancing, like little stars singing. Then he would keep his good eye closed, and even more with his bad eye closed too, see certain beamings like constant gentle explosions, yieldings, which both dimmed and brightened, "visibly" varying in his own darkness, until he opened his good eye again. Somehow these beamings' yieldings felt like knowings.

Now living on Bayou Rd., Drauzin found himself sometimes identifying with both Marcelite and Ernestine, liberated from the supposed Garden of Eden, 116 St. Louis, which had become a premature purgatory. Wide were the possibilities now. And yet, he felt an ominous threat in the otherwise soft, soft air of New Orleans. Color lines and their consequences continued to harden. The Latin painter's palate of multitudes of hues was crystallizing into the Anglo-Saxon engraver's sharp distinctions, mutually exclusive: black or white.

During one crucial visit, Fulsain urged Drauzin to start exploring possibilities beyond New Orleans. "For us, for our people, for our family, for you, this world here is shrinking. Those Anglo-Saxons, the Americans, are always drawing more lines; we are more and more on our own reservation here in New Orleans, Louisiana. Here, we shrink.

"Go, cher Drauzin, far away from here. Take your beautiful wife, your soulmate, and your fine young children. Start anew. Go where you each can become mighty, each take your lives fully in hand. After all, Drauzin, mon cher Drauzin," Nonc Fulsain leaned closer, whispering, "your grandfather Jean-Baptiste did." He smiled, nodding.

Various Creole families they knew had made their ways to Vera Cruz, Mexico, down the western shore of the Gulf. Word had spread: "Wider horizons," "Latin culture," "Gracious living," "White is part of the blend, not binding the colors." Drauzin and Josephine had agreed that after the birth of Eugene, Drauzin would explore south. However, the Mexican-American War had started the year before. And in fact, a week before baby Eugene joined the family on Bayou Rd., General Winfield Scott arrived with American troops and the US Navy on the shores of Vera Cruz itself, to begin a successful twenty-day siege before continuing toward Mexico City. Eugene was a strong, fiery baby, born during the war that kept their family from Mexico.

So Drauzin and Josephine turned their thoughts east to a port that had played an important role in the life of Drauzin's parrain, godfather Hector Beaulieu, as well as many other residents of New Orleans: Havana, Cuba. Drauzin took a ship there and found he loved the land.

"Ma Josie," he reported upon return. "I love the many-hued textures of the people. I love stately, multidimensional Havana, especially its many-layered musics, much like our Vieux Quartier. It seems half the population are slaves, mostly on sugar or tobacco plantations. Maybe a tenth are free people of color. Among the rest, many whites, the leading people, make extra efforts to distinguish themselves from the rest of the people. They segregate themselves in exclusive zones, even in public areas, as we certainly have here at home." Josephine nodded.

Drauzin continued, "But, Chérie, over the days and nights, something both dawned on me and wore on me increasingly: tension between all the people of Cuba and the government of Spain. I realized for the first time that, unlike my father, no matter how our streets of New Orleans increasingly stifle us, you and I have grown up without a king. No king! That simple. I know I have never voted myself, but I know that in most of our country up North, most people do. That is our government—most people vote. Not a little crown on a little head on a big fat throne far across the ocean. In spite of slavery in our South, many ideas of freedom and independence actually affect most people's lives. Chérie," he whispered, "our country is wider than our city."

"Mon Drauzin, you return to the soft air of our New Orleans with hard, new clarity."

"Ma Josie, one day each year here pains me most. That is the day many men stand hours in long lines at the polls. I look hardly any different from many of them. They own property; I own property. They pay taxes; I pay taxes. I *know* I know more and understand more than many, perhaps even most of them. I feel in my marrow that I have the same right to stand in that long line, to exercise my judgment, to make my mark, to cast my vote, to cause my little ripple of influence. We are in the right country, just not the right city.

"The only difference between voting men and me is the color of my skin, and in my case, may I say, that is a sublimely subtle difference indeed." He grinned. Josephine chuckled, nodding.

"I, Drauzin Valsin Bacas, I want to vote. Back in 1815, General Jackson came mighty close to granting the vote to gens de couleur who fought in the colored battalions against the British. After the victory, Jackson retreated on that front. Our Anglo-Saxon Americans resent looking Nègres in the eye, scorn in one eye, fear in the other.

"Now, in 1848, people are dancing in the American streets of French New Orleans, celebrating the overthrow of Louis Philippe. 'Finally,' they cheer, 'the fall of the final French king!' Finally, the French abolition of slavery throughout the Empire, again. After the Revolution of 1789, we had Liberté, Egalité, Fraternité. The ensuing fifty years have included first the abolition of slavery, then our Eternal Emperor Napoleon trying and failing to restore slavery in Toussaint L'Ouverture's Haiti. Then kings, and kings again for a year, a season, a month, a week, one for twenty minutes, until Louis Philippe. And finally now, the Revolutions of 1848, feared by monarchies across Europe.

"Here in our New Orleans, ma chère Josephine, do I have Liberté? Yes, but I am limited in terms of certain restaurants, hotels, business opportunities, transport, and, of course, I lack the right to vote. Do I have Égalité? Non. Fraternité? Limited. How far we have been falling."

⚜

Closer to home, a different fall. Barthelemy Bacas's most-beloved grandson, Joseph's fifteen-year-old Louis Adhemar, wandered down from the Place des Armes to the riverside with some friends. They fished, snacked, smoked cheap cigars. After lunch, their favorite game——taunting duels.

"You're so fat ya can't lie down."

"You're so bones I can't see ya sideways."

"You're so slow you never caught a sunrise."

"You're so weak I could sneeze ya right over," followed of course by a push, then tackling back into the muck. Two and then all, shouting, jumped in, mucked up, the mess soon metamorphosing into slop-hobbling around as they did a mesmerizing chant-dance: "We are the mud-men, we are the mud-men."

Then, up arose in their midst the muddiest of the mud-men, leaping above the others. Louis Adhemar Bacas roared, "I, Loup-Garou, I, Loup-Garou, do hereby turn each of you, mere Mississippi River mud-men, into——werewolves!" And fangs bared, Loup-Garou proceeded to mark each mud-man's neck, completing the conversion of Mississippi mud-men into snarling werewolves as they roiled and tumbled each other into an exhausted pile on the shore. Some even slipped into siesta in the mess.

In time, the weary "werewolves" began washing the muck off their clothes, becoming boys yet again, some standing, some sitting, some rolling in the shale-brown waters. Louis Adhemar stepped further back into the river, scrubbing his pants. Strong undercurrents had carved a sharp drop under the brown swirls. Down Louis Adhemar slipped, disappearing into the curving current before others noticed. He resurfaced twice, calling the second time. The boys had no rope or pole to throw; two held a third back from going after him. One ran down the shore. No third time did Adhemar resurface; the racing Mississippi swallowed Louis Adhemar Bacas without a trace. Stunned stood the boys, helpless.

Two days later, Adhemar's body was found nine miles

downriver toward the Chalmette battlefield, his hickory-han-
dled pen-knife in one pocket and a big hole through the other
and into his leg: crawfish had started nibbling on leftover callas and kept gnawing long after the rice was gone. His face
too, was mostly gone.

Papa Joseph had the croque-mort, Raoul Bonnot Jr., keep
Louis Adhemar Bacas in a closed casket. Barthelemy ordered
him placed in the Bacas vault in St. Louis Cemetery No. 1,
joining Jean-Baptiste Manuel Bacas; his wife, Marie Luise
Catherine Landrony Bacas; and their daughter, Marie Luysa
Bacas Cossé.

On the one hand, the spirit of the '48 revolution inspired Nelson
Fouché, wealthy architect and free man of color, to found the
Catholic Convent School, where children of color could study
English, French composition, history, rhetoric, logic, and
accounting, under the direction of Armand Lanusseal, poet,
publisher of journals. He had edited *Les Cenelles*, a collection of
inspiring verse by free men of color back in 1845. On the other
hand, each year the "enlightened" Louisiana legislature continued to pass more laws restricting the rights of free blacks.

One sunny day after heavy rains, Drauzin walked down
Rue St. Ann with six-year-old Ti-Drauzin in hand, excited to
see the city with his father. Both Drauzins, Père and Fils, wandered past shop windows, savoring scents, watching crayfish
in bowls, sharing a mille-feuilles in the pastry shop. Greens,
blues, golds, oranges, reds on ladies' heads and all the way
down to some fancy feet flowed up and down the streets
among all shades of skin.

Ti-Drauzin asked, "Papa, am I a prince in the Kingdom of
Colors?"

"Si, mon Vieux, you are my prince in the Kingdom of
Colors."

Along the sidewalk-banquette approaching them strode two white Creole gentlemen, their ten-year-old boys in tow. The white men, on a collision course with Drauzin, were in vigorous conversation, punctuating their points with their walking sticks.

Drauzin, firming his grip on Ti-Drauzin's hand, wondered if they saw him. He cleared his throat. The near one's red jowls spilled above the orange waistcoat that barely contained his massive middle. With a half-glance at Drauzin, and without altering stride, he barreled forward, barking, "Out of my way, boy!"

Drauzin knew he was not referring to Ti-Drauzin. He swept his son into his arms, stepping into the street-muck with Ti-Drauzin. The far Creole had never noticed him. The two trailing ten-year-olds, one a redhead, the other dirty blond, were imitating their fathers' struts, noses high. The far one snickered. The near one spat onto Drauzin's trousers. Both snorted.

Back on the sidewalk, shaking their mucky-wet pants cuffs, scraping their mud-caked shoes, Ti-Drauzin asked, "Pa-pa, Pa-pa, pourquoi?" He clearly expected more heroic action from his mighty father.

"Un jour, un jour." One day. Drauzin had hardly answered, bleeding inside with shame, but unable to tell his little boy it was more important for him to have a father than a hero, especially now.

The assumed right of the white had always been there, of course. In the generally civil potpourri of New Orleans of decades past, it had rarely been exercised. Such behavior was being almost summoned by recent legislation, both local and national.

On the way home, Drauzin felt all their morning joy had been erased; he noticed nothing but mud streaming in the streets, slops steaming, reeking in the alleys, and his son's hand, wet and warm, holding on to his father's for dear life.

Josephine could tell that something wrong had happened to father and son. That night when Drauzin reflected with her on their experience, he felt as though he were confessing a sin. "I can not even defend my honor in a duel against a white man."

"Thank heavens for that, at least," said Josephine, placing her hands on his shoulders, pulling his head back upright, assuring him he had acted the best, all things considered. "Better you're my man, and Ti-Drauzin's, than the street's and St. Louis Cemetery's."

"Yes, maybe," Drauzin said, his eye-whites reddening, "but it takes its toll. I wish never to step aside for a white man again. You—know—me. I feel my mother knows me. My father—no, but—ha, he's white, white of course! No. I feel my brothers and sisters know me. My children love me for who I am. Many days I make my way just fine. I'm a man in our world.

"Then along come two whites on the banquette, and what am I? A goat? Sheep? Dog? Ox? What am I, man inside, animal outside? Or a shadow, just a shade outside? Has some Greek god cursed us coloreds, so we've become like that stag who can't tell his own hounds, 'But I'm Actaeon, can't you see, I'm Actaeon?' as they, barking, rip him to shreds. Are we cursed? Why? Why do we deserve to be treated so? Who put a boogeyman Voodoun curse on our whole race?

"Chèrie, can't you get your great Marie LaVeau to work up a mighty gris-gris, a gris-gris spell on every white around, that would blind them each to all our colors, so only their pupils could see, not their irises, only their black, black pupils, where there's no color at all, right into the heart of us, right into the light of us, each? Or maybe get the whites to see all colors as parts of light? Can't you get your grande dame, your grande magicienne, to make that spell we need, Chèrie? I'm so tired of being an animal man—sometimes it makes me wonder if we are then less than men. And I hate wondering that. I hate it the worst.

"How can I not flinch every time I meet a white? I've got to know what's coming. I'm a panther among hounds. And Aline, Drauzin, Lucien—what are the odds they might be taken for slave some day and end up back where my mother began? And if not that, how much might they remain slave within? Oh, Josephine—who knows our children's coming days?"

"Cher, cher, the present pains us, mon cher, but the future, the future is in our hands," said Josephine with a kiss on the back of her husband's head, which made a surprising difference, in spite of his feeling sick. In fact, that simple kiss seemed to rekindle, like a match, the sleeted flame of who Drauzin was.

"And remember, mon cher," continued Josephine, "it's not *all* the whites; brother Samuel likes many he works with up north. Those who are blind to our 'ins' you want to blind to our 'outs.' Remember, there are whites up there hollerin' to break off all iron shackles of slaves, and of mind for us all.

"Mon cher, Actaeon may have been trapped in that stag, but our Compair Lapin, Brer Rabbit, always figures a way out. We will figure ours. That hyena Bouki does not always determine us. And meanwhile, remember, as my Granmère used to say, 'When you see a palm tree, the palm tree sees you.' Our job is to be sure that at least we *see* the palm tree. That's where we start. The present pains us, but the future is in our hands." Josephine bestowed upon Drauzin another kiss, this time in front. Then she prepared a hot cup of herbe tisane for her beloved, frustrated, most handsome husband. Drauzin sipped the herbal tea gratefully.

CHAPTER 18:

LAND OF PROMISE, 1849

Jean-Baptiste Bacas was pursuing interests sparked by his year on the undertaker's crew. He had begun to study with doctors Hunt, Harrison, and Stone in the recently formed Medical College of Louisiana, over at the junction of Common, Baronne, and Philippa Streets.

Josephine's oldest Mathé brother, Louis Francois, opened up a feed store at 251 Bayou Rd. Her oldest Young brother, Samuel Charles, operated his grocery store at 330 Bayou Rd., selling not only vegetables and dairy produce, but also local sugar and cotton all the way up to Ohio and the prairie states, buying directly from plantations and distributing himself. He talked with both Drauzin and Josephine about various trade experiences up the Mississippi and the Ohio Rivers. Davenport, Iowa, up above St. Louis just beyond where the Iowa River joins the Mississippi, interested him as a promising town for trade. And Cincinnati, on the Ohio River, already bustled with business.

Granmère Josephine, the widow Mathé, presided as matriarch over her household, including Philippe Young's four children, Drauzin's and Josephine's four, and brothers Brou Simon and Simon Raphael Mathé, both in their early twenties. As the Bacas household on Rue St. Louis had been bursting in 1846, the Mathé household on Bayou Rd. was fairly overflowing in 1849, though without the same internal storms.

Nevertheless, on May 3, 1849, a Mississippi River levee breached upriver from the city, creating by far the worst flooding the city had ever seen. The flood, known as Sauvé's Crevasse, left twelve thousand people without their homes. Although the Mathé, Young, and Bacas residences on lower Bayou Rd. did not suffer directly, the vulnerability of both the homes and the economy to the whims of the mighty Mississippi River intensified Drauzin's and Josephine's quest for their next step.

Josephine enlarged with their next child, who arrived September 19. Laure Bacas was a slight, quiet baby. Josephine had always identified with Daphne of their ciel-de-lit, Daphne who, pursued by Apollo, had turned into the laurel tree. Now, two girls, one the family's own laurel, three boys in between, and one boy long ago gone to heaven.

In October, Barthelemy's only surviving brother, Leon Bacas, died at sixty-four, out west of the city in his and his wife Marie-Celeste Tègre's home in St. John Parish, Edgard. Perhaps they were one of those couples only meant to be on Earth together, for Marie-Celeste joined him before the year ended. The loss of Nonc Leon reminded Drauzin that no one had heard a word from or about his own younger brother Leon since they had all left 116 St. Louis.

The home at 116 St. Louis St. had been suffering, not from the flood, but from the ebbing of 1846. The two houses there seemed like tombs barely tended. Weeds grew in the pass-through between them. Adelaïde wilted, unsustained by the former teeming streams of children and grandchildren. Barthelemy had to have both Alfonce and Nelson rescue the woodshed work initially, while Barthelemy's bashed hand healed, which it never did properly. He too lost momentum and power.

Joseph Bacas and his Louise had struggled in their own ebbing, the terrible loss of their fifteen-year-old son Louis Adhemar. Plainly, their next step was not working so well. In

1850 Joseph sensed that mutual grief may have melted pride and bitterness in both father and son. He asked his father to meet. Barthelemy sat in the front room, bidding Joseph to sit. Adelaïde brought them tea.

"Our own house feels empty, Papa; our Louis Adhemar's absence looms large."

Barthelemy, who had loved Joseph's boy first and most of the grandchildren, nodded,

"Ours is emptier." Four years had passed since the great evacuation from 116 St. Louis.

"Papa, could you use a hand in the shop?"

"I could. Would you?"

"I, I would; I would like that."

"Son, my first-born, I would like that too. I would."

Adelaïde stepped into the room. "Mon chère Joseph, would you and Louise please consider rejoining us here at 116 St. Louis? If you both would, we," she looked at Barthelemy, who nodded, "would love to have you."

Adelaïde was overjoyed and relieved to have Joseph's family move back in, this time on the third floor of 116 St. Louis. The house hummed and babbled again, now with seven rather than eighteen. Next door, 114 St. Louis became an empty storeroom. Eight-year-old Henry had the rule of the roost, and little five-year-old Albert Paul became the new apple of his Granpère's eye, by his side for hours in the shop, doing much to heal old wounds. Albert Paul and his cousin Lucien were each the "darkies" of their families. Six-year-old Maria was like a second apron on her dear Granmère Adelaïde, singing with her, sewing, embroidering, and hearing tales galore.

Jean-Baptiste Bacas began to practice medicine. Dr. Bacas rented for both residence and professional practice Drauzin's other property on 323 Claiborne, not far from Bayou Rd.

Almost immediately after the United States Congress beleagueredly passed Henry Clay's desperate compromise for keeping the Union together, Drauzin could see the effects of the Fugitive Slave Act. Slave catchers stepped up hunts right in Louisiana; captured escapees from throughout the South and North were paraded like Spanish cattle into New Orleans at higher rates than ever.

Drauzin and Josephine pondered, gathering courage, forces, and facts, reaching both wide and deep. They shared clarity about leaving New Orleans and about heading into the largely unknown north. Through sifting all they had heard, two possibilities were emerging as most likely: Davenport, Iowa, and Cincinnati, Ohio. Brother Samuel Charles Young pushed strongly for Davenport, hoping to make such a move with his family some day. Two families they knew, Laraldes and Lalondes, were considering Cincinnati strongly. Those families liked all their reports.

Drauzin and Josephine lived in a tension of unknowing. "We are a boat without oars or sail," said Drauzin, increasingly restless.

Josephine soothed him as best she could, "We can float for a while."

But the recent flood, increasingly ugly public street behavior, and mild tensions with Philippe's Jamaican wife Adèle all made them feel the clock was ticking. One night before going to bed, Maman Josephine Tassy Mathé whispered in her daughter's ear, "Read the chocolate."

The next day, daughter Josephine offered hot chocolate to everyone in the late morning. She put Drauzin's cup aside before Claire washed the others. It sat all day, all night, the remaining chocolate in the bottom of the cup crystallizing as it dried.

The next morning, she and Drauzin went out to the yard with his cup of yesterday. Looking down at the dregs the way people look up at stars, Josephine could see a long flow-path, with a branch off to the right, to an oval with lots of little uprisings—what looked, in fact, a lot like a crown. A river perhaps, with a right-hand branch. Drauzin could see it, too. Drauzin and Josephine both knew that the Ohio River branched east from the Mississippi. Brother Samuel had said that Cincinnati, on the Ohio, was called by many the Queen City. Something stirred in Josephine, a long-forgotten snippet of a strange childhood dream from when she was about nine or ten.

"In the dream a particularly handsome stranger boy had confided in me, 'Je veux devenir le prince de Cin-ci-nna-ti,' I want to become the prince of Cin-ci-nnati. And I responded, tout de suite, 'Moi la princesse de Cin-ci-nna-tesse!' And this went on and on, back and forth, almost like a madness. 'Je veux devenir le prince de Cin-ci-nna-ti,' 'Moi la princesse de Cin-ci-nna-tesse!' I had no idea what Cincinnati was, though somewhere I must have heard the word. For a couple of days I repeated this mad double ditty to myself hundreds of times, though it quickly evaporated from memory." Drauzin listened, and Josephine's childhood dream rang in him strangely. They slept on it.

The next afternoon, down on Bourbon St. at the Court of Two Sisters, Drauzin heard four slaves singing as they unloaded wagons of furniture:

> They say go north, find us new kin,
> They say go north, find us new kin,
> We try save our folks,
> We never come back again.

Over the next couple of mornings, Drauzin and Josephine realized that they felt mutually clear about what Drauzin's cup of yesterday had revealed about tomorrow. The Drauzin Valsin Bacas family was indeed heading north to Cincinnati, Ohio. Well, almost.

CHAPTER 19:

WHO GOES THERE? 1851

In 1851, the city of New Orleans shut down Congo Square, forbidding music and dancing by slaves on Sundays, thereby eliminating the only place and time in the whole South such regular, public celebrating had been permitted. Dr. "John B. Bacas" was living at 323 Claiborne St., which he had purchased from his brother, Drauzin V. Bacas. As Dr. John B., Jean-Baptiste was clearly charting a professional future in increasingly Anglo New Orleans. Josephine's brother, Samuel Charles Young IV, bought their property on North Roman St.

Drauzin and Josephine supervised the packing for hauling both their Bacas-built furniture and their future down to the wharf of New Orleans to be shipped by packet keelboat up to Cincinnati. Drauzin and Nonc Fulsain spent an afternoon installing a false bottom on Drauzin's sturdy leather-and-wood trunk. In it Drauzin hid three thousand dollars in gold, muffle-wrapped in burlap—silent, invisible, and inaccessible—under books and winter clothing. Into this heavy cabin trunk he also slipped a flute and two clarinets, wrapped in his clothes. His guitar had its own case.

Fulsain gave his beloved young namesake his favorite hand drill and his blessings. With a great hug, his drooping mustache on Drauzin's neck now flecked with grey, Fulsain sent his namesake off with words that Drauzin would never forget. "You are doing what you have to; run while you still have legs."

The necessary clarity for filling out the bill of lading papers forced focus and resolution on another riddle Drauzin and Josephine had been pondering. If they were going to take this step together as a family and venture into the unknown North, they had to commit to going whole hog. New required new. Only two generations earlier, on both sides, ancestors had taken huge leaps to New Orleans. Josephine's Granmère Marie-Françoise Lalande had united with dashing, short-lived French Lieutenant Joseph Tassy. Drauzin's Granpère Manuel Jean-Baptiste Bacas had arrived in the city to begin a new life. None of their "Bacases," they decided, were leaving town. That snakeskin Drauzin and Josephine would shed. What would take its place?

Part of Drauzin, music-man, did indeed wonder about losing "Bacas." Yes, as Apollo, he had vanquished Dionysus-inspired Pan in a musical duel, culminating in the exile of Dionysus/Bacchus, "Va-t-en, Bacchus, va-t-en Bacas!" As Apollo he had indeed pursued his Daphne, "Lady Joo-o-oe," under the canopy of their wedding ciel-de-lit. But something primal sounded in him whenever he was called Bacas. Almost like a cave, or a mouth, "Bah-cah," the *s* silent, like a still serpent in the cave, or a still tongue in the mouth, "Bah-cah," like a chick in an egg breaking out. Nevertheless, break out they would, leaving Bacas behind, a broken shell.

"Valsin," they had both recently learned, was in Catholic Louisiana the French version of St. Wulsin, a tenth-century Anglo-Saxon saint, Abbott of Winchester, Bishop of Sherbourne. Bishop Wulsin had, in fact, crowned English kings in Winchester. Some French boy babies, born on the Saint's feast day, January 8, were given his name, Valsin.

Drauzin said, "Chère, I've been wondering about 'Wul-sin.'"

"'Wul-sin,'" repeated Josephine thoughtfully. "'Wul-sin'—It sounds like—an Anglo cousin to—'Fulsain.'"

Drauzin smiled. "Yes, you're right, it does."

"Drauzin Valsín Bacas. Fulsain Bacas. Wulsin. Drau-zin Wúlsin. Drau-zín Wulsin. It must, I think, become Dráu-sin Wulsin, n'est-ce pas? Drau-sin Wulsin?

"A bit of a mumbling mouthful," continued Josephine, smiling also, "but it's our *own* new secret gumbo; I like it. And please, mon Cher, I pray you keep Drausin. St. Drauzin has always helped protect people confronting danger. Soldiers would sleep near his tomb before battle. We, your family, need you to remain our Drauzin."

Drauzin tried it again: "Drausin Wulsin." Then, accenting both first syllables more strongly, "Draú-sin Wúl-sin." He nodded, grinning. "Si, ma Chère, I will certainly remain Drauzin within, but outwardly non plus, no more Drauzin. I will go north into our future as Drau-sin, Drau-sin Wul-sin," and Drauzin repeated his new name again and again, stepping around the room to the new rhythms, long-short, long-short.

"If you think we can take this step, then we take this step together," said Josephine.

"Yes, I do think we can take this step together." Drauzin—or rather, Drausin—felt the conviction of this momentous action settle in his bones. "Good, ma Chère, *so* good. And I wonder if you think we can take one step more."

"One step more?" Josephine paused. "Dieu de Dieu. What more can there possibly be?"

"Yes, one step more. Look at me, Josephine." And she looked deep into her husband's brown, shining eyes with her green, green eyes as he continued, "Do you think we can——book it?"

"Book it? Oh no, that's de trop. We don't dare book it. However much we *do* dare, that we *don't* dare."

"Look at me, Josie. We just might."

"You might, but look at me—my nose, my hair!"

"I see you, my beauty, and you will be beauty anywhere. Remember, my hexadecaron, you are one-sixteenth black—one-sixteenth, my Mustée, my Mamalouque." He kissed her on her full, warm lips. "I see you, and I think we just might, we just might."

"But the children—Lucien, even Ti-Drauzin?"

"When we all do, each will."

"No, mon Cher, I fear such a step. Bookin' would be our end, not our new beginning. De trop. I fear, I fear."

"I understand, I understand. But Josie, we have a margin of time between our old and our new worlds: a week on the river. Let's watch for signs. Our river will tell us."

Drausin, having strategically jettisoned the z in his name, and Josephine became of one mind that they would head north into the largely Anglo-Saxon world of Cincinnati as the Wulsin family, secretly under guardianship of the two saints, St. Drausin and St. Wulsin. Not *Au revoir, Bacas, until we see you again,* but *farewell, Bacas, and may we Wulsins please fare better.*

Drausin Wulsin went down to the waterfront of New Orleans. At times he could hardly even see the mighty Mississippi flowing by, right to left, through the teeming, living thicket, like a bog of boats: pirogues, light, flat-bottomed bateaux tapering towards the ends; oyster-ligers, flat-bottomed skiffs with a long pole for dredging up ten to twenty oysters at a time; flatboats, called arks; Kentucky boats; New Orleans boats; and "broad horns," powered only by muscle and river current, twenty to sixty feet long and ten to twenty feet wide; keelboats; barges; the gaff-rigs and lanteen sails of various Baratarian luggers; single-masted, double-sailed sloops; two-masted schooners; the occasional three-masted barks with square sails on the foremast; and the kings of the river—paddle-wheel steamboats, both side-wheelers and stern-wheelers, maybe thirty or more.

Drausin saw ropes thick and thin, and different woods, and oars. Iron creaked, groaned, banged, splashed; sails flapped. Captains and mates barked orders. Longshoremen, stevedores, roustabouts, and wags grunted, swore, sang, and sometimes yelped or groaned as a fierce third mate bruised them into faster action with barrel staves or hickory sticks. Vendors chanted their wares. Gulls careened through the air, yipping, shrieking, and chattering, swooping and nipping for fish and scraps. Pelicans poised silent on less busy pier posts. The air along the riverbank was pungent with brackish sea-scent mixed with tar, mud-stench, fish-smell, and man-sweat.

Drausin watched, fascinated, as one crew from Marietta, Ohio, finished unloading a flatboat of its cattle; mules; Monongahela rye; Kentucky bourbon; millstones; plows; skins of otter, beaver, fox, and wildcat; butter; lard; linseed; tallow; candles; iron bars; unbleached linen, and what-have-you. Then these "Kaintucks," a name applied to all Northern boatmen, including Buckeyes from Ohio and Hoosiers from Indiana, proceeded to pull the boat itself apart, starting with the partial roof, then the above-deck walls, then the flooring, the siding, and finally the hull itself, stacking the planks on the wharf for sale.

Drausin began to focus on the keelboats, which would return upriver with a fresh load. One boss, one-eyed and one-eared, bashed the backs and even heads of his Negro roustabouts generously. They winced in pain and shame as they loaded cane, cotton, and other cargo. Most keelboaters had stride with pride, the cocks of the walk; they seemed to own the river. All keelboatmen pushed their pointed boats with pole and oar. They knew, and the flatboatmen knew, that, muscle-hard, they were superior to flatboatmen, mere floaters. Although only nine keelboaters might have brought the boat downriver, twenty-four would take it back up, rowing against the current, shoulder-poling the river bottom as they walked from bow to stern with a shoulder crutch and often an iron tip or knob for the long pole. Rarely, they would sail if winds allowed, otherwise pulling towropes, cordelles, from shore if necessary, even "bushwhacking," pulling along by grabbing overhead branches. The keelboats moved upstream about a mile an hour, managing in good weather about fifteen hours a day. The keelboatmen knew Ole Man River better than anyone except captains and pilots. Indeed, they knew every wave, eddy, shifting sandbank, and nearly every foot of shore. The keelboatmen learned the river and earned the right to own it.

One craft and crew caught Drausin's ear first, then eye. Men were loading cotton bales by boom, block and tackle, and a heisting horse from the dock into the paddle-wheel packet steamboat, Natchez III, which had striking red smokestacks. Once the bale was on the skid into the hold, the screwmen would grab it to screw each bale in a press as tight as possible, to pack in as many as possible, singing coonjines for their rhythmic shuffles. One coonjine went

> Markey faye
> Down the bay
> What you say?

All turning the screw together on "faye," "bay," and "say." Drausin gleaned good esprit in the whole crew.

Drausin hadn't thought of a packet. He'd figured the luggage would go on the slow, cheaper keelboat, while he'd heard that gens de couleurs were often charged extra for the privilege of staterooms on an elegant "touring" steamboat. If there were a large number of gens de couleurs, they might have to dine at an earlier sitting, or, if the dining room weren't full, they might be given a special table in the corner. It hadn't occurred to him that while they might pay a little more than on the keelboats for the convenience of bringing their luggage along, they might actually save more altogether booking as passengers on the working packet rather than on the floating hotels.

From the mate overseeing the operation, Drausin learned the Natchez III was bound for Cincinnati. "Yessir, we have some room available for shipment, ten feet by ten. Mos'ly furniture an' trunks? Cost prob'ly 'bout two hundred dollars. Staterooms? You'd have to speak with Cap'n Leathers, right down along starboard there at the stern."

The captain turned out to be the weathered man oiling the pitman joint on the paddle-wheel shank. "Captain Leathers?" said Drausin.

"Yessir." The man stepped back, swung around, and looked Drausin in the eye, attempting to wipe his hands on a cloth, but realizing that wouldn't be clean enough, he gave up, chuckled, and nodded slightly. "Captain Ishmael Leathers, at your service.—Yes, we do head to Cincinnati.—Yes, we do happen to have two staterooms and some storage space available. Five children, let's see, upstream—that would be two hundred dollars each for you, your wife, and the twelve-year-old, and one hundred each for the three boys, fifty for the baby, and two hundred for storage. That figures to one thousand, one hundred-fifty. All meals included.

"Freight needs to be loaded tomorrow. We'll be leaving in three days, June 15, likely to arrive in Cincinnati about June 23. Jebediah!" Captain Leathers called over a black boy about Aline's age. "Jebediah, show this gentleman the two starboard staterooms on the boiler deck."

"Yassuh."

"If they're satisfactory, sir, come back and we can reserve your tickets."

Drausin was indeed content with the sparse, tight, double-bunk staterooms, one for Aline, Ti-Drauzin, and Lucien, and one for Josephine, baby Laure, Eugene, and himself. Eugene would of course prefer to be with his brothers, but he still needed Maman.

Drausin Wulsin sighed deeply, looked up at Captain Leathers, down at the nib of his pen, and signed the lading papers, making a careful *s* in his name for the first time, not *z*. Drausin paid the patroon, who had by now properly cleaned his hands, a five-hundred-dollar deposit for his reservation. Captain Leathers and Mr. Wulsin shook hands with mutual smiles. Drausin noticed one set of preceding lading papers for cotton being shipped to S. C. Foster, Wadding, in Cincinnati. And Mr. Drausin Wulsin wondered what the odds were that he would ever meet Mr. S. C. Foster in the new world of Cincinnati.

Returning first along the riverfront to his cabriolet, and then through the streets of the Vieux Quartier for likely the penultimate time in his life, Drauzin found himself triply relieved. One, at the better total cost than he had feared. Two, at having all their property with them on the one boat. And three, to his surprise, he had discerned no patronizing or "different" treatment from Captain Ishmael Leathers. In fact, Captain Leathers had not even asked to see his papers ascertaining that he was indeed a free man of color.

Drausin and Josephine had invited Adelaïde Pouponne Beaulieu to 325 Bayou Rd. After Aline Adelaïde, Ti-Drauzin, Lucien, and Eugene ran to greet chère Granmère Pouponne, she and Josephine Mathé greeted each other warmly, respectfully, with embrace and kiss on each cheek, two aging matriarchs whose kingdoms were coming and going in spite of their wishes.

After they all enjoyed tea, croissants, beignets, and festive mille-feuilles, Drausin went for a walk with his Maman, arm-in-arm, in the shade of the giant, spreading oaks up Bayou Rd., almost all the way to Bayou St. Jean and back.

"Maman, come with us up north. You were given your freedom. You chose the bonds of love with Papa. Take the next step. Become fully free with us up north."

"Oh, mon cher fils, mon cher Drauzin, I live free in the bonds of my love. Remember, whoever abandons his own calabash will find that other calabashes leak dry wherever he needs to drink. Do you have to leave?"

"Oh, Maman, that's what you asked me and my brothers five years ago, after the fight with Papa. Did we have to leave then? Yes. Did any of us stay? No. For you to say that to me again today makes it sound like a curse. Are you declaring a curse upon us, Maman? A curse?"

"Oh, non, mon Dieu, non, mon Cher, jamais a curse. Of course I give you and your wonderful family all my blessings."

"Thank you, Maman, thank you—and Papa?"

"Oh—Papa—je ne sais pas. He can't see the sticks of anger in his own eye." She changed the subject. "Veuve Mathé tells me you and Josephine are thinking of leaving your color behind when you leave us behind."

"Yes, Maman—we might well try, passer blanc."

"You want to do what your father did, swallow your color?"

Drausin's steps slowed, and he inhaled sharply. "Yes, I know. It's bizarre. But we feel trapped. The only way out is to become like Papa. How's that for non-sense destiny?"

"Remember, you may manage to get the mbubboo, the jacket, by deception, and even the pants, but fail to get the hat."

"Ha! You should tell that to your husband. Do you remember why we brothers fought Papa in the woodshop? Well, Josephine and I are tired, with everything else, and for our children, of failing to get the hat. Although we love you all, no hat for us here in New Orleans. This town only lets us play the black keys on the piano.

"And remember, Maman ma Chère, as you so often told us, 'Whoever wants honey must brave the bees.' Yes, we just might learn to play the white keys—for the hat, for the honey. Is our blood not just as white as colored, or more? Where do you and I get our broad, high brow? Please, help us with your blessings, Maman. Remember, you once made your mighty choice, first to be free, and then to return to Papa. Well, we're making ours, a different choice, but maybe just as mighty—"

"Yes, of course, mon cher Drusino. I bless you, bless you, bless you, yes, my dearly beloved boy, my ear of all ears, listener always. And Josephine's man. Maybe you two do have the greatest courage of us all." Adelaïde bit her lip; she shone with pride at his subtle strength, gripping his arm, resting her head on his shoulder, giving and receiving soul-transfusion with her soon-gone son.

Just before reentering Veuve Mathé's compound, Drausin whispered into his mother's ear, "And forget not, ma chère Maman, it was you who often said over the years, 'It is better to walk the road than to curse it.' Well, tomorrow, we walk it." Adelaïde nodded, beaming through tears.

Not long after their return, once Adelaïde had recomposed herself, Josephine soon-no-longer-to-be Bacas gave the nod to Drausin, who gave the nod to Adelaïde. Josephine asked Aline to tend to the other children, with Granmère Josephine holding baby Laure. Josephine Bacas then told Claire to follow them. Drausin, with Adelaïde on his arm, then Josephine and Claire crossed the Esplanade to Tivoli Gardens. Under a mimosa tree, Drausin presented Claire with papers of her manumission, as he and Josephine had promised each other years ago. Claire, dumbfounded, looked from Drausin to Josephine, to Adelaïde, each of whom nodded, and back to Drausin. Grateful beyond words.

Drausin shook her hand, like a man's. Josephine gave the new free woman of color a kiss on each cheek, hugging her for the first time. Adelaïde embraced her muscularly, almost fiercely, kissed her on the forehead, and gave her blessings. Yet another bird would learn to fly, lightening Drausin, Josephine, and Adelaïde within. Little did Drausin and Josephine know the actual weight until it lifted. Gravity, always iron, could become air, as Adelaïde knew better than any of them.

Claire managed to look again at each of them more directly than ever before, which she discovered to be, mysteriously, like looking in the mirror and recognizing herself for the first time. *How does this work?* she wondered. *When I look at each of them, I feel I somehow see me more clearly. Strange.*

Back at 325 Bayou Rd., all bade a warm farewell to Claire. Drausin noticed Josephine washing her hands. She noticed him washing his. Equally surprised, the two realized, smiled, and embraced each other, sealing yet another page in closing this chapter of their lives. Both knew their hands were fine; their souls they were purging.

The two Josephines, mother and daughter, then took their walk, leisurely strolling down Bayou Rd., east along Claiborne, up Esplanade, back west along North Roman, and finally down Bayou, several times, circling their Bayou block, savoring the late afternoon light sifting through the ancient oaks, each knowing it likely was their last stroll together. "You will fare well, ma chère fille. Though ton cher Drauzin is not likely to build you a castle."

Josephine fille chuckled. "I know, Maman, but he'll keep our hearth warm."

As both Josephines glanced up Esplanade to where Charles Young II had kept the hearth of his noncastle warm for only a few of his and the elder Josephine's ten years together, Maman said, "Yes, he will; he will. But please remember, as your Granmère so often told me, 'Tomorrow does not have lunch or dinner, but one should put aside its ration.'"

"Si, Maman, she did well; you did well. We Lalande women—I will do well, je t'assure."

"Si, chou-chou, I know you will.... Your brother Samuel is

urging you to pass?"

"It's been our idea, or at least our question, but he supports it. Do you think we can or should try?"

"I understand you both leaning that way. Yes, ma belle, I do think you could try. Should? I do not know. Just remember, no matter how long a log floats on the river, it will never be a crocodile."

Josephine stopped, kissed her mother on the cheek, and with a smile wrapping her mother all around, said, "Si ma chère Maman, si, but an alligator just might become a crocodile. And besides," she continued, her green eyes deepening into her mother's grey eyes, "I may actually be as much crocodile as alligator, n'est-ce pas?" And these two strong women, one who had long found her way in the outer world, one just coming into her own inwardly, enjoyed a long, full-armed embrace, armoring each other for tomorrow's departure.

Returning home, Maman Josephine led her daughter into the garden, where children played while some adults sat. By the lemon tree, Josephine Mathé pulled out a silver cross on a silver chain. She reached down, opened the little cross, sifted some soil into it, closed it, kissed it three times and hung it around the neck of daughter Josephine. "Here, chou-chou, a gift from Granmère to me to you, with some of our soil of Rue Bayou. Not to pull you back here. I kiss you as you fly. But rather to give you strength of your roots where you grew, and now for where you go to."

As afternoon slowly succumbed to dusk, both Adelaïde Pouponne and Veuve Mathé drank in their son and their daughter, their Bacas grandchildren, unlikely ever to see them again. Eyes moist, the grandmothers' voices were tender, verging on breaking at times. Through repeated impromptu embraces of Aline, Ti-Drauzin, Lucien, Eugene, and especially little Laure, the two queens drank in their scents, warmth, giggles, and affection at their oasis, anticipating the imminent desert of separation.

Philippe Young watched his sister and Drausin, wondering but doubting if he and his wife Adèle might ever make such a move themselves. Up the country, yes; across the color line, impossible, with her Jamaican dark skin. Oldest brother, Samuel Charles Young IV, came by, offering tidbits about Cincinnati, of which Drausin and Josephine still knew little. He spoke much of Davenport, Iowa, urging them to reconsider.

At one point Samuel whispered in Drausin's ear, "Pour nous, blanc, ça va marcher." For us, white will work.

PART 2

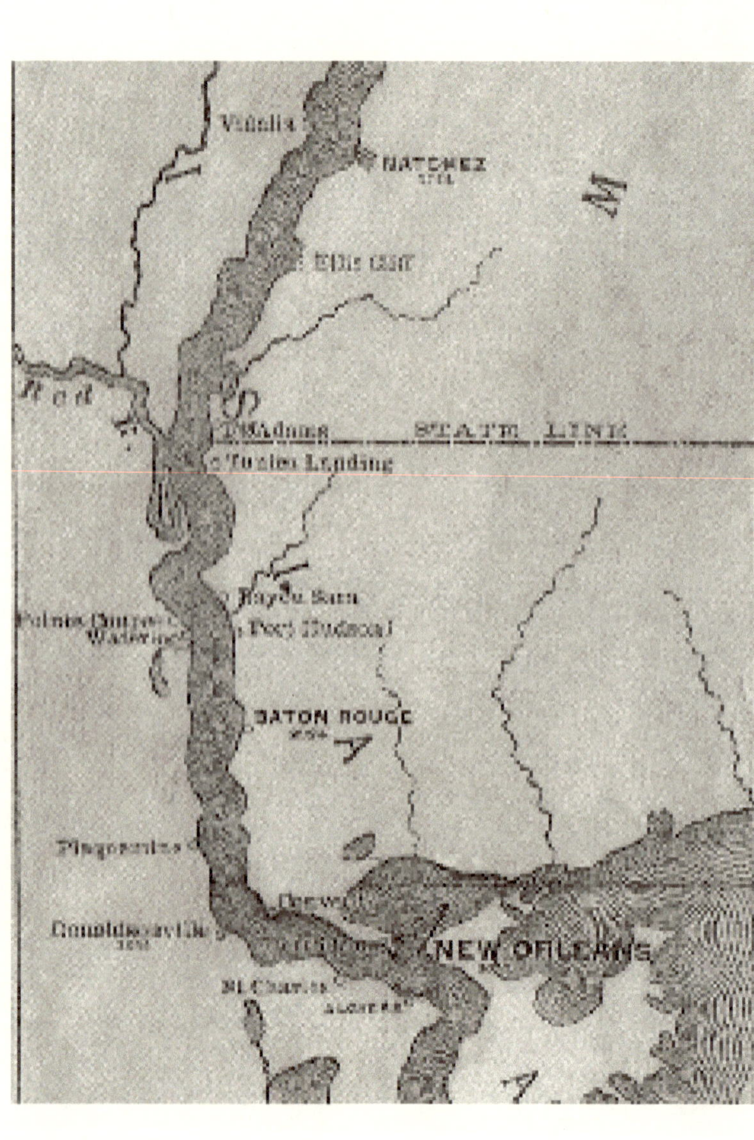

Vidalia
NATCHEZ
Red
Fort Adams
STATE LINE
Tunica Landing
Bayou Sara
Port Hudson
Pointe Coupee
Waterloo
BATON ROUGE
Plaquemine
Donaldsonville
Donaldsonville
NEW ORLEANS
St. Charles
Algiers
M

CHAPTER 20:
UP THE MISSISSIPPI, 1851

Little Lucien had spent the night doing dastardly dream-deeds with his gang of pirate cousins, a brood of Rue Bayou. Then, still half asleep, he was wrapped in a blanket, rolling with his family in the wagon down the streets of New Orleans, still bad-boying with his gang, saving lovely ladies here and there. Sewage scent suggested they must be downtown. Of the children, only sister Aline recognized in passing the stately double-glass door beneath its arched entry-roof, below the filigreed ironwork balcony of Granpère and Granmère Pouponne's sitting room at 116 Rue St. Louis, their own home of long ago. About to exclaim, Aline heeded Maman Josephine's finger to lips.

Josephine had chosen to wear a durable, modest travel dress of dark grey, with a checked pattern, closed at the throat, complemented with a lavender choker. Below the narrowing waist, it billowed slightly over several light petticoats. A short shoulder cape helped for cool mornings and evenings. Her dark brown hair was done simply, parted in the middle, brushed down over her ears and tucked under, a horizontal bun circling the back of her head. For the sun she wore a straw bonnet tied with a lavender ribbon. Never again would she be required by law to wear a tignon. Josephine wondered if she would ever again savor the scent of orange blossoms.

Drausin wore a long, narrow-sleeved, dark brown jacket

over a beige, double-breasted vest, a simple black foulard tied horizontally under his raised white shirt collar. A handsome couple they made. Drausin wondered if ever again he would hear the fascinating music of mockingbirds' variations and improvisations. And he was wondering if, this morning, the birds indeed were mocking these "Wulsins." Aline wore a simple, reddish-brown cotton dress, half-sleeved, hanging naturally with two darker stripes around the bottom. The boys wore loose pantalons down below the knee, and little jackets for morning and evening. A well-wrapped family of seven, heading into the unknown.

Lucien's eyes dawned in mephitic sunlight, leaving him confused to behold a thicket of strange city, which he only gradually realized was the apparently waterless harbor of boats. How could so many boats be so close in one place? He followed brother Ti-Drauzin's eyes, which were following Papa's arm, pointing toward two tall, bright red smokestacks. "Na-tch-ez III," Aline called, making out the red letters on the white main deck walls, far in front of the bright red stern paddle wheel. Bustle, holler, bang, creak, thick fish-mud stench—Lucien clung close to his mother, already held onto by Eugene and, of course, baby Laure.

Papa handed final payment to the ticket man and received their tickets; then the family walked the plank, off the ground, over the water, onto their mighty white steamboat. Lucien saw no pirates, no sharks, just two shining black roustabouts behind, lugging their travel trunks into their two cabins. Simple, with two bunks each, a window each, just enough room for a table, mirror, chair, and of course a travel trunk; the two rooms shared an adjoining door. The children then ran right back out to the railing on the boiler deck, watching the wharf, all a bustle with wagons, carriages, and drays filled with sugar and indigo, fancy folk and poor, vendors and hawkers. Aline, Ti-Drauzin, and Lucien were identifying, in addition to familiar Spanish and French folk, turbaned Turks, white-robed Arabs, Chinamen with black queues hanging from shaved scalps, black Africans, red Indians, swarthy mestizos, yellow mulattos, olive Malays, light Creoles and quadroons, Germans, Yankees, and Englishmen.

"Granmère! and Granmère Pouponne!" There were Josephine Mathè and Adelaïde arm-in-arm, waving red silk kerchiefs at them. Josephine and the children called out, "Au revoir, au revoir!" Josephine was thinking, *How unlikely it is I will ever see Maman again. I might never again experience myself as daughter. I feel a little light-headed, like rising to the top of a cliff with no tree to lean on. Except cher Drauzin, I mean dear Drausin, of course.* She squeezed his arm, hooked at her elbow.

While waving back, Aline pointed out to her parents, over behind a lamppost, like a shadow, what she thought was Granpère, Papa's Papa. Did he wave a finger when she waved at him? Aline noticed Papa's eyes moisten, his jaw tighten, as his hand was hurting hers, till he realized, relaxed it, and stroked her hair ever so gently. Granpère Barthelemy had disappeared.

Lucien pulled on Josephine's hand, two fingers in his mouth. "My tooth gets wigglier and wigglier, my first!"

It had looked to Drausin from afar as though the left side of his father's face had fallen, lost its levity, settling into a signature of sadness, or sneer. Drausin realized that little Lucien neither recognized nor even remembered his own grandfather Barthelemy, and never would. Oblivious to his father's pain, Lucien was feeling like the hero beginning a great adventure, the crowds cheering, calling, crying, clearly waving at him. Aline reached out toward her two grandmothers, pretending to hug them both, feeling them wrap her like shawls. Granpère's finger waving, before he disappeared, Aline would never forget.

The whistles blew and the last brass bell rang as the "can't-get-away-folk" scrambled ashore. Roustabouts drew the staging plank in; longshoremen at the bow and stern tossed "monkey's fist" hemp balls to boat-hands, who reeled in the thin line till they hefted the attached four-inch-thick heavy hawsers aboard, coiling them in growing mountains on the deck by the upright cross-bitts. The engineer's bell tinkled. Captain calling to mate, mate calling to deckhands. Huge fire logs were heaved, rattling into the steam-boat furnace, its fires glittering red on the grey-brown water. Steam whistles screeched, rising and falling in pitches. The "'scape" pipe barked hoarsely.

The mighty leg shafts started to pedal the paddle wheels groaning into motion, plunging, crashing, splashing, dipping, plowing, then breaking out and waterfalling as they rose out of the water at the back, one continuous *wish-wash, wish-wash, wish-wash,* the brown water foaming like a feeding frenzy, as the mighty steamboat cleared, the current helping pull its nose out as the triple rudders straightened the Natchez III upriver. Underway, finding her mighty glide, she pushed so the water seemed to pull her into it, the water in her wake behind strangely calm, as though the storm of the churn had purged it.

A scary-looking Tocko hawking oysters from the Delta last minute just managed to keep his pirogue from swamping in the turbulent side-wash. Lucien smelled the city's smudges, burning hair, horn, hooves, and lemon to keep mosquitoes away as boats loaded in the sooty, glaring sun.

Papa pointed back to shore below Place d'Armes, identifying for Aline and Ti-Drauzin the spot where their cousin Louis Adhemar had drowned. Lucien, overhearing, could hardly remember him, but never forgot that seemingly peaceful spot at the edge of the lives they were leaving, a water-grave. Closing his good eye, Lucien saw a swirl; he thought, *Papa always feels that swirl, where the Mississippi swallowed cousin Adhemar.* Opening his eye, Lucien saw water curl, drifting out of sight.

Papa Drausin wondered what else of their past was drowning behind their stern. Josephine wiped her eyes with a handkerchief from her sleeve. *I can hardly believe I am, we are leaving*

Bayou Rd., my mother, my brothers. For Drausin's and my family I will have to become the Bayou Rd. of the North, become those mighty-armed oaks, my mother and my brothers.

Ahead, ripples and waves burned gold on their edges in the low-rising sun shafts. Leaning on the guardrail, dreaming into the river, Lucien let his good eye almost close until all he saw was dancing dazzle, dazzle dancing. He remembered lazing along Bayou St. Jean with his father in the pirogue, the water light-lit. *This boat's surely going into glory,* felt little Lucien. *Bigger waters, bigger lights, bigger Lucien.*

As Natchez III headed steadily up the current of the big river, New Orleans disappeared behind; both banks widened into vast plantations, mostly dark-striped sugar cane, head-high. Lucien heard a roustabout tell a passenger that "Down here dis ol' man river was jus' 'bout a whole mile wide." This river world was wider than Lucien had ever seen. How wide could a world get?

Papa and Maman called the children into their cabin before descending to the dining room. Lucien was puppy-sniffing blends of old and new smells, especially wet wood, lemon oil, and cigar smoke. With baby Laure on her lap on the lower bunk, Maman said, "Children, line up by age. Good. What a handsome crew. Now, repeat after your father when it's your turn. 'I am Aline Wul-sin.'"

"I am Aline Wul-sin."

"Good—I am Drausin Wulsin."

"I am Drauzin, Drau-sin, Drau-sin Wul-sin."

"Good—I am Lu-shin Wul-sin."

"I am Lucien, non, Lu-shin, Lu-shin Wul-sin."

"Good—I am U-gene Wul-sin."

"I am Oy-jenne, non, Oy-gene, U-gene, Eu-gene Wul-sin."

"Very good, very good, all of you. As you know, we are all

going together into a new world of Cincinnati. Everyone say 'Cin-cin-na-ti.'"

"Cin-cin-na-ti."

"Well done." Josephine chuckled and couldn't help commanding, "And now say 'the Prince of Cincinnati.'"

"The Prince of Cincinnati."

"And now," laughing like a little girl, "'The Princesse of Cincinnatesse.'"

"The Princesse of Cincinnatesse," said the children, giggling, starting off on a rant with it till Papa pulled them back to their mission.

"In our new world, we all get to have new names. In our new world, we will be the family Wul-sin. Wul-sin. I will be Drausin Wulsin. Maman, you will be—"

"Missus José—, non, dJosa-phine Wul-sin. dJosa-phine Wul-sin. Oh, it's hard."

"Wul-sin, what a strange, ugly name. I don't like it. I love Bacas," said Aline.

"Yes, Chère, so do I," said Maman, "but we will be leaving many familiar things behind and finding many new things in our new world; gradually they will become familiar and loved, too. Now, march around the room, all of you together, practicing your new names." Which they each did, like good little soldiers, for a good little while, unraveling eventually, inevitably, into "Prince of Cincinnati," and "Princesse of Cincinnatesse."

"Baton Rouge, Baton Rouge, where're the red sticks?" Lucien and Eugene started chanting. "Where're the red sticks?"

"Dey were dere, dey were here. Ya' jus' don' see 'em no more." The boys were stunned silent. There was the black boy they'd seen running in and out of the kitchen.

"Who're you?" asked Aline.

"Jebediah."

"How old are you?"

"Twelve. You?"

"Twelve. What do you do here?"

"Ah'm de cook's flunky. My daddy's de deckhand boss. Ah'm on break now. Ah figured what you wuz askin'. Way back when, buffalo hunters'd stand up three red sticks to show de boats dere was buffalo hides fo' trade. 'N' way back before dat, de Houma Injuns an' de Bayougoula Injuns had jus' de one red stick, showin' de borderline 'tween dere huntin' groun's. Baton Rouge de Frenchies came to call de place, an' de name stuck, but de sticks're gone. Frenchies like you. But you prolly don't even know what I'm sayin'."

"I do," said Aline, with an indignant humph. "I speak English."

"Me too, a leetle," said Drausin. And they each, in turn, introduced themselves proudly, struggling to get their new names right. Jebediah was amused. When the last, Eugene, introduced himself as le Prince de Cincinnati, the siblings howled, and, of course, Aline asserted she was actually the Princesse de Cincinnatesse, which equally delighted Jebediah.

"An' ya' prolly also don' know, dis mile-wide ribber we been chuggin' up all day, some places along here it's ober two hunnerd feet deep. We been in one ob de biggest chunks ob ribber in de whole worl'. Well, now pretty soon dis here ribber's gonna narrow, like a bottleneck, 'mos' all de way to Cairo an' de O-hi-o. Well, I gots to go. See y'all later."

"Bye, Jebediah," the four children chorused, liking the sound of his name. Eugene and Lucien repeated "Jebediah, Jebediah," many times during the day, even more than, "'mos' all de way to Cairo, an de O-hi-o."

On the boiler deck, the second floor of the packet steamboat, there were men's quarters toward the bow, ladies' quarters toward the stern, and family staterooms amidships. The top two feet of the walls were glass, washing the rooms with sky-light beneath the enclosing roof. Below, on the main deck, the lounge toward the stern served as a dining room. The children learned from their father that most of the cargo had been stored in the hold, below the main deck. Jebediah showed them that passengers' cargo had also been stored aft on the main deck, between the engine room and the dining room, as well as forward between the dining room and the boiler room. Although a working cargo ship, the Natchez's dining room offered some elegance, its patterned tin-tiled ceiling reflecting warmly the candlelit chandeliers, echoed further in wall mirrors behind the mahogany bar, and glass windows all along.

The crew ate in the first shift; Captain Leathers and his mate, Jack Green, ate at the same time as the passengers. Jebediah, as cook's flunky, was busy before, during, and directly after both shifts. Roustabouts shined themselves up to serve passengers fare hearty, not fancy, including platters of breaded cod, boiled and fried chicken, cold ham, hot bread, and yams, with preserved cucumbers, pickled peaches, and big ironstone bowls of steaming vegetables. To drink were coffee, tea, and wine. Desserts sometimes included a beautiful jelly clear as amber, as well as the usual cranberry, apple, and mince pies.

Settling down at their table, the Wulsin family became very aware that always, everywhere on the packet, inside and out, they were wrapped in thick shawls of sounds. There was always the hum of boilers to talk over, splashes of paddle wheels breaking water and dripping up out of it: *swoosh, wish, plash*, and the chug-splashing *chshchshchshgchshchshgchshchshshsh*. Steam released from the boilers, periodically whistling out of the 'scape pipes. Almost regularly would thud the big bass beat, not of a banging deadhead, but of the mud drums blowing out, emptying river silt sifted from the boilers back into the river.

Drausin and Josephine figured their fellow passengers included corn and cotton planters returning home upriver, one in buff trousers, pale yellow nankeen jacket, and Manilla or Panama hat. A couple of them might soon disembark at Baton Rouge. There looked to be a banker with wife and daughter, probably heading on their annual pilgrimage north to escape summertime yellow fever plagues. They thought they recognized two Creole merchants of the French quarter, in coats of claret or blue, with ruffles galore, plaited pantalons, shining jewelry, and light-colored boots. A couple of American merchants wore black cloth dress-coats, black satin shining vests, trousers, calf-skin boots, and definitely no gloves. And they figured that two hard, muscled, bronzed men in new broadcloth and snow-white linen must be riverboat men who probably had, in jean trousers and red flannel shirts, pushed a flatboat some two thousand miles downriver, then had chosen not to walk two months home back to the Licking, the Miami, or the Cumberland Rivers. Those two rivermen were proudly shining, hoping to keep their earnings by arrival. Out of the side of his eye, Drausin noticed the eyes of one of them darting scornfully between large-loaded fork bites, stopping for a moment like a scratch on the Wulsin family. Drausin, not to catch his eye, dropped his, but catching himself in that old reflex, raised his glance back in place, by which time the Kaintuck's eye had moved on around the dining room.

After supper, Captain Leathers rang the bell three times for landing in Baton Rouge. Lucien watched the mighty boat edge its way, swinging right alongside the wharf, gentle as a bar of soap in a bathtub, as deckhands tossed the monkey's fist knot and thin line ashore, leaping the last yard or two of gap, hauling the thick hawsers around the shore posts while two roustabouts aboard pushed the capstan bar around, tightening the hawser in the bow to make the craft fast, then tossing the lighter spring lines from the two-horned cavels aboard to make fast to cavels ashore, bow to stern, stern to bow, a criss-cross-ing X to hold the steamboat snug. Although the corn and cotton planters and a few others disembarked, most passengers stayed on board during the short stop. The Natchez III would travel through the night, notching miles to slice time.

Up toward the bow, the Wulsins found an outdoor perch on the hurricane deck, the open part of the third level of Natchez III. Around a couple of deck chairs for the parents, the children draped themselves on coils of hemp line. The sun fell red-gold into the west. Shadows merged into settling dusk. Josephine pulled on her shawl; Drausin enjoyed one of his Havana cigars, the smoke lazing astern like a mini-"chimley," together with the boat-breeze clearing mosquitoes. Josephine let Laure roll around her feet. Among the hoary tillandsia drooping from the encroaching cypress trees, they heard the "Coo-whoo-a" of a swamp owl. Tree crickets and cicadas were creaking and chirping. A bull-frog tong-tonged, tong-tonged.

"Jebediah was right," said Aline. "The river sure starts to tighten."

And who should appear but —"Jebediah!" hollered the children with delight, surprising into a start both little Laure and her parents, as their new friend seemed to materialize from the condensing night. He introduced himself politely to Mr. Wulsin, to whom he'd shown the staterooms days earlier, and to Mrs. Wulsin, whom he'd been noticing but not met, and then he settled right down between Aline and Lucien on some hemp coils.

"You were right," said Aline, "what's happening to the river."

"Ohh, dis Mississippi, you know why de Ojibway up nort' call it dat?"

"No."

"De Great Ribber, dey calls it. And down sout', some calls it de Mudder ob all Ribbers, 'n' some de Fadder ob all Ribbers. Well, you see, 'dis ole man ribber, as we headin' nort', he jus' keep gettin' younger an' younger, wilder 'n' wilder, trickier 'n' trickier, 'n' narrower."

Lucien asked his father where the huge river came from. Drausin asked Jebediah what he thought.

"Ohh, dis mighty Mississip' be born 'mos all de way up nort', pre'near at de top of our country. An de little bitty crick he jus' keep on drinkin' tousands o' odder cricks 'n' streams, an' hundreds o' liddle 'n middle ribbers, 'n' a few mighty ones, becomin' den de mightiest ob 'em all."

Drausin showed them the Big Dipper, rising slowly up river. "Yep," said Jebediah, "now draw yoursels a line from de bottom o' dat dipper right up tru' de top star, de rim ob de dipper, see, an' follow dat line; what does you come to?"

"The tip," said young Drausin, "of another handle with a littler dipper?"

"Yessiree, 'n' dat star at de tip o' de handle, dat de Nort' Star."

"Right you are, Jebediah," said Papa Drausin. "And, children, thousands and thousands of people have followed that star north, to a land that's new and free."

"Jus' like the river getting younger?" asked Lucien.

"Yes, just like Jebediah's Ole Man Mississippi getting younger. And we, the Wulsin family ..."

Lucien and Eugene eagerly chimed in, echoing, "... we, the Wulsin family, are following that star, too." A batrachian trumpeted, almost barking from somewhere in the night-black shore muck, before slithering back into the river. Above, a bull-bat trebled.

Ever so quietly, almost blending with the swishings of the water and the choruses of tree-toads, Drausin started to sing, to the melody of Stephen Foster's still very new song "Oh Susanna,"

Oh!—Star of Freedom,
'Tis the star for me;
'Twill lead me off to Canada,
There I will be free.

The children joined in, Jebediah with special reverence, as though he were hearing it sung in the night all across the land.

"Are we going to Canada?" asked Lucien.

Papa chuckled, "No, Luche, I don't think so, at least not for a very long time. We're only going to O-hi-o."

"Look," cooed Lucien, a bit in awe, gazing east, "the new moon, with the old moon in her arms!"

"Yes, cher Lucien, dear Lu-shin," said Josephine ever so gently, putting her hand on his head, "the new moon, with the old moon in her arms." By now, Laure had been long asleep in Josephine's arms. Josephine smiled at herself, the old moon with the new moon in her arms.

"Well, I gots to go," said Jebediah.

"Where do you sleep?" asked young Drausin.

"See de Texas, up above dis here Hurricane deck? Das where we all sleeps. De Cap'n in de foreroom. De mate, eng'neer an' cook in de midrooms. An' mah daddy an' me an' de rest ob us in de coon pen back aft. Now up on top ob de Texas, dat's de pilot house. My daddy gots to take ober de night-watch."

"Why is it called Texas?" Lucien was curious.

"That's jus' what it's called, I guess," said Jebediah. "See y'all tomorra."

"Bye, Jebediah, Jebediah," said the children, sounding his name with joy.

And the Wulsin family headed in for their first night as the Wulsin family, in their staterooms on the boiler deck of the paddle-wheel packet steamboat Natchez III on the Mississippi Ribber. Lucien dreamed of the new moon, with the old moon in its arms, which somehow, with the North Star, gave birth up on the top of the country to a little creek, which, with the help of Ojibway Indians, drank and drank and drank to become the biggest river in the world.

CHAPTER 21:
NATCHEZ, 1851

Drausin noticed less golden sugarcane, silvery rice, snowy cotton plants, and sable palms during the hours approaching Natchez. More begonias and coloquintidas stretched from maple to tall tulip trees; creepers crossed a feeding stream with a bridge of flowers. Sweet-scented white magnolia blossoms commanded the forest. He recognized pecan trees and pawpaw, wild plum and buckeye, black willow and black ash, sweet bay, catalpa, persimmon, wild cherry, beech, chestnut, and chincopin. Sumac and trumpet vine often veiled the river road. At times the children noticed black squirrels dashing in the elms, heard mockingbirds, and saw green parrots with yellow heads, purple woodpeckers, and fire-red cardinals in the tops of cypress trees. Hummingbirds sparkled in the jasmine, safe from bird-catching serpents hissing while swinging like vines. Most of the family managed to espy occasional fallow deer, spotted, with palm antlers.

Lucien eyed a water snake, which Drausin showed them to be a "snake bird," or "water-turkey," swimming with only its head and neck above water. And a large shadow and swell turned out to be, according to the deckhand, a huge buffalo fish, a sucker four feet long weighing about sixty-five pounds.

After a while, Papa Drausin asked the children why the legs of all the horses they could see along the shore were red up to their knees. Black, brown, red, white, grey horses—all red to the knees. No idea. "The juice of wild strawberries." The children ohhed, awed, partially seeing some red fetlocks, mostly imagining strawberries two feet deep.

"Yes, y'all," said Jebediah, who showed up after the Natchez III docked in Natchez, as the children eagerly shared their finds. "Daz some bee-utiful shores we jus' been seein'. Now you looks 'roun' here, close, in de t'ick of all dis beauty. All 'bout here, outlaws on de ribber an' de Natchez Trace, what day call de Debil's Backbone, day sets up ambushes fo' to murderin' flatboatmen. Dese waters is t'ick, dang'rus wid shoals, sucks, snags, an' sawyers. Sawyers? D'as sunken trees. Natchez-Under-de-Hill, ober here, be de wildes' hellhole on de ribber.

"See dem Natchez Bluffs? Dey's full of red, white,'n' yaller octaroon whores, 'n' gamblers, drifters,'n' bruisers. See all de hogs, smell all de stenches. Look 'roun' at all de wharf rats, livin' unner dese docks an' wharfs. Dey's collectin' and sellin' drif'wood, sometime two dollar a load o' firewood. You see 'em fishin', collectin' bananas and food trown from de boats. See dat drif' over here, why he'd beg you for your toes off your feet, an' your eyes off your nose. Down here all roun', we gots tramps, beggars, tieves, an artis' here, a fortuneteller dere, all libbin' in dese hobbels, shacks, tents'n' houseboats."

The children's eyes were wide with the feast of sinners and busy-ness. Lucien and Eugene of course hardly understood half of what Jebediah was saying, but they got the feel. Their toes were dangling over the waters of Hell in Natchez.

"Hey, Natchez, our boat, Natchez III!" said Lucien. "Did Cap'n Leathers steal Natchez III from this hellhole?"

"Lucien, no such talk from you," snapped Aline.

Jebediah chuckled, "No, li'l Lucien, he din't steal her from here, but, you almos' right; her granmommy, Natchez I, was built here.

"'N' up here jus' a ways Mike Fink got shot, Mike Fink, King ob de keelboatmen, cock-a- doodle-doo ob de river men.

Why, wid a musket ball he could cut off a turkey's head in full flight at a hunnerd yards. At forty paces he could drive a nail home, jus' to its head. Down below de Natchez bluffs, in a quarrel wif his good friend Carpenter, Fink was allowed to place a tin cup ob whiskey on Carpenter's head an' shoot a hole trough it. De bullet looked to have gone below de cup, into Carpenter's skull. Fink said, 'Carpenter, you done spilt de whiskey.' A friend ob Carpenter's, he shot Fink for killin' Carpenter.

"But den people saw dat Fink had shot between de cup an de skull, to knock him out for a moment wid a crease on his scalp. An dat was de end ob Mike Fink, de big ole buddy ob Daby Crockett.

"Now, ye see dose bucket women an' pan ladies? Dey's a sellin' bull neck, hebby debil, an' stage planks."

"What's hebby debil?" asked Ti-Drausin.

"An' stage planks?" asked Aline.

"Why, hebby debil's bread puddin', hmm; I likes dat. 'N' stage planks, dey's flat ginger cakes. Dey're good too. You aks fo' a 'nigger's lunch,' you gets stage plank an' a dipperful o' ribber water."

Lucien nuzzled Drausin and whispered in his ear. "Luche wants to know if it's the Big Dipper or the Little Dipper."

Jebediah, overhearing, chuckled, "Ohh, preddy liddle."

Josephine had been vaguely recollecting something in her father's past about Natchez. Yes, there'd been talk. She remembered well, of course, that her father, Samuel Young II, had first been married to someone named Anna Francesca Farrar, with whom he had several children, her older half-brothers, who never paid her much mind. Their mother, Anna, had died in 1804. *Yes—then that was it; in 1808 he had married Lydia Armstrong in Natchez, Mississippi. But when he returned to New Orleans a month*

later, she remained in Natchez. Why? What in the world was that story?

And now, Josephine realized, *My father must have helped my mother, then seventeen-year-old Josephine Tassy, to buy her first slave, Catherine, also that same year, in 1808. His second marriage, the almost immediate end of that marriage, and the beginning of his connection, at least professional, to Maman, all in the same year! How strange. Still so much a stranger, my own father.*

And I, I met my Drauzin when I was only fifteen, first from a distance at the slave market, and then on Bayou St. Jean, finally marrying him at eighteen. My Drauzin, grâce à Dieu. My mild-mannered music man sure shows every sign of being more a continuous presence in our children's lives than Samuel Young II ever was in mine. My gentle man for sure. Too gentle?

Looking among the peoples along the shore, Josephine wondered what might have become of Lydia Armstrong Young, her father's wife for a month. *My own mother, Josephine, eventually became his nonwife for ten years and three children. My far-away father, far even in the same house. By the end, he was like a mist, a fog, dank, even toxic, blowing off. Might I have another sibling in Natchez?*

She combed the raunchy, classy, ranging crowds again more carefully, for any chin, nose, brow, hair, or even countenance akin to her own, or to brothers Samuel or Philippe—any sign of herself out there in Natchez.

Gradually the Wulsins became aware of a growing background sound. None could figure it. Engine room? Boiler room? It sounded like low bellows groaning, like chains clinking. Crew scraping decks clean? Hopped-up longshoremen grunting, at organ heads with each other? Anchors aweigh? Not on a riverboat. The whole Natchez III was actually growing silent. The whole riverfront grew silent as the background sounds approached the foreground. Little Lucien saw an army of zombies approaching in a cloud of dust.

Almost like a humming, a droning, like locusts whirring, but low, were sounds that Aline and her parents gradually recognized as a kind of mumble-chant: "Go down, Moses, all de way to E-gypt la-and, go tell-ll, ole Pha-raoh, let my people go."

On a night-black horse, in loose coat, slouching black hat, and coarse boots, rawhide bullwhip in hand, appeared the general of the army. Papa Drausin thought he scowled like Beelzebub. "Soul-driver," whispered Jebediah. Soon Lucien could see more clearly the "soldiers," thick black "John Brown" hair burnt rust-red by the sun, dusty skin, reddish-white eyes bulging, cheeks slack, some necks shackled and yoked to another, all arms manacled and chained, ankles shackled in dusty black iron, ringed red with blood above cracked bare feet. Drausin saw permanent bone spurs already on many of those ankles. The men wore ragged burlap pants, and some still wore rough shirts died reddish-brown from catalpa, with similar shirts and linsey skirts for the women.

"They look like walking dead," whispered Ti-Drausin.

"Yeah, dose be walkin' dead alright, some walkin' in dis copple all de way from Carolinas, mebbe a tousan' mile, mos' days walkin' twenty mile in dem chains, down de Natchez Trace, right along de Debil's Backbone to here."

"Why?" asked Ti-Drausin, though he half-knew.

"Some x-caped 'n' been caught, afer las' year's Fug'tive Slave Ack. Dey'll be returned 'n' prolly chopped somepin' fierce. One slave-mudder got hung from a oak tree in a potato sack an' beaten tree times daily by de master wid a stick. Some lose an ear, or half a foot, so's dey won't never run again. All dese odders, dey jus' been sole down de ribber, all de way to New Awleens, where dey'll get bacon-fattened in de pens, till dey gets sold to work derselves to def on de sugarcane; mos' won' las' sebben years."

Papa Drausin glanced over to Josephine, suddenly reminded that their keynote, the prelude to their first meeting on the bayou, had been slaves being sold at the St. Louis

Hotel market. Josephine, rocking baby Laure, wanted to cover all eight ears and eyes of her other four children. Of course she couldn't, and on the other hand, she thought, *Maybe this searing picture is actually a fitting endnote to the chapters of our past.* She nodded to Drausin, who seemed to be of similar mind. It had better be an endnote. Drausin and Josephine, watching from hell's balcony, were each thinking, they found out later that night, *There, but for the grace of God, go I, go we.*

Aline was in fact imagining their whole family as slaves. She valued her middle name, Adelaïde. Young Drausin remembered how Papa and he had been pushed by uppity whites into the mud of Rue St. Ann. Lucien and Eugene were not thinking; they just became—those zombies.

Then Lucien noticed one brown boy, about his own age, a rope around his chest, tied to a woman's waist. The boy, holding her hand, was looking right into Lucien's eyes, up on the hurricane deck. Lucien knew that boy was no zombie. In a weird, timeless way that he would never forget, he felt that he himself, down on the wharf, roped to that woman, was looking up into his own eyes on the hurricane deck. Everyone else melted away. Lucien did not know that his own grandmother, Granmère Pouponne, could have been one of those zombies long ago.

"What'll happen to them?" asked Aline.

"A few dat are fit might get sol' right down here on de Natchez wharf. Mos'll wait till a flatboat loads 'em like cattle down to New Awleens."

They heard a shriek, and saw that the soul-driver had dismounted and gone to a haggard woman ten rows back. In spite of her howling clutches, he ripped from her chest a bundle that smelled so bad the stench even reached the hurricane deck in the downstream breeze. Clearly the baby had been dead for days. Beelzebub grabbed it by the foot and hurled it into the garbage-eddying river, soon washed out of sight. With the butt of his bullwhip, he bashed the shrieking mother three times hard on her back, where the bruises wouldn't show, as she fell to the ground. When he yanked her back to her feet, she slumped onto the woman chained next to her. Josephine managed to cover the eyes of both Lucien and Eugene, but not in time. Aline blanched. This was more than they'd bargained for. Josephine realized, strangely, that she wanted to bring Laure back inside her, all five of them actually, until they got to Cincinnati.

Lucien saw soap-colored, well-calloused palms of black hands on Jebediah's shoulders suddenly. "Pa!" called out Jebediah, leaning his cheek onto one of the hands; they held Jebediah warm and strong, as though father wanted to shield son from shore. "Pa. Dese are my friends, de Wulsins."

"Pleased to meet you, Mr. Wulsin, Mrs. Wulsin," the man responded, slightly bowing. "Esau Makely. Children," as Jedediah introduced them each. "I hope my Jebediah has not been bothering you," said the deckhand who had identified the buffalo fish earlier.

"Oh no," said Aline and Ti-Drausin.

"He's our friend," said Eugene.

"Esau, you seem to pretty much run the crew," said Drausin.

"Oh nassuh, that's First Mate Green's 'n' Cap'n Leathers' doin'."

"Ohh, I see though; they work well because of you."

"Thank you, Sir, thank you."

"Esau, I've been amazed at all the different trees along the shore," said Drausin.

"Yessir, this one rich stretch. Cap'n Leathers, he like to say, 'bout dis trip all de way from N'Awleens to Cincinnati, 'We's a goin' from orange to apple, from clime to clime, from palm to pine.'"

Aline and Ti-Drausin repeated it several times. "We's a goin' from orange to apple, from clime to clime, from palm to pine." Lucien and Eugene joined in. The children had found yet another chant.

"Pa, since we's in Natchez, tell 'em 'bout Annie Christmas."

The couple of zombies had started to shuffle further down the pier, ready to be shoved onto a flatboat. Drausin's eye caught one man in the ranks.

"Esau, see that man, standing near us in the fifth row? Look at his eyes, and his stance. Tell me what you see."

Esau looked closely. "I'd say—he ben free."

"That's what I think."

"He watch everyone, evert'ing. He awake all over." The man, for a moment, caught their eyes watching him, almost seemed to question them, then slightly nodded and moved on with his riddle among the chained shufflers.

Esau hugged Jebediah all the more strongly, then started to relax, enjoying the feel of this family. He wanted to shift everyone's attention away from the copple. "Annie Christmas—Annie Christmas—" He was pulling himself inwardly back to Jebediah's request. He looked again at each child, then at Josephine and Drausin, nodded, and proceeded.

"Well, I betchya you ain't never seen nobody like Annie Christmas. She stood six foot, eight inches tall, weighed two hunnerd fifty pound and wore a neat mustache, wid a voice as loud an' deep as a foghorn. When Annie snapped her black fingers, giant stevedores 'n' tough keelboatmen jumped. Everybody knew she could lick a dozen of 'em with one arm tied behind her back. Usually she dressed like a man an' worked hard. She often worked as a longshoreman, pulled a sweep, or hauled cordelle. Sometimes she'd carry a barrel of flour under each arm an' one on her head. Once she towed a keelboat all de way from N'awleens to Natchez, alone, widout losin' her breath."

The children, remembering the long, wide, endless stretches between home and Natchez, were imagining such a wondrous feat. Aline listened with one ear wondrous, one ear skeptical.

"Annie Christmas could drink a barrel o' beer, chasin' it with ten quarts uh whiskey without stoppin'. Sometimes in a barroom she'd get mad an' beat up all de men in de barroom jus' for fun.

"You gotta picture Annie Christmas in a red satin gown, scarlet plumes in her woolly hair, an' one mighty necklace, threaded with one bead for each eye, ear, and nose she had gouged from men in fights. Her necklace was thirty foot long, but it only had a bead for each white man she'd fought; there weren't enough beads in N'Awleens for all de Negroes she had gouged."

Esau paused, letting the children conjure that necklace, imagine that black giantesse in red satin, those fights, and those white men she'd gouged eyes, ears, and noses from. Josephine, more than a little uncomfortable with this story for the little children especially, was about to stop Esau. Yet she was enthralled. Such a story she'd never heard. Before she could stop him, he continued.

"Annie had twelve coal-black sons, each seven foot tall, all born at de same time. When she'd have another chile, she'd drink a quart of whiskey, lie down, give birth, drink another quart, an' go back to work.

"When she finally met a man who could lick her, she fell in love, but he did not want her. She got herself all bedecked in finery, put on her famous necklace, and jumped right down into de river-deeps. Later her river-drenched body was lifted like a deadhead into a coal-black coffin. After de ceremony, it was driven back down to de wharf in a coal-black wagon drawn by six coal-black horses. Her sons marched, six on each side, in coal-black suits. On a moonless night, her dozen coal-black sons loaded Annie onto a coal-black barge and floated with it out to sea, vanishing into that night forever."

That night Lucien spent most of his sleep with a six-year-old brown boy in chains, a mirror-image of himself, holding the hand of coal-black Annie Christmas, in her necklace of white ears, eyes, and noses, and her twelve coal-black sons on a coal-black barge disappearing on the coal-black sea into that forever coal-black night.

CHAPTER 22:

MEMPHIS, 1851

The next morning Drausin went for his walk around the boiler deck guard, circling the eight feet of deck skirting the cabins. At one point the Kaintuck in his new white suit happened to be approaching. Drausin kept his course. The Kaintuck stopped, too close to him. "What the hell d'ye think you're doin' here?"

Drausin looked him straight in the eye before responding. He knew Kaintucks notoriously turned coloreds bloody. He knew the keelboatman could knock him over the guardrail with a simple sweep of his oak-oar arm. "Just strolling."

"No, I mean on this damn boat, in that damn dining room. You think you belong here?"

Drausin was struck by the thickness of his eyebrows, chestnut and silver, the left one split by a glaring red scar still healing, that continued onto his cheek. His skin looked over-burnt, browned, peeling into reddish-white. A red-brown mustache drooped over his upper lip like a slouch-brimmed hat. His breath smelled of chewing tobacco and yesterday's rotgut whiskey, a mouth not often cleaned. Drausin wondered if he was actually a Buckeye from Ohio, a Hoosier from Indiana, or a bona fide Kaintuck from Kentucky. What was his story?

Drausin was most struck by his sea-green eyes, similar, he was surprised to realize, to Josephine's. "I, Sir, belong where I'm heading; I no longer belong where I've come from."

"You better damn well watch your step. Don't cross the line—who the hell do you think you are, a damned tour-boater?"

"No, Sir, I am a husband and a father. And I am crossing the border. I'm getting out of where I'm stuck, back home. I can't stand it any longer. And I don't want my children stuck back home. I am taking my family north to make a new life." Drausin knew he had gambled in speaking so frankly.

The Kaintuck's Adam's apple bobbed a couple of times; he quieted, and for the first time looked into Drausin's brown eyes. Drausin recognized pain in his green eyes, some kind of pain that had probably led this man to leave his home, and maybe his family, to work long days like an iron man, to fight hard nights, all to get him and his family, maybe, out of whatever they were stuck in back home. The Kaintuck stepped back, looked at Drausin again, grumbled, "Well, damn you!" and pivoted on his way.

At lunchtime, Captain Leathers stood up from his table and strolled around the dining room, stopping at the Wulsins' table. He remembered Drausin and the unusual spelling of his last name. Drausin rose and shook hands. Josephine gestured to the children to rise, and Captain Leathers urged them to resume sitting. Drausin said how much the family was enjoying their quarters, the good food, the ship, and the whole trip.

"Yes, I love her; she's a good craft. Her mama, Natchez II, was built for me up in Cincinnati, which builds the best and the most steamboats in the whole country. I worked her out of Crawfish Bayou for several years, then sold her so Cincinnati could build me Natchez III, longer at one hundred seventy-five feet, with triple boilers 'n' triple rudders. An' I painted her stacks red, jus' like her mama. She's great steamin' up through jus' 'bout any of the chutes."

"Cap'n, how do you know how to go?" asked Ti-Drausin.

Cap'n Leathers beamed with pleasure at the question. "Well, son, it looks pretty simple, don't it? Jus' follow the river. Well, son, it ain't so simple at all. Why not? 'Cuz this crafty ole river, this mighty Mississip', he's always a changin', always a changin'. You got to always remember how he was last time, and you got to always be readin' him, always be readin' him, to figure how he's become new, now."

He placed two knives parallel on their table. He poured a little table salt inside by the top of the left one. He took a spoon and started her sliding along the tabletop through the chute of knives. "Here's our Natchez III. Las' trip, comin' down, we had a sandbar here, we had to go around. Now, there was a big rain last week and those swollen river waters—" with a third knife he swerved the salt pile down over to the right inside, then continued, "worked day and night writhing, twisting, shifting those sands down over to here, still under the water's surface.

"And we—" he brought the spoon into the chute from the other end, "comin' back upstream now, have to read the ripples on the water, that tell us what's underneath, so's we know how to go. Now, I'd much sooner enter a chute goin' upstream than down. Downstream's much more dangerous, all that strong current a pushin' you behind. You're sure less likely to see me runnin' chutes in low water downstream at night. Yes, our Ole Mississipp' can be mean, an' tease you, but he won't do you any real harm if you handle him right. Well, I've gotta get back to the pilot house. Pleasure to have you aboard; I hope you have a good trip, family Wulsin." Captain Leathers touched his gold-braided hat.

Aline had been translating some for Eugene and Lucien, who never forgot Captain Leathers' spoon navigating the shifting salts on the Natchez III's tabletop. Lucien felt as though Ole Mississipp' himself had been speaking through Cap'n Leathers.

At one point Drausin had noticed, across the dining room,

the Kaintuck observing Captain Leathers's navigation school at the Wulsin table.

At a quick stop in Vicksburg, Jebediah pointed out the many hills of the river city. Then he pointed upriver. "Dere use to be a decent ribberport ober dere, back inland. Now it's shrunk so much it almos' disappeart."

"Why, what happened?" Aline asked.

"De town went to bed one night as a major Mississippi ribber town, on a meanderin' oxbow. Den nex' mornin' dey awoke'n de ribber done darn near gone. Durin' de night, it broke frough de neck o' de oxbow, runnin' in a straight line right on frough. 'N' hardly any ribber, 'n' hardly any boats ebber boddered to run all de ole way aroun' again since. No more ribber port. No more trade, an' almos' no more town at all. Pretty soon, it'll jus' be in de middle ob a cow-field. Why, one cut-frough sliced de ribber off tirty mile; it done shrunk tirty mile shorter! De story is, nex' night one sleepy pilot jus' went de ole way and de whole boat jus' disappeared, still tryin' to chug its way trough de pastures. Yup, it joined de cattle.

"Now, two mile upstream is de town o' Delta. It used to be tree mile downstream, on one long meander. One night de ribber jus' cut on frough, leavin' de whole town now upstream o' Vicksburg.

"Why, way furder up nort, a slave could go to sleep in Missouri, 'n' wake up a free man in Illinois, if ole man Mississippi moved so. Don' dat take de cake?

"Now, downstream we already passed Hard Times, Louisiana, on de West Bank. My daddy say de 'riginal town ob Hard Times weren't dere at all; it was ober on de east side ob de ribber, what's now in Mississippi. Cap'n Leathers say, de ribber done moved so much sideways, lef' here, 'n' right dere, dat de whole Mississippi ole Lasalle floated down in his canoes two hunnerd years ago is solid dry groun' today. So much change ober de long years. Oh, dis ebber-changin' ribber!"

Ti-Drausin could hardly stop thinking about Delta especially, trying to figure just how it could shift from downstream to upstream, all on account of the river's ways. Lucien, who got the picture in his way, dreamed in his next dozing nap about little towns spinning side to side and up and down, like rings on a children's jumping rope, that spiraling, twisting Mississippi River.

In Memphis the shore was thick with all kinds of crafts, inside that long, wide island. Cap'n Leathers swung the Natchez III right in between two flatboats; Esau's roustabouts made her six-inch hemp ropes fast on eight-inch iron rings stone-sunk in the bank mud for moorings. The ropes groaned, Ole Man Mississippi always trying to pull her downriver. Laid stones started pretty near, up the slope to the front street. Southern breezes teased against the current. The children watched roustabouts work a coal barge, prancing all the way along on the gunnels rather than walking down inside the barge. In a flash, Eugene pulled himself up onto a Naschez III guardrail, leaning against an upright stanchion supporting the roof. One group of flatboatmen "belly-to-backing" large, heavy armoires, wardrobes, and other furniture ashore onto the wharf, and then loading barrels of corn on board, sang snippets:

> Whip or whop, whip or whop you-ee,
> We gonna sing and dance and sing,
> Whip or whop, whip or whop, you-ee!

Another gang of keelboatmen unloaded barrels of nails and boxes of horseshoes, singing also:

A hook on a cistern is bon' to rust,
Lots of N'Awleens wimmen is hard to trust.
If we two was like we three,
We'd all git together an' then agree.

A nickel is a nickel,
An' a dime is a dime,
The best work is on de riverfront,
All de time.

At lunchbreak, after unloading and loading, flatboatmen, keelboatmen, stevedores, and longshoremen all sat in clusters along the riverbank, chomping on their bull necks or heavy devil, some making the "nigger's lunches" Jebediah had described out of stage planks. After a while, one bulky flatboatman stood up and hollered, "I c'n outrun, out-hop, out-jump, throw down, drag out, an' lick any man in the country. I'm a salt river roarer; I love wimmin' an' I am chock full o' fight." His cronies cheered as he looked around tauntingly at the other groups.

After a minute or two, a small, wiry keelboatman stood up to the challenge. "I'm from the Lightning Forks of Roaring River. I'm all man, save what is wildcat an' extra lightning. I'm as hard to run against as a cypress snag. I never back water. Look at me—a small specimen—harmless as an angle worm—a remote circumstance—a mere yearling. Cockle-doodle-doo! I did hold down a buffalo bull, an' tar off his scalp with my teeth, but I can't do it now—I'm too powerful weak, I am. But ne'rtheless, I'm the genuine article, tough as bullhide, keen as a rifle. I can out-swim, out-jump, out-drink, and keep soberer than any man at Cat Fish Bend. I'm painfully ferocious—I'm spoilin' for someone to whip me—if there's a creeter in this diggin' that wants to be disappointed in trying' to do it, let him yell, 'whoop-hurra!'" His fellow keelboatmen, who knew they were the bullies of the banks, kings of the ring, royals of the river, cheered their man twice as loud.

Drausin, enjoying a cigar against a stanchion on the hurricane deck guard, was amused, imagining what fun Annie Christmas would have with these bluster-busses. He noticed, two stanchions down, the new white suit, already looking a little worn. The Kaintuck was watching and listening to those other Kaintucks boasting down below. Drausin quietly glided down, two arms length away, reached inside his breast pocket, and pulled out a fine cigar. "May I offer you one?"

The Kaintuck twitched alert, clenched his fist, saw the cigar, then Drausin's eyes; he paused, relaxed, and raised his opening hand. "Why, thank you, I guess."

Drausin struck a match, handed it to him, and returned to his post. The Kaintuck savored the first flavor of fine smoke, looking over at Drausin, who watched the riverfront keenly, then back down at his Kaintucks in their jersey shirts and rough jeans.

After some pause, an unexpected loner off to the side, who looked to have been chewing on smoked catfish, stood up from his driftwood bench in greasy buckskins and, through his salty beard, said, "Boys, boys, puffin' yourselves up like bullfrogs—don'cha know it's allus another fellow what's greater? No real riverboatman ever whupped James Girty in a fight. Why, that man had such a solid boneplate over his chest, no knives or bullets could ever kill 'im. As far as the bes' shot aroun', well, Angus Castleman's better'n all o' you combined.

"One time he fired once, girdled an oak, nicked the epidermis off an Indian's back, knocked over a catamount, brought down a flock o' turkeys from the treetops, laid out a buffalo, blazed a section of lands, split enough boards to cover a shanty, and, if I'd a fired once more, you may say I wasted time an' ammunition."

After silence, sticks beat logs, stones smacked rocks; the assembled rousters and river runners signaled the winner of the day. Castleman raised his hand in grinning acknowledgment, nodded, and sat back down on his driftwood. The

Kaintuck puffed three clouds of smoke in tribute and smiled from his proud perch down at the whole scene.

Drausin smiled, too. He was impressed, even a little proud himself, at the rough-hewn rhetoric of these rustics. At the same time, though, he knew what that gang could do to a darky in the night, all for more to boast on. Then he noticed little Eugene running the guardrail, swinging around stanchions, the whole length of the deck, before Ti-Drausin, who'd been playing mumbledy-peg with Lucien, caught and pulled him down. Papa shook his head and smiled. Some day—that boy—with his already thrusting chin.

Suddenly, the children heard a strange noise, unlike any they'd heard, and it wasn't the steam whistle of the Natchez III. It seemed to make a kind of music, just a little upriver. In minutes a barker came along down the shore, hollering for all to hear, "Showboat, showboat, afternoon matinee, best music from North to South, from source to mouth, come one, come all! Suitable for whole family, three o'clock on the showboat, three o'clock on the showboat, world-famous Christy's Minstrels, first time ever south of the O-hi-o, world-famous Christy's Minstrels!" The children, of course, clamored and pleaded to go. Drausin asked some other passengers, consulted with Josephine, and gave the nod.

As the Wulsin family approached the Floating Theater on its moored barge, they could see the source of the welcoming music, a multicolored calliope, tooting white steam out of its pipes. Inside, the children were surprised when Mr. E. P. Christy brought his Minstrels onstage: a group of burnt-cork-blackened white men, lips reddened into watermelon slices, looking like a bunch of coon goofs. Many in the audience laughed just at the sight. Drausin and Josephine were appalled, regretting their choice.

That is, they regretted their choice until the Minstrels began to sing in exquisite four-part harmonies. Their repertoire included some straightforward parlor romances and some nigger songs. Drausin had already heard a few versions of "Oh Susanna" down in New Orleans.

> Oh, I come from Alabama
> Wid my Banjo on my knee
> I'se gwine to Lou'siana
> My true lub for to see.

> I jump'd aboard de Telegraph
> And trabbled down de ribber,
> De lectrick fluid magnified,
> And kill'd five hundred Nigga.
> De bulgine bust and de hoss ran off,
> I really thought I'd die;
> I shut my eyes to hold my bref
> Susanna don't you cry.

The banjo player was pretty good, twanging a new version of the original African Benze Drausin remembered from his youth at Congo Square, now with a fifth string. Banjo Man made raucous, gutsy layers of melodies, sweetened by the mighty mobile fiddle player. Tambourine Man shook and beat a large tambourine with just a few tin jingles on it. And Bone Man thwacked his sawed-off horse-ribs in whole ranges of rhythms and beats. In various songs Drausin recognized echoes, some of European classical music, some of English, Irish, and Scots ballads, and some of more African rhythms— all music from back home. His heart contracted.

Drausin and Josephine had noticed the older three children twitch their shoulders, gasp and look at each other at the line, "Kill'd five hundred Nigga," in a stanza he'd not heard before. And here they were as a young family, watching white blackface performers singing supposed Negro songs.

Drausin remembered that both he and Josephine at Congo Square had felt inwardly moved, wanting to move outwardly, to join the dancers, but feeling unable to, as free Creoles of color. *And now here are these whites, trying in their clumsy, yet also graceful, ways to participate in something they had to mock, and yet toward which they were reaching nevertheless. And through the reaching, they offered something of beauty that somehow touched us all. This was both new and old. The back-of-the-church blacks were quiet during some of the laughing of the whites, among whom the Wulsins were successfully sitting and blending. And yet the blacks in back, like everyone, swayed to the music, moved by the songs in spite of some offensive words and notions.*

Mr. E. P. Christy introduced a brand-new composition of his own, "Old Folks at Home," a melancholy lament:

All up and down de whole creation
Sadly I roam,
Still longing for de ole plantation,
An' for de ole folks at home.
All de world am sad and dreary,
Eb-rywhere I roam.
Oh, darkeys, how my heart grows weary,
Far from de old folks at home!

Josephine knew that, as hauntingly lovely as the melody and harmonies were, swaying the audience like one breeze blowing through all grasses, *Drausin and I are far from longing for any old plantation, and, though roaming somewhat sadly, we are roaming much more gladly, toward whatever lies ahead of us.* She caught his eye, read him, wondered who was thinking whose thoughts, he or she, and he nodded, agreeing.

The hour-long show culminated with an "Original Burlesque, entitled 'Zachary Taylor and the Battle of Buena Vista in Mexico,'" including energizing martial music such as "General

Taylor's Encampment Quick-step" and "Santa Anna's Retreat from Buena Vista." Drausin remembered how close he had come to exploring Vera Cruz as a possibility for the family's future, instead of their eventual and now imminent Cincinnati. They had almost gone more south, rather than north.

The Christy's Minstrels concluded with a walkaround. Lucien and Eugene marched emphatically back along the riverfront; Jebediah had joined them from the back section of the theater on the way out. He looked up at the gulls flying in circles, then over at horses jumping and snorting on the levee. "Rain's a comin', rain's a comin'." Both Drausins, Aline and Lucien, could certainly see the gulls and the horses, but they saw no other signs in the still-blue sky. Yet Jebediah knew.

Later that night, after supper, Drausin stayed for a while with the older three while Josephine settled Eugene and Laure into bed in the other cabin. First the three older children sang, "All up and down de whole creation, sadly I roam...." Then Aline said, "I wish they'd left out the blackface. I hated that." Drausin nodded in agreement.

Then Ti-Drausin and Lucien started to chant:

We're goin' from Memphis, Tennessee
On the Miss-i-ssip-pi River
All the way to Cin-cin-nati
On the O-hi-O.

Soon, Aline could no longer refrain from joining in. And during the next days the Bacas-children-becoming-Wulsins would march it, Lucien pretending to beat a snare drum. Eugene trumpeted the loudest, marching like a naval cadet, with high step to boot.

MISSOURI
ARKANSAS
KENTUCKY
TENNESSEE
OHIO RIVER
Phelps
Columbus
Dickman
STATE LINE
Dennison
Georgetown
Point Pleasant
Edgington
Seminca
Clarksville
Hickman
Greys Chapel
Belleview
Hickman Point
Airport
Fort Pillow
Fulton
Fort Wright
Randolph
River View
MEMPHIS
STATE LINE
Norfolk
De Soto
Hopewell

CHAPTER 23:

LADY LUCK, 1851

After the children finally subsided into sleep, dark settling in Memphis, Drausin walked ashore from the Natchez III through blazing jacks lighting up gangplanks and piles of cargo, upstream beyond the Floating Theater, toward a fancy steamboat with a casino. He was reflecting on the strange, contradictory experience earlier with the Christy Minstrels. *Why is "blackface" so painful, so embarrassing for us gens de couleur? Since our behavior was normally so confined by whites anyway to limiting cartoons of ourselves, "blackface" is a humiliating double cartoon. It demeans coloreds by cartooning the limiting behavior which itself is already enforced upon us by whites, all to the amusement of the largely white audience. We are being doubly reduced. Too many people of many shades of color are forced to live only "blackface" in relation to whites in our daily lives. But not our children; our children will not—and yet—the music touches us all, from black to white, surprisingly. Strange.*

Boarding the casino boat on the gangplank, Drausin noticed how the new moon had grown some, shedding the old, allowing the stars still to be incredibly bright, reflecting almost mirror-clearly on the water; he chuckled at Jebediah's forecast of rain. Across the river a wolf howled. Familiar with various forms of gambling in New Orleans, Drausin was interested less in the gambling itself than in the gamblers. By the doorways one hawker sold money belts; another offered paper-book lives of Murrell, the Hellbender Pirate of the Mississippi, and Mason, the Bandit of Ohio, and the Harpe brothers, the Thugs of the Green River country in Kentucky. Drausin bought one of each for the children.

No, Drausin's gambling was of a different scope. He knew it was a gamble even to voyage on a steamboat, boiler explosions being a weekly and often deadly disaster. Drausin was gambling even larger, though, betting on Cincinnati with the highest of stakes—the rest of his whole family's lives. No mere coinage this. No gold in his trunk's secret compartment would see light tonight. Tonight for Drausin was a game of gaze.

Inside the white clapboard exterior was a sumptuous palace with red velvet on the walls, mirrors galore, and gleaming brass spittoons polished to mini-mirror again the whole festival. A familiar range of characters flocked to nibble, graze, gobble, devour, and—to be nibbled, grazed, gobbled, devoured. Yes, at one end of the spectrum were Kaintucks, still in jeans and red flannel, with chips on their shoulders as well as on the tables. At the other end of the spectrum were the sportsmen, in their brightest white linens and ruffles, diamonds sparkling in their cufflinks, eyeing the crowd, analyzing, diagnosing, like the keenest of surgeons, studying the skill-weak or the pride-blind, deciding whom they would slice or dice tonight, savoring the ensuing play.

While Drausin gathered that there were billiards and even ten-pin bowling in another room, he could tell quickly that a keen quiet surrounded the games of skill: English whist, cribbage, American poker, and euchre, while a more raucous density of whiskey, smoke, glee, and groans rose and fell in the games of chance: faro, craps, roulette, and monte. For a while he watched card players for signs—unconscious mannerisms—like rising eyebrows, clenched lips, twitches of the nose, finger diddling, or any other clue to what really lay in their hands.

Then, lo and behold, who should Drausin espy but his own Kaintuck's white linen suit, by now somewhat stained and quite rumpled. A half-bottle of unlabeled whiskey accompanied him at the roulette wheel. Drausin's Kaintuck stood up, roaring like a waterfall to proclaim his power and luck. Lady Fortune had just doubled his on an inside bet, a straight—black eleven. "Ooh, my Lady Luck, ohh sweet lady, yuh lak me better 'n muh mama, an' you're just a makin' me lak a king, to go home 'n' make muh sweetheart a queen. Queenie, Queenie, here ah come. Bless me sweet Fortuna, bless me jus' one more time."

And Drausin's Kaintuck pushed all his chips, old and new, out in an outside bet, one ultimate bid for the Wheel of Fortune to land this time on red for him, her favored one, just one more time. Drausin could see that he'd most likely lose it all, returning home empty-pocketed, probably without even his white suit. Glancing around, Drausin dashed to the piano man, flipped him a silver dollar, and asked, "May I, just one?"

"Why sure, Mister."

Before he even settled onto the stool, Drausin banged down loudly a bass chord, then a jangling interval of a seventh, three times, so loud the piano man worried for his piano, and so loud the whole casino snapped out of its obsessions and bustlings for a moment. Drausin played and sang, still loudly, then increasingly tenderly, yet urgently, a tune most people had not yet heard:

The sun shines bright on the old Kentucky home...

Drausin shouted "Ken-tucky," which pulled his Kaintuck's sloshy head around, the half-soused man shocked to find his Natchez III cigar-enemy-friend to be the source of this noise, this mighty disruption in the flow of the evening, in the go of Lady Fortune. Drausin continued:

'Tis summer, the darkies are gay,
They hunt some more for possum and the coon
On the meadow, the hill, and the hay.

The young folks roll on the little cabin floor,
All merry, all happy and bright:
By'n by' Hard Times comes a knocking at the door,
Then my old Kentucky Home, good night!

At the end Drausin repeated his triple chord, but more plaintively. He thanked bewildered Piano Man, strode to the roulette table, helped Kaintuck sweep his still-intact pile of chips into his pockets, whispered in his ear, "After the Wheel of Fortune rises high, it always falls down below," and ushered him out the door. Under the deck roof, in the lee of pelting rain, Drausin lit him a cigar, on which Kaintuck puffed, pulling himself back to his senses.

Feeling the bulk of the chips in his pockets, fickle Fortune's darling realized how close he had come to being emptied. "Oh, Jaysus, oh, Jaysus. Sir, I thank you." He stepped back. "Declan Fletcher." For the first time, he offered his hand.

"Drausin Wulsin." Drausin shook hands with Declan, unsurprised that Kaintuck had hard, calloused palms. "Think nothing of it. Let's cash your chips and get you back to the Natchez." They both knew there was no way Drausin could "ride the tide," give oak-armed, half-addled, silver-laden Declan any trouble between the two boats, even if he had wanted to. Declan looked his savior in the eye, nodded, and cashed in his chips. Then the pair shouldered each other through the torrents back to the Natchez III, managing to keep their cigars glowing through the rain.

Under the boiler-deck roof, Declan paused. Then he said, "Drausin, tonight you saved two months o' hard work an' who knows how many years o' my future. I'll allus be indebted to you." They shook hands again, with a slight, bowing nod to each other, and returned, drenched, to their rooms. On his way, Drausin chuckled, "Oh Jebediah, Jebediah, you wise weather-watcher."

Inside their stateroom, Josephine listened with gravity to

Drausin's whispered reflections on blackface. "I sure see why some folks call minstrelsy the nation's schoolhouse for niggerin'," he concluded.

"And at the same time, how strange," Josephine said, "that while the packaging leaves us aghast, the music nevertheless touches us, still is much our own." Drausin agreed as they pondered the unsettling riddle, which seemed to deepen, to reinforce their mutual vow to do their best to launch their children into unshrunken possibilities.

Josephine then listened with wonder to Drausin's story of Declan Fletcher. "Chère Josie, remember when Ti-Drauzin and I were pushed down into St. Ann St.? Well, that was the last street I ever went down. From now on, I'm only going up, upriver. We're streamin', Josie, we'se a strea-min'."

Josephine looked with pride into her Drausin's eyes. "Cher, tonight you crossed over the border. You danced with the danger. You crossed that border." She wrapped him 'round, her man.

CHAPTER 24:
THE OHIO, 1851

The next night Lucien dreamed a rat was chewing on his bunk, right by his nose. He opened his good left eye to see, to his surprise, his brother and sister opening the porthole. "Psst, psst, come on out, dey're soundin' a shoal!" It was Jebediah, outside the porthole.

Aline, about to go next door to beg permission, decided to skip it. The three older children bundled their coats on, closed their hall door ever so gingerly, and tiptoed out to the boiler guard. "Careful, stay hand-in-hand; it's darker dan inside a cow," whispered Jebediah. Making their way to the bow, they settled in. A lantern floated above the water, while what seemed to be four oars broke up the inky surface, rippling silver and black, which, for a disorienting moment, left Lucien feeling slightly seasick. The children then realized the Natchez III was tied up to a huge cottonwood alongshore. Ti-Drausin turned. "No one's in the pilot house!"

"Oh no, Cap'n Leffers 'n' Mate Green 're dere. We're slicing' time by night trabel. Cap'n Leffers say, 'In a dark, dark night on de ribber, a light, you think he your bes' friend? No, he your wors' enemy. Wid a light, dere's only dark. Widout a light, dere's lotsa differen' darks. He aluss likes jus' as dark as can be, so his eyes can shif' to read de differen' darks de bes'. He don' allow even a ceegar or pipe to be lit."

Aline, Ti-Drausin, and Lucien all started trying to read the different darks of the water. "My pa's runnin' de yawl, soundin' down how deep 'wid a long pole, marked a differen' color each foot, one foot red, nex' foot blue, nex' one white 'n so on all de way down de sixteen-foot pole. Mosly, on de Mississip', we usin' a long cord, 'cuz it can get so deep, but on shoals, an' on mos' ob de O-hi-o, we use de pole. Dey needs a lantern to read de pole, but Cap'n Leffers don' look dat direction; he only listen, lookin' eberywhere else."

"Ten an' half feet, ten—eight an' half feet, eight—" Esau was calling out, having his men row toward the shoal. One of his wags was preparing the buoy, a five-foot plank with a "foot" extending down, and a thin, three-foot upright pole. On it he rigged a paper lantern with a lit candle inside. Esau had him cover the side of the lantern facing the Natchez with a piece of canvas, so Cap'n Leathers would be able to know its location from the light reflecting on the waters away from the candle, while still having dark on his side.

"Seven an' half!"

"It sure gettin' shoalier," said Jebediah. Esau had his crew row over the shoal to find deeper water upstream, and then return.

"Seven! Six an' half! Mark the buoy!" The wag dropped the buoy directly overboard, tied with a seven-foot grass line to a large stone. Esau had the rowers move the yawl forty feet further west-to-east, able to find a stretch of shoal consistently between six-and-a-half and seven-and-a-half feet deep so the thirty-foot-wide Natchez could get through. With a six-foot draft on the Natchez III, Cap'n Leathers would nose the Natchez up pretty close to the shoal—and then, with full power, leap the big ship right on over the shoal. Esau's men dropped a second lit buoy, rare in thousands of miles of unlit river. Then they raised their oars upright, letting the current drift them back down to the Natchez. Invisible Captain Leathers was preparing his approach to the chute.

Ti-Drausin asked Jebediah if there were pirates around these parts, like Jean Lafitte. "Oh dat Lafitte, from down in Barataria, no, he long dead. But once in a while somebody say he's hidin' out in St. Louis under a diffren' name."

"I've been reading about some Mississippi pirates, that Murrell gang," said Aline.

"Oh yeah, dey was bad. Watchya know?"

"Well, the book says that John Andrew Murrell, 'the Great West Land Pirate,' was caught already as a teenager, branded HT for being a horse thief, flogged, and sentenced to six years in prison down in Tennessee." Aline and Ti-Drausin had to explain to Lucien about branding, flogging, and prison, new notions each. The images seared into him.

"Then what?"

"Well," continued Aline, "after he was released, he and his brothers founded the Mystic Clan, anywhere from three hundred to a thousand stealers and robbers. Why, they'd rob almost anything you could think of—houses, stagecoaches, stores, banks. Stealing almost anything you could think of—money, jewelry, cattle, horses. That John Andrew Murrell had such a sweet-looking baby-face; he liked to arrive in some river town as a traveling preacher and get himself to preaching a big sermon on Sunday, filling up the church. Meanwhile his Mystic Clan would be sneakin' outside stealing all the horses, 'cept his, of course." In the dark, Lucien was picturing churches filling with people inside and emptying of horses outside. "D'you know what they got the richest by stealing?" Aline asked.

"Ah t'ink so; tell 'em," said Jebediah.

"Slaves. They'd steal a slave from a plantation and convince that slave to let them sell him again to a new master. Then the Murrells would steal him again, split the profits, and let the slave run free with some cash."

"Sounds good for everyone," said Ti-Drausin.

"Well, that was the plan they talked. Only problem was, the Murrells didn't want any witnesses. So, after stealing and selling a slave several times, they'd kill him in a swamp, gut him, an' feed his body to the crawfish an' alligators. So, you see, this Murrell gang were sort of conductors on an underground railroad going backwards." Ti-Drausin and Lucien certainly needed some help with that notion.

"Remember, back after Baton Rouge you daddy was showin' us all de norf star, sayin' how many followed it norf, to freedom?" asked Jebediah. Nods. "Well, people help dem along de way; dat's called de Unnergroun' Railroad. Nobody can really see it, but it work like a railroad. Murrell an' de Mystic Clan steals 'em free, dat's headin' Norf, and sells 'em back, dat's stuck Souf."

After a pause to grasp that, Lucien asked, "Are we on the Underwater Railroad?"

Jebediah chuckled, "Mebbe, only we ain't slabes. But—mebbe—an, ya never know—hey, here we go!"

The Natchez III had reentered the central flow of the river, all dark except for the two lit buoys; Captain Leathers approached about twenty feet from the "line" between the lanterns, pulled the bell-cords for the engine room to give full steam, and planed the boat over the shoal successfully. She labored through the shallows, shimmying, then sliding on over into deep water with a soothing sigh. The yawl picked up the buoys and joined the mother ship before she streamed on up the dark river until the next shoal.

"Then that Mystic Clan," Aline continued, "was making big plans for a good while, really big plans, all the way to New Orleans. Why, after John Andrew Murrell was captured again and put back in prison for ten years, even so, something big happened. That next year, 1835, on July 4, the red-light districts in Nashville, Memphis, and Natchez all went wild at the same time. Twenty slaves and ten white men were hanged for starting the riots; people called it the Murrell Slave Insurrection and the Murrell Excitement, and people say their ultimate goal was to capture New Orleans. Whites in Vicksburg got so scared they hanged six gamblers, just on suspicions."

"Yeah, dose Murrells was usin' de slaves again to be getting sometin' bigger for demselbes," said Jebediah.

"But John Andrew was in jail?" asked Ti-Drausin.

"Yes, but he was the mastermind," clarified Aline.

"What happened to him?"

"They worked him so hard in prison, and he spent so much time in solitary confinement that he sort of lost his marbles. He worked as a blacksmith, so after ten years in jail he blacksmithed in Pikeville, till he died of consumption, age thirty-four."

"So that was that end of the Murrell gang?" Ti-Drausin and Lucien were looking a bit disappointed to be nearing the end of the hair-raising escapades of the Mystic Clan.

"Well, almost. Some grave robbers dug up his body and sold parts. His head was pickled and showed at county fairs."

"Yup, I hear de mu-seem in Nashville has one ob his tumbs, like dem Cat'lics sellin' Jesus' toes."

Lucien was yawning and a little cold by now; the three siblings thanked Jebediah for helping them watch Esau sound the shoal. As they returned quietly, a woman shrieked off in the dark to the west. The children startled.

"Das a cougar," assured Jebediah, and they were glad to get back in their stateroom bunks. But Lucien had an uneasy night, with John Andrew Murrell's pickled, baby-faced head floating between lanterns, shrieking like a woman like a cougar, all in the dark inside a cow.

The next day, Jebediah informed them that, after passing Point Pleasant, they had crossed borders between Donaldson Point and French Point; the west shore had changed from Arkansas to Missouri, and the east shore had changed from Tennessee to Kentucky. Of course the marching chant resumed, with the children's mounting excitement:

We're going from Memphis, Tennessee
On the Miss-i-ssip-pi River
All the way to Cin-cin-nati
On the O-hi-O.

Drausin noticed that the Natchez III seemed to be grad-ually slowing, at least until Captain Leathers swung her into the western side of the river, which Drausin realized was still mud-brown, whereas the east side had started to become more clay-slate blue. Lucien was the first child to notice. "We've got the brown water and the blue!"

"Yes," said his father, "and do you know where the blue comes from?—The O-Hi-O river." And of course the chant would resume. It wasn't long though before the children's chant was drowned out by Esau's rousters, heartily and proudly singing out:

Hey, ho, hey ho,
Hey, no, hey, no,
We never gonna live in Cai-ro
We ain't never gonna live in Cai-ro
Any ole place in de whole wide worl'
But Cai-ro,
Never gonna live in Cai-ro.

Occasionally one or two would break out of their work, shifting cargo to unload in Cairo, and shift into "patting juba," clapping, slapping thighs, and heel-stomping in a bewildering complexity of rhythms, culminating in cheers from all. Esau would wait till after the display to call his deckhands back into their work lines.

And of course the children, seasoned swags themselves by now, all the way up the river from New Orleans, joined in, hol-lering out, delighting the crew, who had grown to love them, Jebediah's own little gang. And yes, Eugene danced along the guardrail, swinging around the stanchions with familiar ease by now, trying to lead the chant like some marching band drum major, to Josephine's helpless consternation.

And soon enough, Captain Leathers swung the Natchez III back over to the east side, where the waters seemed to Drausin to pop-rise, actually higher than the waters to the west. Then the town of Cairo, Illinois, broke through up ahead, like a rusty axe-head splitting the weak brown waters of the Mississippi to the left from the powerful, blasting bluish waters of the Ohio to the right. Drausin thought, *If the Mississippi at this point flows like a fourteen-year-old boy, lengthening but still boy-lean, the Ohio must flow like a twenty-year-old, bulging, blasting with all its muscle-joy, a full-blown Kaintuck, one Mike Fink of a river, to which the Mississippi here tamely defers. Then, down further, maybe around Memphis, the Mississippi becomes more like an old man.*

And now Captain Leathers had to pull those bell-cords to signal the engineers to give more power, so the Natchez III could make even decent forward progress up what at first seemed like the broken-dam floodwaters of the Ohio. Drausin figured those boilers to be glowing cherry-red.

He said, "Children, say goodbye to the Mississippi River." Lucien and Eugene called out, "Au revoir, Mississippi." Lucien thought, *I really mean, "I'll see you again, M. Mississippi." I wonder what the river might be like upstream, growing younger and younger.*

As the Captain, the crew, the passengers, and indeed the Natchez III herself adjusted to the new world of the Ohio River, Drausin at one point asked the children, "What is high in the middle and round on the ends?" While they pondered the riddle, Aline, absent-mindedly doodling, happened to finger on the sooty outside wall behind them the four letters, "O HI O."

"I got it!" she said, standing over in front of the letters, blocking them. "O-HI-O!"

Lucien and Eugene, of course, were bewildered. Ti-Drausin was starting to get it as she stepped aside, showing them the name, O-HI-O, repeating the sounds of each letter. Aline was delighted. Ti-Drausin too. Eugene couldn't quite grasp it. Lucien could. Saying it again and again to himself, Lucien felt that O-HI-O was one of the most beautiful words he had ever heard, seen, and even tasted. Just saying it aloud opened him.

"Ill-ie-noy," not "Ee-lee-nwa," was now on their larboard side, the north, and "Ken-tuck-y" on the starboard side, the south. Lucien felt he was chewing on smoked meat when he pronounced "Ken-tuck-y."

Drausin had been half-noticing that his Josephine, naturally quiet anyway, had become even more silent in public recently. By now, they were the only passengers remaining on the Natchez III, for whom French was the mother tongue. She hardly tried herself to pronounce these new English words. Was this simply her natural shyness, or actually some kind of resistance to the language now in their air? Had her father, Samuel Young II, been more than just evaporating in her early years? He clearly had spoken French fluently and apparently normally in their family, perhaps only cursing in English. When he was coming undone in his later years, due to too much fruit of the vine, had there been actions more harsh than sounds in the Young household? Drausin did not know; he did not know if Josephine even knew.

At that moment on the deck, Josephine was thinking not about her English-speaking father but about the hot chocolate dregs in Drauzin's—not yet Drausin's!—cup that morning back on Rue Bayou. *Now, here our family actually is! Right on that right branch of the big river, reaching like an arm toward Cincinnati.*

However little interest Josephine may have had in learning the English language all around her (she definitely resisted), she felt fully content behind the reach of this river, whatever might lie in store for them all at the docks of Cincinnati. Josephine reached her right arm to Drausin, taking his left hand in her left, her right arm then resting 'round his right shoulder, feeling the connection complete.

Lucien had been making apparently random references to the dark insides of a cow, to Esau's sounding pole, to lanterns rippling on the waters, to pirate Murrell's pickled head. Drausin and Josephine began to grasp that the three elder children had shared an unknown adventure last night on the Mississippi. A quiet conversation with Aline revealed the nature of Jebediah's generous inclusion of them in the shoal-sounding, while the parents reinforced the rightness of Aline's initial instinct simply to let them know. Papa would have gladly accompanied them, with less risk of any child slipping into the black mouth of the midnight river, disappearing like Annie Christmas's twelve sons. Or, more potently, Drausin realized with a gasp, like the drowning of Louis Adhemar, which had formed a relentless emotional whirlpool for the Bacas family.

A new guide joined the family on deck at unexpected moments, offering seasoned perspectives on the Ohio River—Declan Fletcher, former keelboatman and everlasting Kaintuck. Sometimes accepting one of Drausin's cigars, sometimes offering one of his own, purchased in Memphis, better than any he'd bought before. Drausin found Declan's cigars both a little bitter, of poorer tobacco, and a little sweet, the leaves soaked in molasses and rum, yet Drausin honestly enjoyed them. He savored how their initial enmity was unfolding surprisingly, against high odds.

"Now, right up here to starboard is Paducah, Kaintucky, the lowest port on the Ohio where a riverboat'll never find ice—'n jus' after, yon mouth is the grand Tennessee River, flowin' down through Kaintucky 'cross Tennessee way east almos' to Knoxville. We rivermen used to call it the Cherokee, but they, the Cherokee, called it Tanasi. 'N now we do too—"

"Is the Ohio River high in the middle and round on the ends?" interrupted Eugene.

"Well," said Declan, chuckling, "its name is, 'O-hi-o,' but the river itself ain't."

"Then why's it called Ohio?"

"Well, you're sure full a questions. Alls I know is, the Miami Injuns called it the Ohi, the Great White Water."

"Oh."

Declan chuckled. "Yessir, but the Shawnee called it the Ohio, the Bloody River."

"Oh?" puzzled Eugene.

"And the Iroquois called it the Oyo, the Beautiful River. So—you watch that river like a bobcat watchin' a rabbit, an' you tell me why, when you know." Eugene looked at the hardened riverboatman, gulped, nodded, and got to work at the rail, watching the Ohio River hard.

"—Now up on ahead, on the larboard Illinois shore, ye'll be seein' one strange place, Cave-in-Rock. Why, already back b'fore this cent'ry, that was a den of thieves." As the white cliff surged up, with the dark mouth of the cave widening, the children ran over to the larboard guardrail.

Declan told Drausin, "Big and Little Harpe, two brothers from up on Green River, they joined Mason's gang in Cave-in-Rock for a while. Well, one day they took one suckered flatboatman up on top o' the cliff, stripped him, tied a rope, one end to his neck, the other to a horse, blindfolded the horse, 'n cracked whips over'n over near the rearin', fearin' horse, till it finally trip-slipped o'er the cliff, providin' one real spectacle, with the flatboatman flyin' screamin' behind. All of which skeert even Mason's hardened gang down below. Mason's river pirates boot-scooted them Harpe Brothers right on out from Cave-in-Rock. Yup, I heard tell those Harpe boys might've left more innocent victims on their trail than any killers in our whole nation's history."

As the two men joined the children at the rail, Declan continued, "Yes, children, Mason's river pirates would lure a flatboat or keelboat over to shore with pretty women, fiery moonshine, or jus' a good tradin' bargain, and then rob 'em of everything they could eat, drink, wear, or trade for. Tough'n dang'rous."

"Did you ever fight 'em, Mr. Fletcher?" asked Ti-Drausin.

"Nope, young fella, we wuz allus a heap smarter than messin' with 'em; we'd allus slide by at night, no candles, real silent, squirrel guns ready, but they never knew us to be slippin' by."

"What happened to 'em?"

"Oh, that last year, 1799, Cap'n Young's regulators, called the Exterminators, they rode in and cleaned the whole gang outta the cave, jus' like burnin' out a hornet's nest. The survivors skedaddled on down to the Natchez Trace. They took to leavin' messages in blood, like 'Done by Mason of the woods.' After a few years the Spanish Government officials arrested him and his men in Little Prairie 'n took 'em to New Madrid to be tried."

"Hey, New Madrid!" said Ti-Drausin. "The Natchez III stopped in there to load up on firewood for the boilers!"

"That's right, son—well, Mason told the judge he was just a farmer. But officials found seven thousand dollars and twenty scalps in Mason's luggage. Some farmer. Well, while his killer buddies Harpe and Alston escaped, Mason got shot in the head. When Mississippi's governor issued a reward for Mason's head, well, would'nch'ya know, Harpe and Alston got all excited 'bout a new get-rich-quick scheme. Yup, they went'n brought in Mason's head for reward money. Just before they had that reward in hand, one officer, a former victim himself, recognized 'em. So, they were found guilty of piracy and hanged down in Old Greenville, Mississippi, early 1804. An' it pretty much all started up here in Cave-in-Rock."

"Mr. Fletcher, how old are you?" asked Aline.

"Why, now that you ask—" Declan could tell she was subtracting 1799 from 1851, "guess 'bout a hunnert." The boys were open-jawed, Ti-Drausin a little dubious. Declan leaned down to Aline's ear an' whispered, "But all the rest is true."

The children couldn't stop watching that shrinking black mouth of a cave in the shrinking white cliff. Lucien was starting to get confused about pirate heads, Murrell's and Mason's, which sure seemed to get lost a lot and to get around a lot. Father Drausin couldn't stop thinking about Odysseus, warned by the sorceress Circe to sail on by the cave in the rock, no matter what. Yes, the six-headed monster Skylla would chomp up six of Odysseus's crew as they sailed by. But the only alternative was Charybdis, the maelstrom, which would suck down in its swirls the whole ship, losing the whole crew. Drausin couldn't help wondering who of his crew he might lose on this long odyssey of theirs.

But he shook off his pesky melancholy and held Josephine's hand unusually firmly, so that she wondered. He looked at his five children glowing with growth, and turned his gaze into Josephine's green eyes with courage, confidence, and gratitude. At least he had his Penelope and their little Telemachuses with him on this Ohio River in 1851. *Except we aren't returning home*, he thought. Then, *Thank heavens.*

Kaintuck, with perhaps surprising tact, had stepped back aft along the rail, also watching that last black dot of Cave-in-Rock, puffing on his cigar like a steamboat.

CHAPTER 25:

PRINCE MADOC AT THE DEVIL'S BACKBONE, 1851

Often the Kentucky banks rose high, with blue clay at times caving. The opposite Illinois shore tended toward sandbars covered with poplars and willows, their leaves drooping in the water like so many long fingers. In one Kentucky landing, where the Natchez III stopped mainly to load up fuel at the woodlot, Drausin noticed old papers nailed to walls or trees announcing sperm oil and newer ones offering discounted brown French linens at good prices.

Josephine had Aline ask Jebediah to loan them a bucket, and then she sent the children, led by Aline of course, to fetch a little clay and some river mud. Jebediah would not go with them. Josephine also had Aline ask Jebediah for a patch of burlap, maybe a foot square, which he managed to procure. When the children returned, the boys were a mess, of course, fancying themselves as river pirates and requiring Aline and Josephine to do some cleaning on the dock to transform the dastardly rogues back into civilized passengers.

Aline asked Jebediah why he hadn't come along. "You han't noticed? Pa 'n me, we nebber goes ashore in a slabe state; don' wan' nobody mistakin' us fer runaways, grabbin' us 'n sellin' us down de ribber. We seen it too many times." Lucien couldn't quite grasp it. Starboard side of the river—

slave. Larboard side of the river—free. It sure seemed to him Jebediah was the same Jebediah, whichever side of the boat he was on, whichever side of the river. Still Jebediah. Lucien wondered if the shabbier shorefronts on the Kentucky side were due to slaves, compared to the better-tended "free side."

Along the way upriver the children heard a light, tinkling music. Soon, it became clear that the source was hundreds of strings of thousands of purple, pink, blue, and mauve mussel shells, hanging to dry, jingling in sun and wind, until the mussel-boat divers would pack them in barrels to ship by flatboat to button factories in New Orleans. There were hundreds of varieties of Ohio River mussels.

Drausin heard Caliban's music on Prospero's island:

Sometimes a thousand twangling instruments
Will hum about mine ears, and sometimes voices
That, if I then had waked after long sleep,
Will make me sleep again; and then, in dreaming,
The clouds methought would open and show riches
Ready to drop upon me that, when I waked
I cried to dream again.

What a river, he pondered, wondering what riches these clouds above the Ohio might show them.

"How does it feel to be travelin' the alligator's eye?" That question from Mr. Fletcher caught the children by surprise. They knew they had long ago left the land of palms and oranges, and although they'd not seen much in the way of pines, or apples in June, yet they sure did not expect any alligators way up here on the Ohio River. Lucien stepped toward his father, eyeing the waters keenly. Eugene jumped up on Mr. Fletcher's lap, ready for battle. Declan chuckled reassuringly, "No, no, no worry here, young'uns, ain't no gators in these here waters. But, I'm tellin' ye, we're travelin' through the alligator's eye."

All four children looked at him, believing him, then looked at each other, unable to figure his crazy statement; their parents had no clue.

"Okay now, here's what you have to unnerstan'. This whole great state of Kaintucky, well, on a map she's shaped jus' like an alligator, just a lyin' on top o' flat ole, tabletop Tennessee, facin' west to the sunset." He turned and finger-drew the shape of an alligator's head in the wall soot. "'N right here, right near the mouth of the Wabash River, here near Fairview, Indiana, is jus' 'bout the eye of the gator, the gator of all Kaintucky, an' that's what we're sailin' through right now." All the Wulsins, except little Laure, of course, could see it on the wall.

"We're in the eye of the gator, the eye of the gator!" The pirate boys became the alligator of the Ohio River, leaving Aline amused and intrigued.

"What's Indiana?" Lucien asked.

"Oh, that's the state to larboard now, that shore."

"Why?"

"Why? 'Cuz Shawnee Indians used to live here, not so long ago."

One huge Kaintucky gator, across from a state full of Shawnee Indians, Lucien was imagining. *What a river! Slave gator? Free Indians?*

Josephine gave Drausin a nod, and he said, "Declan, my wife Josephine offers to put a salve on that still-festering wound of yours. She's good at such things."

"Oh, why, no, thank you, Ma'am," he turned to her, slight-bowing awkwardly. "I'm a doin' jus' fine, thank you jus' the same." Which wasn't true; the wound, red, oozing some at the cheek, needed him to tamp it pretty regularly with his kerchief.

Pecan trees started lining the Indiana banks of the river. Sometimes primeval forests alternated with farm fields and villages. The Kentucky side was still often walled with limestone hills, ranges, and bluffs. Approaching the Ohio River Falls at Louisville, Kentucky, Captain Leathers decided to have his mate Jack Green pilot the Natchez III up through the canal around the Falls, where the river dropped twenty-six feet in three miles. Green was so pleased with his slow progress through the canal that, opening up speed afterward, he forgot to mind submerged rocks just downstream of Twelve-mile Island. The trip halted, abruptly. Fortunately, the hull, though punished, was not leaking, at least not yet.

First, Captain Leathers called for the steamboat crutches, a pair of singular spars that Esau directed two crewmen to set on the river bottom, close to the Natchez's head. Then he directed leading the tackle from the pole-top to a ring on deck. Roustabouts heaved on the windlass, hoping to lift the boat bodily off the rocks, but to no avail. Unfortunately, neither full steam in reverse nor shifting as much weight as possible, including moving all passengers to the stern, could lift the bow sufficiently.

The Natchez settled in for a long wait. Captain Leathers ordered the cook to double the desserts and bring out special wines. After supper, Declan joined the Wulsin family on deck for cigars. Touch-tamping his cheek, he quietly allowed as to how he might accept Josephine's offer after all. Very soon, in the dusk under gathering clouds, he was holding a poultice of clay and river mud wrapped in burlap, soaking a wad of cotton onto his wound.

Declan spoke of how, just upriver by Charlestown, Indiana, on the Devil's Backbone, a long, high plateau, early explorers had found blue-eyed Indians. "Story goes, locals say, that way back in the twelfth cent'ry, a Welsh prince, Madoc, left his feudin' brothers, sailed all the way over the ocean to this new world, 'n' settled right there, marryin' with the mound-makin' Indians of the time, leavin' blue-eyed descendants among Indians evench'ly from Tennessee all the way up to Lake Erie, an' 'specially right there on Devil's Backbone."

Declan put aside his poultice so little Eugene could climb onto his lap, riding his legs, as Declan said, ever so gently, "Ts, ts, ts, ts—this is the way the ladies ride, ts, ts, ts, ts." Then Declan slightly sped up his pace. "An' this is the way the gentlemen ride—t-dum t-dum, t-dum t-dum, t-dum t-dum, t-dum." Then, slowing and quieting both legs and voice, he said, ever so slowly into Eugene's ear, "And this is the way the farmers ride—" then exploded into a riot of crazy legs, Eugene bounding around with screaming delight: "Hobbledy-hoy, hobbledy-hoy, hobbledy-hoy!" Of course Lucien ended up trying the rides, too. Ti-Drausin was a little big for them, which he regretted.

Lucien whispered in his father's ear that they'd already been to the Devil's Backbone. After a pause, Drausin realized Lucien was remembering Jebediah's reference to Devil's Backbone way back down by Natchez. When he explained Lucien's concern to Declan, the Kaintuck said, "Yes, my boy, anywhere you go, it's possible for the Devil's Backbone to just pop up right here 'n' pop up right there. Any time it does, you jus' look 'em in the eye, spit on the ground', rub it roun', stand up straight, an' say, 'I.' Look 'em in the eye 'n' say 'I.' You look 'em in the eye 'n' say 'I,' 'n' you'll be jus' fine."

Drausin joined a pick-up band with his mandolin, and it wasn't long before people of all ages, children included, were enjoying various reels and squares. Declan took the poultice to his room and returned with a clay jug, which still smelled of Tennessee whiskey; he played the jug like a tuba, joining the band with surprising versatility and even expressiveness in his instrument, fascinating the Wulsin children and many others.

After a while, Jebediah sang along, with increasing confidence, weaving in and out among the verses, the choruses, and the instruments, improvising all sorts of harmonies, like some combination of mockingbird and nightingale, leaving tender tenor tones in the air, touching some women and even some men to tears. At one point Declan asked Drausin to sing the Old Kaintucky Home song, which he did. All the passengers went quiet, listening. At the end the Kentuckians cheered and huzzahed, and many others applauded.

After the music ended, Drausin and Declan enjoyed what might be their final cigars in each other's company. "What're ya gonna do?" The Kaintuck asked the man he'd wanted to pummel early in the trip.

"We don't know. Find our way."

"The way you handled this trip upriver, I know you'll make your way," declared Declan with what Drausin sensed as an extra-knowing assertion in both his glance and voice. Was this Kaintuck implying something about the "success" of this trip as harbinger of what lay ahead? Was Declan giving some go-ahead signal? Drausin could not tell. "You have a fine family, and you're a man of courage."

"I'm not a strong man, Declan."

"You're a man of courage—that can beat stupid strength. I haf to tell you, at first I 'us just blind, sniffin' color under your fancy garb. An you, right away you could see under my new suit, see me, true me, higher than any duds. You didn't just save my chips; you gave me back my real me."

"Thank you, Declan," acknowledged Drausin sincerely, thinking with a wry smile that his father might have disagreed with Kaintuck about courage. "I could here find you, inside of you, in spite of your fists. —And you? What are you going home to, if I may ask?"

Declan drew a thick, rich cloud of smoke from his cigar. "Well, 'bout thirty mile up Lickin' River is Rollin' Crick. I work mos'ly in lumber roun' there. I got my sights set on a sawmill on Rollin' Crick. You should see the paddle wheels turnin' differn' gear wheels, jus' like bein' inside one hefty Swiss Cuckoo clock. Purtiest thing I know, 'cept fer my sweetheart, Katie Simmons. I wan' ta buy that mill an' settle down with her—she's a widow with two girls, so I'd be graftin' a family. She's not all so strong herself. In a way her clock's tickin', but for me that clock slows down'n' stops when I'm with her. I'm her man, 'n' now's our time, which, thanks to you, Mr. Piano Man, I think might jus' happen after all."

"Well, Mr. Kaintuck, those are three lucky ladies—I guess we're all crossing lines, aren't we?"

Declan grinned, remembering his first angry warning to Drausin, back before Vicksburg, back when he'd sniffed the stench of color in that family and saw Cap'n Leathers treating them as well as everyone else. Now, he just saw Drausin, and each member of the family he was coming to love. He shook his head, stepped forward, paused, then grabbed Drausin in an oak-hard bear-hug, whispering, "You'll make your way jus' fine, Drausin, any which way." He released Drausin, and the two men nodded to each other and retired. As he walked toward his cabin, Drausin shook his head, smiling at it all.

Back in the stateroom, after Drausin shared the conversation with Josephine, he tickled her ribs gently. "Josie, Chère, is we a goin' booker?" Then he took her chin in his hand and, looking deeply into her eyes, repeated, "Is we a goin' booker, ma Josie Chérie? Brown soun' goin' down—me'n' you, we's a goin' booker?"

"Oh, chou-chou, carbon zames va done la farine. Coal will never make flour. You can't wash a Negro white, but—" Josephine gulped. Then she nodded, beaming. "Si, mon Cher, all signs on this river trip of ours, these two rivers, the Mississippi and the Ohio, seem to be sayin', yes, we's a goin' booker. I guess we have to try. Oh, mon Dieu." She lay wondering long into their last night on that long river trip, approaching the end of the journey her beloved's chocolate dregs had mapped, wondering and praying. *It was, she realized, a white cup.*

Did Josephine wonder where they might end up living? Yes. Did she worry whether Drausin would get beaten down, or be able to find his way, his chosen way, whatever that may turn out to be? Yes. *Will our boys find work? Will our girls find mates? Can we all "book?" Will our children even survive? Will they shrivel, or thrive, in such Anglo air? Will they keep their faith in the Protestant North? What will we lose, leaving our known world behind? Will I, will they, ever see again Maman, my Young brothers, my Mathé siblings?* Josephine knew she had no answers to most of her questions. But she also knew these questionings played a crucial role in piloting her family into their new harbor as safely as possible.

Around midnight the clouds poured down their riches. This meant that, sometime well before dawn, the rising waters lifted the Natchez III enough for her to shift off the rocks and drift downstream till the engineers fired the boilers enough for her to resume streaming upriver toward Cincinnati. Lucien slept through the liberation of the Natchez, dreaming of a blue-eyed prince drifting down the Ohio River, saying "I," and making families among copper Indians on the Devil's Backbone.

Early the next afternoon, as the Natchez III navigated the narrowing river by North Bend, Ohio, Captain Leathers sounded the steam whistle without landing. The children, seasoned by now to the usual signals and rituals on the steamboat packet, looked about quizzically. Jebediah appeared, as if summoned. "Oh, dat be Norf Ben'. Eb'ry steamboat whistles at Norf' Ben'. Why? Well, de Presiden' Will'm Henry Harrison, he done died pretty quick, only thirty days in 'at White House, 'n' his body got brought down de ribber from Pittsburg all de way to Norf' Ben' to be buried, mebbe back in '41. Eber since den, ebry steamboat toots in tribute to de Presiden' Will'm Henry Harrison, bof acomin' an' agoin'."

Jebediah, always naturally scanning both the waters and the shores, like any river denizen, suddenly hollered out to Captain Leathers, "HO, Cap'n, starboard shore, jus' b'low de crick!" Few could see what the fuss was about. Cap'n Leathers slowed the Natchez, easing, angling over toward the Kentucky shore, where gradually more and more people could discern something rotating slowly in an eddy, just below the mouth of what Esau identified as Potato Creek. Realizing the nature of the floating object sooner than most, the Captain ordered Esau to lower the skiff and head to it. Since the shore offered no large landing, Captain Leathers resolved to idle in the current, in the lee of the point, dropping a bow anchor to ease the task. Groans and moans started to sound along the starboard decks as more passengers could see what floated—a body.

"A man float face down; a woman face de sky," offered Jebediah, who seemed to the children to know something about everything. It was a woman, brown flesh intact. Eyes open, still glistening. Drausin knew that meant pretty "fresh." Some piece of cloth floated like a banner, arm-long, rip-tangled from her wrist. Almost at the same moment, Aline and Josephine gasped, realizing that cloth must have wrapped a baby. They held each other, hardly daring imagine the scene. Jebediah at first started to nod, slowly, then shook his head side-to-side. "Unnergroun' Railroad."

Declan had quietly appeared. "I reckon you're right, son, usu'ly where the river's narrowest. She must have drowned in the strong current, tryin' to swim it, probly chased. She, they, came so close." Jebediah, who early in the trip had watched the Kaintuck warily, had grown gradually more trusting of him. Now he nodded. Something had gone all wrong. Where had the pickup skiff been? Esau and his crew brought the body aboard, wrapped in canvas, to be iced and delivered to Cincinnati, at least part of the runaway's mission accomplished. Lucien wondered if the Natchez III was the Underwater Railroad. Lucien tentatively touched Declan's scar, which was less red, more dried, and no longer dripping.

225

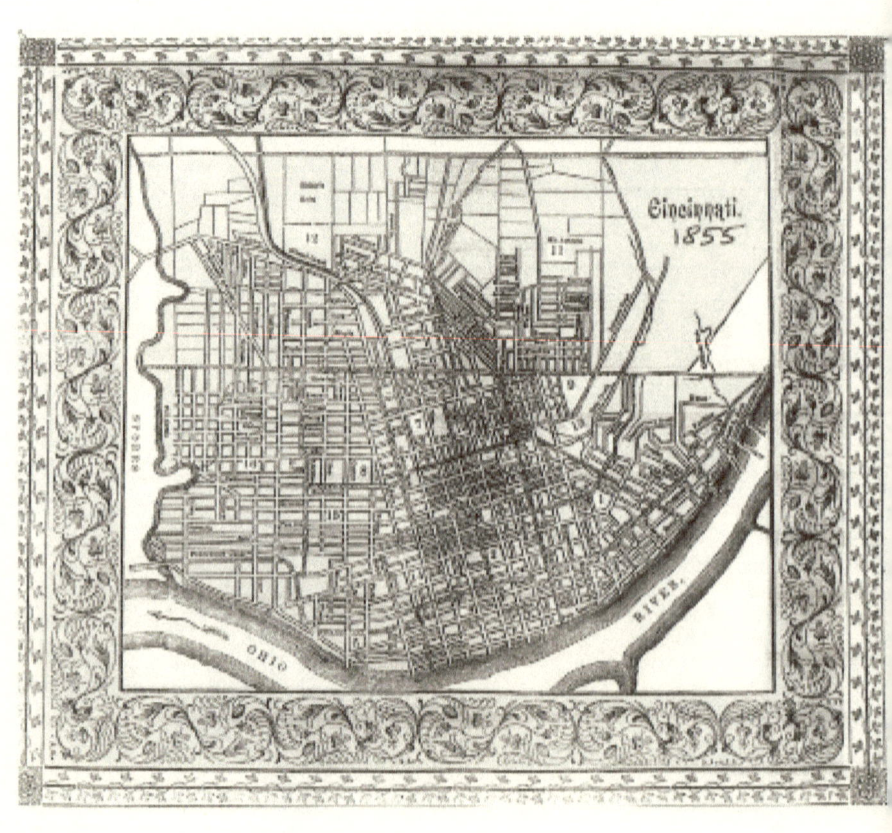

Cincinnati.
1855
OHIO
RIVER

CHAPTER 26:

RAGTOWN, 1851

The Natchez III was bustling. The Wulsin family luggage was carried down to the main deck guard, lined along the railing with other passenger baggage. Drausin smoothed his dark brown jacket, allowing Josephine to straighten his black foulard over his white shirt and beige vest. Josephine also smoothed her grey-checked travel dress, puffing up her lavender choker and perking her straw bonnet with its lavender ribbon. "Well, are we ready to meet our future, Mrs. Wulsin?"

"Why, yes we are indeed, Mr. Wulsin, we are indeed."

The children were back to marching along the decks, chanting, "From orange to apple, from clime to clime, from palm to pine—" and "We've gone from Memphis Tennessee/ on the Miss-i-ssip-pi River/all the way to Cin-cin-nati/on the O-hi-O." Captain Leathers, striding by, stopped. "Mr. Drausin Wulsin, your family has made this a better trip for all of us. I wish you well in your new lives in Cincinnati."

"Captain Leathers, Sir, I thank you, in many ways. You run a fine ship, a fine trip, which has been more important for us than you can know. We arrive in Cincinnati not simply who we were when we left New Orleans. It's a privilege for us and for our children to know you. I think we'll never forget the journey of the spoon around the salt and down through the knives. And may I say, Esau and Jebediah are two fine crew."

"Yes, I agree; they're fine. I wish Esau could be my mate. Good luck to you all." Captain Leathers tipped his captain's hat to Josephine and nodded to each of the children.

At another point, Esau Makely made his way over to Drausin. "Good luck to you, Sir. And thank you for suffering my son. He loves your whole family."

"Thank you, Esau. We love Jebediah; you're raising one fine fellow. And what happens to you both now?"

"Oh, we stay home now for a week, before the Natchez III heads down to Chattanooga on the Tennessee."

"And what do you come home to here, if I may ask?"

"Oh, we jus' stay in a boardin' house. No, no family. Jebediah's mother died bringin' him in. When he got old enough to sail, we hit the river. That's his schoolin', the Ohio an' the Mississip."

"Well, he sure knows more about life than most school-boys."

"I think so, too, but I need to get him some proper schoolin' soon. Cincinnati's got some good schools for the colored, like Gilmore, but I'd have to give up the river. Maybe jus' in winter. I don' know—"

"An' how did you come to Cincinnati, Esau?"

"Oh, an' you might jus' mean how come we's free? Well, my daddy got bought by a Quaker in Pennsylvania, back in Lafayette, 'n' freed, and he made his way to Cincinnati right before I was born. I worked a lotta pork here in the city, but followin' the river's the life for me."

"Yes, I can see that. And you're good. Captain Leathers wishes you could be his mate."

"I do too. I do too—an' you all? What's your plan now?"

"Oh, just find a place and find our way."

After a pause. "C'n I make a suggestion?"

"Why, certainly."

"The colored folks live mos'ly up in Bucktown or east in Little Africa. I'm thinkin' you might want to look to settle in over on the west side of town, down by the Mill Creek, where many newcomers get their start. Over in the Sixteenth Ward. Take a look an' see what you think. Good luck to you all."

Esau looked extra straight at Drausin, before moving on, and Drausin figured he was giving a silent message, which Drausin got. "An' if you need a place to settle while you're looking, you might try Mrs. Griffin's boardin' house over on 421 East Fourth Street."

"Thank you, Esau, thank you. That's mighty helpful. We Wulsins wish you well." Drausin, touched by this conversation, realized he was starting to get used to "Wulsins." He might have missed only one beat before saying the name in the flow of the sentence.

When Jebediah came by, Ti-Drausin went up to him first. "Hello, I am Drau-sin Wul-sin, Prince of Cincinnati. Pleased to meet you."

Jebediah formally raised himself up straight, shook his hand, and said, giving a slight nod, "Pleased to meet you, Sir."

"Hello, I am Lucien Wulsin, Prince of Cincinnati. Pleased to meet you." Handshake, bow.

"Pleased to meet you, Sir."

"Hello, I am Eugene Wulsin, Prince of Cincinnati. Pleased to meet you." Handshake, slightly deeper bow.

"And I—I am Jebediah Makely, the original Prince of Cincinnati. Pleased to meet you, good Sir." Eugene bowed again in response.

"Hello, I am Aline Adelaïde Wulsin, Princesse of Cincinnatesse. Pleased to meet you, Sir." With a curtsy, she extended her hand.

"Jebediah Makely, Original Prince of Cincinnati," he said as he took hers and lowered his head to it. Aline blushed, pleased. The boys clapped. Jebediah was aware that when Declan Fletcher was just *that Kaintuck* back in Natchez, he might well have busted Jebediah's chops, most likely more, for playing this role. Then, having this thought, Jebediah realized he was regarding Aline as white in her role as Princesse. Would Declan?

"An' hey, if you ever gets lost in Cincinnati, I gotta secret fo' you. Come 'roun'." The four older Wulsin children huddled on the deck with Jeremiah, arms on each other's shoulders; his voice lowered. "'Big strong men will very rarely eat pork chops,' he said solemnly. "Repeat affer me."

Baffled, they repeated, "Big strong men will very rarely eat pork chops."

"Das it, das all ya needs to know." Leaving them bewildered, Jebediah shifted quickly into his final stretch as their river guide, pointing out on the Ohio side first Muddy Creek, then Rapid Run, Chippy Run, Boldface Run, and finally Mill Creek.

Declan appeared, reaching into his coat pocket and handing Drausin five cigars. Drausin reached into his own pocket and handed Declan five cigars. Declan pointed to his healing cheek and said, "Thank you, ma'am, an' God Bless."

Josephine nodded with a smile. "And bless you, Declan. You're a good soul."

"Thank you, ma'am."

"And Declan—"

"Yes, ma'am?"

"You can make a good life for you and yours, I can tell. But Declan, you'll make a better life with your hands than with your fists."

"Yes, ma'am, I know. Thank you," he said, his eyes moistening. He tousled the hair of each boy, including Jebediah, and shook Aline's hand. Then an especially firm handshake and a strong, silent look at Drausin.

Noticing Declan's Adam's apple moving in that muscular neck, Drausin said, "Good luck with your mill and everything, Declan," and they nodded, parting. Drausin thought, *How the river always changes, and how the river changes its people. And here goes this Wulsin family, soon to step onto northern, Cincinnati land, to make our new home.*

Drausin and Josephine, approaching Cincinnati, stood hand in hand, finger by finger; Drausin was well aware that Josephine clenched tightly at times, apparently randomly. She huddled close, sheltered below his shoulder. *This trip ends.*

She leaned forward, shading her brow, then gasped and pointed, in a whisper, "Cher, look, the hills surrounding the city— the crown, of the Queen City." Drausin saw and smiled, feeling their future in her green eyes. *Now, the real trip begins. Who knows?*

The Ohio River opened wide. Several sloops glided with curving sails in sweeping arcs. Lucien, his back to the rail, was day-dreaming into the mouth of a smaller river across the river, with buildings and homes on either side, a couple of skiffs wending their ways. As he was wondering which cluster of buildings was Cincinnati, Ti-Drausin pulled his brother's gaze back to their own larboard shore. There it was—a huge city, with fortresses ringed by mountains behind. And down on the shore stood a forest of burnt-black trees, which Lucien quickly realized were steamboat stacks. Even in New Orleans he'd never seen such a dense collection of so many steamboats, moored not head to toe along the shore, but "parked" perpendicular to it, all in a row, shoulder to shoulder, bows out, twenty to thirty of them. Ti-Drausin and Aline read aloud some of the names: New Orleans, Creole Queen, Mary Cole-Licking Packet, the Jacob Strader, New World, Car of Commerce, Telegraph I,

Telegraph II, Brilliant, Messenger, Embassy, Chrystal Palace, and Monongahela. The Natchez III cruised slowly past them to the public landing where there was room for her to nose in, still facing upstream, and unload before shouldering back in among the phalanx of others.

When the hawsers and gangplank were made fast, the Wulsins and all passengers disembarked first, the children and Jebediah waving to each other. After collecting their travel luggage up the sloping shore, they created a pile while Papa Drausin went to make arrangements for storing their cargo until they were settled.

Esau, holding the long canvas-wrapped bundle at one end, was cutting through the crowd, one of his roustabouts carrying the other end. Cutting up to the left, they met at the edge of the crowd two husky men of color accompanied by a third, older, in a suit. The transfer happened, the three men and the bundle disappearing quickly. The children, watching, were impressed with Esau's somber demeanor. Aline, turning to Maman, asked, "Is that—the Railroad?" Josephine nodded, taking her hand.

The children, familiar by now with disembarking, were scanning the town. Ti-Drausin was the first to notice, further up the shore slope atop a two-story front building, a huge model of a steamboat, with two decks and black stacks. The children were in awe. Lucien and Eugene remembered hearing about the great floods of '49 back in New Orleans, so they knew unusual things were possible. They were trying to imagine the flood that put that steamboat up on the roof. Eugene wondered if the Natchez III had ever been up there. Lucien didn't think so. Aline and Ti-Drausin enjoyed their young siblings' perspectives, or lack of.

Just near the roofed boat, atop the next building, flew a huge American flag. With how many white stars on the blue night? The children set to counting. Aline and Ti-Drausin pretty soon came up with the same figure, in spite of the breeze swirling the flag. "Thirty-one!" Josephine asked how they were arranged. Again, Ti-Drausin and Aline figured it out. "One row of seven, one row of six, one of five, one of six, and a bottom row of seven again. Seven, six, five, six, seven. Thirty-one," Aline said. "One for each state of the Union."

Lucien asked, "What's a Union?"

Aline, looking at her mother, said, "All of us together." Josephine nodded. Lucien liked that idea, *That flag, for all of us together.*

With all the passengers and personal luggage ashore, the children heard the crew back at the Natchez singing. Josephine, presiding on the throne of luggage with Laure, gave Aline permission to lead the boys back down the stone-paved riverbank to the base of the gangway, as long as they stayed in sight. Esau's roustabouts were emptying the hold and the deck of passenger trunks, furniture, mahogany planks, barrels of sugar, and cotton bales. Individuals and pairs or trios would take turns singing lines:

> Ah bin mos' eberywhere,
> Ah 'd seen mos' eberyting;
> Shoot craps wid de president,
> An' played kyards wid de king
> All—night—long!

> You wanna know whah we is from?
> It suah will make you shivah;
> We's from dat dar ol' Ragtown
> On de ol' Cincinnati ribber!
> All—night—long!

The Wulsin children joined in the chorus, shouting louder after each verse, delighting the roustabouts.

> Mah job am hustlin' freight
> On de packet Minnie Snow.

Ah'm at de big forward hatch,
An' holler "Look out down be-low!"
All—night—long!

Now, niggahs, roll yoh cotton,
An' rousters, tote yoh corn!
An' listen for de heavenly trumpet
Ob ol' Gabriel's tootin' horn,
All—night—long!

Esau led them to repeat—with special boisterous gusto inspired by the children:

We's from dat dar ol' Ragtown
Un de ol' Cincinnati ribber!
All—night—long!

The children trumpeted, hollered, almost screaming, clapping hands, others too. A few passengers pursed lips, turning away, clearly uncomfortable with the exuberance rising from the hold.

Drausin finished his business and descended the slope, placing hands quietly on Lucien's and Eugene's shoulders. He'd noticed that Esau's singing roustabouts hadn't missed a beat while moving their loads.

As the hired carriage, followed by the luggage wagon, made its way up Broadway, Drausin noticed on 22 Broadway, between Front and Second Streets, a sign for Irwin and Foster, Commission Merchants. He remembered seeing under his lading papers with Captain Leathers back in New Orleans some papers for "S. C. Foster, cotton, Cincinnati." He wondered if this office might belong to that same Foster. Signing those papers had been his own first deed as Drausin Wulsin.

Yes. After just a week, Drausin's name was already feeling less like Declan's brand-new suit.

Mrs. Griffin was a slightly worn, taut lady, whose boarding house was neither in Bucktown nor in Little Africa, but at 421 East Fourth St. She beheld the distinguished gentleman entering in dark brown frock coat and double-breasted vest. She looked out through the dusk at the rest of the family of seven in the carriage, looked back at him, and welcomed him, to Drausin's great relief. "It's thinkin' I am we might just manage you all. We could put a third cot in with the children, if you'll be havin' have the baby in with you. How long?"

"Likely a month."

Later, Drausin helped put the older children to sleep, Aline in one bed, Ti-Drausin in the cot, Eugene and Lucien in the other bed, after a hearty meal of pork and potatoes, a little heavy for the rice-accustomed Creoles. The Wulsin family's first night in Cincinnati. Lucien asked his father, "Am I going to be the Prince of Cincinnati, or the Prince of Ragtown?"

"Good question, mon Vieux. Maybe both, maybe both—"

Aline and Ti-Drausin chimed in, "All—night—long!" Eugene was already snoring.

PART 3

CHAPTER 27:

FIRST PERCH, 1851

Josephine, in an auburn cotton dress, led her family like a raft of ducklings four blocks north to the St. Peter in Chains Cathedral, at Plum and Eighth Streets on their first Sunday in Cincinnati. Its mighty size matched St. Louis Cathedral and seemed to her like the heart of their new city. Arriving early, the Wulsins were fortunate to find room in a back pew to squinch into together. Grand with Greek pediments and pillars, the cathedral was soon full to overflowing.

As soon as the mass began, Josephine thought, *What a relief. The frankincense, my timeless Latin ritual—here, my home away from home. The Latin feels like an old godmother of our own French.* She drank in the priest's words: "In Nomine Patris, et Filii, et Spiritus Sancto—et Mater Dolorosa." In her own prayers she thanked Mother Mary and Jesus himself for having helped them to journey safely. She asked for their blessings in the Wulsins' new lives in Cincinnati.

Watching others, Josephine wondered if any other family in the church might be from Louisiana. Most seemed either German or a strange kind of English she hardly understood, which Drausin clarified for her as Irish. Were any others people of color? It did not seem so. Any others? *Oh, mon Dieu.* She caught herself, chuckling. *It's one thing to remember we're Wulsins. To remember as well we're bookin'—ain't colored no more, so far anyway. Hard work.*

As they departed, she turned toward the altar, knelt, and crossed herself, thanking St. Peter that the Wulsin family was doing its best to shed its potential chains. She thought of Drausin's mother, Adelaïde, freedom-bought by her sister, freely giving herself to Barthelemy. She thought of her own mother, Josephine, and her mother's mother, Marie-Françoise, glad she had such able, independent models, owners of property, and yes, owners of slaves. Josephine said a prayer for Claire, hoping she was finding her way "unchained." Aline knelt even more deeply, crossing herself, moving her lips in prayer, clearly touched in this new yet familiar sanctuary.

After Sunday lunch at Mrs. Griffin's boarding house, Aline helped Josephine settle the children for naps, and father Drausin headed back out into their new city. Having noticed Richmond St., one block north of St. Peter in Chains, and remembering Esau's advice, he followed it west, finding himself drawn gradually south toward that Ohio River he'd spent several days and nights on, both respecting and fascinated by it. Walking down Carr St., he found the Whitewater Canal, a bit like a busy bayou, heading due west all the way into Indiana. He liked this pocket of town, near both the restless river and the gentle canal.

In the coming week, Drausin returned with a realtor, sans famille, and chose 139 Carr, a white, narrow clapboard house close to other similar houses, with three floors and a stoop in front; a living and dining room and kitchen, on the first floor; three bedrooms on the second; and two on the third. There was a small alley in back for an eventual horse and buggy. Rent was monthly, the lease year-by-year. The whole transaction went smoothly, helped no doubt by his distinguished appearance and manner, clinched by gold.

Gold whitens, he reminded himself on the way back to Mrs.

Griffin's. *Our gold whitens our secret race as we strive to pass. Gold is our silent key, making our way.* His smile curved up on his right, down on his left. How would he have fared in the Sixteenth Ward here without the gold?

I am glad it is good gold, from selling instruments, selling property I alone, and then Josephine and I together, had purchased. No bad gold; we never sold Claire, thank heavens, just gave her her freedom. And Maman Adelaïde secretly, and Josephine's mother Josephine discreetly, each gave us five hundred dollars in gold. So it's three thousand dollars in good Bacas gold, ballast for this Wulsin family's life-voyage.

Josephine was thrilled. Their first home as a family. It lacked both the surrounding spaciousness under the grand sheltering live oaks of Bayou Rd. and the simple elegance of 116 St. Louis, but nonetheless it was the first home of their own, eleven years after their wedding. A good enough place to start their new lives. They would be able to move in a month. Their furniture would come from storage.

The children loved the July Fourth parade celebrating independence, which proceeded up Vine St. to the Miami Canal, chock full of freight barges and lined with spectators, then went west along it for four blocks, then turned down Western Row to the real waterfront. Lucien was amazed at how wide, fast, and swirling the Ohio River looked from the side—that river that had been their home for several days and nights. They could not find the Natchez III's red stacks among the flotilla of steamboats along the bank.

"Jebediah and Esau must have already embarked on the Natchez III's next journey to Chattanooga," Aline recalled.

"Chatta-chatta-chatta-chatta, chatta chatta-nooo-gahh!" chanted Lucien and Eugene incessantly.

Drausin and the older four children followed the parade all the way, circling back up from the river to Mrs. Griffin's.

They saw many American flags, with, yes, thirty-one stars, which Lucien found he could count. Some veterans of the Mexican War, and even the War of 1812, were marching in front of the bands. Drausin thought of his father Barthelemy and Nonc Drauzin, his father's cousin. *Nonc Drauzin, my name-sake. Papa Barthelemy, with his hatred of all things American, would certainly not be marching today. Nonc Drauzin, our good uncle, perhaps.*

After supper, settling into sleep, Lucien was dreaming of wars and cannons when he was shaken awake by Ti-Drausin, who pointed out the window to a sky of exploding suns and stars; they watched for what felt like hours. Papa and Aline joined them, assuring that they were not being cannon-blasted. No houses fell. No wounded shrieked. Eugene climbed onto the windowsills, jumping onto beds, arms stretched out, shout-blasting as he sputtered flames down onto those assembled in the room. Aline wondered aloud if Mount Vesuvius might have looked anything like that when it erupted back in Roman times. "Maybe, but redder," said Papa.

He later learned from Mrs. Griffin that a Mr. Diehl had built a wooden platform, called the Pyro Garden, on the top of Mt. Adams to set off fireworks for the city, which he hoped to do annually for many years.

As the children settled back toward sleep with fireworks continuing to explode in their minds, Josephine, who with little Laure had watched the parade go by Mrs. Griffin's, said to Drausin, "Well, we are certainly living in a white town."

"Yes," he smiled, nodding.

"And many shades of white," she said.

"Yes. One of the boarders was saying that, in addition to the buckskinned squirrel hunters from the hills, we have horny-handed Ohio and Kaintuck farmers, Pennsylvanians, Virginians, Marylanders, New Yorkers, New Jerseyans, and not only many Germans, Irish, and Italians, but many Jewish people too, from different countries in Europe. But, among gens de couleur, I saw as many shades of brown as we have back in New Orleans. Remember, Esau's rousties sometimes sang, 'Shallo Brown,' about passing over a darker woman for 'a bright mulatto, she's from Cincinnati'? Now I see why."

"Cher, how are we going to cross over, all of us? Lucien? Me? All of us?" She laid her head on his shoulder. "Lucien's got thicker lips and darker skin than any of us, and I, with my widish nostrils?"

"And you, and you, chou-chou, are my beautiful, green-eyed Daphne, Oh-o-oh, Mah Lady, Oh-o-oh, Mah Lady, Oh-o-oh, Mah Lady Jo-o-oe." Josephine melted into laughter and into her beloved Drausin. He continued, "We will cross over—Lucien, you, all of us. We'll make even more shades of white." And he stroked her naturally wavy dark brown hair, which she still always wore up in public after years of the habit of the tignon, although in boarding the Natchez she had allowed the bonnet to serve the transition. Now, in Cincinnati, Josephine might wear a hat or nothing at all on her head. She loved the breeze blowing through her hair, fresh-tingling. "How, mon Cher, how?"

Drausin continued, "Chèrie, I do not know. We're rabbits trying to trick the trickster, Bouki the hyena. All I know is, I didn't know if Captain Leathers would take our tickets. I didn't know if Captain Leathers would let us eat in the Natchez III's dining hall. I didn't know if the Kaintuck would bust my nose. But we ended up dining with the captain and swapping cigars, even making music, with that Kaintuck." They chuckled, recalling Declan bending notes on his Tennessee whisky-jug, his healing cheek wound having cracked off the clay caking of her compress.

"Yes," Drausin continued, "we're new people—Wulsins. Our Bacas has gone silent, like your Young. But we're still Drausin and Josephine. We're only shifting from dusk to dawn—you know, from orange to apple, from palm to pine—just from dusk to dawn, like your beautiful, dawn-colored skin. You'll see, you'll see," Drausin repeated.

Occasionally, in the broad daylight of ensuing days, Josephine noticed Mrs. Griffin observing the children and her closely. The landlady stopped greeting the children by name, kept her distance. She no longer looked Josephine in the eye. Josephine, worried, told Drausin of Mrs. Griffin's cooling behavior toward them.

That evening after supper, Drausin sat down at Mrs. Griffin's piano and started wandering around, meandering wherever his fingers, ear, and mood led him. Eventually, he started playing some pieces popularized by the Christy Minstrels, such as "Old Folks at Home," which led into everyone's favorite, closing with:

I say, I'm comin' from the South,
Susanna, don't you cry.

The children and some of the other boarders joined in on the chorus. Drausin remembered the banzes played by Senegambian slaves at Congo Square back in his teens. He also knew he had no intention of going back to Lou'siana himself ever again. He wondered how Declan might be faring with his Kentucky widow by the mill. Which led to Drausin singing,

... my old Kentucky home, good night.

Mrs. Griffin, standing right by the piano in her usual grey basketweave dress, was beholding Drausin as a wonder. After some moments she said, "Mr. Wulsin, do you know where 'Oh Susanna' was composed?"
"Why, no."
"Right on this piano you are playing."
Drausin was stunned. "Stephen Foster, here?"
"Yes, he lived in your boys' room for three years till he

moved back to Pittsburgh early last year." Silence all around. "And may I say, Sir, you make his songs sound like him." Drausin, touched, nodded in modest and surprised appreciation. "But that last song you just played, 'My Old Kentucky Home, Good Night,' I think he has not even published yet. How do you know it?"

"Mrs. Griffin, I heard it sung by stevedores on the docks of New Orleans."

"Oh yes, of course. After a day's work bookkeeping at his brother's mercantile office on Front St., he'd often go down by the steamboats to listen to the cooks and roustabouts singing. Sometimes he'd sing them one of his pieces, hear them sing it, and then make adjustments. His songs traveled up and down the rivers."

"Like a liquid telegraph. Are you referring to the office of 'Irwin and Foster,' at 22 Broadway?"

"Yes, that's it; they moved from Front St. in '49."

"Not S. C. Foster, by chance?"

"No. Stephen's brother, Dunning, is still Irwin's partner." Drausin looked at this Reuss piano's keys, the white ones and the black ones, with new respect and affection, his own fingers following patterns Stephen Foster's fingers had found on them.

That night Drausin reflected with Josephine on the mysterious coincidence of starting their new life in the same boarding house in which Stephen Foster had both lived and composed. Drausin kept imagining young Foster listening in the steamboat galleys and on the docks, singing back and forth with the stevedores.

"Josie, I think many of these river songs, however diluted and disturbed visually by the ridiculous blackface performers on the stage of the Floating Theater, have nevertheless been imbued with the spirit of the roustabouts who work the rivers up and down the main arteries of the land. Stephen Foster, crafting their songs onto paper, gave them voice through the years, the decades—maybe even centuries. Through all their labors, Josie, these workers become co-composers of many songs of the land, songs which move all kinds of souls, black, all colors, and white, all up and down the whole creation."

"Mon Cher, what you say rings true to me."

Mrs. Griffin gave the Wulsins a week's free rent so long as Drausin played each night, which he did. And Mrs. Griffin became more gracious to Josephine, tending to Aline and Laure especially affectionately, usually giving each of the four older children an extra cookie. On the Wulsin family's last night in her boarding house, Mrs. Griffin mentioned that Stephen Foster told her once that he was reaching for, listening for, some kind of "African-white music, some night'n' day blend."

"Mrs. Griffin, I think Mr. Foster just might have succeeded."

From the new center of their lives, 139 Carr St. in western Cincinnati, it did not take Josephine long to find a close enough place of worship, the brand-new St. Patrick's Church, one year old, about five blocks east on Third Street and Mill. Lacking the majestic grandeur of St. Peter in Chains, St. Patrick's nevertheless shined, already showing twelve stations of the cross around the nave. The window glass was simple. But Josephine was pleased, proud of this new church in their new neighborhood.

Most of the parish sounded and even looked Irish, sons and daughters of St. Patrick. Fair to ruddy complexions. Red hair and freckles sprinkled generously among them. The Wulsin children, who had never seen so many freckles, were sad not to find a single one among themselves. Father Matthew Mackey welcomed the Wulsins warmly, a cue followed by the good Catholic families at church.

In those early weeks, Drausin walked and walked, exploring the city, scouting what work he might find, often taking Aline, Ti-Drausin, and Lucien along. Sometimes Eugene came too, usually leading them as he scrambled. Often enough though he stayed at home with his mother and Laure, content to be king of the new castle for a while.

Shops galore offered exotic fare: sweetmeats from Havana, sealskins from the Pacific, oysters from Philadelphia. At newsstands, Aline noticed ladies buying *Godey's Lady's Book* and *The Ladies Repository*. Men bought *Harper's*. This midwestern city had four German-language newspapers! The Wulsins often heard German conversations passing them by on the sidewalks. Among various signs for astrologers, fortune-tellers, and healers, Aline was particularly intrigued by "Miss Tennessee Claflin, 'Magnetic Doctress,' who can see past, present, and future, make paralytics walk, and cure cancer in four to twenty-four hours." The boys were more interested in John Hunt's Apple Butter wagon rolling by.

Cincinnati's markets were huge, seeming to go on for a mile on some streets. Typically, chickens cost twelve cents a pair, eggs six cents a dozen, beef eight cents a pound, and pork four cents a pound. Drausin learned that at certain times of year spareribs were given away free at the packing houses. Come fall, the newcomer Wulsins would certainly learn why. Peaches, pears, apples—all cost four cents a pound.

"Hey, from orange to apple, from palm to pine! Finally apples, hooray!" shouted the children with glee, renewing their old chant on the street. And they started to understand Mrs. Griffin having served meat and potatoes three times a day. There were tripe and pigs' feet, hasenpfeffer—peppered rabbit—sauerkraut, smoked sausage, mackerel, shad, and gemisch—ham bone, cabbage, and potatoes cooked together. Potato pancakes, cinnamon kuchen, steamed apple dumplings, cherries, strawberries, red bananas, and blancmange made with Irish moss.

Blancmange soon became the children's favorite. "Warm

the almonds," the plump frau told Aline, who listened keenly, so Maman could do it right. "Let them steep in milk overnight, dear; thicken it with powdered almonds until it jells. Serve it cold, with raspberry sauce, and you'll have a happy family." Aline soon made blancmange herself.

Sometimes Drausin walked the children east along the river so they could cruise the shipyards, most of which were down beyond the public landing, by Delta Avenue and the Rookwood Crossing. They loved the smells of the woods, the sawdust, the glues, and the caulking tools. They loved the music, the beats of banging hammers and mauls, the regular rhythms of the fletch saws, and finally, the brilliant use of levers and pulleys maneuvering steam engines into place.

They passed the Lithreebury Co., the Marine Railway Dry Dock, and Samuel Humbleton. The James Mack yards had built the Reuben Springer, which made it from New Orleans to Cincinnati in five days, twelve hours, and forty-five minutes, a legendary race the children had heard of on their trip north. Little Lucien felt he was observing an ant farm or a beehive, fascinated by how well all the workers seemed to dance together at their various tasks. Drausin was not surprised to learn in the coming months that their new city supplied more steamboats for the United States of America than any city other than Pittsburgh.

Further on, a sign in the window of Niles & Co. informed the public that, having made sugar mills, stationary engines, machine tools, and rolling mills since 1834, it was now commencing to build locomotive engines. Did Drausin imagine how locomotives would soon replace steamboats? Probably not. But his sons certainly would. Lucien asked, "If a steam engine can go on water, can one go on land?"

"It seems so, little Lucien," Papa replied. "Men here are learning how."

Walking back west, the Wulsins passed brewery after brewery, including Herancourt and the Eagle, housing huge copper vats, hundreds of barrels, and mallets thumping in cooperages galore. Drausin was not surprised to learn that Cincinnati was the nation's largest producer of beer and liquor.

They passed furniture shop after furniture shop, most impressed by one; they gradually realized, watching through the window, that the various workers were ordered, coordinated, and directed by the master, who was—black. "Henry Boyd," said the sign. The children were fascinated by the spinning lathes, curving elegant legs, pedal-run band-saws and press drills, the whole ranges of colors and smells of various woods, thoroughly familiar, of course, to Papa Drausin, but only a memory of Barthelemy's shop for Aline and Ti-Drausin. Lucien was particularly impressed by the harmony of the work of the people with their tools and their machines.

"Lucien, your grandfather Barthelemy and his sons, your uncles, were all fine furniture makers in New Orleans."

"And you, our own father," said, Ti-Drausin.

"Yes, and I, your father, that is true."

"Are you going to work for Mr. Boyd, Papa?" asked Lucien.

"I, oh no, I don't think so." Drausin knew that his most marketable craft, woodwork, would never emerge to support the Wulsin family. It had been shattered like that chair in that fractured scene with the furious father and the four persistent, resistant sons. That page had long been closed for Drausin no-longer-Bacas Wulsin.

Maybe I will some day, thought Lucien.

Nevertheless, Drausin was impressed to read weeks later in *The Cincinnati Enquirer* that Cincinnati had more than a thousand woodworkers in one hundred and thirty-six furniture shops, making the city the chief furniture maker in the Midwest.

Back home, Josephine received regular visits at 139 Carr St. from street vendors and merchants. The butcher came daily, cutting chops on his wagon tailgate. The dry goods vendor offered bolts of gingham, flannel, cashmere, and silk; he fitted corsets, taking measurements and returning the completed garment the following week. Josephine had noticed that women in Cincinnati tended to wear long "street-sweepers," with gores, flutings, braid, and bead trimmings. The classy ladies wore silk or luster, a silk sunshade, and elegant boots of light bronzed leather. Josephine held back for now on a street-sweeper, feeling that would be presumptuous.

The drayman's beer wagons rolled by constantly, even though the secret Creoles of 139 Carr St. continued to prefer wine to the ubiquitous, sour-bodied German beers. The whiskey seller came by twice weekly. The tea and spice men aspired to put a library in each home, offering coupons redeemable in books with each purchase.

At night Drausin and Josephine reflected on their scouting reports of the day, both what they went out to discover and what presented itself to 139 Carr. "Chérie, this city breathes," said Drausin. "It moves at a different pace."

"Yes, I've noticed. Even out the window. Back home people amble, relaxing, enjoying the walking, the air."

"Yes, like the waters of the bayou, seeming not to go somewhere. By contrast, these Queen City streets hustle, busy, bustle, push, rush, buzz, hum, chugga-chugga twooo, twoooo." Josephine smiled as Drausin continued. "Cincinnati's in high gear, as though its people pulse with the beat not only of the steamboats but even already with the new railroad engines.

"Chérie, do you think so many men in their cassinet coats wear congress gaiters, those ankle-high boots with elastic at each side, to sustain the race of the streets?"

"Perhaps. Will you buy a pair of congress-gaiters?"

Drausin smiled. "I think not. I'm not ready yet to chugga-chugga twooo, twoooo."

"Well, I have ordered a pair of those bronzed boots," Josephine declared. However, she did not speak of one of her motivations, which was that she felt they might lighten her skin by contrast.

CHAPTER 28:

WALKING, 1851

Josephine overheard in the markets some women of color speaking of the Negro public schools in Cincinnati, active since 1844. Then the State of Ohio had officially granted an Independent Colored School System, one of the first in the nation. She wondered if that might not be, in fact, the best learning environment for their children. She and Drausin wondered together if they should reassess their options.

One night Drausin went to the Wesleyan Church to listen in on the Second Anti-Slavery Convention of Cincinnati. Drausin stood in the shadows of the church interior, not wanting to identify with or be identified with the anti-slavery movement, although his own anti-slavery sentiments were key to his family's move to Cincinnati. Henry Bibb, a large mulatto man, spoke of having been betrayed back into slavery in Cincinnati years ago while trying to rescue his wife. One eye shone wide open; the other almost squinted closed. Several times he had been re-enslaved down south, escaped and recaptured before his "final," current freedom. In fact, seven times in the 1830s and '40s, Henry Bibb had been bought and sold, each time by one "Christian" minister to another.

A distinguished statesman then stood, looked out upon the audience—seemingly all the way back to Drausin—and spoke, sounding to Drausin like a combination of Moses and his brother Aaron. Stuttering Moses had received the word of the Lord; his brother had communicated it to the chosen people with both heavenly eloquence and earthly force. Drausin thought of this strong Frederick Douglass, *Here is a man, chiseled from hickory or oak, who serves as the best model for anyone. His words shine with hard-earned truth, like the well-sharpened blade of an axe, yet sometimes flying, soaring with the beauty of a brilliant bird.* Drausin was bewildered for many days and nights by some nagging association triggered by both the sight and sound of Douglass.

Finally, one afternoon, upon entering a high-ceilinged room at the Mercantile Library, Drausin got it: The elusive connection surfaced from memory, like some sea-creature into daylight. Tree-straight Douglass's firm jaw, almost hatchet nose, and broad, furrowed brow, with eyes tirelessly reading the audience, had reminded him, he now realized, of a certain young white man in straw hat and blue trousers whom he had noticed in the rotunda of the New Orleans Hotel St. Louis over twenty years ago.

Certain of Douglass's words kept returning to Drausin like a refrain, resounding musically. Douglass had said, "A contest had in fact been going on in my mind for a long time, between the plausible makeshifts of theology and superstition, and the clear consciousness of right. The one held me an abject slave—a prisoner for life, punished for some transgressions in which I had no lot or part; the other counseled me to manly endeavor to secure my freedom."

Once Drausin had brought into clarity his memory's association between Fredrick Douglass and that young white man decades ago in the Hotel St. Louis, he remembered that at Douglass's anti-slavery convention the previous week, Drausin had also been deeply impressed with a man who had not said a single public word that night. Up on the dais with Bibb and Douglass now sat that white man with a brow broad as sunrise, his strong, warm eyes clearly lending the support of his presence to the occasion. Drausin could sense the mutual respect among the three men, especially a relaxed, affectionate regard between Douglass and the white man. Drausin had whispered to his neighbor, "Who is that next to Douglass?"

"Oh, that's Mr. Salmon P. Chase, our US Senator for the State of Ohio; we've long called him our Attorney General for Fugitive Slaves. Back 'mos' ten years ago, he he'ped Lydia Mott 'n' others start the Cincinnati Orphan Asylum for Colored Children."

Drausin walked home from the library that warm night, gas lights illuminating moving shadows; he felt his will reinforced, his conviction re-rooted. He and Josephine had chosen wider skies of liberty, had chosen a place where they could walk anywhere, anytime, north of the Ohio River. Inwardly Drausin declared to himself, *My manly endeavor may be small; but it will be devoted to assure that our Wulsin children must not be burdened, shadowed by the risks of enslavement themselves.* Josephine's and his initial intuition, their gamble, was now being affirmed.

That night in their bedroom, Josephine listened to Drausin's recent reflections. "Since, back on Bayou Rd., we first conceived of 'bookin'' up north," Josephine said, "we have been digging down through layers of soil, layers of possibility in this bold, unfamiliar venture of ours. At each layer, we have found ourselves, one or the other or both, reconsidering, wondering. Now, through this question of the children's schooling, you and I, husband and wife, father and mother, we feel to me like two birds in one tree, of one mind, singing one song, maybe even 'bob whites.'" Josephine smiled.

Drausin chuckled, "Bob whites. Oh, ma Daphne, ma Josie, Ma Joe-oe-oe," kissing her on the forehead and holding her hard.

They were ready to root, to put in the final topsoil, and tamp firmly. Their only way to assure the freedom of their Wulsin children was indeed to stay in the shadows of the anti-slavery movement in order to secure the sunlight of life-long liberty for themselves, and, above all, for their children.

"Our Wulsin children will go," concluded Drausin, "not to the good colored schools, but to the 'regular' Twelfth District School, not far from home. Like some others fleeing north, they will 'pass' into the light of being white."

"Or," Josephine realized as equally valid, "claim their right, being in fact more white than not."

"Ma chère," said Drausin, "I notice my growing ability to read signs, to recognize other people of light color living the other side of the almost invisible gauze scrim of the white world. Subtle signals, like a gambler's 'tells'—mutual recognitions, a moment's glance followed by lowered eyes, the slightest nod, the barest ripple on the waters of normal circulation, or even the kind of night breeze so slight it shows no ripple at all."

"Yes, mon Drausin, I too. So slight the signals, but clear it seems. Unfortunately, I feel often that, of course, there are always darker people who can clearly read our passing, in ways the whites can not."

More uncomfortable for Drausin and Josephine were these experiences, which largely they chose to ignore, though they always pained inwardly, pain they accepted however as their sacrifice, the 'pound of flesh' they had to pay, part of the price of 'bookin'.' The loss of the lake of brown, as they learned to swim in the sea of white. And of course in their pond at home, they were each other's familiar South, familiar French, familiar Catholic, and familiar shades of brown, however light.

"Ma Josie, I have also realized that, perhaps since freeing Claire and leaving the port and world of New Orleans, I have had no recurrences of that old nightmare, the grimacing, torturing slavemaster and the grimacing, tortured slave, in their interchanging waltz of mutual agony—so far."

"Ahh, grâce a Dieu; that sounds like a blessing in our progressing."

❧

254

Having resolved the question of their children's schooling, Josephine remembered how they had oriented the children on the Natchez III, practicing to become "Wulsin." By now, the children had settled comfortably into their new name. Only Aline, now twelve, at times silently longed for the music of "Bacas," reinforced by the rich texture of cousins, aunts and uncles, and grandparents associated with it; many of her memories had continued evaporating, though, since the ruptured exodus from 116 St. Louis St. five years earlier. The boys, Ti-Drausin, Lucien, and Eugene, immersed themselves in their new world, today and tomorrow having more currency than yesterday. Little Laure had no memory of New Orleans anyway.

"Children," said Father Drausin, "You may or may not have noticed that most Negroes, and our gens de couleur, usually look down, sometimes up to heaven, but almost never straightforward, horizontally, eye to eye—certainly not with the whites, but often not even with each other. We have the right, we have the white, and frankly, we have the need to look anyone in the eye, man or woman, white or colored. We, and you, when you go to school, shake anyone's hand firmly; look everyone in the eye. Speak clearly. Answer directly. Your mother and I will ask you the color of the eyes of your teachers and your classmates. Do you each understand?" Heads nodded.

"Now, as we did on the Natchez, and as you all did so well, I want each of you to step forward to each of us, look us in the eye, introduce yourself, shake our hand, and tell us each the color of our eyes." Which they dutifully did, Laure still too shy, five-year-old Eugene gigglingly exaggerating into an over-bold glare. Aline, Drausin, and Lucien maturely, even naturally, obliged. For the week before school began, the family practiced its greeting ritual, training the soldiers to go forth.

Another day Papa added, "Children, slaves answer questions, but don't dare ask them. Make sure you ask questions at school. Each one of you, each one of us, has the right to ask any question that comes to mind, as long as you think twice first and ask respectfully. When you go to school, each one of you must ask at least one question every day. Do you understand? Now, after you shake our hand and tell us each the color of our eyes, ask us a question, any question."

Like the rest of the walking city of Cincinnati, the Wulsins walked everywhere: to school, to shops, to church. Each morning Josephine brushed hair and inspected the children for their proper clothing. On Lucien's face, arms, and legs, she always put some Shea butter, which the others hardly needed. Aline was proud of her rose matelasse dress, with its almost knit weave, trés chic. On the first day of school, Drausin walked his three older children several blocks north and east to the Twelfth District School at the corner of Eighth and Donnersberger. Their new school fed into Hughes High School, a few blocks down on Fifth and Mound; its first graduating class of high school seniors that very year had six girls and four boys.

Aline, young Drausin, and Lucien listened keenly to their teachers, and to their classmates, absorbing every accent, pronunciation, intonation, syllable, word, phrase, and accompanying gesture with full focus. Aline loved the day, except she realized on the playground that girl classmates regarded her rose matelasse as suspicious. It never left the closet again that fall. Aline relied on a plain white poplin dress and a light pink sateen most weeks.

Now spending most of their days immersed in English at home, the children loved speak-playing with their new words and phrases, which seemed to Papa almost dripping wet, fresh expression. "I would like to intro-duce you to..." became a favorite one week, introducing everyone and everything in the household to each other, most graciously, always eyes directly on their audience. Within days, weeks, and months, their English became almost indistinguishable from their classmates', Lucien imitating most malleably, then Ti-Drausin, and then Aline, with non-schooling Eugene imitating them all.

Cincinnati's school system had long offered and even required German for all students, so the Wulsins' German led them to some of English's non-Greco-Roman/Latin vocabulary, words like "machen" (make, machine), "lernen" (learn), and "nacht" (night). Each of the three young scholars strove, and even competed with each other proudly, to fashion their penmanship as artfully, clearly, and consistently as their spoken words, aiming to become worthy scriveners.

At night, Drausin said to Josephine, "The ways our children learn English, we all learn White."

Replied Josephine, "I think you all are learning both far better than I am."

Among the Cincinnati youth, some typical childhood tendencies effectively constrained at church spilled onto the school playground. Fourth-grader Drausin had a knack for appearing the moment any of Lucien's big, Irish, first-grade classmates teased him about his knickers, lips, skin, or accent. "Don't ye wash? Don't ye wash?" Lucien would stand still, enduring, eyes moist with hurt, but stoic. Sometimes, he instinctively closed his good eye; then he could hear in the taunter's voice something subtle—fear. And he wondered why: Who had hurt that bully-boy?

Drausin would appear right near, timely, silent. The second time, young Drausin's strong look, like a spear, put an end for good to any teasing that might have monstered into bullying.

Drausin's own English was quickly good enough, and he was game enough in the games, especially town-ball, hitting with a broomstick a stone tied into a rag-ball, that he fast earned his place in the class and school, excelling in everything, which allowed Lucien to settle into his place more quietly.

In those first weeks of school especially, it was not unusual for the children to walk home, fall asleep after a snack and then, after supper, fall asleep pretty early, so tired were they from their keen attention to everything new, every sound they heard, every gesture in the people around them hinting at the ways to make their way, to navigate, as though they were learning to breathe new kinds of air. After the first week of shepherding the children back and forth, Papa Drausin felt confident in assigning Aline to captain the walking crew both ways.

Over the ensuing weeks, the walking crew began exploring their walking city on their own after school. Of course, inevitably they got lost one day, confused about what went where. At a certain point, Lucien blurted out, "I've got it! 'Big strong men'!"

"What?" said the others, clueless.

"'Big strong men.' Remember, Jebediah's secret just before landing? What street are we on?"

"Sycamore."

"And we crossed, back a block...?"

"Broadway."

"And look ahead a block..."

"Main."

"'Big strong men' means B, S, M—Broadway, Sycamore, Main," declared little Lucien. His older sister and brother were amazed. And the rest?

Ti-Drausin remembered, "Big strong men will very rarely—" and Aline, "—eat pork."

"Big strong men will very rarely eat pork!" The children raced west on Eighth St. to find, block by block, "will—Walnut!—very—Vine!—rarely—Race!—eat—Elm!—pork—Plum! Hooray! That's it, east to west: 'Big strong men will very rarely eat pork'—Broadway, Sycamore, Main, Walnut, Vine, Race, Elm, and Plum!"

In front of St. Peter in Chains, their first church as strangers to the city, the three Wulsin children huddled, arms on each other's shoulders, and for a moment, disturbing the pace and peace of the pedestrians as they shouted, "Oh, Jebediah, thank you! You gave us the key to navigating Cincinnati!"

Then Lucien said, "Hey, we forgot somethin'. Wait here." He ran off west along Eighth St. and returned huffing in five minutes. "Yup, we forgot 'chops.'" The others were quizzical. "Big strong men will very rarely eat pork-chops."

"You're right! And what did you find?"

"Central Avenue. Pork then chops. Plum then Central."

And one final time, all chorused, "Thank you, Jebediah!"

CHAPTER 29:

PORKIN' AND POETRY, 1851

Another afternoon after school, the three elder children ventured way up to the Miami–Erie Canal, Aline in her white poplin dress, Drausin and Lucien in grey cotton knickers and vests. Pretty far east, they noticed a gang of about ten boys in a motley array of worn knickers, frayed vests, and old anklejacks, about Aline's age, each holding a four- to five-foot stick. Not looking for trouble, the Wulsins kept moving, dawdling here and there alongside canal boats. Some homes and factories were just tossing their garbage out on the streets. At times balcony-emptied buckets would have slopped them with rot-food if they weren't watchful.

At one point strange sounds stirred behind them, bizarre, increasing. Another army of zombie-slaves, like the one in Natchez? No. Instead, sloughing, grunting, and snorting, scores of black, white, red, and brown pigs appeared around the corner, knee-high, waist-high, some even shoulder-high for little Lucien, who sheltered behind his older brother as the pigs licked up slops on the cobblestones, driven forward by some of those same boys with sticks, a few on each side, several in the back.

"Hey," called Drausin, "where ya takin' those hogs?"

"Langton's Porkhouse, right up the street, this batch."

"Whatya get?"

"We each get a penny a herd." One cocked his straw hat, reached into his pocket, pulled out a copper, and flipped it in the air, catching and re-pocketing it with a proud smile. "We're the Princes of Porkopolis."

At the same time the pigs were cleaning up the slops in the streets, they were leaving slops of their own. For months in the fall, hogs and cattle dominated the streets of Cincinnati. As the slaughterhouses went into full operation, the children had noticed the canal waters going red, with pigs' tails, hooves, knuckles, and even occasionally heads floating by. Aline stepped the streets ever so gingerly to avoid staining her shoes red or brown. Drausin and Lucien looked at each other.

"They don't know we're already the Princes of Cincinnati," said Drausin with a grin.

"Yep," replied Lucien, "but I'd sure like to become Princes of Porkopolis, putting proud pennies in our pockets." Drausin nodded to that.

Papa Drausin had heard that Cincinnati packed more pork than Belfast or Cork. Its pigs came to market in Cincinnati from all around southern Ohio, Indiana, and northern Kentucky; its pork went out to the world. One day he took young Drausin and Lucien back to Langton's slaughterhouse, just above the Miami–Erie Canal, to observe the whole process inside the factory. The wide-eyed boys didn't miss a thing.

First, after the Princes of Porkopolis drove the herd to the ramp, Driver-men drove the hogs up the ramp to the top floor of the slaughterhouse, where Hammer-man knocked each on its head with an eight-pound sledge. Two Hanger-men then manacled the usually unconscious hog by its hind legs to hang head down from a six-foot-high moving rack.

In the next chamber, Slice-man slit the throat, blood pouring into a large vat. Then Boiler-man released the hog into a vat of boiling water, rolling it to scald off the bristles. Fork-men rolled the denuded hog onto a huge, multipronged fork, lifting it onto a large bench, where Scraper-men shaved off the remaining bristles, tossing them into buckets for plaster-binding or brushes.

At the next stage of the process, Lift-men hung the carcass back up on a moving rack. Knife-men flayed off the hide using the finest knives, then sent the carcass on for the tanners. Lard was bucketed for lamp oil and candles. Other knivers sliced the hog down the middle, anus to throat, to gut the innards, dropping intestines into one big bucket, livers into another, and kidneys into yet another.

Emptied and sponge-swabbed inside, the carcasses went back on the moving rack down to the next floor, where butchers awaited with their cleavers. Pig on the table: *Whack*—off with the squiggly tail. *Whack, whack, whack, whack*—off with the feet, into one bin for pigs' knuckles, another for pigs' feet. *Whack, whack* into the neck—off came the head. The carcass was pivoted. Then Mighty Man—the Paul Bunyan, the John Henry of porkers—raised his cleaver highest and split the carcass right down the spine.

Now the artists started. *Chop, chop, swish, chop, swish*—off with a leg, here a prime, there a shoulder, each cut into different bins: hams off to Mexico, loins to Bordeaux, chops all round the country, bacon to be pressed in great slabs, spareribs dumped in a bin for locals to pick for free, some skins in bins for cracklings, for soap. Other cracklings and knuckles and feet were barreled in brine to be shipped south for slave-food on plantations.

Lucien recalled the Princes of Porkopolis chanting in the streets, "And everybody kno-ows, everywhere you go-o, the Queen City is—the Kiiing—of Pork."

Once he shifted from feeling "pig" to thinking "pork," Lucien was fascinated, impressed, even mesmerized by the rhythms, the order, the seeming harmony of all these toiling, sweating men working together on various stages of the process like one big machine, all its parts humming as they thwacked and splattered, magically turning pigs into pork for all the world. From the hammer-thwack on the head to being "ready for the barrel"—three and a half minutes!

Ti-Drausin found himself less interested in the particulars of gristle, fat, and bone than in who was paid what and how, from the farmers to the herders, from the slaughterhouse workers to the packers and shippers.

For weeks Lucien's sleep wound through endless cycles of pig turning into pork and then, stage by stage, back into a pig, and onward, over and over, again and again.

Father Drausin, entertaining the possibility of going into the business himself, realized after listening to the porkers instruct, clarify, and banter with each other that he couldn't do such business in his modest English. He was okay with certain conversations with cigars, and was familiar with Shakespeare's *Comedy of Errors*, *Twelfth Night*, and *Othello*, but even the adventures of *Tom Jones* weren't enough for him to feel confident he could manage business amid the world's busiest porkers. In the practical world, his literary English was a limiting tool rather than a strengthening one. Drausin realized that instead of getting down to the business of supporting his family, he'd better go to school first himself and make his lingo a usable tool.

At St. Xavier College on Sycamore St., Drausin took two courses, including one that covered basic English spelling, vocabulary, and grammar, designed for the many immigrants in the city, mostly German and Italian, and some scarcely literate Irish. But he could not resist his second course: English Literature, taught by a passionate Jesuit priest-professor, with a few smatterings of American writings. Drausin worked through Pope's translations of *The Iliad* and *The Odyssey*, and he enjoyed

Chaucer's French-flavored *Canterbury Tales*: "and bathèd every vein in swich licour,/Of which engendered is the fleur—"

Drausin read some of the poetry aloud to his family at night. He learned some by heart. Some poems he made melodies for on his mandolin, while speaking them again and again until he could sing them. One that filled the house for weeks and then recurrently, randomly, was "a poem I like by a little-known English poet named William Blake":

Why should I care for the men of Thames
Or the cheating waves of charter'd streams;
Or shrink at the little blasts of fear
That the hireling blows into my ear?

Tho' born on the cheating banks of Thames,
Tho' his waters bathèd my infant limbs,
The Ohio shall wash his stains from me:
I was born a slave, but I go free!

Drausin would repeat the poem-song several times, shifting the emphasis, playing with the rhythms, and the final two lines:

The Ohio shall wash his stains from me:
I was born a slave, but I go free!

Sometimes he whispered the final line, and sometimes he came close to shouting it to his family. "The Thames is the most famous river in England, where the great city London is," he reminded them, "and the king's castle. And our country fought its way free from that king and that England."

One night, Eugene asked, "Were we a slave?"

Drausin looked at Josephine, whose right eyebrow arched

emphatically, while her left leveled, offering Drausin the response. Moments of mutual silence. Then, "Ohh, my boy. We are free. You children are free, and always will be."

Drausin caught Aline starting, "But—" and with a keen glance at her, then a sweeping look over the children and back to his daughter, he stilled her impulse to no doubt interject about her Granmère Pouponne Adelaïde's childhood and youth as a slave. Aline, caught, caught herself.

That silencing gesture was the beginning of the end of Drausin ever saying much about his family in New Orleans to his children. He thought, *My mother was born a slave and freed. I was born free, as free as a man of color can still be in New Orleans. But I will be no mind-slave. This Ohio River, with its swirling, clay-blue waters, shall wash all stains from me and mine.*

"But, inwardly," said Drausin to his children, "we could still all be slaves." None of the children understood. "In another poem, 'London,' in fact, Mr. Blake speaks of 'mind-forged manacles.'"

Only Aline knew what manacles were. "Shackles, hand-cuffs."

"You mean, like what the slaves in the copple in Natchez wore?" asked Lucien.

"Exactly."

"Some with spikes?"

"Even. Imagine such shackles and spikes inside you, around your mind, around your thoughts, your feelings." The children gasped and moaned at the image.

Josephine put a hand on the neck of Lucien and of Eugene, massaging them warmly, "Children, you do not have those, in you or outside you."

"No, most certainly not," affirmed their father, "and we will make sure you never will. We came to Ohio to make sure that you can, and always will, look any person in the world right in their eyes. Right?" They all stood, looked him directly in the eye, and called out, "Yes, Sir!"— masters by now of the greeting game, yet sensing in their bones that it was more than a game, maybe even a matter of life and death.

Drausin read a strange, brand-new book by the popular author of *Typee*. In *Moby Dick*, Henry Melville devoted one long chapter solely to the mysteries of "Whiteness." What Drausin most wanted to share with his family was Melville's distinctions between light and pigment. "What do we see when we hold a prism, a crystal, in a beam of sunlight?"

Drausin detached a piece of the crystal chandelier and held it up to an incoming sunbeam.

"Red!" shouted Eugene.

"Yellows, and greens," said young Drausin.

"Oranges," called Lucien.

"Blues, indigos, and violets," said Aline.

Lucien said, "The prism shows the colors—in the white light."

"Precisely. In light," Papa Drausin continued, "white holds all the colors. In light, you see, black is the lack of color. Now, in pigment, in paint, how do we make black?"

Aline looked at him, then lit in recognition, nodded, and took out her paints; on her palette-board she proceeded to add color to color to color.

"When we mix all the colors, we—finally make—" said Aline, mixing,

"Black!" gasped Eugene.

"Exactly," said Papa. "Pigment, paint, is physical. We can touch it. In our bodies, the darker we are, the more color we have.

"Light is not physical. Light is like our souls, our spirits. We cannot touch our souls. In our souls, inwardly, the whiter, the lighter we are, the more color we have. That's one thing Mr. Melville, the whaler, helped me understand about black and white."

It's not that the children understood it all. Aline did, clearly. Young Drausin grasped some. Lucien never forgot his own translation of Papa's whaler-talk: 'The darker our bodies, the more colors we have; the lighter our souls, the more colors we have.' Lucien knew he had the darkest body in the family. He did not know what souls were. But he did know that when he closed his good eye, he saw many colors in and around people, not on them. Young Lucien felt rich in colors himself.

Meanwhile, Papa Drausin began taking in music students on piano, flute, clarinet, mandolin, and guitar, setting up in the drawing room. The Wulsin children were growing up with music permeating their home, one way or another. Yet, as is often the case, Father was not the patient teacher with his own children that he was with others.

Drausin found a young man, Mr. D. H. Baldwin, up on Richmond St., who started coming once a week to give piano lessons to the older three children. Baldwin was tall, gangly, good-willed, and mild-mannered. Aline was persistent, a bit plodding, but respectably musical on the piano. Young Drausin was diligent, but lacked his father's deftness. He seemed to think his music more than feel it. Lucien was decent, looking forward to refining violin. Eugene—not so interested. Although, when he absentmindedly let his fingers play among the keys, Eugene found tunes the other three struggled to learn. Then off he'd skip. Baldwin looked forward especially to Eugene in the future.

Papa Drausin and Baldwin respected each other's musicality; increasingly they enjoyed playing together. Selections from Bach's "Well-tempered Clavier," Mozart's "Piano Concerto no. 21 in C Major" and his "Clarinet Concerto," Schubert's piano sonatas, and soon Liszt's new "Piano Sonata in B Minor," and Chopin's "Preludes" and the "Polonaise in G Minor." Baldwin always stayed with the piano; Drausin moved easily from piano to flute to clarinet to guitar. Sometimes they even took turns at the piano within one concerto. They liked occasionally to play Bach's "Polonaise in G Minor" and then Chopin's

"Polonaise in G Minor." Baldwin had two pianos at home, so they played double concertos there.

One cold night by the fire in late October Drausin read the children Edgar Allen Poe's story, *The Tell-Tale Heart*. When the narrator cut up the corpse of the old man, the children huddled with each other under blankets, groaning. Lucien couldn't help thinking of the porkers chopping pig into pork. Then, as the murderer babbled nonchalantly to the relaxed, unsuspecting police inspectors, the ever-louder beating of the buried heart under the floorboards, or of his own guilty heart, drove him to hysterical confession of the secret he had been so blithely hiding. Drausin, hearing himself read that passage aloud, wondered, *Am I hearing my own heart? Is just one secret I am hiding, banging my own heart's drum?*

Aline applied herself to her studies industriously, enjoying her growing fluency in English while becoming more self-conscious of differences between her dresses and those of her classmates, which Josephine would remedy gradually by Christmastime. The Wulsin family enjoyed its first Christmas tree, a custom brought to Cincinnati by the substantial German population, only beginning to spread across the rest of the land. A young blue spruce served them well.

A brown glen plaid wool dress set Aline for the winter, and a bright red-and-white gingham dress armed her for spring. Then, to the surprise of all the girls, what should appear one day on a girl whose family had just visited Paris but a lavender dress in elegant, loosely woven matelasse cotton, right off the streets of high fashion, no doubt. Oh, the slow pace of this midwestern Porkopolis! Amused, Josephine thought, *Cincinnati* may be ahead in terms of industry and liberty, but New Orleans far outpaces the Queen City in terms of chic fashion. Aline's own rose matelasse immediately saw the light of day, and she enjoyed a season in the know, at least until she outgrew it.

269

CHAPTER 30:
WHAT'S DE MATTAH? 1853

Josephine gave birth to her sixth child, a small, delicate boy, fine-featured and thin-haired, on August 20, 1853. He seemed to her like a ray of light, perhaps even as fragile. Josephine realized she had often wondered during her pregnancy how Claire might be faring. *Had that called to me his name, "Clarence"?* Only later did she also wonder, *With a son already named "Lucien," might I be calling light, or lightness, into our family?* Although Clarence would gradually darken in eyes, hair, and skin, his mother always felt him to be a ray of light, however delicately embodied.

Aline continued to be ever her mother's faithful helper with baby Clarence and little Laure, now walking and talking, in her gentle, quiet way. Aline's form was also beginning to swell from girl-straight toward woman-curve. Although her eyes were onyx black, unlike her mother's green, Aline shared just as deeply Josephine's devotion, her innate piety.

Christmas mass in St. Patrick's Church was the occasion of Aline's First Communion. In the chill air, the brothers noted their sister's grave demeanor as she shed her grey wool coat; as Aline stepped forward from the pew in her white wool dress with plain bodice over her expanding chest, Lucien wondered if his eldest sister was leaving them and her childhood behind.

Her brothers were unaware that when she kneeled beside her mother, hands open to receive the host, Aline felt the candlelight glow in the cold December dark like Christ's angels. When the priest placed the holy bread into her mouth, she felt it melt and merge, the body of her Lord, informing, illumining her own. If any brother had had the mischief or audacity to soil the sanctity of the moment with such a secular question as "Who's your sweetheart? Who you gonna marry?" Aline would have responded without hesitation, "I will be the bride of Christ." But none thought to ask, hardly there yet themselves.

Banging at St. Patrick's front doors broke Aline's rapture. A red-faced, red-haired young man, panting, whispered to several others; the word spread—into a rumbling exodus of thirty to forty young men and teenage boys. Father Matthew continued with Mass, as did the remaining congregation. All that brothers Drausin and Lucien had been able to hear amid the whisperings was something about Germans attacking the Cathedral. Young Drausin, seated at the end of the pew, slipped out the front door, asking a racing Irish teen, "What's the matter?"

"What's de mattah? More mattah'n you can scattah all over Cincinnata!"

Only the next day did the family learn the source of the rupture of Aline's rapture. Pope Pius IX had sent Cardinal Bedini all the way from the Vatican to Cincinnati to help with questions of church property. But many recent German immigrants were "Forty-Eighters," Protestants, liberals, having left Europe after the Revolutions of 1848; hence they identified Cardinal Bedini with aristocratic, oppressive old-world regimes, whose members they felt should have no right to own property in the new world. There had been a march to protest at the local bishop's home four days earlier, leading to arrests. The mayor had heard of possible further rioting but assumed nothing would occur on Christmas Day.

The German Forty-Eighters and the nativist "Know-Nothings" had united around ten o'clock at night, with five hundred men and a hundred women marching to St. Peter in Chains to protest, and possibly even end, the Cardinal's presence and influence. Both Irish and German Catholics had rushed to defend the Cathedral and the visiting Cardinal. Police charged, arresting about sixty German protesters. Catholics trod more carefully for a while. The Wulsins trod carefully always, southerners blending north, French-speakers Anglicizing, coloreds passing white, Catholics in a Protestant town.

Josephine said to Drausin one night after the children were in bed, "My mother used to say *her* mother used to say, 'Tomorrow does not have lunch or dinner, but one should put aside its ration.'" She prodded her husband to better secure their futures in this surprisingly turbulent new city of theirs. Music lessons brought in some regular income, but it was modest.

In 1854, Drausin Wulsin uncharacteristically "went to town," using a portion of his three thousand dollars in gold. First, he bought from the Cincinnati Western Railroad Co. lot number thirty-three "on a plat of Avondale," on the east side of Cincinnati. Then he bought lot twenty-two on Carr St. between Whitewater Canal and Budd St. Then he bought their own rented residence, 139 Carr St., between Sixth St. and Whitewater Canal. Finally, he bought four more lots—sixteen, seventeen, forty-nine, and fifty—in Home City, further west in Delhi Township, down by the Ohio River.

It was a busy year for a formerly not-so-busy man, purchasing land spanning the city, from east in Avondale to the West End on Carr, to further west in Home City. Josephine was proud of her husband's purchases. "Mon Cher, I know ma mère, Josephine Tassey Mathé, and my long-gone Granmère,

Marie-Francoise Lalande Perreault, are proud of me and of my husband for our new real estate, securing our new future. My dear husband, of almost twenty years now! We have been together longer than either of them ever stayed with a man, white or colored. We can be even prouder of that."

Drausin and Josephine enjoyed more wine than usual and more of each other than usual that night. Rentals began bringing in much-needed income for the music teacher supporting a family of eight.

During this year, the children made some new friends, children of a man of far more substantial property. One day after school Aline had gone off with a classmate. The three boys headed to the Whitewater Canal to watch the boats loading and unloading their freight: coal, grain, pork, salt, nails, and cases of beer and wine. They loved to spend time around the horses and mules that waited to pull the canal boats along the towpaths, heading west to Indiana. Lucien remembered "Indiana," and Mr. Fletcher's stories about blue-eyed Indians and the Welsh brother Madoc at Devil's Backbone. None of these canal boats' crews were heading to Devil's Backbone; only riverboats went by there, and fast.

"Sonny, no canal boat'd ever make it through there alive," exaggerated one boatman.

"Betchya we could," hollered Eugene.

"Good luck," the guy chuckled.

Up ahead a captain barked, "Scat, skedaddle on outta here, ya pesky muskrats. Don't ya tangle no ropes no more or we'll tie ya up'n' squeeze the juices outta ya." A tow-haired boy a little bigger than Lucien helped a smaller boy to his feet as he limped back off the towpath away from the water and the snarling captain.

"Hey, is he alright?" Drausin asked the bigger.

"Yeah, he'll be fine, just got tangled hurdling the tow-lines."

"Wow, hurdling the tow-lines?" lit up Eugene.

"Yup, it can get tricky, 'specially when two mules are pulling close enough together. You gotta get the rhythm. Sorta like jump-rope. But you gotta go when neither the crew from the boat nor the mule leader up the path is looking."

The Wulsin boys were impressed, intrigued. They spent the rest of the afternoon with the two new boys, getting the hang of it further up the canal, where the crews weren't on the lookout already. Nick was a year older than nine-year-old Lucien. His brother Landon was Eugene's age, seven. Little Eugene was quickly as nimble as Nick at tow-line hurdling, as long as the ropes weren't too high. Landon shook off his limp and didn't fall again that afternoon. The five boys became sporting otters, following each other in their jumping rhythms along the muddy banks.

Nick's and Landon's father, Joseph Longworth, felt that his children learned most through playing in the woods at their home, "Rookwood," up on Mount Adams. So they didn't go to school. At night their father read to them from Pope's *Iliad* and *Odyssey*, Shakespeare, Dickens, Thackeray, and Scott, feeling no good work of literature was too good for his children. On Wednesdays, their father spent the day tending to one of the family warehouses on Horne St., near both the Whitewater Canal and the Cincinnati, Hamilton, and Dayton Railroad.

So the five young fellows often found each other on Wednesday afternoons. When the Wulsins realized that their five-year-old sister Laure was the same age as Nick and Landin's sister Mary, the girls often played together at tea-time for snacks at the Wulsin home, sometimes venturing out later with the boys. The Wulsins' new friends loved hearing stories of New Orleans and the Mississippi River. The urban Wulsins loved hearing stories of their new friends' lives in the woods.

"One day," Nick accounted over freshly made blancmange, "Landon and I were out in the woods, not far beyond the big old hackberry tree, when all of a sudden we found ourselves face to face with a huge black bear." The Wulsins could hardly imagine, in civilized Cincinnati. "And Landon—he was only your age, girls—called out, 'Run, run, Nicholas! You will have time to get away while the bear is eating me.'"

And then Landon chimed in, "And, and Nicholath thaid, 'No, let'th both run. Perhapth if we go very fatht, he can't catch uth.'"

"What did you do?" asked Eugene.

And Nick and Landon spoke almost in chorus, "We ran very fatht." The Wulsins were stunned, in silence, trying to picture themselves in front of a wild bear, right here in Cincinnati.

"It turned out the bear was not so wild," said Nick. "It was eventually caught and returned to the circus."

"Oh," the Wulsins collectively sighed, only half-relieved. Josephine, quietly present in the background, asked, "Landon, why did you tell Nicholas to run?"

"Oh," he said, very matter-of-factly, "I knew Nicholath wath alwayth the favorite." The Wulsins looked anew at this selfless young soul.

Occasionally, on a Saturday, Nick and Landon invited the three Wulsin boys and Laure over to play for the day. In the fall, one of their favorite activities was running through Nick's grandfather's vineyards along the river side of Mount Adams. "Some of them grow all the way upriver as far as Ripley," said young Nick. They loved plucking and popping into their mouths, like Antony and Cleopatra, the green Catawba grapes, juicy fresh, foxy and musky flavored, endless. What the Wulsin children did *not* like was the bottle of sparkling Catawba wine occasionally given to Mr. and Mrs. Wulsin by Mr. Longworth. Nick agreed. "Just because we grow more wine than anywhere in the country, and just because our Catawba is popular around the world, doesn't mean it tastes as good as grapes."

One Saturday, after hours of harmonious play, including making a couple of plays to perform, Nick and Landon got into a fight, passionate, right down to hair-pulling. A distinguished gentleman guest ambled by, with a tomahawk nose and silvered temples. "Why the fight, boys? What's the matter?" he asked them with interest.

Through his tears, Landon lisped, "Nick thays that Clytaemnethtra hated Orethtes, and I thay that it can't be true 'cauthe Orethtes wath her little boy."

What manner of child is this? wondered the grey gentleman, amused, touched, and impressed at the issue sparking battle between the wild Ohio River boys. As he gently placed a hand on the head of each boy, they calmed. He had given a public address on friendship the night before at the Mercantile Library. Lucien felt in him the wisdom of a grand, benevolent oak tree.

Only years later would Lucien learn the national stature of the Longworths' frequent guest, Ralph Waldo Emerson.

CHAPTER 31:

TO VOTE, HIGH AND LOW, 1855

Drausin felt he had been waiting all his life for this day. He, Mr. Drausin Wulsin, was finally going to vote, in 1855, at the age of forty-two, in his new city, in his new state, in his new state of mind, in his new country, or rather as his new self in this new part of his old country. No, Ohio did not allow people of color to vote. Yes, so far Drausin Wulsin was passing successfully as white.

The issues in Cincinnati were not simple, but in some ways they were getting simpler. The nativist Know-Nothing party, many of whom had allied with the German Protestants against the Catholics in the riots of '53, was shifting its focus to a broader spectrum, including all "immigrants," targeting above all the largest immigrant population in Cincinnati: their former allies, the German-Americans. The loudest spokesman for this populist party, the editor-in-chief of *The Cincinnati Times*, James D. Taylor, was running as candidate for mayor of Cincinnati. Anti-Catholic always, Taylor was now blasting all immigrants, even Jews who had lived in Cincinnati since the 1820s—anyone who hailed from elsewhere than the Eastern seaboard of the still-young United States of America.

Drausin relished the opportunity to participate in the voting process, to make his quiet mark, whatever the disagreements around town. The opportunity to vote had been one of the crucial reasons he and Josephine had chosen to leave New Orleans. He brushed his dark hair smoothly across the top down to a gentle swirl of curls just above his ears. With tallow oil he brushed his still-new congress-gaiters into a proclaiming shine. Josephine ensured his white collar and black cravat were symmetrically situated.

After straightening his black frock coat and brushing his black top hat to a sheen, Drausin kissed his wife. Josephine, proud, nevertheless let her hand linger on his lapel, "Fais attention, mon Cher." Drausin clicked his heels with a grin, took his silver-ferruled, ebony walking stick in hand, and headed off to the polls. The air was cool, the sun warming. Hyacinth by the door, honeysuckle afar. Drausin wondered, *Am I savoring the sweet scent of this new morning, of this new season, or indeed of a new era?*

Josephine, on the one hand concerned for the safety of her beloved, on the other hand could not help wondering, *Might I ever get to vote myself? Now wouldn't that be something? Or at least my daughters?*

Outside the election center for the West End's Sixteenth Ward, all kinds of people milled around the stately entrance, notably some scarred snarlers with clubs in hand, inspecting, daunting, taunting voters. Drausin thought of his dear Kaintuck, Declan, saw Declan in each snarling guardian, and tipped his top hat, an acknowledging nod. As he paced past, they nodded back, clearly taking him for a legitimate local gentleman, exuding no alien stench.

Drausin entered the hall and paused. When he recovered his breath, he felt the reverence of entering a new church. He signed his name and address. The election attendant did not look at him twice, in fact closing with, "Thank you, Sir." When Drausin didn't know certain names on the ballot, he voted mostly Democrat. For mayor he marked the box for James J. Faran. Faran offered a hand, Know-Nothing Taylor a fist. After marking all boxes, he signed the ballot, folded it, and inserted it in the slit atop the ballot-box. Solitary, the room solemnly silent, Drausin felt his swerves of the pen to be as important as the swerves of a musketeer's sword in service of a queen. Yet, so simple in the Queen City, sans queen. *En garde! Touché!*

Stepping outside, he lit his last cigar, savoring a new pride. Drausin Wulsin, voting citizen of the United States of America, found himself walking toward City Hall to observe the process at the center of the city. As often when walking, he whistled between puffs, almost unconsciously.

Policemen secured stability as voters flowed in and out of City Hall in what Drausin already felt to be a familiar process. His eye was drawn across the street to the grand Greek columns of St. Peter-in-Chains, the Catholic Cathedral whose tall steeple rose, or perhaps descended, ancbored by its cross high in the heavens.

Here stand I, Drauzin Valsin Bacas, free man of color, who cared but never dared to vote in New Orleans. Now I, Drausin Wulsin, have finally cast off my chains, St. Peter, and have indeed cast my own vote in Cincinnati. I have cast my vote. A few marks. Such a little matter; such a mighty matter.

Drausin stamped his cigar stub into the soil beneath a young sycamore and strolled on to Fritz Brothers, just across the canal, to purchase a dozen of his favorite Marguerite cigars from Havana. The blacksmith Mörlein had recently started making beer, his brew growing increasingly popular. Drausin found himself drifting up to the smithy on Elm St. to enjoy the melodic ringing of Mörlein's percussions, the lager, and the gemütlichkeit, the warmth and friendliness around him, often in German, but also in all flavors of English. Unlike most blacksmiths, Mörlein had a knack for chat with customers while he bellowed, fired, banged, twisted, and soused his irons. Drausin savored his dark malt beer and the light cigar smoke curling, rising. The afterglow of having finally cast his first votes melded with the warming forge-coals inside and the goldening afternoon outside. He never imagined what adventure his children were just beginning, as his was coming to a close.

Aline Wulsin, now sixteen and studying at Hughes High School on Fifth and Mound Streets, always carried coins in her reticule. She met her three younger brothers at their school with news she was treating them to a sweet. They crossed the Miami Canal at the Vine St. Bridge, heading "Over the Rhine" for the Charles Doerr and Sons Bakery, the best in the heart of Germantown.

Each soon armed with cinnamon kuchen, they sauntered along, enjoying the lingering spring warmth, crisping with sun-downing cool, crumbs and powdered sugar trailing. Sparrows, pigeons, and wrens swooped in to street-clean behind them. They heard occasional canal-boaters' mournful songs. Like their father, the Wulsin boys were whistling, as Aline improvised harmonic hummings to their tunes.

As they started across Main St., Lucien was first to notice no bird-chat, no canal-song, just strange silence. He stopped; they stopped. South toward the canal, he saw at first nothing, then a flood pouring not under but over the Main St. Bridge. Not water, but men, roaring. As soon as the mob reached the first buildings on Canal St., clashes bashed, glass cracked, shattered, tinkled. Shouts arose, then *thwack-thwacks* of hardwood, and a round, white-aproned, white-haired man crumpled to the sidewalk. Some of the mob kicked him.

The children only slowly grasped what was happening. The shopkeeper struggled to his feet, making his way toward the Wulsins, groaning, red with blood and apoplexy.

Some breakers and beaters spotted them. "Look, up ahead, Piggy-Schwein's runnin' to dem Dutch runts—let's snuff 'em, float 'em back down de river an over de ocean. Come on, Herr Piggy, Piggy-Piggy, we gonna beat you tender into sausage—c'mon, little Piggy-Schweins, we gonna chomp ya, chew ya—gonna make you de wurst, ha-ha! Gonna make you de wurst, ja, ja!"

As the shopkeeper hobbled toward them, the Wulsins ran north too, Eugene scooting on ahead, followed by Lucien; Aline and Drausin tried to help the bleeding man, wobbling as he was. The disheveled, red-faced, broken-toothed mob, swinging staffs and iron bars, shouted and surged forward, distracted by windows or doors to batter.

Aline called, "Help! Help us, please! Someone, please help us!" They ran across Liberty St., angling up Hamilton Rd. in the growing dusk. Lucien, eying the closing crowd, did not notice a strong arm till it yanked him inside a door. Eugene, who'd been pulled in just before, was already swinging his fists. Drausin, grabbed next, was quickly helping Aline pull in the fat man. A strong young man bar-locked the door from the inside. When he finished, he turned, picked up hitting, kicking, sputtering Eugene, and chuckled, raising him to eye level. "Well, well, good evening to you, Eu-gene, you Prince of Cincinnati."

Eugene, face to face with the black man, not so long ago still a boy, was dumbfounded till he looked in those dark brown eyes. Then Eugene wrapped his arms around that strong neck, his legs around that mighty chest. "Jebediah! Now you're a man!" Aline, then Drausin and Lucien recognized him, all astonished first at being saved, and above all by Jedediah, whom each boy hugged in turn. Aline blushed rose at the young man in front of her; Jebediah blushed crimson at the young woman in front of him.

"First I heard the noise in the streets; then I heard a voice hollerin' for help, a familiar voice. So, I did. Now—come. That iron-wood door might hold till judgment day. But jus' in case, we got to disappear. Mr. Weissman, Sir, can you walk a little further?"

The fat old butcher, his own blood brighter than his apron stains, wheezed, groaned, and nodded.

"Then, follow me." Jebediah raised his lantern, ushered

them through a door, down three steps, along to a hole in the ground, showing the tip of a ten-foot ladder. He had Drausin pull the cover back from the hole, then handed the lantern to him. Jebediah proceeded down the ladder, so he could help the bloody butcher down. When all six were down the ladder, Jebediah took the lantern and led them through an opening into a large room with a bricked-arch ceiling. The Wulsins were amazed at their subterranean chamber, and then even more amazed to see, over in the lantern-shadows, six white eyes in three black faces. Two of the people were wrapped in worn shawls; one wore a coat and hat.

Jebediah said to them, "Ain't no worry; these're mah friends, so they're your friends—Walter, his wife Ruth-in-the-Alien-Corn, and their daughter Jessie"—the latter of whom, about the age of Lucien, watched the children with large dark eyes. To Lucien they looked weary, wary, yet sympathetic, and grateful. After all, the Wulsins had just escaped, too.

Turning to the Wulsins, Jebediah explained, "I'm jus' helpin' this family get on up north." The Wulsin children nodded to the family. Jebediah continued, "This is the Schmidt Brothers Brewery. They allow us shelter from time to time. Mister Weissman, Sir, I recommend you settle in here with these Wulsins till that crazy crowd cools down or falls back away. Aline, we got water here an' some bread. Here. Would you take care of him, while I get these folks on to their next stop? I'll be back to get y'all in a little while, an' help you get back home alright."

The butcher nodded. "Tank you, Jebediah. You alvays been gut boy. Tank you, tank you ferry much." As he lowered himself down the wall to the ground, the man groaned, eyelids heavy. Aline started to tend his wounds with a cloth Jebediah gave her. She daubed the cuts, wiped off blood, tried to rearrange his broken nose, and felt no other bones broken. The left eye-socket, with much blood around it, was hard to tell. Lucien helped her as best he could.

"Hurry back, Jebediah," said Eugene. He took a bite of the bread Aline had passed along to him.

Jebediah grinned, tousled the boy's hair, nodded, and stuffed more bread and two goatskins of water into a burlap shoulder bag. He looked at Drausin, realizing he was now about the age Jebediah himself had been on that river trip four years ago, and asked him to come along as he lit a new lantern.

Ruth-in-the-Alien-Corn had been watching Lucien intently. Rising, clearly fatigue-frayed, soles peeling from the toes of her boots, she had a "lazy" eye; she held Jessie's hand strongly in her right. As they turned to go, she nodded to Lucien, raised her left hand, licked her thumb, drew a circle in the air, crossing it in the center, and said, "Bless you, Chile. You see."

She nodded, almost bowing to him. Puzzled, Lucien would never forget that gesture. He watched Ruth-in-the-Alien-Corn and Jesse disappear into another arched opening, led by their friend Jebediah, followed by their brother, Drausin, with Walter bringing up the rear.

Drausin was amazed that all of them were walking, upright, through a tunnel, rough-walled but solid-ceilinged, at least thirty feet along, before the figures in front of him started floating up a ladder. Up the ladder all, and through a door, they took stock. "Did we just walk across under Hamilton Rd?"

"Yessir, Drausin, you called it," whispered Jebediah, listening through an outside door. "We're on the other side now, in the ice house."

Drausin felt the bone cold and smelled the damp sawdust wrapping what he now could glean were mighty blocks of ice, gleaming in the torchlight, with saws, axes, and arm-long ice-tongs hanging on the beams.

"From what I can tell, those crazies out there have done their damage, retreated, prolly back on across the canal, back on out of Germantown. We got to go though, silent like shadows. Ready?" He looked at each of the runaways, who nodded. "Ready?" he grinned at Drausin, pulling the big boy up beside him, putting his finger to his lips. Drausin nodded, now following directly behind the leader, always sensing Walter the recent slave-man right close.

At the far back door of the icehouse, Jebediah lifted the iron bar, opening the massive door. Drausin snuffed the torch, left it, and slipped outside into the night, as Jebediah re-locked the door from the outside. Almost hand in hand, the five shadows headed to the alley behind the Hamilton Rd. buildings. They wafted in halting rhythms, like gliding crows, from tree to tree, from building to building, stretching apart, then coalescing.

After slow-spying about eight quiet blocks, they found themselves in thickening woods, mostly tall tulip trees, oaks, and locust. Early honeysuckle sweetened the cooling night. Jebediah stopped in a small clearing in a ravine, not far from a railroad bed. He reached into an old fox den and brought out a wrapped bundle. He whispered to the runaways, "Here's your place; here're four blankets. Here's more bread and water for the night," shedding his shoulder-bag.

"Settle in. Sleep well tonight. Those lights through the trees belong to the house of Mr. Zebulon Strong. Tomorrow, his children'll come out in the woods to play. They'll leave you food an' drink, under that largest beech tree. You stay silent in this ravine all day. Tomorrow night, your next guide'll find you here, to lead you not far away, to the Miami Canal, where you'll board a boat to head north to your next station, prolly Hamilton or Middletown. Good luck an' blessings be with you, Walter, Ruth-in-the-Alien-Corn, and dear Jessie," he said, taking in turn each one's hand in both of his.

"God bless you, Jebediah, and thank you," they said, overlapping each other. Drausin nodded to each.

"And we," whispered Jebediah to Drausin as they melted back into shadows, "still have work to do."

Back in the catacombs of the Schmidt Brothers brewery, Aline had sent the boys scouting for spiderwebs, which they found in abundance, and which she placed generously on Herr Weissman's wounds. His nose looked wobbly but was no longer bleeding. His left eye, already bluing toward black, had swollen closed like a large plum.

Lucien, after eating his bread, had slipped into slumber of his own. Eugene had climbed almost up the walls to the ceiling, exploring two other large chambers full of shiny copper stills, tubing, vats, and ladders, and then Jebediah's tunnel all the way to the top of the ladder under the closed board. Eugene had then returned near Lucien, and was also just beginning to drift off.

When Drausin appeared in the dark archway, Lucien, having first heard them coming, whispered, "Drausin." Eugene called out, "Jebediah," as he appeared. Herr Weissman opened his right eye. Drausin and Jebediah shared their adventures, which fascinated all three children.

Aline watched and listened to Jebediah closely. Then, at the end, she said, "Jebediah, you have changed."

"Yeah, you got a man voice," added Eugene.

"Yes," said Aline, "but you speak differently, too."

Jebediah smiled. "I know. My Daddy's got me goin' to Mr. Peter Clark's School for the Colored. I'm learnin' all kinds of things I didn't know. An' my talkin', yeah, I guess it's sorta like straightenin' out a winding crick. I'm straightenin' some. Now—we gotta get you home, an' that's startin' with you, Mr. Weissman. Can you manage?"

"Ja," he grunted onto his swelling ankle, but Jebediah shouldered him along the tunnel, and helped the butcher struggle up the icehouse ladder. Drausin had gone ahead to light the way and lift the lid. While they got Herr Weissman to his nearby home, the streets seemed quiet, and his wife remained wary behind the door at first.

"Schatzi, hier bin ich," he called. Flinging the door open, the butcher's wife embraced her husband in tears as Aline enumerated his wounds to her. Herr Weissman said, "Jebediah und you, Miss Aline, I vill gif you each free pork efery Christmas for ze rest ov my life." His Frau nodded.

As Jebediah and the four Wulsins made their way west along the dark, smaller streets, they noticed more and more German men leaving their homes, also heading west. From all over Germantown, they were funneling, it soon became clear, into the doors of the Turner Verein Gymnasium on Walnut St., the center of gymnastic sports education for the whole city of Cincinnati. For the safety of their journey, Jebediah had to find out why.

He and the Wulsins managed to slip discreetly through the dark into the back hall. Aline could glean from the speakers' German, first of all, that several men had died so far in the riots and that the Know-Nothings had destroyed ballot boxes in two German wards. The Germans were planning to build barricades that night at the Vine St. Bridge, to be ready by dawn, organizing their militias with weapons and ammunition, to repel any Know-Nothing mobs at any near bridges: Main, Walnut, Race, and Elm. Some recent immigrants, veterans of the Revolutions of 1848, were savvy barricaders. The Over-the-Rhine community would allow no more invasions.

The eavesdroppers were impressed with the force of feeling in the hall, but also with both the clarity of the planning and the unanimity of all the men being galvanized into action. Then Jebediah took the Wulsins to cross the canal above the Plum St. bend at the Fifteenth St. Bridge, which was clear and quiet.

On the other side, Aline and Drausin insisted they could make their way home unguided. "We're all the way down by the river at 139 Carr," Aline said.

But Jebediah insisted more strongly, "I know."

"How do you know?" asked Aline.

"Oh, 'cuz I been keepin' an eye on you all, from time to time these years. Now, les go." The children were stunned to imagine that, and touched.

When Aline knocked on her home door, Josephine opened it to see her older children arrayed before her. "Oh, mon Dieu, oh, mon Dieu," she said, inspecting and hugging each of the four in turn, crying tears of relief and joy.

"Where's Papa?" asked Drausin.

"Out looking for you." Aline then stepped back out and brought in the young black man, which quieted Josephine. When her children went to him affectionately, she looked in his eyes, exclaiming, "Jebediah?!"

The children chimed in together. "He rescued us—" Breathlessly they began telling their mother of their experience.

"Wait, wait," said Josephine. Young Drausin stoked the coals in the fireplace while Josephine prepared hot mulled bier douce for all and reheated their long-cold supper. Then the young Wulsins started recounting their adventures.

After about twenty minutes, they heard the key in the door, and silenced each other. Weary Papa backed in, put his hat on the rack, and turned to a shrieking, jumping bundle of children, who swarmed to him. When he noticed the young man who had put down his cup and stood, hat in hand, Aline formally announced, "Papa, I would like to introduce to you Mr. Jebediah Makely, Prince of Cincinnati." And of course the stories bubbled forth again, new details emerging.

Finally, Jebediah stood to go. Josephine embraced him, with moist eyes, and gave him a loaf of freshly baked bread. Drausin looked him in the eye, shook his hand. "Jebediah, Jebediah, thank heavens for you, and thank you, immeasurably. Where is your father, Esau?"

"Oh, he just started the season again last week, with Cap'n Leathers on the Natchez III. But he's keepin' me here for school."

"And where do you live, if I may ask?"

"Oh, I board wit' a good family over in Bucktown."

"Well, good luck to you, and let us know any way we can ever help you."

Jebediah thanked him, nodded in slight bow, and said, "Mr. Wulsin, your children did well tonight." Young Drausin shook his hand. Then Aline took it, and to everyone's surprise, including herself, tiptoed up with a kiss on his cheek. Lucien and Eugene each wrapped a leg and would not let him go, until Papa gave them the signal. "Good night." Jebediah disappeared back into the dark.

After the children went to bed, Josephine, rocking by the fire, said, "How can we be so fortunate?"

"Yes—and so foolish," said Drausin, letting his cigar help him digest the day's dangers. "I never imagined—the day I cast my first vote, the Know-Nothings try to deny the Germans their vote, and we're all still denying Ruth-in-the-Alien-Corn's family's right to vote. We should have warned our children to come right home from school." The next day the Wulsin schoolchildren did stay home, safe.

The next evening Papa Drausin shared what he had learned. The Know-Nothings had indeed destroyed two ballot boxes in Germantown before retreating. Several men had indeed died in the fights. This morning, the Know-Nothing mob had surged up Vine St. to discover impressively solid barricades of overturned wagons, barrels, and lots of planking. The German militia units were prepared to fire their muskets and reload in well-disciplined, alternating rows, at the near bridges as well. A single cannon had fired once across the bridge right down the center of Vine St., clearing a furrow like a plow; the whole mob retreated in mayhem. By midday Cincinnati was beginning to breathe normally. Nevertheless, Drausin accompanied his children to school and back the next three days.

In ensuing days, one fact became clear: Know-Nothing Taylor had lost the election for mayor to the Democrat, James J. Faran. The *Cincinnati Enquirer* said it could "find no language capable of expressing our indignation. Words could but faintly translate the abhorrence we feel that the ark of our safety, our ballot boxes, the very covenant of our freedom, should be ruthlessly seized by sacrilegious hands, and destroyed before our very eyes."

In ensuing weeks, most accounts suggested that the Know-Nothing party in Cincinnati had sputtered to its ignominious end in 1855. *Ahh, the freedom to vote,* thought Drausin. *How sweet, and a bit of a beast.*

CHAPTER 32:

ADELAÏDE POUPONNE, 1855

The day before the Wulsin family's fifth Christmas in Cincinnati, ice and snow bleached everything white. Icicles hung from eavestroughs, sparkling in the icy sun. The coldest weather the Wulsins had ever known was actually the coldest winter Cincinnati had known in sixty years. Papa Drausin and the boys kept feeding coal to the ravenous fireplaces.

At midday, Papa arose from his armchair at the head of the dinner table to the sound of the knocker at the door. The younger children, Eugene, Laure, and Clarence, hardly paid attention. Josephine, seven months with child, moved slowly these days. She and Aline certainly noticed Papa's unusually slow return, holding a Western Union telegram from his eldest brother, Joseph Valmont Bacas. He settled into his chair. As Josephine watched, Drausin raised his eyes, his voice low. "Maman died last night."

Josephine gathered the children; she and Aline led a prayer for the departing soul of Adelaïde, age seventy-two, on her journey through purgatory to heaven. Drausin couldn't help thinking that his mother would find few sins in her life to purge, that she'd have a smoother trip than most to St. Peter's gate. Laure and Clarence never imagined Papa even having a Maman. Eugene could vaguely, and Lucien a little more clearly, remember Granmère Pouponne, with her queenly warmth, mostly from when she visited the family at Granmère Josephine's house on Bayou Rd. Aline and Ti-Drausin had the strongest earlier memories of how Granmère Adelaïde Pouponne Beaulieu had gracefully conducted the whole Bacas household, overflowing with families at 116 St. Louis. And how she frequently soothed volcanic Granpère Barthelemy.

Christmas day, in spite of the delicious pork loin provided by Aline's ever-grateful Herr Weissman, felt grey due to Papa's mood. Christmas night was white, all night. With winter solstice just days earlier, the night was long. Moonrise met sunset, moon-shadows heading west, sun-shadows heading east, dueling on opposite sides of each tree, each building, each gaslight pole, each winter walker, as sun surrendered. The moon, still full, poured like the mouth of a milk bottle, lightened all around, except darkening shadows. Horses, dogs, and cats slowed like ghosts across the white, sparkling ground. The longest full moon in the longest nights of the year. In fact, this Blood Moon was also Wolf-eating Moon. At one moment in the middle of the night, Drausin could see out his window the Blood Moon being "nibbled" by the wolf of the eclipse. Everything seemed to melt, like reflections on a pond. Everything was its opposite. What should be dark was light. The night was a photographic negative of its usual self.

In his dream-sleep, Papa Drausin felt doors, windows, and roofs melting open, allowing Adelaïde to visit him, all night long. Her presence permeated. He felt her citrus oil and cinnamon smells, her warm breath, her slight, unspeaking sounds, felt her hand on his neck, her arms around him, her hair wisping his ear. A kiss on his forehead. Little bits of her singing wove in and out like breezes. The nights continued white; Adelaïde permeated Drausin's Holy Nights, all the way through to the day of the original Jean-Baptiste, January 6. Drausin knew, especially through Josephine, that January 6 commemorated John's baptism of Jesus by water, when the dove of the Holy Spirit descended, entering Jesus, who then became Christ. *Maman feels so present these Holy Nights, I can't help wondering how she may have participated somehow in my own slow, informal, invisible baptism, as Drauzin has become Drausin.*

Josephine's mate spent much of his days reflecting, as he hardly had since waving farewell to his mother from the Natchez III four and a half years ago. Although he had uprooted his own family, his own roots actually remained way down south in generations of soil, swamp, bloods, and blends. Maybe for the first time ever, he wondered about Adelaïde Pouponne Beaulieu. What had life been like for her Wolof people in Senegal, generations back? *Although Maman never talked of Africa, many of her words, phrases, and snatches of song formed the natural fabric of my childhood.*

Drausin remembered conversations Adelaïde had with their slave Marcelite back in their Rue St. Louis courtyard, while he, in his teens, played mandolin in the jasmine-musked dusk. He re-heard unseemly groans wrenching out of his mother after Marcelite walked out the front door of 116 St. Louis, freed. *Had Maman been caught by surprise, this explosion of her own childhood slave-pain? Did she groan, feeling still partially enslaved in her bones with her beloved, bad-man Barthelemy?* Whatever the source, she had kept her other slaves until manumitting Ernestine years later.

I always loved Maman's freeing of Marcelite and later Ernestine, a model for Josephine's and my later freeing of Claire. Why, why, then, did my mother, former slave, own slaves at all? Not unusual, though among free people of color in New Orleans in those days. Nelson and Alfonse belonged to Papa Barthelemy. But Chloe, Rose, Betsy—Maman's. Our household had certainly been bustling, nine children, and then children's children as well, overflowing—hence the need for help. Had it felt strange to Maman to have slaves of her own, doing her every bidding, serving her life, rather than leading their own? Could Josephine and I actually be tempted again, with our seventh child soon to arrive, to have slave help if it were legal here? I think not. Do I know for sure?

Adelaïde Pouponne, the harmonizing queen. Drausin looked, atypically, into the bedroom mirror. *How much of my own brow, high and wide, came from hers, whether Chaouchas Indian, African Wolof, or Quebecois? How much of my thin lips, my aquiline nose? How much of my own priority of harmonizing in life has embodied, through music, her essential, harmonizing gesture in the family?*

One evening, as Papa Drausin was smoking his cigar in his armchair by the fire, Aline walked by. Touched by his rich grief, his mood of reflection, of gratitude, she kissed him on his forehead. He looked up into her shining black eyes, realizing that Josephine had been close to Aline's age, sixteen, when he and she had first met. At Aline's age, Josephine had already been offering sweet crackers, bière creole, and grenadine outside her front door for potential suitors. He kept this thought to himself, not wanting yet to invite such rogues as himself into Aline's life.

Taking her hand into his, he pulled her gently down onto the arm of the chair. "Thank you, ma chère Aline Adelaïde. You have your grandmother's name, you have her brow, and, like your Granmère Adelaïde Pouponne, you help hold all together. She always loved you especially, her first granddaughter, and she would be especially proud of you now. What a blessing you are to your mother, to me, and to us all." Smiling, she kissed him again on his brow, and he kissed her hand before she sashayed on her way.

Drausin remembered asking his mother after the wood-shed blowup, just before all four sons left their home, "Maman, how could you give back your freedom for that tyrant?" She had smiled, a little painfully, it seemed to him.

"Simple. I loved him—and I still do. Remember, mon cher

Drauzin, a man is a lion when he puts on his pants, and he becomes a lamb when he takes them off. That has always been true, believe it or not, of your father."

Have I long felt guilty, Drausin wondered, leaving her unprotected in that big, suddenly empty house? Yes, certainly, some. How much of her freedom did she surrender to our father? Has the fact that my mother, Adelaïde Beaulieu, has never been allowed to assume, to wear, to identify with the name Bacas made it easier for me to shed that name when the time came to leave New Orleans? I think so.

Young Drausin's fourteenth birthday was celebrated with pleasure by all Wulsins on January 10, 1856. The young man was rising tall. His request: his favorite gumbo, with chicken, andouille sausage, and ochra. Papa and all sang and played.

Younger Lucien's eleventh birthday was celebrated, not by all, on January 19. Lucien, still slight and small, but with notably large hands, requested wiener schnitzel. His most exciting gift: a sun-bright orange. The difference between the two celebrations? At Lucien's, others sang, but not Papa.

An envelope had arrived on January 15 from Joseph Valmont Bacas. Papa Drausin had retired into his studio to open it. Hours passed. When Josephine finally joined him, he seemed to her like a zombie, the light out of his eyes, the blood out of his veins. He looked at her from afar and rose, nodding toward the documents on the desk. He closed the study door behind him, donned his coat, scarf, hat, and gloves, and left for a long walk in the bracing cold.

Josephine noticed several pages of a letter from Joseph, mostly about his mother's protracted illness, followed by a copy of Adelaïde Pouponne Beaulieu's will, dictated by her two weeks before she died.

Pouponne Adelaïde Beaulieu
City of New Orleans
State of Louisiana

Today, this fourteenth of December Eighteen Fifty-Five, year Eighty of the Independence of the United States of America at around twelve-thirty p.m, I have before me Octave de Armas public notary at the residence of the said city of New Orleans, duly committed, in presence of Mssrs. Felix de Armas, Jacques Alfred Charbonnet, et Louis de Roche, witnesses known as residing in this city.

With company of Miss "Pouponne" Adelaïde Beaulieu, a.72, F.(emme) (de)C.(ouleur)L.(ibre), resides in this city, street St. Louis in between Bourbon and Dauphine, for which we, the said notary and his witnesses have found at her home, the above mentioned (Pouponne Adelaïde), lying in her bed, sick of body, but with healthy memory and understanding, as it appears to me, the named notary, and the said witnesses, and the said "Pouponne" A. Beaulieu has required me to receive her testament that she has dictated to me as is.

1. I declare to have six children named Joseph Valmont Bacas [a.48], Jean-Baptiste Valcour Bacas [43], Drausin Valsin Bacas [42], Adelaïde Emilia Bacas [38] = Madame Belmont-Heno, Marie-Josephine Felice Bacas = Madame Livermore [35], Elizabeth Coelina Bacas [29] = Madame LeRond, who all have their majority, the named ones instituted as my sole heirs and universal receivers.

2. I give to my daughter Marie-Josephine Felicie Bacas, independently of her portion of heritage the amount of two thousand dollars, for the purpose of helping her improve her land situated on street Claiborne.

3. I give freedom to the cost of my succession to my slave Chloe, negresse of around 34 years old, recommending her my children to replace me.

4. I leave to my children hereafter named, the five children of Chloe: to Mme. Heno, the little mulato Felicite; to Mme.

Livermore, Gabriel who is around 8 years old; to Mme. LeRond, Sannon, who is around 6 years old; to Joseph Valmont, Sam, who is around 2 and a half years old; to Jean-Baptiste, Edward, presently wet-nursed. These slaves' value will be estimated by the evaluators named by the law. The evaluators will reimburse to those of my children who will receive less in "slave value" the difference whatever it is. I desire as well that those slaves always remain at the service of their family, and never be sold.

5. I am giving and bequeathing to my three daughters my armoire with its possessions, with the recommendation to give to my daughter-in-law Sizandre, Louise Essayleme, wife of Joseph Valmont Bacas, mother of Henry, what she may desire from the possessions contained, and I am giving to my grandson Henry Bacas my gold watch.

6. I want that my two slaves, Rose and Betsy be sold for the benefit of my inheritors, wanting that Betsy be sold for the countryside and that the entrance of my house be refused to her.

7. I am bequeathing three "billets" mortgages in the hands of my daughter, Marie-Josephine for the total sum of 3,200$. The "billets" once paid, will be divided equally between my inheritors, to the exception of 400$ dollars, who will come back as "billets" to her.

8. I name as the executors of my will and possessors of my "goods" Mssrs. Barthelemy Bacas et John Dawson both from this city, either jointly or separately.

This is how this testament has been dictated to me, notary, by the testator in presence of the witnesses named and under-signed, as dictated by the testator in presence of the said wit-nesses. With a high and intelligible voice, she the testator has declared in the presence of these witnesses that she was hearin-gand comprehending well.

The action required and granted in New Orleans, in the dwelling of the testator the days, month and year above men-tioned in presence of the named Sir Felix de Armas,

Jacques Alfred Chabonnet et Louis de Roche, witnesses

who have signed with me notary but not the testator, who has declared not knowing how to sign her name and hasmade her ordinary mark that would represent her individual "signature" after the reading was completed.

Signed Pouponne A. Beaulieu and her ordinary mark
F. de Armas, J.A Charbomet, Louis de Roche, Octave de Armas, not. pub.

Josephine, stunned, reflected, trying to digest what she had read.

First, Adelaïde Pouponne Beaulieu has six inheritors: Joseph Valmont Bacas, Jean-Baptiste Bacas, Drauzin Valsin Bacas (not Wulsin), Adelaïde Emilia Bacas (Heno), Marie-Josephine Felice Bacas (Livermore), and Elizabeth Coëlina Bacas (LeRond). Louisa had been long dead of scarlet fever, and baby Felix too, of course, but it was clear now that youngest brother Leon was deemed dead. A hard blow for his closest brother, Drauzin, in spite of their eight-year difference. The other five surviving siblings remained in New Orleans, so far.

Second, Marie-Josephine would receive some money to help improve her Claiborne property.

Third, thirty-four-year-old slave Chloe would receive her freedom.

So far, so good.

Fourth, Chloe's five children were to be given to Drausin's five local siblings, one each, "to remain in service—to the family, never to be sold." Josephine was shocked. Mulatto Felicite (maybe five years old, maybe fathered by—Nelson? Alfonce? Please not Barthelemy?) to Adelaïde Emilia; eight-year-old Gabriel (maybe fathered by who knew?) to Maria-Josephine; six-year-old Sannon to Elizabeth; two-and-a-half-year-old Sam to Joseph Valmont; and still-nursing Edward to Jean-Baptiste. Chloe, the mother, is to be freed, but her children are to be kept in slavery, separated from her and from each other as well?

Was only one, Felicite, mulatto? Who was her father? Leon had not been seen since '46. Barthelemy? And the others? Nelson? Alfonce? What could Adelaïde be thinking, feeling, intending? Why spread Chloe's children evenly among Barthelemy's and Adelaïde Pouponne's own children?

Fifth, the two slaves, Rose and Betsy, were to be sold to provide inheritance. Betsy specifically to be sold to the countryside, never to reenter 116 St. Louis again. A house slave sold to become a field slave would likely not survive more than several years chopping cane.

Sixth, Adelaïde, not knowing how to sign, had made her mark, for "Pouponne A. Beaulieu"—Josephine had never thought twice about the fact that Adelaïde could neither read nor write. Having so loved to read in her own father's library, Josephine was now surprised to realize that the mate of former City Councilman Barthelemy Bacas, the mother of the well-tutored, literate Bacas children, had never either asked nor been helped by Barthelemy, by tutor Basil Crockère, or by any of her own children to learn to read and write.

And, finally, Adelaïde had left nothing to her beloved Barthelemy. Because he had never been formalized as her husband? Because, it had always been clear, he would leave nothing to his own children? So she had to do the bequeathing?

Josephine could now understand why her husband had looked like a zombie. She felt in shock herself, almost as severely as he must feel himself to be. Was this really Adelaïde's official will? Was she really of sound mind? Did this will reveal another Adelaïde beneath the surface of the ever-warming copper queen all those years? Where was Barthelemy in all this, other than being one of two executors of Adelaïde's will? Was Drausin discovering, in her death, a new mother? What can he possibly be thinking and feeling? She knew he must feel poisoned at least. She felt poisoned herself.

Drausin, meanwhile, had walked halfway across the Ohio River before realizing that strong currents under the ice might open it at any moment.

Upon his return and throughout the ensuing weeks, Josephine did her best to warm Drausin, any way she could. In bed, she wrapped herself around him under an extra duvée. New wool socks, new wool vest, new wool gloves. At tea-time a cup of hot buttered rum with a cinnamon stick by the fire. After supper, cognac with his cigar. As the weeks passed, he became less a zombie and more a sleepwalker. It seemed to her as though, when he looked in the mirror, he saw either a monster or the familiar image shattered.

When he awoke in the morning, he lit his first cigar. By midday he had often smoked five, by tea-time ten, by bedtime, sometimes twenty. He was not pickling himself in spirits, but he was smoking himself dry.

Drausin wondered relentlessly, *Who was my mother? Freed slave? Freer of slaves, three at least? Faithful non-wife? Mother of nine? Ever "Pouponne"?* According to Valmont's statement on the death certificate, Adelaïde was the "wife of Barthelemy Bacas, his Surviving Consort, —She was a Pouponne—" *Wife? Consort? Pouponne? Copper queen, matriarch of the Bacas clan? Perhaps all that, but also a wreaker of vengeance, indifferent to slaves' sufferings? Punisher more than nurse? Depriver more than nurturer? In fact, a sham pouponne? Destroyer rather than harmonizer, scatterer rather than uniter? Was she somehow as much a monster as Barthelemy? She private, he public? Was she, in fact, as bad a master as she had had? Worse? Did these dying deeds of hers reveal some twisted bitterness, implying she remained, in hidden ways, the slave of Barthelemy Bacas?* Smoke clouded and stung Drausin's lifelong experience and notion of his mother.

Was my mother somehow an original source of my most long-forgotten but most haunting nightmare? When I, Drausin, alternated between slave whipper and slave whipped, back and forth, back and forth, the grimace of each the same, like a knife slice. And my strange obsession to go down to the slave markets until I met Josephine?

Confounded after days and nights of inner solitude,

Drausin finally felt he could, *must*, consult with his wisdom tree, his beloved laurel tree.

"Ma Josephine, tell me, *tell me*, why had Maman's own son Joseph signed her death certificate, not her 'husband' Barthelemy? Do you think Adelaïde Pouponne must have always lived split, having given her freedom to the man who could not marry her, and with whom they continued to own and command other slaves?

"My own father has been the boogeyman, the loup garou of my youth. And now, later in my life, it turns out that my dear mother is the boogeywoman, the loup garou for her own slaves?

"Am I, now forty-two, actually blinder than I was in my teens? We all saw our father's tyranny. Were we all blinded by our mother's tignon? Am I, Drausin, from two monsters, not one? From what in me might I, might *you*, my Josephine, might our children need still to escape? Oh, Josephine, I do not know. I fail to understand."

Josephine, his perennial laurel tree, was wise enough simply to listen, and to embrace him, mildly rocking.

In spite of his obsessive ponderings upon his mother, or perhaps because of them, Drausin never mentioned her again in the family. Adelaïde Pouponne Beaulieu, long beloved by Aline, Ti-Drausin, and Lucien, now became ghosted, banished, by her own child. Perhaps as her own son, sons, had been ghosted and banished by his father nine years earlier from the family at 116 St. Louis.

Acid often corroded Drausin's stomach, his throat, even his veins. When his mouth burned and his throat was too raw, he sucked, chewed, unlit cigars. He carried on normally around town, teaching his music students, yet he couldn't help wondering at times, *Can strangers in the streets, or my students close at the keyboard, tell not only that I am actually a man of color, but even that I am the progeny of two beasts, hence a demon myself, dangerous in terms of what might lurch forth unbeknownst? Should, or* do, my own children actually dread something dark lurking within their own father, the apparent harmonizer of the North? How much might I, Drausin Wulsin, in fact, be the wolf eating the moon?

CHAPTER 33:
FADED FACES, 1856

Quite early one late January morning, Aline was awakened by the bright, almost daylight of the full snow moon, still well before dawn. Stirred, unable to slip back to sleep, she dressed warmly, pulled on her rabbit-fur coat, and slipped outside, drawn toward the moon hanging low now in the western night sky. The whole basin of the city seemed to shine, night though it still was. And the greatest brightness came from the river, the Ohio River, which beckoned Aline, as though sleep-walking, so entranced was she.

All the way across to Kentucky, the vast hard-pan of ice looked to her like a second moon itself, reflecting the light of the actual moon, which reflected the light of the sun still behind the earth—rebounding echoes of light. The wind swirled snow into paisley patterns on the ice.

Aline found herself thinking of another young woman and ice—Eliza and her baby in *Uncle Tom's Cabin*, which she had bought from the tea and spice man just four years ago when it first appeared. She remembered her own Papa, recently driving her and her brothers in a carriage past the white house up in Walnut Hills, where Harriet Beecher Stowe had written much of the novel, after asking many runaways and slaves their stories. Who could match the desperate courage of Eliza, leaping, baby in arms, onto the blue-green ice floe as the slave-catcher, hounds baying by his boots, watched from the Kentucky shore, her shoeless feet trailing scarlet as she jumped from floe to floe, miraculously reaching the Ohio shore, and freedom for both? A much colder night this.

She remembered as well how Eliza's husband George had passed as a Spanish gentleman in inns and hotels, making his way north through slave country to join her. He had succeeded because he imitated so masterfully the imperious manners of his master. *Our Wulsin family is living a version of the same, imitating the whites around, yet with less life-or-death, freedom-or-slavery intensity, so far anyway.*

Then Aline smiled, both amused at her forgetfulness and impressed with the power of Eliza's story, as told by Mrs. Stowe. She was just remembering Harvey Young, the strong Negro servant of their new friends, the Longworths, the man who took care of their household, horses, and surrounding grounds. Young Nick had told her and her brothers that it had actually been Harvey Young who, alone, clad only in tattered jeans, had leapt from floe to floe in his escape from slavery. Reaching shore, he had veered and raced up Pike St., where a man pruning trees told him to jump in the cellar window. The old pruner, questioned by pursuers, pointed up north, where they fast ran past.

That old pruner had been Nick's grandfather, Nicholas Longworth I. Hearing Harvey Young's story, Longworth had gone to Kentucky and purchased Harvey's freedom. Harvey devoted the rest of his life to helping the Longworth family. Aline liked imagining Mrs. Harriet Beecher Stowe interviewing Harvey Young. Mrs. Stowe had clearly concluded that Harvey's actual deed would live longer in the literary incarnation of Eliza and daughter.

While pondering, Aline's eye naturally scanning the white expanse, she half-noticed a stark darkness like an inkblot on the far Kentucky shore downriver. In the dawning light it was growing larger. She wrapped her scarf several times around, shielding her face except her eyes; hugged her chest, holding in as much warmth as possible; and stamped her feet gently. Her breath steamed.

Soon she saw two high heads, with high ears. She was watching a wagon, pulled by two mules, crossing the Ohio River! The huge wagon seemed loaded, and people walked alongside on the ice, right over the frozen middle of the river. She started half-walking, half-running in their direction along the higher Ohio north shore, counting more and more people on and off the wagon. *Eleven it seems now. Oh, Lordy.*

She worried about the ice at the shoreline. Wouldn't it be less thick than the rest? But the driver got the mules trotting. Yes, some ice cracked under the weight of the wheels right at the edge, but the mud was rock hard, and the momentum of the wagon took it right on up the bank near the summertime ferry landing. By now a number of people had appeared, seemingly out of nowhere, to meet the wagon. Six more clambered out of the wagon's back. All the travelers were colored, dark to light. *Runaways*, Aline realized. Quickly, greeters led the seventeen off in different directions. One family headed further west toward Mill Creek. And suddenly the Ohio River was white as before, except for tracks catching shadow across the ice.

Aline hurried home to help with Laure and Clarence, Maman larger and more uncomfortable each day. The family was amazed at Aline's story as, shivering, she sipped choco-chaud by the fireplace. Yes, Drausin, Lucien, Eugene, and, of course, Maman and Papa remembered Captain Leathers pulling the Natchez III over toward the Kentucky shore as Esau had pulled out the body of the mother clutching a baby blanket, a body that had been discreetly secreted away immediately at their arrival in the port of Cincinnati.

The Wulsins realized that the famed, and in some circles infamous, Underground Railroad was far more active here in Cincinnati than they had thought. Although, of course, the older children had already witnessed it in action last Election Day with Jebediah.

The newspapers refrained for several days. Drausin figured there might be an understood, self-imposed public silence in order not to endanger both runaway slaves and the people helping them, colored or white. It was Aline's teenage grapevine, her high school mates, who, having heard her account, gradually gathered facts.

The party of seventeen had been led by a slave, Robert Garner, who had stolen his master's wagon and gun earlier that night. Right in Boone County, right across the river—Maplewood Plantation, owned by Archibald Gaines, known as A. K. "Practically our neighbors!" one of her classmates had said.

Garner; his parents; his pregnant wife Margaret, called Peggy; and their four children had sought shelter on Mill Creek at the house of Peggy's uncle, Joe Kite. While their host had gone off to Levi Coffin for advice, US Marshalls and slave-catchers had surrounded the house to take the whole runaway family to jail and back into slavery. The other nine successfully traveled the Underground Railroad north to Canada and certain freedom.

What had happened next, none of Aline's classmates nor family initially believed. As the posse stormed the house, pregnant Peggy grabbed a butcher knife, stabbed her two-year-old, and then started on her other children, intending to finish off them and herself, rather than let them grow up as slaves. The shocked slave-catchers and marshalls jumped her, interfering, but her two-year-old died. Her husband, Robert, had shot a marshall in the arm before being subdued. The wounded family was taken to jail.

The owner and the catchers were ready to take the runaways right back to Maplewood, but local abolitionists hired John Joliffe to plead the Garners' case, which caught the attention of the newspapers. A. K. Gaines's lawyer argued that the Federal Fugitive Slave Act of 1850 made the case clear: property, namely the Garner family, must be returned to their owner. Joliffe argued that the state of Ohio had the right to protect its citizens. He hoped to attack the Fugitive Slave Act itself.

A classmate loaned Aline a copy of Joliffe's recently published *Belle Scott, or, Liberty Overthrown; a Tale for the Crisis*. Aline was haunted by main character Edgar's realization that slavery was just a form of soul-cannibalism. In Edgar's dream, the sellers had shrieked, "Ha! Ha! We sell the souls of the slaves and buy the souls of the purchasers. Ha! Ha!" before fading away as fiends.

Drausin gleaned over the unfolding weeks of the trial that if all else failed, Joliffe's last hope was that Peggy Garner would be tried as a person, not as property, convicted for murder. Then Ohio's new and first Republican governor, Cincinnati's own longtime "Attorney General for Fugitive Slaves," Salmon Chase, could pardon Peggy. Maybe.

Unfortunately, six-year-old Laure, playing around the corner, had overheard some of the initial story. She'd poked her head around the doorway, looking at her parents with horror. Josephine, the first to understand, had drawn in a deep, sympathetic sigh and swept her into her arms, saying, "Oh, ma petite chou-chou, non, non non, t'en fais pas." Maman looked around at each of their children reassuringly. "We, *you*, have all been born free, and you will grow free in Cincinnati." And she hummed an old Creole lullaby, rocking Laure in her lap.

Later that night, Drausin and Josephine reflected on both the story and Laure's fear, returning to a frequent debate about whether Drausin should read *Uncle Tom's Cabin* to the children at night. Josephine remained adamantly opposed to the idea. She had not, though, resisted Aline reading it herself. Josephine confided in her mate, "I prefer to have the children not even think about such things."

Drausin, sympathizing, said, "I want them to forget or not know what is in them. But I *do* want our children to know what is outside them, so they can navigate the world. Can we do that?"

"I don't know. I do not know." *Uncle Tom's Cabin* was left to the ready individual. Maman and Papa rarely let themselves remember that their own romance had begun when they first laid eyes on each other at the slave market of the Hotel St. Louis. Both Drausin and Josephine avoided exposing the children to the slave auctions across the river in Covington, Kentucky.

On the final day of the trial Aline played hookie with a few classmates, slipping into the crowded courtroom. Mr. Joliffe called to the stand a short young woman named Lucy Stone. Aline and her friends giggled, trying to see if she might be wearing her famous bloomers under her long skirt. Aline hoped so, in this coldest of weather. They knew Lucy Stone was the first American woman known to keep her own name in her brand-new marriage. Aline was impressed with her modest beauty, brown hair brushed and bound back tight, broad brow, lovely brown eyes, uplifting nose, and clear chin, all composed in pleasing balance, bespeaking harmony. Aline knew Lucy was becoming famous as an anti-slavery activist. Before speaking, she looked directly, it seemed, at every person in the courtroom, a match for anyone. She spoke with the clarity of a silver bell.

Lucy Stone pointed to black Robert Garner and mulatto Peggy Garner. "Peggy is likely the daughter of her previous owner, John Pollard Gaines, Archibald Gaines's older brother. Behold the eldest Garner child, six-year-old Thomas; he is dark like his father. He would have been conceived before the Garners had been sold to their master's brother, Archibald Gaines. Now, look at the other three children, Samuel, Mary, and Priscilla. Yes—they are lighter than their mother. Each of these three lighter Garner children was born exactly five to seven months after three of Archibald Gaines's own children; each Garner child was conceived when Gaines's own wife would have not been 'available' for sex, fathered no doubt by the only white male on Maplewood Plantation, Archibald Gaines."

At one point, Aline felt Lucy Stone was speaking directly to her alone, as she seemed somehow to be focusing on her, Aline. *Probably everyone experiences that,* she thought. Listening, Aline thought of her own publicly reticent mother, Josephine, and realized that for the first time in her own life she was listening to a woman speak officially in public.

Lucy Stone explained to the court how, in the institution of American slavery, mulatto women often suffer doubly severe mistreatment. "First, like all their fellow dark slaves, they are treated as subhuman. Second, they suffer a painful contradiction. While the mulatto woman is more likely than other slave women to be the object of the white master's desire, catalyzing forced sexual intimacy, nevertheless that same lightness of skin serves as a continuous, irritating public announcement of the master's infidelity, of his sexual transgressions, to the humiliation of the master's wife and family, and of himself, often catalyzing doubly harsh punishment—

"Now, picture, each one of you, the face of Archibald Gaines, master, and then picture, each one of you, the faces of young Samuel and Priscilla Garner, two of his surviving slave children. The faded faces of the Negro children tell too plainly to what degradation the female slaves submit. I am afraid, gentlemen of the court and ladies of the audience, that we have to say and hear the name of what this family both shows us and lives—systematic plantation rape. Yes, *systematic plantation rape.* And everyone, I repeat, *everyone,* knows that to be the truth. Rather than give her daughter to that life, Margaret Garner killed her. If, in her deep maternal love, she felt the impulse to send her child back to God, to save it from coming woe, who shall say she had no right to do so?"

Aline, aware of the general advantages of lighter skin in general society, was shocked that she had not gleaned such disadvantages inside slavery itself. And she herself, with her family, had jumped clear to the other side by passing as white. From disadvantage to advantage? It certainly seemed so, at least so far.

Judge Pendery in the end deferred to the Federal Fugitive Slave Act of 1850. The surviving members of Robert and Margaret Garner's family were returned as lawful property to Archibald K. Gaines, who gloated, plucking the folds of his neck with his right hand.

Aline was seared. She spent more and more time in St. Patrick's Church, not hiding from the world, but rather burrowing, digging, mining for meaning, through kneeling, through praying for Mama-sliced Mary Garner, for mother Peggy herself, for the whole family, for all slave women, for all slave children, for all slaves. Aline remembered someone saying of Eliza's escape across the ice floes, "Lawd, dat woman got seven debils in 'er." Did Peggy Garner have seven devils in her? Or angels? How could one know? Aline prayed too for Granmère Adelaïde Pouponne, Granpère Barthelemy, Granmère Josephine, and for all owners of slaves to open their souls so widely that the only question left would be, "How could we?"

Lucy Stone, the little lady, became for Aline the picture of a self-possessed woman, standing quiet but strong in her own name, with the steadiness of a boulder, at rest in herself. At the same time she was lucid, light-clear in her thinking, in her gaze, in her speakings.

"Lucien," Aline told her little brother, "this woman, Lucy Stone, is name-kin to you. Lucy. Lucien. You would do well to learn someday to speak as clearly, as strongly, as Lucy Stone." Eleven-year-old Lucien, hardly verbose, did not much understand what Aline meant. But in ensuing years he would keep eye and ear out for news of Lucy Stone.

The Garners' experiences of family, conceptions, births,

slavery, murder, and capture roiled Aline's own feelings in relation to romance, marriage, mothering, and child-bearing. Aline Adelaïde Wulsin deepened her wish to become, some day, the Bride of Christ, to help all His children who suffer unduly.

The next Sunday at mass, Aline removed her garnet earrings, a long-ago gift that once belonged to her grandfather Barthelemy Bacas's mother, Marie Louise Catherine Landrony. Aline placed her blood-red earrings onto the silver offering plate.

CHAPTER 34:

POSSIBILITIES, PRAYERS, AND PIRATES, 1857

Josephine was grateful she did not suffer Peggy Garner's tragic trap in relation to her own children. As Josephine birthed her eighth child, she remembered her first-born, short-lived Barthelemy, always a keynote of sadness in her bounty. February 29, 1857, was a leap year, which seemed fitting, as though the baby had slipped into life between the ordinary calendar months. Josephine gazed at a little pixie with slanting, darting eyes, nose rising like a flower petal, and pointed ears; she named her baby daughter Lillie Alice Eve. Drausin thought his new daughter seemed more the flower fairy than the flower itself. He couldn't help noticing a family name-sequence extending: Lucien—light, Clarence—clarity, Lillie—white. A conscious, deliberate choice? Or unconscious? But he refrained from questioning.

Whereas little Laure continued quiet as dusk, Lillie quickly became, and evermore remained, a little mocking bird, flitting and flisking this way and that, ever improvising in response to whatever she might notice.

Partially to wean themselves of the habit of slave Claire's help, Josephine and Drausin had been trying in the North to manage their home sans slave. Aline, of course, was the supreme second mother and housekeeper. But with Laure at six and Clarence almost three, Drausin and Josephine decided they did need extra hands and so hired an Irish servant girl to help with children, cooking, and cleaning—what Aline called the three Cs. Caitlin (the fourth C) Hennessey, age twelve, hailed from rural county Sligo, having arrived with her family in Cincinnati (the fifth C!) two years ago. Caitlin was slightly saucy, but she lightened the workload and was grateful for this family, all things considered. Both her parents struggled to make a living, her mother with laundry, her father with horses in a livery stable. Caitlin needed work, and the Wulsins needed Caitlin. Drausin and Josephine were grateful they needed to pay their new servant.

Drausin, due partially to the icy winter, coughed often. Josephine noticed he was easing off his constant cigars. His inner grey remained. Adelaïde's will continued to weigh heavily on him. Josephine, with the passing of weeks and in light of Lillie, developed new perspectives. "Cher, do you think your mother loved Chloe?"

"I do. I think Chloe delighted her. She touched something in Maman's heart."

"So she freed her?"

"Yes."

"Can you imagine her wishing to punish Chloe, even to torture her, we might say?"

"No, I have tried, I have tried, and I cannot find it; I cannot."

"Can you imagine the pain of Chloe being separated from her five children?"

"I can imagine my pain being separated from five of my children. Can I imagine hers? Probably just partially, not wholly; it must be twice or ten times mine. I can hardly imagine."

"Do you picture how Chloe will make her way, suddenly free?"

"Oh, I don't know; she has a flare with hair. But, though

a delight, she's flighty. It's likely to be a winding road, I'm afraid."

"Is it more likely that your mother would disregard the well-being of Chloe's children, or intensely consider their well-being?"

"Intensely consider, intensely consider—surely that would be more likely. That's why this kills me."

"Can you imagine that, in spite of the pain of separation, Chloe might know she would struggle mightily to feed all five of her children, might be relieved for each child to be safe and secure in the known homes of your five siblings?"

"Yes—I guess."

"Can you imagine any brother or sister of yours being able to take all five children together?"

"No, no. I can't see that working."

"Can you imagine the possibility that your mother, ill as she was, wrestling with the riddle of the future of Chloe and her children, and painful as this outcome was, felt unable to secure their futures any other way?"

"Oh, Josie, Chère, ma Lady Jo-o-o-e, I would so like to think so, *so* wish to think so. I just don't know."

"And desiring that those child-slaves never be sold does not imply they could never be freed, right?"

"Why, you're right. I had not thought of that. Yes, I think that is certainly true."

"Mon Cher, did Betsy and Rose respect your mother?"

"Of course."

"Are you sure? Think."

"Well—I guess not like Marcelite, Nelson, Evangeline, and Chloe."

"I remember their snide looks and side-whispers, though never in Barthelemy's presence. I remember their slow responses. I always felt they resented being owned and mastered by a former slave."

"Now that you mention it, I do recall some such hints,

innuendoes, gestures. Did Betsy do something especially foul that got her sent to the country and banned from 116?"

"Maybe, maybe. In fact, I would say most likely. Because this is so unlike your mother. But remember, it takes two wings to fly. Your mother was so warm. Perhaps she had to have a hard, even cruel-for-truth side, to be able to *be* so able all those years."

"I don't know, Chèrie, I just don't know. But I do know that just pondering these new possibilities feels like rubbing one of your liniments, your calendula-arnica blend, around my heart, which has felt so torn, so twisted these months. It's been hurting me so I could hardly breathe sometimes. I've felt at times mad. But you're helping me, soothing, comme d'habitude."

Drausin's voice was raspy, and he coughed with a rattle. But he smiled at Josephine, his eyes brightening for just the second time in more than a year—the first being when he held his bright little pixie, Lillie.

Later that spring, as the ice was finally melting and the river swelling, word was that the State of Ohio was seeking Margaret Garner to extradite her, to try her for murder. Joliffe still hoped for both judicial conviction and the governor's pardon. Slaver A. K. Gaines became the hunted, moving his property—the Garners—from place to place, city to city. Ohio authorities missed Peggy by hours in Covington, then again in Franklin, and found their master in Louisville—but he had just shipped the Garners down river to his brother's plantation in Arkansas. Their steamboat, the Henry Lewis, collided with another boat, throwing Peggy and her baby girl overboard. Peggy was glad her daughter had drowned, even though she was dark like her father, Robert. Peggy was sorry her effort to drown herself had failed. After a short stint in Arkansas, the

Garners were sold as house servants to a Gaines family friend in New Orleans. Aline prayed daily for the Garners all.

One morning later that summer, as the river sighed back into its banks, Harvey Young removed from the Longworth warehouse on Horne St. two old birchbark canoes that Grandpa Longworth had traded from Shawnee Indians for axes back in the twenties. Harvey wagonned the canoes and seven voyageurs a few blocks west to the shore of Mill Creek. The youngsters had brought along a basket of bread, cheese, chocolate, wienerwurst, some early apples, and several Longworth wine bottles of well water.

In the stern of one canoe paddled Ti-Drausin, now thirteen; Eugene, eight, sat in the bow, with Laure and her friend Mary, both six, in the middle. The other canoe held Nick, eleven, at the stern; Lucien, ten, in the bow; and Landon, also eight, in the middle. All were armed with paddles, and the boys had pocket knives. The younger boys brought a couple of sling-shots as well. Barefoot all, they were headed north, upstream. "Thank you, Harvey," called Nick.

"Bless you, children. Keep your heads."

"Bye, Harvey," chorused the voyageurs, who all knew he was the actual hero of Eliza's legendary Ohio River ice escape.

"We'll fetchya a gator!" hollered Eugene. Harvey chuckled.

Birds sang variously and profusely. Mourning doves provided bass notes. Bobwhites called Bob-Bob-White. The sun glowed. The adventurers knew they'd start against the current but enjoy an easy float home at day's end. After some tipping, but not over-tipping, in both canoes, Drausin and Lucien quickly had the hang of paddling, recovered from younger trips back on the bayou with their father. Nick and Landon had paddled before. Eugene, as always, picked it up quickly, paddling vigorously, each bowman setting the pace. The girls paddled off and on as they talked, staying still and trying not to shift the balance in the canoe. Drausin and Nick switched paddles to the opposite side any time their bowmen did, keeping an increasingly straight course. The current in fact was hardly noticeable; the brown waters lazed between the green-leaved banks, like Bayou St. Jean. Nick respected the steady, rhythmic pulls of his bowman, Lucien; the beat of the paddles on the gunnels made a music like gentle drums as they pulled, gliding, dividing waters, cruising.

Lucien started imagining himself as René Robert Cavalier, Sieur de La Salle, the first Frenchman to paddle the waters of the Mississippi from the Illinois River all the way to its mouth, claiming all the lands west for France, hence "Louisiane." But Lucien knew its true name to be "Lucianne." Lucien La Salle, paddling new waters along new lands, meeting new Indians, learning new tongues.

At one point they pulled over on the west shore so Drausin and Nick could rig lines on poles, trolling from each stern. The creek flowed gently under overhanging willows, ashes, poplars, even lazier when it veered east on a long oxbow, meandering around the peninsula. They spotted a west-shore clearing with slight bluffs for their picnic.

The boys skinny-dipped; the girls gathered clay from the banks, layered blue-grey. Mary and Laure soaked slabs, working them with their wet hands into growing batches of workable clay. Butterflies started appearing, a cat, a resting robin. When the boys shimmied themselves dry and pulled on their knickers, a boat, a bear, a catfish, and even a horse had joined the clay creatures on the flat shore stones. Then bowls and cups were set under the high sun to dry, some even with finger-handles. The potters dripped, satisfied with their work.

Nick and Lucien offered a huge, spade-shaped catalpa leaf to each voyageur as a plate for their feast of wurst and chocolate. Nick had brought along a couple of dried corncobs. Cutting them and boring a hole, Drausin, Nick, and Lucien then cut hollow reeds, inserting a stem into each bottom. Next they pinched, poured, and packed some tobacco filched from their fathers, managing to light a rough, exciting smoke. The girls retreated from the smoke and sun to the comfort of shade, making little fairy gardens with moss, acorns, and leaves.

The Wulsin boys patched together stories of pirates, especially the Green River's Harte Brothers and the Cave-in-the-Rock gang down in Illinois. Landon soon had them all as pirates, the girls playing damsels in distress, enticing unsuspecting river travelers to their cave so the gang could take their goods. Eugene made clear they were Mason's river pirates, honest to goodness—no scaring horse and stranger over the cliff like those awful Harte brothers. These pirates helped hungry locals and runaways too, being regular Robin Hoods of the West.

Before returning downstream, the girls placed their clay-pieces out of sight to further dry, to be fetched another day. Mary, though, couldn't resist stowing a bowl, a cup, and a butterfly, wrapped carefully in the muslin picnic cloth, under Drausin's stern-thwart.

On the way home, Lucien and Drausin pieced together a verse of one of their father's old voyageur songs:

Parmi les voyageurs—lui y à de bons enfants—
Et qui ne mangent guère (who hardly eat)—mais qui
    boivent souvent; (but who ofen drink)
Et la pipe a la bouche (the pipe in the mouth) "That's
    us!" Nick hollered,
et le verre a la main (and the glass in hand)—
Ils disent: camarades, versez-moi du vin. (comrades,
    pour me wine)

They all got the hang of it quickly, as the Longworth children were well tutored in French at home.

Then it rained. Under the sun. And the girls noticed pebbles in the bottom of their boat.

"Scram! Outta here! This is our shore! Steer clear o' here, ya bums!" Four or five half-wet, half-dirty boys were hurling pebbles, mud, and stones from the west shore.

"Girls down!" Drausin called. "Pull, pull!" Drausin and Nick each called hard, shoulder-stroking deep, as Lucien and Eugene paddled fast and shallow to speed the canoes by. Landon was hit in the shoulder, but just by a pebble.

Once in the clear, the two canoes pulled over to the east shore. The children stocked up on little stones, bow and stern, in case of any more attacks, and made plans. Nick stripped off his shirt, emptied the picnic basket remains into it, stuffed it under his stern-thwart, and switched places with Lucien. Mary lay flat in their canoe, ready to supply Landon with stones. Laure did the same for Eugene. Silently, they proceeded downstream.

Sure enough, it wasn't long before Nick heard another west shore gang attacking Drausin's canoe up ahead. He slipped overboard on the east side of the canoe. Lucien tossed the basket upside down on the water. Nick raised his head into it, and, slow and low, with no show, breast-stroked his way down toward shore. "Ha, they lost their basket! Yippee," whooped several ragamuffins ashore. "Ha! If you take dat dare, you'll steal a hawg an' eat his hair. We're de West Side Gang, an' donchya forget it!"

Drausin and Lucien first swung their sterns out, less target for the gang. Laure handed stones to Eugene, who'd slid down in the bow, sling-shot at the gunnel. Mary and Landon kept his sling-shot busy, too. Lucien threw stones and batted away incoming ones with his paddle. Then Drausin, who had already tied his stern line around his waist, pulled into the shallows, stepped into the water with his fishing stick, tossed a stone just in front of him and whacked, stone after stone, at the attackers, just like town-ball, only now he was trying to hit them, rather than avoid them. One antagonist yelped at the zing on his thigh. Eugene, hawk-eyed, hit two more on arm and chest.

Meanwhile, Nick, having landed downstream and loaded stones in his pocket, crept back up behind the gang and pelted them from the bluff above. The blusterers, some screeching, hightailed it upstream, and Mason's Pirates hooted in victory. After the children retrieved the picnic basket and counted noses to be sure everyone was at their assigned position, their trip home was smooth. It was one fine expedition for the young Longworths and Wulsins on Mill Creek, many details of which they shared with Harvey Young, and many fewer of which they later shared with families.

Two years earlier, a weak suspension bridge across Kentucky's Licking River had collapsed, further discouraging Cincinnati's longtime hopes to bridge the mammoth Ohio River. This September, though, a Pennsylvania engineer named John Roebling was finally able to begin digging the holes for two massive stone towers, one on the Cincinnati shore, one on the Covington shore, to support a suspension bridge over a thousand feet long. The boys, especially Lucien, were fascinated to watch the struggles of the excavating crew to empty the pit of water, mud, and stone through pumps that Roebling had devised for the task. Then, down on the gravel riverbed, the construction crew laid the foundation of thirteen layers of oak beams, each set perpendicular to the one beneath it, all bolted with iron and then cemented into place.

Such a massive base, from which wire would reach south across the river, when so many people have reached north. Lucien knew something of South and North, and the river between. To this curious child, fascinated by the challenges of bridging such a river, it did feel odd for North to be reaching South.

CHAPTER 35:

REUNION, 1857

Papa Drausin found himself turning in a direction he had never imagined. His initial grief over his mother's death, followed by the shock of her will and ensuing confusions, had been leading him to consider trying to see his father, who he'd heard was ill at age seventy-seven. Drausin surprised himself with a growing urge to visit New Orleans. He did not want to go south. He did feel the need to remeet family. And yet ...

Both the successful trip upriver six years ago, and the Wulsins' success so far in passing as white in Cincinnati, gave Drausin confidence that he could manage such a visit, despite the risks. He knew that soul-snatchers haunted the Underground Railroad.

Josephine hesitantly supported Drausin's surprising urge, recognizing his need. With baby Lillie and little Clarence, she was relieved she could not go herself, although she would have loved to see her mother, brothers, sister, and family.

What a difference now to be Drausin Wulsin from Cincinnati, he thought as he took his place on the side-wheel packet Buckeye State. He knew the ropes, the rivers, the lingo. His destination was no longer the unknown future but the over-known past, now just a visit.

At times the ride down the Ohio felt like a whaler's "Nantucket sleigh ride" compared to the sleepy, brown Ole

Mississippi, which was more like a huge bayou by contrast, though he knew its currents and snags could destroy. Drausin noticed that, heading downstream now, the captain ran no shallows at night. As humid as Cincinnati's summers could be, Drausin felt the further south they steamed, the more he was returning inside the cow's—no, the alligator's—mouth, so moist the air. And he noticed that while no soul treated him with other than respect, he felt like a stag; his eyes darted, his ears keened, his breathing shallowed, quickened; this old world's serene surface felt loaded to explode.

At the pier in New Orleans, Drausin hired a livery to deliver his baggage to JB Bacas at Franklin and De Lord Streets. He chose to walk the fifteen blocks to St. Louis Cemetery No. 1, avoiding 116 St. Louis St. by walking mostly up the parallel Toulouse St. As orange blossom blended with lavender, jasmine and rose, Drausin smelled less sewage-stench in the streets than formerly, though mosquito-wrigglers still flurried the air. *The night-soil men must work more efficiently now, emptying latrines.*

His memory in Cincinnati had been accurate; here in New Orleans, pedestrians still ambled, in spite of Anglo-Saxons picking up the pace. At one point Drausin hardly noticed a dapper young blond gent step aside to allow him to keep his course on the sidewalk. Drausin nodded in acknowledgment, realized the monumentality of what had just happened, savored the moment with a chuckle, and carried on.

Entering the gate of the high-walled cemetery, Drausin pictured a boatyard, white tombs like hulls above the ground due to the saturated Mississippi Delta soil. His eyes wandered, and in time he noticed a white marble tomb with two names: "Jean-Baptiste Manuel Bacas, né Genes, décédé le 10 fevrier, 1817." And "Louis Adhemar Bacas, décédé 1848," his nephew, Joseph Valmont's eldest. Drausin remembered pointing out to his children the spot where their cousin had drowned at age fifteen as the Wulsin family embarked for Cincinnati on the Natchez III six years ago. *So far, except for our own first baby Barthelemy, we have lost none of our own. I have though forgotten the hollow in me left by Adhemar's drowning.* Otherwise the long marble face of the tomb was blank.

Where was his mother, Adelaïde? He looked on the sides of the tomb, and on the back. Down on the ground. No sign of her. *Where is Maman? Has she not been buried at all? Or does she lie with anonymous paupers outside of town?* He remembered the city allowed no graves to be dug in soil within the city limits.

Born enslaved, Adelaïde had been given her freedom. She had given her freedom back to her beloved Barthelemy. *Did Maman, in her death, just disappear? If so, did Barthelemy, our own father, let her vanish?* Starting to fume, Drausin kicked the corner of his grandfather's Bacas tomb, hurting a toe. As he pivoted to leave, a name slid by his left eye—"Adelaïde." On a brick tomb about twenty feet away, across the path, was a wooden plaque reading "Adelaïde Beaulieu, décédée Dec. 24, 1855." *Just there, all by herself, away from the Bacas tomb, but there, after all. Waiting for marble?*

Relieved, then puzzled, then angry again, Drausin kissed her name on the cypress plaque, tried to pray as Josephine would wish him to, and stuck in the soil a white rose he had plucked on his walk.

Drausin's closest brother, Jean-Baptiste Valcours Bacas, now practiced medicine as "Dr. J. B. Bacas." Back in 1840 JB had married Rose Celina Saulay; their child, Richard Thomas Bacas, was now about Ti-Drausin's age, fifteen. Drausin made his way to brother JB's house and pulled on the knocker. As it was by now settling into dusk, JB was home from his practice and opened the door. The men regarded each other for only a moment before embracing, JB exclaiming, "What! My long-gone brother returns!"

Drauzin and JB had been close both as boys and as men, and now their comfortable familiarity rushed back. How delighted they were to see one another, even as they recognized in each other's faces road maps of newly earned gravitas.

That night, Rose's sister, Louise Celie Saulay, and a Dr. Louis Roudanez joined them all for supper, a delicious Cajun étoufée. Louis had attained a medical degree in Paris, enjoying life there virtually free of racial prejudice. He had just completed another medical degree at Dartmouth College in New Hampshire, and had recently returned to New Orleans to assume the practice of medicine. At one point Dr. Roudanez said to Drausin, "Your brother has the reputation of being a fine doctor—a great help to the sick and a credit to his people."

"I'm not at all surprised," responded Drausin.

"But he is restless; he wants a larger suit of clothes than New Orleans can give him."

Drausin looked from the large doctor to shorter, leaner JB, and raised an eyebrow.

"I offered to exchange suits to keep him here," said Dr. Roudanez.

Jean-Baptiste chuckled. "Ohh, mon cher Louis, I do feel that here I am a man of matter. I love my work. But mostly gens libres de couleur and slaves come or are sent my way. I'd like to help anyone. I've taken a huge step, becoming a doctor. I'd like to take one huger. I want to go all the way," he said, looking most now at Rose, whose face revealed no clear clues.

"The original Jean Baptiste lost his head, served by dancing Salome on a silver platter to King Herod. I do not mind having my head served, but let it be on a platter large enough for all in need. I want to be no lackey doctor, no lesser doctor; I want to be any man's doctor, any woman's, any child's—. I want to be able to care for any one sick in any hospital."

After a moment Dr. Roudanez said, "That I understand well, Jean-Baptiste, though it saddens me. For me, it's time to root, here; my work, my people, my city will be more than enough. Maybe we need more help here today than everybody out there does tomorrow."

"Yes, Louis, that may well be, and thank heavens for you, for our people. I still feel I need to extend my hand further than I'm allowed to here."

"I've come back here to reclaim my color; I sense you may be heading out there to surpass yours."

"Maybe, maybe."

"As has your esteemed brother Drauzin."

"Yes, as have I," echoed Drausin.

"And may I ask, if you do not mind," broached Dr. Roudanez with careful respect, "would you say that you and your family are *passé blanc*, it has just happened this way, for you? Or are you *blanc fo'cé*? Have you chosen actively to make this change?"

"Yes, of course," said Drausin, trusting their guest's experienced sincerity, "That is not all so clear a distinction, I'm afraid. I think I must say we are *blanc fo'cé*; Josephine and I considered, experimented, and then chose definitely for our family to try to pass in Cincinnati. Yet, I must say, every day we realize we are also *passé blanc*. We are allowed, by the perceptions of others. We are keen in our efforts; we are fortunate so far in our success, so far..."

Dr. Roudanez nodded, grateful for the honesty of Drausin's response, hearing the implied delicacy of danger.

Rose could tell that her sister Louise drank in deeply the words and the ways of the light-skinned Creole who, educated both in the streets of Paris and the hills of New Hampshire, was choosing to re-root in his home soil of New Orleans, as challenging as that would be. She also thought their distinguished guest to be quite aware of his hostess's sister's attention.

Although Drausin could see JB's own riddle tighten his jaw, he, above all, felt how JB's confidence permeated his ambition.

His brother was finding his pace.

Later that night, as JB and Drausin sat alone in the back-yard, enjoying cigars, JB asked his brother to share some experiences of passing: challenges, choices, dangers, failures, benefits, costs. Which Drausin did his best to offer, speaking of Captain Leathers's graciousness, the Kaintuck changing from fisty bully to kind guide on the trip upriver, Mrs. Griffin's ambivalence at their first boarding house, their choices of home, of schooling, their purchases of property, his first vote, the Know-Nothing riots and the children's harrowing escapade, Aline's pained and prayerful experience of Peggy Garner and the Underground Railroad.

"Do you think I, we—Rose, Richard, and I—could?"

Drausin looked at his brother's parchment-colored skin and relatively aquiline features and thought of JB's wife, Rose, and their son Richard.

"Yes, Jean-Baptiste, your family, like Josephine and me and ours, have the tickets; you can play each way. I do think you could. In different contexts, you have many possibilities. Your family and mine, we light Creoles are indeed 'nations;' we can be seen in this light, in that, and in another."

That night Drausin reflected on the worlds and seeming decades he had experienced in this one day. The Bacas tomb, with Maman's humble one nearby. Louis Roudanez returning to New Orleans and his people. Brother JB hankering to leave, as his brother Drauzin had already done.

In the end, one simple thought touched Drausin the most: his double kiss and long embrace of his brother, and the casual touches of hand on shoulder, arm on arm. This was the first man-warmth he had experienced in six years in their cold, white northern world of proper handshakes, other than with his sons, still boys.

The next day, a Saturday, JB and Drausin walked over to 62 Marais St. Joseph Valmont Bacas, now forty-nine, certainly looked the oldest of the brothers, more lined in face, heavier set, even slower in movements, his hair salted and peppered. He beamed, holding Drausin long to his chest, soaking him in. Joseph's wife, Louise Essayleme, welcomed her brothers-in-law, especially the "prodigal," freshly returned from the North. Henry, fifteen like JB's Richard and Drausin's Ti-Drausin, had his father's roundness in eye, body, and soul. Henry asked questions about life in Cincinnati. Maria, thirteen, was noticeably bright, while Paul Albert, twelve, like Lucien, was also noticeably dark.

Brother Joseph seemed to Drausin a good-hearted horse, strong, steady, loyal, but bruised, at least inwardly, by an abusing master. Joseph had endured the most scorn from, and yet remained the most loyal to, their father. Several years after the four brothers had left, Joseph and his family had returned to 116 St. Louis, to help the elders. "After Maman's death, though, we left 116 St. Louis for here," said Joseph.

"A great relief to be finally free again from Rue St. Louis," added Louise.

"Most days, though," clarified Joseph, "I do go to work in the woodshop, since Papa can't anymore."

Drausin looked at his two brothers, dear Joseph and dear Jean-Baptiste, being with them like bathing in a childhood stream. "Any news of Leon?" Chill silence.

"Not a word," said JB as Joseph shook his head. "Just a ghost, long gone."

Then JB confirmed Joseph's statement that Adelaïde, though born enslaved and having mothered nine, had died at age seventy-two, largely of old age. "Her organs had begun failing, and her breathing weakened," the doctor said. "Maman stopped eating ten days before her death, when her heart finally stopped."

When Joseph brought out their mother's death certificate, Drausin pointed to the fact that Joseph, not Barthelemy, had recorded and affirmed it. The statement declared Adelaïde Pouponne Beaulieu to have been "the Wife of Barthelemy Bacas, his Surviving Consort—She was a Pouponne—" What stumbling ambivalence in this document. Someone had drawn a line through "Wife of Barthelemy Bacas, his Surviving Consort, " leaving "She was a Pouponne." Drausin looked at Joseph, who looked at JB, who looked at Drausin, nodded, and clarified, "Later, *he* drew that line. Of course they could never be married legally. But unlike some people in civil unions, he never called her his wife. Officially, outwardly, he kept her, the love of his life, the mother of his children, at Pouponne distance. Did we ever hear him call her wife?"

Both Joseph and Drausin shook their heads—though Drausin had not realized that before. And "Surviving Consort"? What did that mean for someone just dead?

"During the last year of Maman's life—" Joseph, starting, shook his head.

"He drank himself to her death," JB concluded. "As her breathing worsened, his drinking worsened."

"It seemed that, instead of breathing air," said Joseph, "he drank wine."

"And he of course worsened."

"And—he started using Betsy."

JB reflected, "Our Papa Bacas fell not into Greek Dionysus, bestower of the mysteries of wine, but into fat, Roman Bacchus, who sloshed himself dumb in wine, too sloshed to record Maman's death certificate."

"Remember," Drausin reminded his brothers, "years ago, I played Apollo, winning the musical contest with Pan? Then you, JB, farcically portrayed Dionysus/Bacchus being banished from the kingdom, as the family chanted, 'Va-t-en, Bacas, va-t-en, Bacchus!'"

"Papa Bacas, imbibing, embodied Bacchus in the end," said JB.

"Now—I see," said Drausin, the picture coalescing. "Hence Maman's banishment and sale to the countryside of Betsy in her will, sending her from house slave to field slave, to an early death hacking cane." Drausin gritted his teeth. His brothers nodded. "And Rose?"

"Betsy's companion in scorn."

"Oh, Dieu de Dieu," muttered Drausin, shuddering at such misery in their mother's final year. "And I have to ask: Chloe's children?"

Long pause. Joseph nodded again to JB. "For Maman, that may have been the hardest of all. She talked with Chloe about her own death, about Chloe's freedom, about her children's future. Chloe was scared for herself in freedom, but far more frightened for her children. Together they were unable to see any surer way. So, they agreed. Chloe felt ripped, but relieved, grateful. Maman felt ripped; she hated it but considered it best, at least until Chloe found her way, as we all understand."

"Not freed?" asked Drausin. "I do not understand no freedom for Chloe's children."

JB continued, "It fulfilled her that in *her* will—unlike that of her mate—she was leaving something for their Bacas children. And she only said Chloe's children could not be sold, *not* not be freed. After Maman dictated her will, she stopped eating and drinking."

Drausin felt ripped himself, but relieved to better understand his mother's unbearable choice, although he would never understand why such forces should be at sway at all to cause such a choice. His eyes grew wet and he saw his brothers' eyes tear up as well, and Louise Essayleme's.

"Who established Maman's tomb separate from the Bacas tomb? The law? The priest? The non-'husband'?" asked Drausin.

"I'm not sure who determined, but yes," responded Joseph, "after I nagged him, Papa ordered me to arrange Maman's tomb and temporary plaque there."

"Where will Papa go?"

"Oh, sans doute, with his papa, Bacas," said Joseph. "When my time comes, I'm joining Maman, not Papa. I returned to 116 St. Louis for *her*, not him."

"Even though your Adhemar is with Granpère?"

"Si, even so. Papa loved him better than he could love us. Adhemar will be fine with them. The old man kicked us out in life. I'm not rejoining him in death."

Another day, Drausin walked up to what had become his own family's home after leaving 116 St. Louis St. back in '46. There stood Josephine Tassy, the distinguished Veuve Mathé, queen of southern Bayou Road. Now sixty-seven, silver-haired, fine-jawed, grey eyes glistening, light skin olive-oiled smooth, shining. She wore a black-and-silver-striped tignon, and her long dark dress glowed red-tinged like breezed coals, open-collared, flowing out from the golden ceinture below the bust. Down near the hem, embroidered peacocks glistened golden-green, scores of eyes opening at every furl. The queen presided over her silver-tipped, black walking stick.

She greeted her long-gone son-in-law warmly, graciously, feasting on news of her daughter and grandchildren. Laure had drawn scenes of the large Wulsin family for her. Granmère Josephine's daughter Josephine had now given birth to as many children as she had, eight each, seven living each. Aline had scissored black profiles for her of the new ones, Clarence and Lillie. Josephine had sent along long letters about her family.

After his visit, Drausin thought about how his mother-in-law had weathered well, her Creole quadroon beauty still clear. *What attracts, pleases, timelessly, agelessly?* Drausin wondered. *Like a magnet. Aphrodite—and Hera of the hearth? Her home glistens. Her clothes glisten; her tignon is always a bold color. She is not just beautiful to behold; she quickens beauty around her. And yet, regal Maman Josephine lacks vanity even as she invites and enhances beauty around her.*

I feel blessed with my own Josephine, with her own beauty. I do wish the world here were such that our family could bask in the beauty of Bayou Rd. But since the world is not such, I feel fortunate and content for our family to bear such beauty within.

Here on Bayou Rd., one home opens to another, sharing almost two blocks of the family compound, including gardens. The Mathé world opens wide here. In Cincinnati, we Wulsins enjoy our own life in our narrow lot, with only each other. And yet we are free to enjoy the rest of the wide white world of possibilities, at least so far. Whereas much of dear New Orleans remains dangerous, and closed to people of color.

Josephine Young Wulsin's brother Philippe and his wife, Adèle Young, brought their brood of four over later. Drausin's nephew, Samuel Charles Young V, now a mature nineteen, was working at his father's grocery store just up the road, learning the trade, while his father, mother, and seven siblings had been settling into their new life in Davenport, Iowa—also passing as white, also passingly well, so far.

Josephine's now-adult Mathé half-siblings came by—Louis Francois, thirty-two; Matilde Macerte Dawson, thirty-one; Brou Simon, twenty-six; and Simon Raphael, twenty-four. Brou Simon and Simon Raphael were helping Louis Francois with his grocery business. Drausin could tell that Simon Raphael was the most interested and enthusiastic about their business.

For a rare interlude, Drausin reflected, quiet in the garden. *We up north have lost most of our color, but we have gained, our children especially, widened horizons. We pay a price for wider lives. In New Orleans we colored live in constant fear of our color landing us enslaved. In Cincinnati we colored passing white live in constant fear of our color being revealed, of losing our white liberty, as opposed to our colored liberty. Will our choices always include such pain?*

At one point, on a walk with brother-in-law Louis Mathé, Drausin stopped, noticing Fulsain Bacas' property on Bayou

Rd. Louis noticed Drausin's sadness. "When Fulsain died earlier this year, as you know, he left his property to the six of you surviving Bacas nephews and nieces. However, you may not have realized that he divided it in sevenths, deeding you an extra portion. He cared for you especially."

"No, I had not realized that." Drausin felt honored, blessed, and moved to have had Nonc Fulsain, his namesake, Drauzin Valsin Bacas, in his life as a counterpoint to his own father. Drausin said, almost to himself, "Though not much, our uncle left us what our own father would not." *How much*, he wondered, *have Nonc Fulsain and I actually chosen, and how much has life in fact forced us, to change our names?*

CHAPTER 36:

BARTHELEMY, 1857

Drausin approached 116 St. Louis St., the house his mother had borne him into and his father had banished him out of. He bit his cheek and clenched his fist, bracing for bad weather, a habit throughout his first three decades. On the other hand, he reminded himself that *for the last decade, especially these six years north, I have been the tall tree of my own family, at rest in my own gentle authority, at least within my family, behind our front door.*

Alfonce greeted him at the door with joy; Drausin noticed his brown skin had gone sallow under greying hair, but his warmth was undiminished. In the hall, Drausin loved the simple stateliness of the rising banister. Yet he felt stifled by old air, as though the house had been too long sealed. Alfonce nodded toward the living room door, which Drausin opened, to find the old man bedded there. That always dominating oak now lay bloated like a beached manatee, yet blotchy red and white. Barthelemy lifted his head, snowy hair disheveled, looked at the figure hesitating in the doorway, and barked, "Va-t-en!" Then he turned away. Drausin felt punched, then realized he wasn't surprised.

Alfonce gently said, "Michie, he does not recognize you."

Spying a mandolin in the corner of the dining room, which opened to the living room, Drausin crossed to it, picked it up, and started to play, tuning in to soothe old Barthelemy. He sang softly. His father listened intently, then turned toward him, looked again, and said, "Mon fils? Mon cher Drusino?" Barthelemy sat up, trying to see him more clearly.

"Si, mon père, c'est moi."

Barthelemy opened his arms wide. "Ahh, my son, you have come to me; come to me." Drausin sat beside his father on the bed, twisting in an awkward embrace. A low moan droned in his father's chest. Drausin felt his own right shoulder dampen. When they leaned back from each other, the bad old brute was crying. Drausin pulled a chair near the bed and sat. Barthelemy swept his hair back with a hand that had one finger angled outward, never properly reset after the woodshop chair-bashing incident ten years ago. Barthelemy then gestured at himself almost helplessly, and said with an embarrassed chuckle, "Plus ça change—ça change."

Then, "Peut-être je suis bâtarde, et ça me fait de la peine, la peine que je t' ai causé. Mais, ta mère et moi, nous nous aimions comme deux colombes et je crois, toi et Josephine aussi—deux colombes. Cela, ça vaut quelque chose. La peine, ça vaut la peine." Maybe I have been a bastard, and that pains me, the pain that I have caused you. But, your mother and I, we loved each other like two doves, and I believe, you and Josephine also—two doves. That is worth something. The pain, it's worth the pain.

Drausin did not speak, simply nodding. He felt touched by his father in a way he had never remembered.

Barthelemy took a deep breath and continued, his bloodshot eyes holding his son's clear gaze. "Adelaïde—my one and only—Drauzin, when your mother, first freed, left 116 St. Louis, my life shut into shade. I was lost in limbo. Weeks later she reappeared, shining, white-gowned, with a sky-blue ribbon; I saw my bride for always, though we could never marry."

Drausin was touched by the fresh depth of his father's memory. "Yet, Papa, she was only ever 'Pouponne'?"

Barthelemy eyed his son, like his old hammer about to strike a nail, then inwardly he laid down his "hammer."

"A minor matter in our strangely arranged world."

"Minor to her?"

"I was willing to cross certain lines but not others. Your mother was my peace."

"And Betsy?"

"Oh, Betsy, oh—my son, you may not believe me—fear of losing your mother drove me to so much more drink, and—so much more drink drove me to Betsy."

"Again and again?"

"Yes, that was my worst. Your mother gave me her life at age twenty, and then she gave me all of you, and I, in her final, ill year, I sloshed into Betsy. That—my worst—Salaud, quel salaud!" Bastard, what a bastard!

After a pause, Drausin asked, "Have you considered surrendering Genoa, Papa, before you die? You still could."

Barthelemy seemed confused. Then he grasped Drausin's meaning, and his glance revealed the hammer again. "Never."

"But you've lived white, Papa; why do you have to die white?"

"Ha! What a question, coming from you! Are you ready to reclaim Gonaïves? And you aren't even Bacas any more!"

"Yes, you're right. We live white, like you, not as Bacas, but as Wulsin."

"Wulsin, Wulsin, Valsin. Wulsin. Yes, Joseph told me. I see. ... Mon cher fils, my Drusino, will we ever be able just to live as we love?"

"I hope so, Papa. I do wish so."

Barthelemy suddenly cried out, holding his swollen right knee in pain. Alfonce rushed in with compresses. After a few minutes, Barthelemy seemed mildly relieved. He called Drausin back over to him. "My dear son. My gout takes its toll. Thank you for coming back to me here. It means more to me than you can know. I fear I fade fast." He reached up gnarled hands and brought Drausin's face close, looking into his eyes. "My son, I've loved your mother. And I've been selfish and cruel to you all. Can you forgive me?" Barthelemy's hand, almost a claw on Drausin's arm, was careful, like an eagle to its eaglet.

"I tell you," Barthelemy continued, "we loved each other like two doves, you know that. She gave me her life. She gave me *your* lives. I was so scared to lose her. I hate myself for hurting her. I begged on my knees, weeping for her forgiveness. 'I forgive you, my dissolute Cher, bitterly,' she finally half-smiled at me. Did she die a little lightened? I do not know. I hope so. Life for me after Adelaïde has been hell as I feared, hell from which I pray deliverance. Me! Pray! For deliverance!"

Barthelemy grimaced, tightened in a vice. Alfonce reentered with a vial. "Ici, Michie, for the pain in his long days and longer nights. Ten drops."

Drausin put his arms around his father, hands resting on his shoulder blades. Drausin felt a firm warmth on his own neck. Not Alfonce. His own Josephine? His own mother, Adelaïde, who could forgive. "Yes, mon terrible, mon cher Papa, you bastard, you're my father. I forgive you, with all my heart. I forgive you."

"Je te remercie infiniment, I thank you infinitely. Bless you, bless you, my son—please— more music before you go."

Drausin administered the laudanum to Barthelemy. As he lowered his father's head, Barthelemy's eyelids closed. His relaxed mouth reflected a kind of peace Drausin could not recall in him before, like a bow unstrung.

When Drausin would finish a song on the mandolin, his father would slightly nod, so his son would start another, peacening the old storm, soothing him soon to sleep.

The next day, watching the brown waters laze behind the stern of the steamboat headed back up north, Drausin realized certain storms had subsided within him. *All the music I've ever played has failed to soothe me as well as has this visit with my father, to my utter surprise.*

CHAPTER 37:
PANIC, 1857–58

Drausin took gifts up the Mississippi River, past the Ohio, to Davenport, Iowa. From his Josephine and children, and from Granmère Josephine, and from Philippe Young's family especially, all for the family of Josephine's brother Samuel Charles Young IV, who had tried to convince the Wulsins to move to Davenport in the first place.

Josephine had sent young Drausin, now fifteen, down the Ohio River from Cincinnati to join his father at Cairo for the trip north on the Mississippi. Davenport dripped summer humidity almost as thickly as both Cincinnati and New Orleans. Three years ago the Youngs had settled in on the steep West Bank among the Germans, seeming comfortable. The seven children were picking up English quickly, some with traces of German accent because of their neighbors.

Samuel had capitalized on earlier connections, thriving, spreading his grocery business, especially coordinating with young Samuel V, guided by his Mathé uncles back in New Orleans. Although Samuel IV was thriving, Drausin could tell that his wife, Marie Louise, was neither content nor healthy. Samuel interested Drausin in investing in both a lumber company and some land. The town did seem to prosper, though Davenport was far smaller than Cincinnati. In August the smell of the Mississippi mud permeated, pickling the little town on the river bluff, drenched in much more stench than the Queen City.

The previous year, the Rock Island Railroad had succeeded in building the first bridge ever to span the Mississippi River from the west bank across to Illinois. One local captain drove his steamboat, the Cincinnati-built Effie Afton, into one of the buttresses, enabling its owners to sue the railroad company after the boat burned.

"My boy," Drausin explained to his son, "we're looking at the consequences of war, yes, war between the old mode of travel, steamboats, and the new upstart, railroads. In fact, the courts appear to be in the process of requiring the railroad to dismantle the bridge to ensure safe river traffic forever. This revolutionary Rock Island Railroad is being represented in the suit by some unknown Illinois lawyer named Abraham Lincoln."

Although Drausin was tempted to invest in land, he was not tempted to move his family from Cincinnati to Davenport's floodplains.

When father and son Drausins returned to their family in Cincinnati, hours passed with presents and stories of various relatives in New Orleans and Davenport. That night, as Aline walked down the hall toward the outhouse, she overheard her parents talking in their room about Drausin's Bacas siblings' perspectives on Adelaïde's will. Aline had heard no details before.

Later that night Josephine noticed Aline's light still on. Stepping silently to the door, she heard a voice and realized Aline was praying. After a while she tapped, then quietly opened the door to find Aline kneeling in her dotted Swiss cotton nightgown at her bedside, hands folded. Aline continued but shifted into silence. Eventually Aline parted her hands, crossed herself, and rose toward her still mother, who opened her arms. "Oh, Maman, oh, Maman."

"Ma Chère, ma Chère; for what, may I ask, do you pray so fervently?"

"Maman, I heard you and Papa speaking about Granmère Pouponne's will, about Betsy and Rose."

"Si, Chère; that poisons me, and your father especially."

"I pray for Betsy and Rose, for Chloe and her children. And I pray for Granmère Pouponne, that whatever her reasons, she may be forgiven."

"And Granpère Barthelemy?"

"And Granpère Barthelemy—and Granmère Josephine."

"Si, and Granmère Josephine—You are right, my child." Josephine brought her green eyes closer and closer to Aline's burning black eyes, as they used to do so often in Aline's early childhood, merging finally into one, cyclops beholding cyclops, almost nose-to-nose, warming them each into glowing smiles. They pulled back.

"You are right, my wise adult Aline Adelaïde, you are right in your mighty labor," said Josephine, thinking of their own purchase and eventual freeing of Claire before coming north. She realized she was gouging the back of her left hand with her fingernails. "Would you like to know what Marie LaVeau told me, about praying for 'bads' back in the family?" Aline nodded.

"She told me—the Voodoun Queen of New Orleans, who went to mass every morning—she told me to try to 'pray back,' pray back in time from today to yesterday, from this year to last year, from this new sin to those old sins, from this generation back to those generations."

Aline breathed in deeply. "Do you know why?"

"Oh, she only said it was the spirit's way. Our time flows back from us. In the spirit time comes from the future to us." Josephine had stopped gouging her hand; she took Aline's hands into her own, forming a double church, fingers pointing high. "We pray back—God, outside of time, enspirits those deeds, those people, those lives—I will pray too, to Notre Dame, to Marie Madeleine, to St. Michel, Dani, to Jesus Christ Himself, to forgive us all our such sins, to free us each of any such curse, for the sake not only of the slaves, but also of our children's children's children." Josephine and Aline touched foreheads as partners in prayer.

"Yes, I pray, too, for all of us, Granmère Pouponne's descendants," said Aline, "so we may not bear the curse for generations, for centuries, of her buying, owning, and selling others, enslaved though she had been herself. I pray she be forgiven, for the sake of all her ensuing generations, that we may not be burdened by the curse." Maman left daughter to her labors.

On the morning of August 24, 1857, the president of Ohio Life Insurance and Trust Company declared that its New York branch had suspended payments. The Ohio Life bank had failed due to fraudulent activities by the company's management. This failure precipitated a run on banks across the land.

In March that year, the Supreme Court had declared in its Dred Scott decision not only that Dred Scott, being Negro, had no rights under the Constitution, but also that the government had no right to ban slavery in western territories. The railroads had been expanding westward feverishly, but many would-be settlers grew suddenly hesitant to settle in territories that might include slavery. The railroad expansion bubble burst, as the bank bubble burst, engendering the Panic of 1857.

On the one hand, Drausin explained to his eldest son, the Iowa Supreme Court had ruled after all that in Davenport the Rock Island Railroad's bridge linking East and West across the Mississippi would be allowed to stand. On the other hand, the nation's double bubble-burst meant in Cincinnati that Herr Roebling and his crew had to suspend their efforts to bridge the Ohio River to the South.

As winter approached, Papa Drausin's cough worsened in the river damp. Brother JB, having noticed the cough in July, had conceived aid; Brother Joseph delivered it, having nephew Samuel Charles Young V ship a case of Louisiana lemons each month throughout the winter. In November, Drausin found his family a new home, further from the river, out of the flood-plain, eight blocks north up Horne, at 349 Richmond Ave., not far from the Mill Creek's oxbow. The family was able to move before Christmas.

Several factors drew the Wulsins to this new address. First, of course, was to move further away from the river-damp, though in some ways the nearby Mill Creek oxbow was more like a bayou than the Whitewater canal had been. The new house was still in the West Side, in the Sixteenth Ward, still inviting to new arrivals seeking a fresh start. In fact, two friend-families from New Orleans, the Laraldes and the Lalandes, had been inspired partly by the Wulsins' success in passing so far, and had settled recently within several blocks. And the children's piano teacher, D. H. Baldwin, lived just around the corner. A pleasing constellation.

The house itself pleased, enlarging Josephine even more than 139 Carr. Its handsome red Cincinnati brick felt to her substantial, secure, even serene. A shallow porch fronted living room and studio, then came dining room, followed by kitchen and laundry room. Cherry panels warmed the walls. A base-ment offered storage and a modest workshop space, as well as several coal bins. The large back porch was a joy, with some garden ground and a barn for horse and buggy. There were four bedrooms on the second floor, two on the third. Southern light warmed the rooms in front. Josephine especially enjoyed the rocking chairs set near the fireplace and on the back porch where, on warm days, she'd sit shawl-wrapped, swaying, gently rubbing her mounding belly clockwise, then counterclockwise, humming this child along. In their new home the Wulsin family felt they, like their suffering patriarch, could breathe anew.

Josephine Young Wulsin was glad to be comfortably resettled by the time she gave birth in their new home to their new child, their ninth, on February 13, 1858. Aline was a great help, learning from and assisting the midwife at each step of the way, guided as well by the veteran, Josephine herself, "the Captain Leathers of the birth-journey," as her eldest daughter decreed. Drausin was emphatic that la petite should bear the name Josephine, which pleased Josephine, thinking of her own mother, whom she daily emulated and missed.

Aline, joyful to have as many girls in the family now as boys, pleaded strongly for "Marie." Aline had not forgotten about Peggy Garner's Mary. In fact, she had heard of Peggy's recent death in a typhoid fever epidemic on the Bonham plantation at Tennessee Landing, Mississippi. Just before dying, Peggy had urged her husband Robert to "never marry again in slavery, but to live in hope of freedom." For two years, Aline had been praying for little Mary Garner, the daughter whose mother's only way to save her from slavery had been to kill her. Liberty through death. Josephine intuited the source of Aline's wish. Mary Josephine Wulsin was baptized in St. Patrick's church.

One late-summer day at the market, Josephine overheard a spectacled woman with tan skin and a light-green dress urging several other mothers to school their children. Josephine noticed a stack of papers for the taking and discreetly slipped one into her bag. With no people around, she read the notice from Cincinnati's Colored School Board:

The duty of the colored American mother is to educate her children. Other duties are important, but none more important than this. If you wish to keep your children out of jail, the penitentiary, the poor houses, and dens of infamy, educate them. Nine-tenths of all the crimes perpetrated grow out of idleness and ignorance. If you consult the calendars of our State prisons, the estimate I have made will appear small. Go to our police court and there see the black eyes, the bloated faces, the ragged clothes, the haggard emaciated features of the one and twenty that are brought there from day to day, and the truth of our remark is vividly spread out before you.

Always the question for us, reflected Josephine. Ever and again the question. Have we chosen right? Are we doing the best for our children?

That night in their bedroom, Josephine renewed the conversation she'd been having with herself, now with her husband. "Mon Cher, have we chosen right? Are we doing the best for our children?"

"It seems to me so, ma Josie. They make their way well enough."

"Yes, they seem to. But, the price? Will the product be worth the price?"

"We are educating them, just not in the colored schools."

"Exactly, but do they thrive? Do they really prosper? Have the Twelfth District School and Hughes High School these seven years been preparing them to find their way? Will doors open for them?"

"It appears so, so far. Too soon to tell, I suppose."

"Do our children really have each other, really have their father, their mother?"

"Oh, I think so, unlike my family. I believe they have each other and both their father and their mother, such as we are." Drausin kissed Josephine, who smiled. "As little as we are, that is a lot."

"But are we enough?" asked Josephine. "Does our family suffice, living out white as we do?"

"It appears so."

"Or do they starve, thirst in soul out there?"

"You fear they suffer more than we know?"

"Maybe our children's lives are blank, colorless."

"No. Maybe. But I think not. Maybe they have more colors available to them than those living colored, or at a least more shades of grey out in the white world in which we live, in addition to all our tints of color at home."

"Are we all enough colored community for each other at home? Does our combination allow them to breathe, in balance?"

"I think so."

"Or do we fool ourselves?"

"Oh, ma Josie, you ask such hard questions. I do not know. How can we know?"

"What I do know is that these questions flow always, in my blood, in my mind."

"Yes, I guess in me, too, sometimes more dreaming, sometimes more waking. Maybe all we can know is we give all we can to make it go."

"Yes, mon Cher, I do trust, with you, I have to, that our family is sailing its proper course, all things considered, from Bacas with limited future to Wulsin with limitless future."

"Bullseye, Chérie, those are the stakes of our white Wulsin gamble." Drausin leaned over, snuffed her candle with finger and thumb, and kissed her long, "— Ever my Lady Jo-o-oe."

Drausin received a telegram on August 29, 1858, again from his brother Joseph, this time informing him of the death of their father, Barthelemy Bacas, age seventy-eight. Two weeks later a copy of his will arrived. It included record of neither marriage nor children. It bequeathed one-third of his property to his niece Josephine Cosé Berthelot, daughter of Barthelemy's sister Maria Louisa Bacas Cosé; one-third to his niece Aimé Bacas Cambre, daughter of his brother Leon; and one-third to the minor children of his nephew Anatole, deceased son of his brother Leon. Nothing was given to any of his six surviving sons and daughters. It freed his two slaves, Alfonce and Nelson, awarding Alfonce five hundred piastres for his good services—a bonus received by none of his own children. The executor of his will was not one of his sons but a M. Charles Genois. And yet, just before his signature, Barthelemy informed that a copy of the will "is left in the box of my father-in-law of the state of Louisiana espouse Adele de Beaulieu. Barthelemy Bacas."

After the conversation with Nonc Fulsain and the ensuing family rupture in the woodshop eleven years earlier; after the bewildering shocks of Maman Adelaïde's will three years earlier; and after the many-layered, even touching, yet contradictory rapprochement with his father the previous year, Drausin was not surprised by his father's will. Nevertheless, the coexistence in the document of no marriage and no children on the one hand with "father-in-law of Adele de Beaulieu" on the other hand was strange.

Joseph's accompanying letter described the new, somewhat massive marble Bacas tombstone that Barthelemy had commissioned in St. Louis Cemetery No. 1: BARTHELEMY BACAS on the top in large letters, and his father "Jean-Baptiste Manuel Bacas, né a Genes(Genoa)" below in smaller letters, along with his deceased nephew, Joseph's son, "Adhemar Bacas." "Adelaïde Beaulieu" remained across the pathway in her brick tomb, the placard still cypress.

Early one morning Drausin opened an eye, catching the full moon settling through sycamore trees on Richmond Street, opposite the dawning day. Half asleep, half awake, he wondered, *I and our moon-people of color, are we at the end of reflecting the "sunlight" of the whites, as we have had to do in so many ways for so long? We Bacases in New Orleans, we Youngs in Davenport, we Wulsins in Cincinnati.* Shutting his eye, he dawn-dreamed scores of young men and women of all shades racing east through the trees to fill their back-sacks, their reticules, with their own fresh sunlight.

He pictured their own Aline, chest growing, heart swelling, carrying little Mary Garner, and Granmère Adelaïde, Granmère Josephine, and so many others, eventually no doubt the whole world, in the light of her prayers. He chuckled—he himself could hardly run east anymore like those youngsters. Opening an eye again briefly, Drausin noticed white-patched sycamore branches still clutching the setting moon. He wondered, *How free are we, Wulsins and others, actually free to shine our own lights in our daily lives? How much are we still, not black-facing, like white minstrels, but white-facing? How much are we in fact still jangle-dancing on our stage up here in the North?* And he sank again into sleep, dreamless this time. When he finally opened both eyes, the sun showed no more moon.

CHAPTER 38:

MOCKINGBIRD, 1859

Father and son Drausin kept a brisk pace paralleling the parade. Now seventeen, slender, with brown hair brushed flat across, springing into curls by his ears, Ti-Drausin had his father's clear brow over broad cheekbones, scarcely thick lips, and a keen chin. He, like his father, wore a black cravat, black vest, and black frock coat, plus congress gaiters—a young man now, well composed. On this pleasingly cool, mid-September Saturday evening, they had left the less- interested rest of the family at home. They'd first walked to the train station of the Cincinnati, Hamilton, and Dayton Railroad by the Whitewater Canal. Now they were forging ahead to find a good place to stand in the audience at the Fifth Street Market. Bonfires had lit the station entrance. Now torches accompanied the paraders.

Father Drausin, as often when sauntering, was whistling. As the carriage of honor caught up alongside father and son, the guest of honor stopped the driver, stepped down, strode through the roadside crowd, and stood right before them. Young Drausin felt he was beholding a tall elm tree, thin, but likely with knots of steel under that top hat and loose morning coat.

"Sir," the man bowed at father Drausin, "forgive me, I could not help hearing your whistling. You cannot imagine how that melody has soothed me in times of undue darkness. 'Listen to the mocking bird, listen to the mocking bird, still singing o'er her grave—' I thank you for weaving it into this torch-lit night."

"Oh—'The Mockingbird,' yes, I was not even thinking—at your service, Sir. Drausin Wulsin, and my son, Drausin Wulsin," as each bowed in turn.

"Abraham Lincoln, at your service, Messers Wulsin."

Young Drausin, mouth agape, could not help blurting, "Mr. Lincoln, Sir, I've been wondering how you've been passing your time since your loss last January to Senator Douglas, who spoke here earlier this month."

"Ahh, yes, long gone, that limelight. Well, mostly splitting rails and telling tales, I s'pose." The man grinned. But looking directly into Drausin's eyes, discerning depth in the boy's question, he continued, "Actually, I have returned to my offices of law, where I try to do right by the laws of the ship of state. And you, my good young man?"

"Oh, Sir," said Drausin, blushing, "I am just beginning to make my way, as a bookkeeper."

"That is fine, young Drausin Wulsin. You might remember that you and I are likely to do more with the pen than with the axe—and thank you, good father, for your soothing music. 'Listen to the mockingbird, still singing where the weeping willows wave.'" He quoted another line of the song as he shook the hand of father and son and regained his carriage, allowing the parade to resume its flow.

In the dancing lights and shadows of bonfires around the marketplace, a cannon saluted the lawyer from Illinois. The next two and a half hours passed surprisingly quickly, with young Drausin understanding little of Lincoln's legal references. But the bookkeeper strongly felt that the man was speaking directly both to the people of Kentucky, from just across the still-unbuilt bridge, and to the people of Ohio, addressing both sides of the Mason-Dixon Line. While issues were complex, such as slavery in the South, in the North, and in new states, Drausin could tell that Mr. Lincoln was doing his best in relation to the laws of the land—from way back to the Ordinance of the Northwest Territories in 1787, forbidding slavery in these lands which became the states of Ohio, Indiana, Illinois, Michigan, and Wisconsin, right down to the Fugitive Slave Act of 1850. Drausin understood that Abraham Lincoln was striving to navigate according to lighthouses of the law, however complex and challenging the seas might be.

Father Drausin was touched that Abraham Lincoln was so deeply soothed by "Listen to the Mockingbird." Drausin was doubly touched because he knew that the author and composer of the song was not actually the alleged, and assumed white, "Alice Hawthorne." Although white Septimus Winner did write the lyrics, he acknowledged the melody to have been created by "Whistlin' Dick," a colored Philadelphia street musician named Richard Millburn.

> Been inside a coal mine,
> Been inside a whale,
> Been inside a grief just like a jail—
>
> Listen to the mockingbird
> And know that life goes on.

That Saturday night in Cincinnati, Whistlin' Dick and Whistlin' Drausin had combined to soothe the soul of Abraham Lincoln, with Winner's words embroidered in the melody, like clear thread.

Both Drausins could feel, though little did they know, that the Saturday night speech on September 17, 1859, to thousands in Cincinnati by the still little-known Illinois lawyer from the fledgling party, the Republicans, might do much to alter the nation's political landscape.

⚜

Over ensuing days and nights, father Drausin could not help being almost haunted by the visage of Lincoln, and he could not understand why. Finally, about a week later, it came to him in the middle of the night. That jaw, even slightly bearded now; that long, lean figure; those eyes of the man who shared he'd been soothed by the Mockingbird melody—they belonged to the lanky young man in blue trousers and straw slouch hat years ago in the rotunda of the St. Louis Hotel in New Orleans! The man who had looked in at the slaves being sold, unlike any other whites there. That young man, almost twenty-eight years ago, was Abraham Lincoln! Drausin then remembered that ten years ago, in 1849, the author of a Congress bill to abolish slavery in the nation's capital, Washington, DC, was a one-term representative named Abraham Lincoln. The bill had failed.

And Drausin then recalled another dimension of the puzzle. Soon after the Wulsins had arrived in Cincinnati, Drausin had been inspired by Frederick Douglass, whose brow, eyes, nose, and chin, and something within, had reminded him of that young man in the blue trousers and golden slouch hat back in the rotunda of the St. Louis Hotel. Frederick Douglass and Abraham Lincoln. What spirit-sculptor was crafting such mighty individuals out of similar clay, enthusing them with such similar breath?

Young Drausin was fascinated to hear of these strange coincidences, the recent part of which he had been able to witness. Josephine had been fascinated to hear of her Drausins' evening, then remembering her husband's account of the young white man in the Rotunda before Drausin and Josephine had met there. And Aline, Ti-Drausin, Lucien, and Eugene were especially fascinated, slightly horrified, and yet deeply moved to hear, in painful detail insisted by Eugene, about that first time their father and mother had seen each other. The key-note of their mutual melody had actually been a slave auction!

Until, that is, Josephine had lavendered into view on the Bayou, when Drausin's brown and her green eyes first actually met. That's when their real melody actually began, leading to their future "Wulsin" family.

Josephine was glad the younger children—Laure, Clarence, Lillie Alice, and Mary Josephine—were already in bed, as such conversations happened less likely around them. Of course—normal tact, sensitivity, good judgment for the sake of pro-longing innocence. But Josephine was starting to realize another nuance, another layer of discretion unfolding uncon-sciously in the dynamic of the Wulsin family.

Conversations about color simply did not happen around the young children. To spare them? Yes. *But,* Josephine won-dered, *as well perhaps for the question of color not even to be in the light of their days?* The older children had crossed over from free color to white, navigating so far successfully. For the youngers, even ten-year-old Laure, only age two on arrival in Cincinnati, color was hardly a question. The Wulsin family in Cincinnati simply had its timbre, assumed, by most people at least, to be shades of white. And that was that. For the littles.

In bed, Josephine rolled over to face Drausin, placed her hand on his shoulder, and whispered, "Cher, on the bayou you saw lavender all round my green eyes, right?" Drausin nodded, eyes closed but smiling. "Do you remember what I saw?" His smile straightened, then he shook his head. "All around your head, gilded splinters, the gilded splinters." He smiled, eyes still closed, as he drew her to him.

One afternoon, Eugene shared with his older brothers, sister, and parents some news a classmate had heard from his par-ents. One slave, Bright Sam, had sold his master, Black Matt, to a slave-owner near Philadelphia. Finally, Black Matt had produced the papers proving his "whiteness." Meanwhile, Bright Sam had boarded a ship and disappeared. And another slave called Malato John had passed as white, working as a freelance carpenter all the way north to his freedom.

Months later, Lucien and Eugene were out back playing mumbledy-peg, letting their sheath-knives fall from their hand, nose, shoulder, elbow, ideally spinning just right, to land point in ground. When Lucien came inside, ,Eugene had stayed out, working on throwing his knife as accurately as possible into the elm tree.

Now Lucien was using his unusually large but nimble fingers to needle a blueberry onto each of three black threads. He arranged two chairs back-to back, about a foot apart. He tacked one blueberry thread from chairtop to chairtop. The berry hung in the center of the thread between the two chairs. Then he tacked another blueberry thread two inches from the first, watching the arc of that berry's swing, so it would hit the first berry. The third string he adjusted for appropriate tautness on the other side until one berry would hit the center berry into the third. He played with how far to pull a berry away.

Young Drausin and Aline were having fun with verses of the Mockingbird song. Drausin would sing, "when the charms of spring awaken, and the mockingbird sits singing on the bough," and Aline would improvise some mockingbird trilling song. And little Lillie, only three, would first imitate Aline exactly, then vary the mockingbird's song in ways surprisingly true to mockingbirds' actual, endlessly varying songs.

The door-knocker sounded, and Josephine opened the door to reveal a mutton-chopped, short old man with papers on a plank under his arm. He tipped his hat, warmly introducing himself as "Mr. Gentry, here to take the United States Census for the year 1860." Josephine, nervous, signaled Aline to bring him tea. Young Drausin stepped forth, shook his hand strongly, and explained that his father, the music teacher, was out.

Lucien was adjusting his blueberry strings, wondering about replacing the blueberries with stones, the threads with wire; one ear was hearing a sincerity and genuine interest in Mr. Gentry's voice. When Lucien closed his good eye, the Census Man felt to him less a hunter than a gatherer, less a falcon than a quail. Nevertheless, aware that he himself might pose the greatest risk for the family, Lucien kept his face angled away from the visitor. Enjoying his tea, Mr. Gentry took notes as Drausin and Aline informed him of the ages of all in the family, including the housemaid, Caitlin. "No," caught Ti-Drausin. "Not Wilson, it's W-U-L-S-I-N."

"Oh, forgive me," said Gentry.

"Quite alright, Sir," said young Drausin. "Everyone makes that mistake with us. We correct our name daily."

Eugene came in, casually flipping his knife in single spins, beech-handle landing in hand. Shifting it to his left hand, he shook Mr. Gentry's and asked if he had a good knife. Mr. Gentry smiled, producing his bone-handled clasp-knife, impressing Eugene, and expressed equal respect for Eugene's sheath-knife.

Drausin proudly announced his own employment as a bookkeeper, also clarifying that, while very much a part of the family at 349 Richmond St., he now had as well his own official residence two blocks east, six blocks south at the southeast corner of Harriet St. and Whitewater Canal. In 1860, 349 Richmond St. officially included Drausin Wulsin, Music Teacher, forty-six; Josephine Wulsin, forty-two; Aline Wulsin, twenty-one; Drausin Wulsin, bookkeeper, eighteen; Caitlin Hennessy, house-maid, eighteen; Lucien Wulsin, fifteen; Eugene Wulsin, thirteen; Laure Wulsin, eleven; Clarence Wulsin, seven; Lillie Alice Wulsin, four; and Mary Josephine Wulsin, two.

The older children, having been imbued at school with the importance of beautiful, clear penmanship, were impressed with the care with which Mr. Gentry formed his letters and numerals. Ti-Drausin, standing opposite him, saw in a glance that the census-man had inscribed *M* in each box under "Race." Drausin gulped; his heart skipped a beat; he felt his whole family submerging in an undertow. Then he reminded himself that he was looking down on Mr. Gentry's sheet, on which he had actually marked a clear *W* in each box. Drausin then realized that Census Man had not even asked.

"Thank you for the tea and information, and blessings upon you all, Wul-sins," said Mr. Gentry as he bowed back out the door, onward to the next house.

Josephine sat pale in her rose-colored dress, feeling faint. She looked to Drausin and Aline for assessment of how they had fared. News of the *W* slightly surprised and deeply relieved them all. Another test passed. Monumental, in fact. They each looked at each other, almost anew.

"Félicitations," Aline announced. "We are officially white Wulsins." They bowed and curtsied to each other again and again. Each kissed Maman, who kept fanning herself, repeating, "Dieu de Dieu. Dieu de Dieu."

When Father Drausin returned and heard of the visit from the census taker, he kissed Josephine back into some color and offered young Drausin a Marguerite cigar, refraining himself. He also opened a bottle of 1848 Beaujolais and poured some into a glass for each in the family, including little Lillie, who soon continued elaborating variations on the Mockingbird song.

CHAPTER 39:
CANDLE, 1860

Papa Drausin had missed the census visit because he was visiting the doctor for his continuing, debilitating cough. The prognosis was not good. Although the Wulsins had moved north to Richmond St., out of the Ohio River floodplain, the Mill Creek basin still exuded damp that combined with the pollution of hundreds of coal-heated houses in every direction to fill Drausin's lungs. Although some thought of Cincinnati's ring of seven hills like a crown, for Drausin they combined with the basin to work more like a witches' kettle, boiling a brew that was killing him. To make a more drastic move was, in fact, a matter of life and death.

Eugene came home from school one day with a purpling eye and a slight limp. Out on the playground, some of the boys had been dueling boasts. Eugene outdid himself. He had boasted that his great-grandfather, the French Admiral de Tassy, had defeated the British navy at Trafalgar, killing Lord Nelson. Some of the boys had laughed because Lord Nelson, though fatally wounded, had indeed defeated the French-Spanish Armada. Then had swelled from the boys, "Tas-sy, Tas-sy, Eu-gene, Eu-gene, sas-sy Frenchy Tas-sy!" Eugene, hurt by his classmates' taunting laughter, had swung at one, who'd punched back and kicked him before others could restrain them both.

Eugene, both eyes burning reddish-black, was still furious. Drausin and Josephine sat him down by the coal-fire. Aline, Drausin, and Lucien receded to the periphery of the room, bearing quiet witness to their hot-headed younger brother's parental education. "First, mon chou-chou," clarified Josephine, rubbing arnica around the eye and on the shin, "your great-grandfather, Joseph Tassy, was a lieutenant, not an admiral. That was his uncle."

"Second, young master Wulsin," Drausin followed, "your great-grandfather, Lieutenant Joseph Tassy, was guillotined in Marseilles in 1794 by a Revolutionary court. The Battle of Trafalgar was not until 1805. You need to get your facts straight. And the Admiral de Tassy had long disappeared. And yes, Lord Nelson's British Navy not only defeated, but soundly crippled the much larger French-Spanish Navy on that windy Trafalgar coast. You were right only that Lord Nelson died of his wounds in that battle." Eugene's jaw, almost like a muscled arm, relaxed. His lower lip even twitched a bit as his eyes lowered.

"Eugene Wulsin, it is high time you learn what may be the most important lesson in your life. The heart—the hear—caagh—" Drausin exploded into a cough, the noise both silencing and weakening him. Josephine took over, hardly losing a beat, though with one arm on Drausin's shoulder, her eyes on Eugene's.

"One's heart, Eugene, is the heart of the world; what holds the heart healthy is truth. The truth holds the heart healthy, Eugene. However early a lie sets out, even if truth sets out in the evening, truth will always catch up with the lie, always. Tu comprends?"

Eugene nodded with his whole being, looking up into his mother's emerald eyes and then into his wilting father's brown ones. "It is good that this happened today," Josephine continued. "The fastest way to truth is—to let yourself fall. Honesty is your best amulet; always wear it over your heart."

Eugene understood indeed, in ways he would never forget. Yet a small part of him held a question, like a candle in a cave.

"Well, what about our passing white? Is that truth?"

"—You are right to ask, Eugene." Drausin had recovered his voice. "Yes, passing as white is a truth we choose. We are white as much as black. We choose the truth of our whiteness."

Eugene could hear the words; he didn't know if they worked for him. It felt like he wore a white suit whenever he left the house. *Wouldn't it be more truthful to wear whatever color I want, wherever, whenever I wish? But I do know there's all kinds of people around us, old Know-Nothings, cotton-dealing Democrats, Irish fresh off the boat, Kaintucks, who would not let me go wherever I want, whenever I want, without my "white" suit. That is a truth too, I know.*

Later, Drausin wondered how well their conversation with Eugene had worked. Josephine asked, not of him, but of them both, "And the truth of our color?"

Drausin shook his head. "How do we choose among all our truths? I can't help thinking of flitch, not the sides of a hog, but the pieces of wood Papa taught us the craft of arranging on the surface of support wood, to offer the veneer to please the eye. How much are we Wulsins choosing our truth, and how much are we simply arranging our veneer to please the world of white? I wish I were more certain." Josephine worked his shoulders, seeking to soothe him.

"What truths of ours are catching up with what lies?"

"Oh, I do not know, Chérie. Only time will tell, and maybe generations."

CHAPTER 40:
KENTUCKY, 1861

Josephine had Lucien carve out of linden wood a six-inch rudimentary statue of St. Joseph the house builder, his saw down along one leg, his plane in the other hand. Aline painted it in browns. On St. Joseph's Day, March 19, Maman made three different types of St. Joseph's bread, shaped as crucifix, heart, and flower. That evening, Lucien dug a hole in the back yard. Aline placed St. Joseph into it on a bed of moss with some crocuses, his head facing south, slightly east. Josephine added a pinch of each of the three breads. Then she prayed, thanking her name-saint, Joseph, for his protection in their dwellings over the years, asking for his guidance and blessings as they sought their new, urgently important home. *Amen.*

Lucien covered St. Joseph with soil. Laure placed a goldfinch feather, upright.

The Wulsins found land, a forked ridge sloping south to a creek and low pastures, across the river in Kentucky. Lucien remembered how Jebediah and Esau had never debarked in Kentucky on the river trip north. No taking slave-risks for them. Eugene asked their parents if the Kaintucks would be more like their Kaintuck in Natchez, ready to bash Papa, or also like him, Declan, changed by the time they'd reached the alligator's eye on the Ohio, tousling Eugene's hair while telling them tales. After ten years in Cincinnati, Drausin and Josephine were confident they could cope with Kentucky.

Drausin had gone exploring. He'd shown Josephine three possibilities. She and he both preferred this farm, just below Cold Spring, twelve miles south of Newport. They brought Lucien and Eugene one day to see it while young Drausin was at work. Aline stayed home with les cacouettes, the peanuts, helped by Caitlin.

The farmhouse, high on the ridge, faced south in good light, with an almost constant breeze, near no water other than the well and a creek, a good way down the hill. Forest and fields extended as far as the eye could see. *Just what the doctor ordered*, thought Josephine. Since the original house had burned, the present two-story home felt as clean as a new tool. Further north up the ridge stood a small yellow cottage, the former Negro quarters. At one time the farm must have been a modest plantation. Probably hemp. Lexington had long had slaves making rough bagging for cotton bales.

Walking along the ridges, Lucien looked down at his hands, which had become so large, even for a young man of sixteen, that they seemed to cry out for work. As he crossed the lower pastures he felt his thighs tingle as though they were singing. It did not pass. Lucien felt his arms and legs hankering, hungering, thirsting to work this land.

In their room back home at 349 Richmond, Drausin pondered the necessity of moving to the farm; he lamented his situation with a slight chuckle to Josephine. "I admire that this Northwest Territory of ours was given to families of officers as reward for their service in the Revolutionary War. I admire that many of our early settlers were members of the Order of Cincinnatus. I admire that that celebrated Roman general had retired to the pleasures of his farm, and then was recalled to bring order to Rome, which he accomplished, immediately returning to his plow. I just wish we were going to the farm because of my strengths, not my weaknesses."

Josephine arose, swishing in her nightgown over behind his rocking chair, and put her hands firmly on her husband's shoulders. "Mon amour, we are going because of your health, *your health*. That is reason good enough. And it will be good for the children, for us all." Her own strength, her own love for him, certainly helped him accept this necessity. She knew better than he how crucial the move was for her beloved Drausin.

Seven southern states had seceded from the Union. On April 12, 1861, Confederate General Pierre Gustave Toutant Beauregard fired on Ft. Sumter in Charleston Harbor, South Carolina. Union Major Robert Anderson surrendered on April 13 to his good friend and former West Point student.

Josephine remembered the general who struck the match of the war between the States as her childhood Creole playmate, obsessively building forts as a boy, persistent in his periodic visits and teenage attentions to her, bitterly struggling to be gracious about her marriage to Drausin. *Would P.G.T. Beauregard have destroyed our union then as he is starting to do now with the United States? Perhaps if he knew how, back in 1836. I wonder who, among our many family strands in New Orleans, sympathizes with the Union and who with the cause of the southern states, defending their slave-sustained status quo.*

In a strange, unpleasant moment, Josephine imagined having walked down the aisle on P.G.T.'s arm instead of walking past him on Drauzin's. How close she may have come to having children become slave-state seceders rather than northerners buying a farm in Kentucky! She shuddered, squeezing the arm of her music man, resting her head on his shoulder, his shoulder that was hers.

Although some Kentuckians owned slaves, many abhorred slavery. Kentucky and Ohio were both border states, and the Ohio River was the Mason-Dixon Line. Ohio was on the north side of the Mason-Dixon Line; that was pretty clear. Kentucky was on the south side; that was not so clear. When the war started, Kentucky was a neutral state. And when, two days later, the Wulsins signed the papers for the farm, Kentucky was still a neutral state.

On April 15, 1861, Josephine Wulsin, wife of Drausin Wulsin, purchased two adjoining eighty-acre plots, one for three thousand dollars and one for one thousand six hundred. Drausin Wulsin bought sixty contiguous acres for two thousand dollars, totaling two hundred twenty acres for six thousand six hundred dollars in Campbell County, just south of Cold Spring, Kentucky, on the dirt road—the Licking Pike, then Route 9— toward Alexandria.

Drausin recommended appropriate teachers so his music students could continue. Piano students he urged to learn with his own children's teacher, D. H. Baldwin, gangly but earnest, artful, and patient. Baldwin had loved teaching the Wulsin children. He would miss them all. Aline was the most earnest, while young Drausin the most technically proficient. Lucien preferred violin. Laure was the most sensitive, so delicately attuned. But the least disciplined was in fact the most naturally talented. Eugene, hardly aware, would hear a tune, find it among the keys, then run off into the woods whistling it on some adventure.

The family moved, leaving behind St. Joseph, who had helped them well to find their farm, in charge of 349 Richmond, which waited as a weekend retreat or in case the farm failed. Young Drausin remained at Harriet and Whitewater. Inspired by meeting candidate Lincoln two years earlier, he had begun studying the full course of law school in the legal office of French & Cunningham.

Josephine, Aline, and Laure placed pungent pennyroyal in the farmhouse rooms to cleanse the aroma. Laure asked, "The broom, Maman?" Josephine remembered that a young couple moving in can't bring the old broom unless throwing it in handle first. But an old couple moving in must bring an old broom, or one of them will have bad luck. Josephine asked Drausin, "Cher, are we a young couple or old?"

Drausin kissed her on the cheek. "You're young. I'm old."

Josephine smiled. "Cho co! I've borne nine children—I'm old, too, chou-chou; we bring the old broom." However, when they arrived, the handle had snapped when a trunk shifted in the wagon. Josephine crossed herself. Aline gathered alder branches to make a new broom.

Josephine had Aline plant sweet basil on either side of the doorstep and a pepper bush in the yard, all for good luck. She had begun to glean what she had yet to share with Drausin. She was once again enceinte. By now, she could certainly read the signs. She remembered her mother Josephine saying siblings were like fingers on a hand. Well, in this case, the Wulsin siblings would be up to two hands, minus the original little baby Barthelemy. Likely due in November; she'd be forty-three. She prayed to Notre Dame, Mother Mary, for the well-being of the child, and asked, if it be God's will, that she might survive, to care for her failing husband as well as Clarence, Lillie Alice, and Mary Josephine. *Thank heavens for Aline and Caitlin.*

Carpenter though he had been, and music teacher though he was, a farmer Drausin was not. Yet, back on Bayou Rd. in New Orleans, he had learned from Josephine's Young brothers how to harness a plow to a mule. Now Drausin helped Lucien harness the farm's mule, Shadrach, to the plow. Lucien looked into black Shadrach's brown eyes, saw his blue pupils, and rubbed his chest, speaking softly to him. Then he took up the reins, clucked, shook the reins, and the mule started forward.

The plow bit, sliced, some soil started to peel over, and *thwunk*, the oak handle knocked Lucien's jaw hard, leaving him bruised and slightly dazed. Drausin said he had borne down too hard, making the blade bite too deeply. Lucien pulled up the blade, started Shadrach again, and began to control the depth better, gliding a little more steadily along. When he finished his row, he looked back; the plowed line wobbled left and right, a giant thread unfraying. Lucien was tired already, and he'd hardly started.

Eugene, meanwhile, had leapt onto the chestnut mare, Flame, who also had come with the farm, riding her bareback with a halter and rope, venturing farther and farther, up and down, gradually all around the farm.

Drausin got hit by a coughing fit, which sent him reeling, lightheaded, back up the hill into the farmhouse.

Sweating, grunting, cursing, trying to hold some kind of line with the plow, and worrying about his father, Lucien occasionally thought he saw a human shadow in the trees.

CHAPTER 41:
SOWING AND REAPING, 1861

Lucien loved casting seed, especially as the late afternoon slow-glowed into dusk. Just after the first day of light rain was usually best. He'd reach in the burlap seed sack on his left hip, swing out his right hand, and open his fist, spraying, raying round. A circle in front and a circle in back as he walked, figure eight, sometimes a four-leaf clover, tinting the brown ground gold with rye, wheat, even oat seed, as evenly spread as possible. With corn he had to be more careful, planting each seed every three to four inches.

In contrast to his family of ten living in close proximity within their house, Lucien loved the solitude of working in the fields. He could make wind freely as he walked, plowed, or swung an axe. Whenever possible, he made water right in the garden; he even, when no one else was around, preferred to make his earth there. When several of the boys were working, they enjoyed making water together, "crossing swords" with their arcs. Eugene could usually arc the farthest distance, Lucien the longest time. Ah, the simple pleasures of being made in the image of the creator, making earth, water, and wind.

All horse and cow manure around the barn they pitched into piles, along with the seasoned chicken guano, autumn leaves, cut grass from around the house, and ashes from the fireplaces. Later, they would spread the blend on the field. Although "Feed it to the pigs" was usually the first response to leftover food, most nights Lucien took half the kitchen scraps out to the chickens after supper. One night he glimpsed a white stripe near his right ankle. Resigned to being stenched, he was surprised when the stripe moved on along. Many nights Lucien and the skunk crossed paths outside the chicken coop, yet the young man never once had to sleep in the barn, skunk-stunked; that skunk knew his provider.

Lucien had a knack on the ground with the animals that came with the farm. Eugene had a knack on their backs and could ride anything. In the ring he liked to grab Flame's mane in his left hand, swing onto her back, spring toward her withers on the balls of his feet, pivot, march along the walking horse's back to her tail, then pivot again on her rump, pretending to run in slow motion, while clucking the horse into a trot. He'd slip down onto Flame's bare back, shift her into a canter, and swing himself down left, his hands on the mane, toe-touch the ground, spring back up, then do the same on the right side, all without the agreeable mare losing pace.

But a stubborn calf on the ground, that frustrated Eugene. He couldn't push it or pull it toward where he wanted it to go. Lucien, instead of pushing or pulling, would slip his finger between the calf's lips and simply suckle it along where he wanted it to go. Always quiet, he'd move slower than the animal, somehow adjusting to its rhythm. Lucien found that, especially when he closed his good eye, he could attune himself to the animal, learn its lingo.

The head-butting, frisky-horned goat would chew on Lucien's forearm without biting him, then let him slip it into harness for the goat-cart, responsive to all his commands. The mule, Lucien discovered to his surprise, loved onions like apples. Stubborn as any of his kind, Shadrach learned that Lucien could outwait him. The mule always understood Lucien's wishes and discovered that the sooner he obliged, the sooner that onion would appear for a bite or a mouthful. One grey colt, frisky, shy of bridle and saddle, loved walls of water poured down his sides from a bucket, calming, smoothing him into compliance, eventual alliance. Soon enough each animal would come directly to Lucien, any time he attuned to it.

One evening Josephine and Drausin saw Lucien walking along the ridge under the setting sun followed single file by a horse, a mule, a donkey, a goat, a cow, and a calf, all unroped, "like Peter the Hermit leading the Children's Crusade to the Promised Land," remarked Drausin. That silhouette belonged, agreed Drausin and Josephine, on the background of some stage set.

As the first shoots started to green the ground in the garden and cornfields, Papa, Aline, Lucien, Eugene, Laure, and Clarence would stir at dawn, still moist and cool, to weed the rows by hand or hoe. Lillie Alice liked to say, "I'm only one, younger 'n' baby Mary Josephine. Where are my other years? I jus' leaped right over 'em, 'cuz I'm a leap year." And she was right. The family had properly celebrated her birthday for the first time just last year, February 29, 1860, although they had settled for March 1 the years in between. Mary Josephine, only three, stayed inside or on the porch with Maman while the housegirl Caitlin prepared breakfast.

The children were proud, some to be part of the Farmer's Army, while others liked the Army of Farmers better. They sang as they plucked the rows clean, Aline, Lucien, and Papa keeping an eye on Lillie to be sure she picked just weeds, not the pretty flowers. Lillie found faerie treasures of pearls of dew in the pea leaves. Some days Lucien wished he could garden in the morning dew all day long.

Laure directed the animal hospital. Patients included a red-winged blackbird with a broken wing; a sky-blue robin's egg to try to warm and hatch; and still-featherless wren chicks with white-lipped beaks. She also rescued a chipmunk dragging a mauled leg after escaping a fox; a bull frog, a whole leg lost to a catfish; goldfinches and black-capped chickadees stunned from flying at the invisible living room window; a brood of baby squirrels, and bunnies whose mother a bobcat had likely caught. Some birds woke to resume flight in minutes, some hours later, some never again. Laure held animal funerals galore beyond the garden beneath a mimosa tree, offering a ceremony, prayer, and song for each departed creature. A baby crow she named Jezebel limped around the barn.

Lillie was the Ophelia of the family, perpetually gathering little bouquets of wildflowers for this room or that, for this person or another. She made faerie glens of various mosses, including reindeer and star, using walnuts as chairs and ferns as fans. Sometimes she brought in a corn's tassel or an unripe cauliflower, but most of her game was wild. She loved all plants, from milkweed, its seed parachutes flying on the wind, to skunk cabbage that unfurled purple-green along the creek. Wild blue irises. Maroon Lady Slippers. Jack-in-the-Pulpit by the swamp. Forget-me-nots. Trillium in many changing colors. Later in the summer, Lillie watched chrysalises under the milkweed leaves peel back to unfold wet purple, then orange, yellow-eyed monarch butterflies emerging to dry their new wings.

Clarence and Eugene caught their share of frogs, turtles, leeches, slugs, and orange salamanders. Clarence kept a medicinal leech farm in a bucket by the creek. When someone would get a cut, nurse Laure would summon Dr. Clarence to clean it with a leech. The boys showed the girls how to numb their tongues by licking a slug, a good trick for pain.

One day, out by the barn, they unearthed a mess of white, squishy, indented eggs, about half a finger long. Over the days they watched little brown snakes shed their soft shells. The boys whooped with joy. The crows had noticed too, along with a raven and a red-tailed hawk. Eugene and Clarence became heroic defenders of the snake babies, Davy Crockett and Jim Bowie at the Alamo, defending the future of the Wulsin farm. At supper they proudly announced both their find and their defense to the family, promising that their brown babies would become mighty black snakes sure to keep their barn and basement free of mice and rats.

Laure, eyes big, recalled shrieking at a four-foot-long shining piece of night draped in the rafters of the basement. *Maman quieted me by helping me to notice the shiny black diamonds of the scales, the beautiful head, the white throat and belly, the black eyes ringed white. Maman shifted me from my fear to admiring the black snake's beauty.*

The boys liked to track raccoons and possums—even owls, by flight, to their nests to be watched in the dusk. After one good day's work the boys took along a net, tracking a coon far along the east ridge to a tall tulip tree. With the help of a close beech tree, Eugene was able to monkey-climb forty-five feet up to the large notch that nestled the coon's den. He hollered, "Whoa! The mama's in here!"

"Get on down fast as a flash!"

"Nope! I'm gettin' 'em!" While Mama Coon clawed and even bit at Eugene, he grabbed her, pulled her out, shook her off his arm, and let her drop. She landed like a cat and started to climb right back up, hissing. Eugene grabbed one kit from the nursery, held it out, and dropped it into the open net of the coonsters. Then he grabbed and dropped a second kit, leaving two in the den.

Lucien insisted, "That's it, now get on down 'fore you're her meat!" As she hissed and climbed, and he descended, the mama seemed torn between the two in the net down below and the two in their nest above. She headed for Eugene but he spiraled to the other side of the tree, swung out on a branch, and dropped to a branch below her, then continued monkeying down to the ground. The hunters hauled their catch back toward the barn.

Eugene looked forward to a coonskin cap someday. Lucien insisted on taking the kits live to market on Saturday—let customers decide: pets or pelts? The hunters detoured over to Clarence's leech farm at the creek, where Lucien applied leeches to Eugene's scratches and bites. In the barn they added spider webs, hiding what wounds they could.

Later that night, Laure was furious to hear, then find, the kidnapped raccoon kits whimpering. She gently put them in a stall and got them sucking a rag soaked in warm cow's milk.

Whenever young Drausin came out for the weekend, he would lend his back to tasks in the morning. Then, if it was Saturday, he would get the family into a pickup game of town ball in the afternoon. One time Eugene, now fourteen, was pitching. He had tossed a hemp rag on the ground behind the pitcher's mound. When brother Drausin stepped back from batting to wipe his eyes, Eugene bent, turned, slipped his hand under the rag-pile, and then stood to face forward again, looking innocent. When Eugene delivered his pitch, the ball looked slightly larger and definitely greener than usual. Drausin gamely thwacked it with the broomstick. Instead of the glory of a home run, white spattered all over him, though he managed to run to first base. Milky, sticky, he could not get it off, but Eugene, screeching with laughter, nevertheless could not throw his brother out. The "ball" had shattered.

"What?" demanded Drausin.

"Osage orange!" shouted Eugene. "Osage orange! Gotchya!" Drausin had to laugh. After the game he washed off the milky juice in the creek.

Those evenings after a hearty supper the family would bring out instruments, led of course by Papa, sometimes on clarinet, mandolin, piano, or guitar. Songs flowed in French and in English, even some in German. Aline and young Drausin both played cello, taking turns with piano. Lucien played violin while Eugene alternated between piano and boudlin drum, Laure played the flute, and Clarence attempted the piccolo. Lillie, most like her father in musical versatility, harmonized intuitively with voices and instruments, able to pick up tunes even more facilely than Eugene.

After one such evening, glowing, Josephine said to Drausin in their bedroom, "Eh bien, mon Cher, have we chosen right, to buy this farm, si?"

"Oh, ma Josie, si, si, si. Although I cannot shoulder my share, our children, our children, they open out like—like a peacock's feathers fanning."

"Whoa—easy now—" sounded from afar; it felt forests away. Had he been mugged? Lucien slid out his Bowie knife, rolled onto his back, pointing up. "Ownwh," he groaned, his head like rocks in a box.

"Easy now, son, don't you go slicin' me up. Ah'm your help. You were leanin' down so low, tryin' to push-plow through that walnut root, you got thwacked to kingdom come. Course, mebbe you're lucky. Most men standin' behind a plow'll get herniaed when the point jams on a stob. You might recover faster jus' gettin' knocked out. James Gray," he said, reaching out his hand, both to shake Lucien's and to pull him up. Still wobbly, Lucien felt the rocks stop sliding in his skull when he at last stood still.

"I'm Lucien Wulsin. Thank you. Forgive me for the knife—" Lucien took in the man's brownish-red-beard, his smooth-skinned face. His grey eyes smiled like his mouth, slight and natural. *Fittin'*, Lucien thought, *like he wore it most of most days.* He wore a grey linsey-woolsey shirt, blue, stained canvas pants, and well-worn brogans. His stance? *Resting like a tree, when he's not active like a man.* Hands strong, calloused, scratched, dirt-nailed. *Hmm. Looks familiar.*

"—You're the one!—You've been watching me."

"That's right, young man, for weeks."

"Hey, Mr. Gray, I don't know what you have in mind, but we're keepin' this farm; we'll get there—"

"Of course you are, and you will. And I'll help make sure of that. Now you jus' lay yourself down under that paw-paw tree, an' take time to pull yourself back in like a kite. Here's some tea." Gray handed Lucien a powder horn. "Ole Shadrach here, he turned in his track an' come back to shade you when you fell." Gray tied the mule to the paw-paw tree.

Then he swung his axe on that walnut root until it let go, and he proceeded to walk the edges of the field, chopping up any more roots. When Gray got all the way back to the paw-paw tree, Lucien asked, "Why have you been watching so much from the shadows?"

"Why? Why, Lucien Wulsin, you don't know it, but you're a young lion, a picture of courage. You inspire me. This land needs your hands. In fact, so does my land. You keep knockin' your head against all the oak trees of this farm, and they're gonna up and move along to the next hillside, jus' to leave you be."

Stunned in several ways now, Lucien protested, "But I don't know what I'm doing."

"You may not know what you're doin', but the ways you're doin' let you learn how the things need doin'. You listen while you work. Speakin' of trees, I've noticed somethin'. You not only listen, you speak—to your trees."

Lucien blushed. "Yes, I'm afraid so, when I think I'm alone. I guess I feel they're something like the guardians of our farm. Does that sound loony?"

"No, not at all. I think you're right. Know what else I notice? You don't speak to 'em in English. Sounds like French."

Lucien caught a breath, smiled, nodding; he'd not quite realized it. "You know, French just feels closer to their lingo. I don' know."

"You might jus' be onta somethin', Monsieur Lucien." Gray reached into his pocket and handed Lucien a stone.

"Thanks for—the rock."

"Lucien, what I found under one of your walnut roots is not just some rock." The man turned the gritty conglomerate of four smooth stones cemented together in a composite of shells, quartz, fossils, clay; he rotated it up to his eye and peered at Lucien through a hole in the middle of it all.

"I see you, through and through. This, young lion, is a hag stone. Any stone you find with a hole through it is a hag stone. You place that hag stone in the crook of a nearby tree. That hag stone an' that tree'll work extra better together, as guardians of this land." Lucien rolled his hag stone around in his hand, listening to it through his skin.

"Now, here's an ole song fer you ta try, next time you plow, young man. Sing it to ole Shadrach to get you'n' him in tune any time the goin's rough, 'n' your plowin' 'll smooth out sooner:

Got to get behind the mule
In the morning and plow.
Got to get behind the mule
In the morning and plow.

With Papa half-working, half-wheezing, Drausin lawyering in town, Eugene half-working, half-galavanting, Aline majorly tending the garden, and Mama rounding toward melon again, Lucien wondered if, strangely, he might not be so alone as he'd felt. James Gray? Out of the shadows?

"Thank you, Mr. Gray. What kind of walnut was that root?" Lucien asked.

"Call me James, son. Oh, that's black walnut. Beautiful wood, and the nuts—bitter skin, but sweet meat. No white walnut or butternut up here; they're all down deep South. Up here, jus' black walnut—an' us Grays." Gray grinned, showing strong white teeth.

CHAPTER 42:
MOON SHINE, 1861

"Farming's all timing," started James Gray after pausing at the end of the tenth row of corn they were doing together one day. "Like one big symph'ny orchestra. Conductor up there's givin' the signals, what sounds should come in when, to make the whole piece the best music. We have to see the signals. Watch the breeze in the leaves, on the stream or pond. Watch the clouds, at several levels. Weather up high can move opposite of our low clouds down here. Yeah, weather's allus changin'; we rarely know jus' how, try as we may. But there's major beats goin' on no matter how the rhythms may change.

"Everything that lives grows by sun'n' moon. Everybody knows sun. Most folks no-count moon—'cept for romance. You look out there, we don't see much water. But there's puddles, ponds, streams 'n cricks o' water inside us, and in 'mos' everything round us. An' that's what the moon moves. Yessir, mind that moon. Mind the moon, an' the sun'll work better for you." James looked at Lucien, who was open, but clearly needing more.

"Lucien, why don't you meet me at sunset in your garden Monday night? Eat an onion like an apple that afternoon; muskeeters'll steer clear, 'less you'd prefer bear grease, of course," Gray grinned.

First Monday night:

As they walked in descending dusk along the garden paths, James spoke. "See that thumbnail shinin' up there? New Moon means sun 'n' moon 're mos'ly on the same side o' the earth, pullin' together. Water's risin' in the earth, so the plants, the trees are givin' their best growth. Seeds can swell an' even burst. Now's the best time t'plant all those annuals t'make their seeds outside their fruit: spinach'n' lettuce—the leafers; celery 'n' rhubarb—the stalkers; broccoli, cabbage, 'n' cauliflower—the flowerers, of course; 'n' grains—the seeders."

And Lucien went to work accordingly that week.

Second Monday night:

The garden was quite visible, like dark daylight. James continued his lessons. "—Second quarter, see that moon jus' waxin'? Moonlight's juicin' up, strengthenin', good time to plant, make healthy leaves grow. 'Specially two days 'fore the full moon. Now's when you wanna be plantin' your above-ground producers, but especially them that form their seeds inside their fruits: your beans'n' melons, your peas'n' peppers, your squash an' to-ma-toes. Now sing that little ditty. 'Your beans'n' melons, your peas'n' peppers, your squash an' to-ma-toes.'" Lucien gamely sang the ditty.

"Atta boy," said James, chuckling. "Mos' farmers got lotsa ditties to remember by.

"Now, full moon's when tides ride highest, moon'n' sun in a tug'o war from each side o' the earth. So, more moisture in the soil. An' here's a little secret I think you can handle: the spirits of these little plants, helpin' you to help them grow, they don't mind a wee bit o' milk on a wee bit o' bark at the end o' the row on one of these whitenin' nights."

"Mr. Gray—I mean James—may I ask you where you've learned all this farm savvy?"

"Oh, when my family come out from Virginia 'bout turn o' the century, they lived their first three years in a hollow syca-more tree eleven foot across. While they cleared nearby woods into fields an' built their cabin, a part-Shawnee family called Parks befriended 'em, helpin' 'em with all that grows. I fell in love with Parkses' daughter, my Margaret. They'd been farmin' these parts for generations. My Daddy picked up a lot quick, an' worked hard, careful 'n' slow; an' our ground gave forth.

"But—aroun' here, liquor's as thick as chiggers—if you walk in the woods, you get some. Wan't long 'fore my daddy couldn't plow a straight line anymore. Margaret's daddy died. We been makin' do as best we can. Some of that land you bought used to be ours, but last owners knew nothin' 'bout farmin.' We been scrapin' along next farm over. Some day I'll show you a buffalo skull Marg'ret's grandaddy kept from way back 'fore we whites took over on the buffalo traces." And Lucien went to work accordingly that week.

Third Monday night:

Margaret Gray appeared too—quiet, shadowing James to the side. Shining black hair with a tint of auburn, cinnamon skin, hazel eyes glistening like light on the water of a well. She wore a modest maroon linsey-woolsey gown, and mostly watched and listened. When they visited at the house, Josephine read something sad in her, glowing like shining moss, and nodded, almost indiscernibly. Margaret looked into Josephine—and nodded back. Josephine knew Margaret knew they weren't each just Josephine Wulsin and Margaret Gray.

Aline took Margaret's hand and led her inside to a chair in the living room, where they talked, embroidered, sometimes read to each other over ensuing evenings. Aline soon savored the company of the "older sister" she'd never had.

It wasn't long before Margaret came over some days as well. In time Aline learned that Margaret, her mother's last gift, had never known her. Margaret liked just to be near Josephine, her presence like a sheltering willow tree.

In the garden the plants, though dimming, were still visible in the late dusk. "—The third quarter begins just after full moon," James continued, as though a moment, not a week, had passed since their last evening garden session. "Everythin's wanin', not waxin'. Moonlight goin' down, decreasin', but right on down, into those roots, so, more life-juice into the roots. The seeds soak up most water now. Good time for plantin' roots, like taters, carrots, beets, radishes, 'n' onions. An' good for plantin' perennials, 'n' bulbs, an' for transplantin'— but not carrots. Carrots don't like you uprootin' 'em to try to transplant. Jus' let carrots be. You can't transplant carrots."

"Mr.— James, my first time walking this land, my thighs started tingling, my hands felt hungry to work, hankerin' to have at it. Is that corny?"

"Son, you plumb fell in love with this land of yours, love at first sight," said James, chuckling, shaking his head. "Nothin' corny 'bout that—that's in fact what makes corn grow best. You're hooked for sure now, Mr. Love-struck."

Lucien chuckled, too. "Well, I'm sure getting my fill now."

"Yessir, you're fill-in', alright. Look atchya; you're broadenin' at the shoulders like a chestnut tree." James looked at Lucien, spat tobacco juice in the path, and almost whispered, "Lunar Lucien—yup, Lunar Lucien," the last repetition a little louder.

"I don't get it," said Lucien, who as usual had listened closely to everything James uttered.

"'Lunar Lucien,' that's you—'Moon Light'—no, moonshine. Ha, that's it—'Moon Shine'! We got us our very own, pretty spankin' new Moon Shine!" Lucien stood still, having long forgotten the meaning of his proper name. Feeling strange, slightly revealed, slightly renamed, his dusky cheeks shining, Lucien smiled.

And Lucien went to work accordingly that week.

Fourth Monday night:

Lucien had to feel his way in the dark, shuffling to stay on the path and crush no plant, sometimes his hand on James

Gray's shoulder. "—Now, your fourth quarter, there's pretty much no moonlight, so, no moon-pull. 'Less moonlight—let' em rest.' Say that." Which Lucien did. "Mainly, jus' let rest. No plantin'. You might cultivate, harvest, even transplant— but not carrots—maybe prune some. But no plantin.' Moon down—one thing you do do is, pull up weeds, 'cuz they're too weak to spread."

And Lucien went to work accordingly that week.

Many nights over the following months, Lucien started feeling like the ground in the garden, in the fields. Various fragments James had said while working would re-sound in his sleep, like seeds brought by the wind, settling in.

"Yessir, Lunar Lushe, you Moon Shine, you—Mind that moon. Moon risin' makes everythin' rise within. Moon fallin' flattens all.

"When moon rises, plant what grows tall; full moon, trim but don't cut.

"Plant anything that matures underground, like your taters, in the dark of moon; an' what matures on top in full moon.

"Now, you do your fencin' in the dark of the moon if you don't want your fence to settle.

"Ya brand and castrate on the decrease o' the moon; slaughter on the increase.

"Chow down before you plant fruit trees; you plant on an empty stomach, trees'll bear no fruit. Plant on a full stomach, trees're fruit-full.

"Where the soil shivers, plant thickets with roots like claws, sweet-pea, local pea. Oak leaves size of squirrel's ear— time to plant corn. When dogwood's in full bloom, plant corn.

"Plant your pepper when you're mad, or let a red-head plant it." (Lucien would let Eugene plant the peppers, figuring he was a ginger man inside.)

"Never plant okra standing. Always stoop, and the plant'll bear while still low.

"Your vegetables and melon seeds be planted only by a growing child; they'll grow as a child grows. Not your Aline, even not you, but your Eugene, your Laure, your Clarence, and your little Lillie, God help us." James chuckled at that.

"Plant four seeds for each you want to grow: 'One for the blackbird, one for the crow,

one for the cutworm, and one for to grow.'

"Watch your bees waterin' at the creek. Follow 'em to their wild hive. Smoke 'em with wet leaves. Get honey, leave enough for the bees for winter, an' keep the bees. 'A load of bees in May is worth a load of hay. A load of bees in June is worth a silver spoon. A load of bees in July is not worth a fly.' Say it. An' here's another:

"'If the oak is out before the ash, it'll be a summer of wet and splash; if the ash is out before the oak, it'll be a summer of fire and smoke.'

"For meat, spare yourself hours and days wanderin' the woods. Deer graze more 'round dawn an' dusk, 'specially when the moon's closest to the sun, the 'minor' moon. An' fish graze then most, too. Best huntin' and best fishin'—'major' moon, when moon's farthest from the sun, full. You boys'll become good hunters under the minor moon: squirrels in the fall, turkey and deer in the winter, rabbits all year.

"Slingshot prepares for the rifle, for the shotgun.

"Before a death in the family, a little white dog often appears in the house and disappears, passin' through a wall."

Outside of his dreams, too, Lucien often found himself pondering James's proverbial guidance.

Many months later, James Gray noticed Lucien wrestling with some big riddle, maybe between farming and fighting, and said to him, "Moon Shine, you ready for one more secret of the moon?"

"Yessir, Mr. Gray, I mean James." Lucien, pain-tinged, grinned. "Of course I'd be grateful for one more."

"Well, this I learned from Margaret. When you find yourself in some mighty quand'ry, mebbe 'bout a woman, or work, or war—the three big Ws in a man's life—or mebbe somethin' else, try to keep your questions in mind, especially to the new moon. Place your question in that slender silver bowl up there, give it up, and let it be. Mebbe you'll sleep better. Let your sleep work on it. Your sleep works on things, you know, like the moon does plants. Let sleep do its share. In fact, best forget your overriding question.

"Then, come full moon, bring it back to mind. Look at that full moon, Lunar Luche. Listen. Watch everything. Look for what you can't usually see. Listen for what you can't hear. An' you just might find, during the course of those several days of the full moon, that the round silver bowl up there has spilled you some clue, a response to your question. Just mebbe, if you don't miss it."

"Thank you, James Gray. I will surely ask, look and listen— so mysterious, your lunar moon."

Papa Drausin lamented his place on the periphery of Wulsin farm life. But one night he put his hand on Lucien's weary shoulder as the young farmer was heading to bed.

"Son, I'm sorry you're losing your schooling after tenth grade. But I'm glad you seem to be receiving an education worthy of Plato's Academy."

"Si, mon Père, I believe you might just be right."

CHAPTER 43:
MARKET, 1861

Lucien loaded the wagon with the first harvest of June on a Friday afternoon for delivery to market on Saturday. He slept in the hayloft that night, awakening to a barred owl's "whu-whit-too-whooh" several hours before sunrise. A darkness in the dark, the still-limping but now larger black crow Jezebel pecked some seed from his hand. Lucien harnessed Shadrach, onion-led him out of the stall, backed him between the wagon poles, and cinched the stay-straps, talking low all the time. Lucien chuckled, remembering James Gray snorting in disbelief, "I've never known any horse, donkey, or mule to be anythin' but allergic to onions. That Shadrach has an iron stomach as well as head, but good taste." Hemp bags covered bounteous baskets of peas and lettuce from night dew. Even though it was June, Lucien wore his shawl and straw slouch-hat against the night damp.

He "hop-on-up-now"-ed Shadrach, who turned from Gray's Hill down Murnan Ln., then onto Route 9 to start the journey north, past Low Gap Rd., rolling about four miles up to Cold Spring, crossing Ripple Creek Rd., then eventually St. John's Hill Rd. Occasional does crossed, still-spotted fawns scampering spindle legged after. A screech owl's long gravesong tremolo descended into almost a horse's whinny. Lucien imagined not-so-long-ago herds of buffalo migrating by, tuft bearded, mountain shouldered. He wished he'd known Margaret's Shawnee grandaddy and father. He felt James and Margaret Gray had entered his life partially from that grey zone of timelessness. Those Grays again, grey-ing—

Sometimes coyotes yipped like kids at a party, maybe celebrating a kill, then silence. Later, he pulled Shadrach to a stop, hearing a woman scream, being beaten. As he reached for his shotgun, he realized it must be a wildcat in heat, and resumed their way down through trumpeting roosters finally to the Newport shore, where the ferry was loading just as night was lightening.

Lucien had loved the Andersonville ferry as a younger boy, especially from where they lived closer to the river on Carr St. But to wagon north from beyond Cold Spring, it was more direct to catch the easternmost ferry, in Newport at the mouth of the Licking River. By now Lucien had shed his shawl. Shadrach balked at stepping from firm land onto the swaying ferry floor. But the onion proved stronger, and ensuing weeks would prove easier.

Shadrach was also calmed by the quiet presence of the two blinded horses, a black and a bay, treading the treadmills to power the paddle wheels to pull the ferry, the Simon Kenton 2, across the Ohio River. The currents swirled and spun as the ferry swish-splashed its way, gentle and slow compared to the mighty steamboats, but steady. The ferry angled upriver to end up down at Yeatman's Cove.

"Ferry—off!" The price: two dollars for the wagon, ten cents for himself.

Cincinnati's docks bustled already with loadings and unloadings, but the streets lay quiet as Lucien adjusted to the coal-soot-tinged air and the stench of old food and sewage, sweetened by poplar and honeysuckle. Sometimes, as weeks passed, if roustabouts were singing some loading song, Lucien couldn't resist joining in heartily on the chorus, "All ni-i-i-ght long," leading some loaders to turn their heads and wonder at the grinning young wagoneer who tipped his hat and moved on. Shadrach, relieved to be back on terra firma, shouldered heartily up Broadway until the riverbank slope leveled to a steadier pull.

Shadrach pulled the wagon thirteen blocks up to the Erie-Miami Canal bridge at Main St., then nine more blocks into the heart of Germantown to Findlay Market, still shining new, serving numerous communities. The long journey was worth all the blocks for good business. Papa had rented a stall for every Saturday, a fascinating, exhausting marathon. Lucien aimed both to sell all his produce and to purchase certain goods at better prices than in Cold Spring or Newport.

Lucien came to love his stall, all day, even though the day was long. Findlay Market was Lucien's New Orleans in Cincinnati, his window into the world. After his mostly solitary week farming, he enjoyed casual interchanges with all sorts of people: children, parents, servants, young men, young women, hillbilly squirrel hunters, gentleman strolling. The interchanges were short and limited in scope, but a bit like bathing in the Miami Canal, getting drenched with the town-folk. Children played hoops, hop-scotch, and jacks.

Yes, Lucien was the front man, but he was at the same time usually invisible, disregarded until transaction. Ladies talked of prices, rivals, and beaus, sometimes whispering about husbands with chuckles or sneers. Men talked of business, war, horses, or women. A quiet outsider, Lucien valued these glimpses inside people's lives.

One market day, two fresh young men filled their grey porcelain steins with Möerlein ale and sat nearby at one of the many small tables scattered throughout the market. They wore normal day coats and waistcoats, both enjoying cigars. One had a rounded brow, slightly olive skin, and slightly pouchy cheeks. His eyes listened; his whole face smiled. Called Resor, he was speaking of his widowed cousin, Julia, who had last year married twice-widowed Seth Cutter Foster, and would soon give birth to her first—something about raising Foster's four-year-old boy George as well. Resor called the other fellow—square-jawed, large headed, black haired, fair skinned, and handsome—Chatfield.

Foster, thought Lucien. *Back our first month in Cincinnati ten years ago, staying at Mrs. Griffin's boarding house, Pa had learned that Stephen Foster had lived right in our boarding house, composing on that very piano songs like "Old Folks at Home" and "My Old Kentucky Home." Pa had played them nightly, later telling us that Mrs. Griffin had given us a week's free rent for playing Foster's music. But that had been Stephen Foster, not Seth C. Foster.*

Chatfield was asking Resor about Seth Foster. "Well, he left the family farm in Kentucky and came across the river, 'bout sixteen years old." *Just my age*, thought Lucien. "He started as a sweep and errand boy for Lewis Dry Goods store. He soon became one of Dr. Ray's best students at our night school here, the first, you know, west of the Alleghenies. After he met George Stearns, the cotton wadding expert, Foster started selling cotton goods over the counter. Back in '46, they started the Stearns and Foster Mattress Company, the first in the whole country, right down on Clay and Liberty. Right now, their company is the biggest consumer of cotton in the whole country."

Chatfield, impressed, wondered aloud, "I suppose Mr. Foster, like many cotton dealers, may well be a Southern sympathizer at heart. Do you think there's any chance your new family member may be active in the Golden Circle?"

"Look here, my dear Chatfield, look in my dark brown eyes. Do you actually think my cousin would marry herself to a copperhead? No, fear not, my friend; Julia says Foster, in fact, voted for Abraham Lincoln. As for the Golden Circle, you mean that crackpot conspiracy to unite our southern states with large swaths of Central and South America into one large slave nation?"

"Yes, Resor, that's just the one."

"Well, as far as I know, though I'm afraid our Queen City did give birth to that madness back in '54, I'm pretty certain the father of it, that lunatic General Bickley, was run out of town on a rail several years ago."

"That's true," agreed Chatfield, "but let's not forget that anti-abolitionist sentiments run as deep as Mammoth Cave around this Ohio River Valley. We never know. I'm glad to hear your Resors' new family member, Seth Cutter Foster, voted for Lincoln." Resor and Chatfield blew blue smoke and lightened their steins. Thinking of Seth Foster's story, Lucien wondered how his own might unfold.

During the course of the summer, Lucien's weekly Saturday cargo gradually shifted. In June he brought to market strawberries, along with eggs and butter. He remembered the horses south of Natchez, legs red to the knee in wild strawberries, back on the steamboat trip a decade ago. His domestic strawberries here were a strain developed by Nicholas Longworth's grandfather for the Ohio River Valley region.

By July Lucien was adding squash, tomatoes, green beans, peppers, asparagus, raspberries, onions, and radishes to his farm wagon. August: corn, corn, and corn. September: blackberries, grapes, chokecherries, beets, carrots, wax beans, more radishes, potatoes, jams, pickles, sausage, and Indiana bananas, known also as paw-paws. October: pumpkin squash, walnuts, hickory nuts, acorns, chestnuts, apples, some apple cider and some pearry—pear cider, which Lucien liked just as well.

The Findlay Market merchants generally started to close the stalls late afternoon. With an hour to return to the river, and another to wait for the ferry, and three hours to make his way back to the farm, Lucien often did not get home until well after dark, sometimes even midnight, if he stopped in Newport a while. Market day made for a long Saturday. Shadrach was always glad to return to grazing in the fields. Some Saturday nights Lucien just relaxed, staying over with brother Drausin at 22 Carr St., then heading home Sunday morning, occasionally joining the family for mass in Newport on the way.

Father Drausin was intrigued to hear of the Foster conversation between those two young gentlemen. Drausin reminded his children that back in '51, when he purchased their tickets for New Orleans to Cincinnati, a lading notice for cotton for Mr. Seth C. Foster, Wadding Merchant, Cincinnati, had caught his eye. Drausin, wheezing, wondered again if they would ever meet. *It seems Mr. S. C. Foster may be looming just over our horizon.*

CHAPTER 44:
BORDERLINES, 1861

Young Drausin, hard-working in his law studies, could hear from Lucien's occasional overnights, and could see on his own periodic farm visits, that Papa was only managing a couple of hours of work a day, in hopes of re-strengthening. Their sun was receding from the center of their lives, becoming increasingly a peripheral planet.

Brother Eugene was both strengthening and maturing, more helpful on the farm, as wild a child as he remained. Late one busy day, Lucien felt Eugene's absence. Failing to find his brother around the farm, Lucien searched the house and found on Eugene's pillow a scrawled note that read, "Family, I've gone to win the war. Love, Eugene." Aline and Laure couldn't imagine. Maman feared and prayed, like mothers across the land.

Weeks later, Papa left the farm. A day later he reappeared at the door with Eugene, whose arm was in a sling. Eugene had been injured on picket duty, slipping on wet rock and fracturing his clavicle. His commanding officer had discharged his injured soldier from the Eleventh Regiment of Ohio Infantry, by reason of extreme youth, sending for his father. Eugene was fourteen years old.

On the way home, Drausin stopped the buggy by a stream. Father and son chewed on bread and sausage and talked.

"Why, Eugene?"

"Because you and Maman would not let me, I know."

"True, but why, even so?"

"Why?" All teary. "Papa, You can't. Drausin won't. Lucien can't."

"Can't what, Son?"

"So I have to. I won't let any Rebs take us, all or any of us, back down south as slaves."

"Oh, my dear, dear boy." Drausin's arm gingerly rested on Eugene's shoulders, holding him close. "That is not our fight. First of all, dangerous rag-tag Rebs lurk in woods all over Kentucky. And you, my boy, are just that, still our boy. That's a man's fight. We need you home, where you belong. Your Maman needs you home. Your brother Lucien needs you home to do more young man's work on the farm. You know, I can do less. I need you, Eugene, when your shoulder heals, to do more because I can do less. I, we all, need you to do more, my young man at home, not our boy at war. Do you understand, my dear, brave Eugene?"

Eugene, snuffling, looked at his father through his tears, hearing his summons for help much needed. His father was calling for a home-hero. He nodded, going soft in the shelter of his father's shoulder, then sitting straight up anew.

Maman welcomed him home tenderly, with kisses galore. "It's good and right to have our boy back where you belong." Eugene looked at his siblings and mother, nodding as she took him in her arms. He knew they were getting back more than a boy.

That night, Josephine confessed to Drausin, "Mon Cher, I feel fear. Our Eugene gone to soldier and back, and him only fourteen. I fear the wolves are at our gate. How can we protect our fold?"

"I do not know, Cherie—but we will."

❧

Aline helped, especially with children and garden. Laure was coming into her own, ever quiet, inward turning, increasingly reliable. A modest laurel tree. Maman Josephine, growing larger, could do less and less. James Gray was generous beyond measure with his time, but his farm had its own needs, with which, at times, the Wulsins helped. But the main labors of the Wulsin farm fell on sixteen-year-old Lucien's growing shoulders. How could he possibly manage it all?

One warm day, Lucien was forking hay they had scythed the day before, enjoying the open air on his toughening feet. Suddenly he could not lift his pitchfork. James Gray stood on it. "Brogans, Moon Shine. You choose: boy-fool, or man-tool? You lose your foot, you lose your harvest, you lose your farm. Brogans, boy!"

Reluctantly, young Drausin, now nineteen, decided he'd better let go of his legal studies and give all to help the family make a better go of the farm. In July, hoeing was constant in garden and some fields as market harvests expanded. The dog days of summer, the hottest, were also the dampest, saturated in soft, steady "she-rain."

Then autumn gave occasional frosts before sunrise, summer heat at noon, chill at night—each day a whole year's weather. At first frosts, they dug up potatoes and put them in a hill of dirt. They dried beans on strings from ceiling beams and rafters. They dried fox grapes and wolf grapes.

The cooling fall yielded a riot of chestnut yellows, poplar golds, maple oranges, oak reds, sumac rubies, and Virginia creeper purple-whites. Preparing for winter, the fellows bundled pine knots and spent long hours swinging axes from can't see to can't see, cutting hardwood firewood of beech, maple, oak, chestnut, sycamore, and walnut, and hewing yellow locusts for fence posts.

The boys knew their wood should have been cut and stacked back in spring, to season for fall. But they'd been so scrambling just to catch up with plowing, planting, and harvesting they'd not yet thought of winter wood. So they started collecting deadwood, and then they cut and cut, knowing first wood would still be green. Some old slumping wood stacks, greyed black, had long lost most of their heat, but they'd fill in for fall's transition.

On November 21, Josephine Young Wulsin came perilously close to seceding from her union with her beloved Drausin and family. Although the exhausted mother of ten had a short, relatively smooth five-hour labor, the baby almost drowned when the placenta followed him—and then, not a twin but, with a shuddering groan from Josephine, the whole uterus. Margaret Gray handed the baby boy to Aline while she focused on Josephine. Aline, veteran helper of five births, and Margaret had prepared well, boiling water in the cast iron kettle for numerous sterile cloths.

Was Margaret herself barren? No, she'd suffered two miscarriages. Margaret had been her own mother's last gift. Over recent months Josephine had gradually become the closest person to a mother Margaret had ever experienced. She had watched Josephine increasing with both nervous concern and joy. And Margaret often hovered around little Mary Josephine, tending a flame she knew could sputter.

Now, when the uterus unexpectedly appeared, Josephine and Drausin started silently saying farewell to each other, Josephine with a weak smile surrendering. "I am so sorry, chou-chou. I was supposed to hold the family. Ça me fait de la peine. Je t'ai manquée." It pains me. I have failed you.

Drausin, molars grinding, could not remember feeling so afraid, not in the streets of New Orleans, not seeing the copple in Natchez, not from the Kaintuck's clenched fist, not during his first voting. He had not quite grasped what an oak, what a spine his Josephine had been to him especially. *I always knew she was to the whole family more like a mesquite tree even than an oak. Modest looking, yellow flowers yielding delicious honey, root as deep as seventy-five feet in deserts, always finding water, making for one of the strongest of woods. And finance manager to boot. How can I possibly—?*

"Non, ma Chère, you have not failed; you have given a garden of Eden, a tribe into the new world."

I'm the one who's been fading. I'm the tree that feels leaning to fall before my time. If she goes, and I follow, will Aline and Laure bring up Clarence, Lillie, Mary Josephine, and now this little fellow? Would it mean going back to Bayou Rd? Would it mean going back to Bacas for the Wulsins?

Drausin felt his Eurydice fading toward shades of the afterworld. He began humming around and through Josephine, his hand holding hers. He felt her rising like a cloud. He shifted into intervals, a long sequence of fifths, to try to hold her together. Then he shifted down to thirds, trying to bring her back down, and in. He began sounding her name, "Jo-say-pheene, Jo-say-pheene," surrounding her with the *o*, laying her down with the *ay*, initially finding her with the height of the *ee* and increasingly trying to root it down, like a tree. "Jo-say-pheene." Gradually, slowly, what had seemed to be evaporating began to settle, like dew.

Margaret had Aline send Eugene to gather all the spider webs he, Clarence, and Lillie could find. She soaked cloths in winter bloom, tea tree, and lavender to keep the area clean of infections. Aline sent Laure for Angelica archangelica from the herb garden, a few light-green flowers like a ball of many little blossoms, roots strong, adding it to the pot. They replaced cloths every half hour right between Josephine's legs, right at the opening of her birth canal. Each time she removed cloths, Margaret pushed more spider web inside, to help mend flesh-tears.

"Why's it called Angelica archangelica? What kind of name is that for a plant?" asked Laure.

"The story," Aline replied, "is that the Archangel Michael

told us to use the plant for staunching bleeding in wounds. Michael, the 'Countenance of Christ,' helps the Archangel Raphael guide us in healing."

Lillie brought in a gift for her mother and one for her brother. "Look, Maman," she said, holding it up and looking through the hole, "a holy stone! Good luck for you, and for the baby, too. I keep finding them!"

Lucien, smiling, said, "Lillie, how right you are. You have found two good hag stones. And they *will* help, will bring good luck for your mother and your brother."

Lillie's eyes went wide. "Hag stones, hag stones," she said, kissing each stone, then placing one near Maman and one near the baby.

Lucien was struck by how pale his new baby brother was, and how pale his mother Josephine was—and also how pale was his father. He remembered how pale Clarence and Lillie had been at birth. Lucien felt more like earth; his family were more like sky. He recalled the saying, "Blackberries are red when they are green." *Will any or all of us young Wulsins become blackberries? Am I already? Aline? Drausin? Eugene? Laure? Clarence? Lillie? Mary Josephine? Our new little brother? Are we all still passing red? Could that at any moment change to black, at least for some of us?*

About a week later, Drausin, Margaret, and Aline began to feel confident that Josephine was indeed settling back in, this side of the other side. Drausin asked if they might name the boy after his brother Joseph's son Adhemar, who had drowned in the Mississippi at age fifteen. Josephine was glad to be able to mother Adhemar, whose birth had rubbed shoulders with her death. Drausin, savoring her joy, felt she had dipped her feet in the River Styx, then withdrawn them, dripping dry, thank heavens.

When Josephine regained enough strength, she determined to participate in Sunday mass at the Church of All Saints in Newport, in spite of the long carriage ride. She had thanks to offer their Savior, Mère Marie, and the Archangel Michael. She had commitments to make for having survived the birth of Adhemar; for Adhemar himself; for her husband, ever ailing; and for the other younger children especially—Clarence, eight; Lillie, five; and Mary Josephine, three. The elders, Aline, Drausin, and Lucien, could take care of the middles, Eugene and Laure. Josephine lit her candles and said prayers of gratitude, prayers of confidence, and made commitment anew.

Drausin and Josephine felt joy in their relief that, at least for now, their fold would remain whole.

One evening James Gray informed Papa Drausin in his library that Kentucky representatives from sixty-eight of one hundred and ten counties had met at Russelville, calling themselves the "Convention of the People of Kentucky." There they had passed an Ordinance of Secession back on November 20, 1861, the day before Adhemar's birth, establishing a Confederate Government of Kentucky, with its capital in Bowling Green.

Papa shared the news around the fireplace with Aline, Drausin, Lucien, and Eugene. His blue-grey cigar smoke rose near the orange flames and grey smoke of the hearth. Josephine had long gone to bed. Eugene, face initially crinkled as though too close to fire, became strangely still, sitting ramrod straight. Papa looked at each of his four maturing Wulsin children. Ten years ago they had left New Orleans.

James Gray said, "The US Capital of the state of Kentucky remains in Frankfort. We're neutral. Remember, although Jefferson Davis was born here in Kentucky, so was Abraham Lincoln. This state of Kentucky will hold. Sleep well." James departed.

Papa Drausin did *not* sleep well, pondering his three older sons in a state of war.

CHAPTER 45:

WHO COMES? WHO GOES? 1862

Young Drausin Wulsin gave his older sister a red leather book with ornate gold embossing and the words *Wreaths of Friendship*. Inside, he inscribed "To Aline Wulsin, by her brother Drausin, Cincinnati Jany 1, 1862."

The next page showed an engraving by J. Santrov of "Escape of Carrara." In it, a sword-bearing man consoled a woman on a saddled donkey, accompanied by a woman and at least three other men along a precipitous cliff road, with a castle high in mist far behind them. The title page opposite showed a wrecked ship sinking, with people on broken timbers clinging to a high rock jutting up from stormy seas.

> *Aline: My Dear Sister;*
>
> *Let this Album be a casket to gather the sentiments of those with whom you are associated in this your golden age, and who have contributed to make it, so far, a happy one.*
>
> *May it go forth and be filled with gems of friendship and of love. And when you shall be weighed down with cares and troubles, then, turn to this memento of bygone days and hold sweet communion with the ever regretted past.*
>
> *Your brother,*
> *Drausin*

After New Year's Day, young Drausin, confident that he was no longer needed to help run the farm, returned to Cincinnati to resume his studies of law in the office of French & Cunningham.

Rain and sleet fell and fell. Cold winds turned rain to needles of ice. Creeks rose. The Ohio River rose, swelling more than fifty-seven feet above flood level by the end of the month. From Cincinnati young Drausin reported that the Whitewater Canal had flooded in Indianapolis. The Indianapolis and Cincinnati Railroad bought the whole canal, to drain it completely and turn its bed from water to railroad tracks. Drausin and Josephine were glad to have their brood high on their farm in Kentucky rather than down by the river on Cincinnati's Carr St., or even up on Richmond St. near Mill Creek.

One evening, Papa Drausin informed the older children that the Supreme Court of the State of Ohio had decided that "a preponderance of white blood constituted a person a white man in the eye of the law, and entitled him to the exercise of all the civil rights of a white man." That felt to the Wulsins like good news. What a relief.

"I guess that would apply to Peggy Garner's children," said Aline.

"Yes, it should," replied Papa.

"If any of them are alive to take advantage of it," continued Aline.

"What does 'preponderance' mean?" asked Eugene.

"Now there's the rub," replied Papa. "To most people, 'preponderance' means 'majority,' 'most of.' But it could be open to interpretation."

"Does that include us?" asked Eugene. Papa and Maman looked at each other, at Aline, Lucien, Eugene, and Laure, nodded, and smiled.

"Apparently." Yes, the two parents were thinking each other's thoughts simultaneously. *Eleven years have proven the pudding. We are indeed apparently white.*

The children smiled, Lucien just slightly. He thought, At least, *so far.*

One night in April, young Drausin rode up to the door, to everyone's surprise and delight. He washed his hands and face, shed his boots, and relaxed at the table in front of a bowl of rice, crawdads from the stream, chicken, ham, andouille sausage, aged bell peppers, chili peppers, and cayenne—Kaintucky gumbo! While the whole family feasted on his presence, Josephine noticed how his flat-combed brown hair poured into sideburns from the curls above his ears down to his lobes. Young lawyer Drausin was shifting from mannish boy to still-boyish man.

He informed the family that General Grant, through Admiral Farragut, had just captured New Orleans for the Union. The North now controlled the supply lines and traffic of the Mississippi, splitting the South from its western front.

The little children could hardly understand. The middle children, Eugene, Laure, and Clarence, cheered immediately for this significant Union victory. Papa, Maman, Aline, and young Drausin were conscious enough to simultaneously feel joy at the victory and to wonder how that might affect Bacases still living in New Orleans. Lucien was quiet. He was so involved with shouldering the farm that New Orleans seemed quite far away. Still, its atmosphere continued to permeate him enough that he felt longing at times, occasionally at night. But home was definitely here.

Lillie, her black hair framing her white face, asked, "Is the North going south, everything upside down?" Eugene and Clarence chuckled. Laure and Lucien smiled. Aline could not help wondering if they might end up going back home. *Would that still be home? Would New Orleans become at all like Cincinnati?*

Papa Drausin knew his father had detested the effects of the American Anglo-Saxon influence on the former fluid freedoms of the many gens libres de couleur in New Orleans. *Is this news heartening, giving hope for an early end to the war? Does this mean no more slave markets, no more slave pens in New Orleans?*

"Well, dear Lillie," responded her news-bearing oldest brother, "not exactly. North will still be North, South will still be South. But remember, we Wulsins came from the South to the North. And we have changed at least our own lives up here. Only time will tell how General Grant and Admiral Farragut going to New Orleans may change lives down there. And only time will tell how we might change others' lives up here." Young Drausin looked at Aline, Lucien, and Eugene with not a question mark, but rather a dash: —

Lucien felt brother Drausin was throwing down the gauntlet, for them all.

Father Drausin was better, his fever mostly gone by the end of June. He thought, *I'm ready to engage the rest of my life.* Did he feel it? He was not so sure. But the tribe's eldest had definitely improved. The youngest, however, remained too warm to get well. Adhemar waned.

In July Margaret Gray continued waxing, for the first time in her life, like the moon in slow motion. She had worked gently these last three months. Lucien had been helping James in the fields and with the larger animals. Aline, Laure, and little Lillie went over, weekly at least, to help the Grays with chores; house cleaning; laundry; and some cooking when timely, with some

Wulsin leftovers to ease the cooking. They brought in fresh daisies, roses, and tiger lilies after weeding and tending the garden. Josephine visited regularly, helping with special teas, rubbing Margaret's shoulders and feet, telling her stories, singing her songs, and keeping her relaxed in her primary task.

Margaret listened, received, absorbed, and gradually embraced her primary task with growing confidence. James watched Margaret shift from anxious shadow to quiet shine. Her black hair glistened. Josephine both saw and felt that Margaret and the baby within glowed, healthy. "My Cleopatra on her barge," said James fondly. He felt his wife dawning.

Margaret grinned at the ridiculous comparison. "I *am* the barge."

When the time came, Margaret's team was ready: Josephine, Aline, and thirteen-year-old Laure, almost the age Aline had been when helping with Clarence's birth. The labor became intense, but her crew guided her through the narrows and she gave birth to a boy. Margaret hardly believed her eyes. The scent, almost of crocus; the unfamiliar sounds, like sound itself first giving birth, before names had been given; the whole aura sanctifying the room, their whole home heaven-evanescent. The little baby, with strong grip, looked glad to have arrived after all these years. He tasted her tears before her milk. Margaret wondered if joy-tears were as sweet as salty.

She looked up at beaming James, who nodded. Then she asked, "Josephine, would you please do us the honor of naming our boy?" Josephine was stunned silent. Had she heard correctly? Margaret nodded. "With you by our side, our child could arrive. We have already agreed. We would like you, Josephine, to name our child."

Dieu de Dieu, thought Josephine. She closed her eyes and prayed to Notre Dame for help naming this long-awaited son. When she opened her eyes, she saw out the window the full moon, up soft, like an eye in the sky. Night light. Moon shine. To her surprise, she inwardly heard "Lucien." *No.* She looked again at the baby boy—then around at Margaret and James. She heard again "Lucien."

"You asked. Something comes. But please, you choose his name."

"What comes to you?"

"Lucien." They looked at each other, smiled, nodded.

"Yes, Lucien," both parents said heartily, together, "Lucien Gray." Margaret then announced, "Lucien James Gray."

The Grays' baby Lucien bubbled and babbled, fat and happy, a little prince. The Wulsins' baby Adhemar simmered, silent, an afternoon shadow. Josephine tried cilantro teas. On especially dripping hot days in July and early August, they bathed Adhemar in the cooling creek. She wished Marie LaVeau were here to consult.

Josephine recalled when her mother and she had visited Marie LaVeau during the yellow fever and cholera plague of '32, when Granmère was dying. What a grand, blessing presence had been the Voodoun Queen of New Orleans. Josephine missed such consoling wisdom. And such strange advice sometimes—horsehairs and red pepper on an axe-head blade in a tub under the bed, for example. She shook her head, smiling.

Josephine wondered what her mother Josephine would do. Aline and Margaret had their suggestions. Among the three, with help from Laure, Lillie, and housemaid Caitlin, they settled into a routine of hourly refreshed cool cloths, apple cider vinegar compresses on forehead and feet. In the morning they tried to help Adhemar drink bone broth, often chicken, and basil tea with ginger and honey. Midday they boiled garlic in water for him. Evening—peppermint tea.

All this effort was to help bring down his fever, but as time passed without dramatic change, Josephine found herself seeing their first baby, Barthelemy, in little Adhemar's countenance: listless, no expression, peeking at life over the rim of the day. Adhemar drank little when nursing. His soul was sweet, his smile slight, as though the world was too bright. Unlikely he would fulfill the life of his drowned namesake.

So consumed was Josephine with Adhemar that she was fully surprised when her family celebrated what turned out to be her forty-fourth birthday on August 11.

Josephine remembered that the Voodoun Queen had also counseled the Josephines to pray to Mère Marie and Dani, St. Michael, for help preparing her grandmother's soul for her departing journey. Josephine and Aline prayed powerfully to Mère Marie, her son Jésus Christ, and Dani for Adhemar.

On August 13, the moon looked new in the hours-before-dawn dark, an almost flat cradle, glowing orange in the aura of the earth, yet floating above it. Adhemar had absorbed every-one in this large family: Papa, Maman, Aline, Drausin, Lucien, Eugene, Laure, Clarence, Lillie, and Mary Josephine. Each was gentled, slowed by him, softened, silenced. He re-minded them.

Adhemar, ever too warm, expired almost without notice. His breath just left, without finding its way back in. Adhemar Wulsin evaporated, leaving his short-lived body, finally, to cool.

From my own birthday to my youngest child's death day, Josephine thought. *Is the Wulsin family coming to the end of its rainbow?* Josephine had prayed galore at Adhemar's birth and through-out his short year. Had she been heard? Part of her angered at her loss. She overheard Aline in prayer, thanking their Lord for the blessings of His bounty. Josephine winced to remem-ber how their cup nevertheless overflowed, and she wept with gratitude far surpassing her grief. "Not my will, but Thy will be done."

Josephine realized that the sliver of orange moon she had seen in the predawn east had actually been the last of the old moon, not the first of the new moon. Baby Adhemar, gone with the old moon. The night sky now moonless. "Thy will be done."

"Maman, Maman," said Lillie. "I had a little dog in my room last night."

"Oh," said Josephine, hardly listening, washing and oiling little Adhemar for the grave. "What color?"

"White." Josephine stopped. There were no white dogs around. She turned to Lillie. "Where is he now?"

"Oh, he left last night."

"How?"

"Right through the wall." Josephine looked at Aline and Lucien. They were not surprised, though Eugene scoffed silently. And they were not surprised that Lillie would be the one to see it. The old lore, "A white dog appears at a dying," had been confirmed.

The next day, young Drausin came out from Cincinnati in his black frock coat, white vest, and short black cross tie; he brought the priest, Father Patrick, from Newport. James, Margaret, and little Lucien Gray joined the Wulsin family. Josephine and Aline wore black silk. Young Drausin was struck by how yellowish grey and hollowed his formerly handsome father looked. The Wulsins buried little Adhemar in his wee casket beneath the catalpa tree, halfway between the farmhouse and the yellow former slave house up the ridge. Mourning doves cooed.

CHAPTER 46:

THE BLACK BRIGADE, 1862

Word spread through the city fast as a plague. On August 30, Bull Nelson's Union Army had been soundly defeated by Major-General Kirby Smith in Richmond, Kentucky. General John Hunt Morgan's guerrilla cavalry and General Henry Heth led several armies of eight thousand Confederate troops, cutting up the Lexington road north through Kentucky, heading for Cincinnati. On September 1, Union Major-General Lew Wallace took charge of Cincinnati, marshaling its defense.

Everyone north and south of the river knew the stakes were high; whoever held Cincinnati would hold the Ohio River Valley all the way to Pittsburgh. The Union had split the South by seizing New Orleans. The Confederacy would not be allowed to seize Cincinnati and split the North. On September 2, the mayor called on the people to organize and prepare for the defense of the city:

In accordance with a resolution passed by the City Council of Cincinnati on the first instant, I hereby request that all business of every kind or character be suspended at ten o'clock of this day, and that all persons, employers and employees, assemble in their respective wards, at the usual places of voting, and then and there organize themselves in such manner as may be thought best for the defence of the city. Every man,

of every age, be he citizen or alien, who lives under the protec-
tion of our laws, is expected to take part in the organization.
Witness my hand, and the corporate seal of the city of Cincinnati,
this second day of September, A.D. 1862.

GEORGE HATCH, *Mayor*

Jebediah Makely, age twenty-three, like many colored men in the city, went to the streets. He wanted to fight for freedom with the North, but his intentions seemed thwarted. "Where? We have no place of voting. Where do we go?" Black residents did meet here and there without resolving the questions of how to help.

Jebediah knew of the judgment that Drausin had told his older children about, how the Supreme Court of the State of Ohio had recently judged that "a preponderance of white blood constituted a person a white man in the eye of the law, and entitled him to the exercise of all the civil rights of a white man." That judgment raised hope for better treatment for many mulattos; however "preponderance" was interpreted.

On the other hand, Jebediah knew well that just one month ago, the city of Cincinnati's own Mayor Hatch had allowed local police, serving in roles of Special Provost, to beat Negroes and destroy their property in riots. Then, only word of Morgan's cavalry being forty miles south of the river had pulled those low whites away from beating local blacks to meeting alien Rebs. Then Morgan had inexplicably retreated. Now, that same threat again loomed, but larger.

On the morning of September 2, spotting a policeman newly appointed as Provost Guard, Jebediah approached him cautiously, deferentially. "Excuse me, Sir, does the Mayor desire colored men to report for service in the city's defense?"

The Provost Guard snarled, "You know damned well he

doesn't mean you. Niggers ain't citizens."

"But he calls on all citizens and aliens, Sir."

"The Mayor knows better than you do what to write, and all he wants is for you niggers to keep quiet." Jebediah heard distant church bells chime nine o'clock. Already the morning felt long. The message was clear. Colored help was not wanted.

The sneering white Provost Guard had final words for Jebediah. "This is not your war; this is not your city. This is a white man's war, a white man's city." He spat on the ground, just missing Jebediah's worn shoe.

That night in the Plum Street mule pen just across from the Cathedral of St. Peter in Chains, Captain Homer gave orders to his special police, Mayor Hatch's Provost Guards. "Now, then, I want you fellows to go out of this pen an' bring back all the niggers you can catch. Don't come back here without niggers: if you do, you'll not have a bit a grog. Now be off, you shabby cusses, an' come back with niggers or don't come back at all."

Jebediah's door banged open, broken. Yanked from his bed, trying to gain his senses, he was forced to dress fast as the Provost Guards stabbed his mattress with bayonets. Then they poke-jabbed him along with more colored conscripts to the Plum Street pen. Men in the holding pen sat on stacks of bricks and blocks of wood. Captain Homer entered, took a look, shouted, "Rise!" and marched them to another area in the pen. There he shouted, "Damn you, squat! Now, Provosts, shoot the first black hog to rise!"

By that time, since Roebling's bridge had stopped construction back in '57, a pontoon bridge had been assembled with oak boards over coal barges stretching from the Ohio shore all the way across to the Kentucky shore in Covington, barge ends chained to cinderblocks. Four hundred colored men, not allowed to volunteer, were force-marched across the river.

Jebediah looked down at those apparently placid, mighty waters of the Ohio and remembered one of the many Indian meanings of "Ohio"—bloody river. He wondered, *if these waters soon go red, will it be with whose blood—ours?—and if so, shed by Rebs or fellow Cincinnatians?*

On the far shore, in the middle of a dusty road, he heard the same command: "Damn you, squat! Men, shoot any who rise or sit!"

Jebediah and the conscripts were marched up above Kentucky's Ohio River bluffs to swing axes on trees, heave picks into soil, push shovels to dig trenches and rifle pits, and build bunkers from dawn to dusk. The work was hard, the weather muggy. The air sweated. The whole Ohio River Valley sweated. Once a day, midday, they were given water, corn pone, and slops. Then back to work, the special police riding them like plantation foremen. Jebediah swung his axe and dug his shovel just as hard as anyone. But when no provost could hear, he sometimes muttered, "Don't sit, don't stand. Halfway hunker, halfway sit, halfway stand. Halfway men, in our halfway land. No longer slaves, not yet free."

"Amen," Powhatan Beatty next to him said, "but shush down for now. We need you swingin', an' not from a tree."

Finally, after three days, the *Cincinnati Gazette* decried the mistreatment of the black workers who were preparing the defenses of the city.

> *Let our colored fellow-soldiers be treated civilly and not exposed to any unnecessary tyranny, not to the insults of poor whites— for no one but poor-spirited whites insult a race they profess to regard as inferior. It would have been decent to have invited the colored inhabitants to turn out in defense of the city. Then there would have been an opportunity to compare their patriotism*

with that of those who were recently trying to drive them from the city. Since the services of men are required from our colored brethren, let them be treated like men.

Judge William Dickson, outraged to learn from the *Gazette* of the behavior of Captain Homer's special police, went immediately to Major-General Wallace. Equally shocked to learn of the Provost Guards' brutality, the general charged the judge to form and lead the Black Brigade as Colonel Dickson. Captain Homer and the special police were relieved of their duties as Provost Guard.

Thursday afternoon, Colonel Dickson rode up the bluffs to Fort Mitchell and summoned the four hundred black men who had just been working thirty-six hours straight. "Men— men, you have been treated wrongly," he said, his voice carrying over the assembled. "You have been working hard and well in the face of the Confederate threat to our city. I hereby officially relieve you of your duties. Go home. Be with your good families and friends. Rest, recover.

"Is the work over? No, far from it. Is the threat over? Not at all. Any of you men who freely choose, who *freely choose* to volunteer for the Black Brigade, may meet at the Plum Street pen tomorrow at five o'clock in the morning. Now, thank you for your work, and return to your families." Jebediah strode with the others back across the pontoon bridge to his boarding house, feeling weary yet lighter.

The next morning, as Jebediah walked in the predawn dark toward Plum Street, he thought of the muddy waters of the Nile, not sure he had ever seen so many coloreds flowing through the streets at the same time. Quiet, once they arrived at the pen they arranged themselves in rows and columns on the street, facing south. When over six hundred volunteers had been organized into two regiments of more than three hundred men each, Colonel Dickson stepped into the light of two torches and addressed the men, whose black, purple, brown, and yellow faces shone and receded in the flickerings.

The white man with ivory skin, clear jaw, and wide cheek-bones above a generous mustache proclaimed, "I have the kind permission of Major-General Wallace to hand you, without formal speech or presentation, this national flag—my sole object to encourage and cheer you on to duty. On its broad folds is inscribed 'The Black Brigade of Cincinnati.'"

Colonel Dickson's voice commanded with warmth. Jebediah felt that his words, while important, were less so than the fact that Jebediah, and likely each man of the Black Brigade, felt their leader was speaking directly to them individually.

A white aide stretched out the flag on its pole as another held a torch in front so all could see the white stars on night-blue, and the thirteen stripes alternating red and white. On the first white stripe below the stars, bold black letters announced THE BLACK BRIGADE OF CINCINNATI. Those who could see the flag and those who heard the speech realized they were making, and changing, history.

"I am confident," Colonel Dickson continued, "that, in your hands, your flag will not be dishonored. The duty of the hour is work—hard, severe labor on the fortifications of the city. In the emergency upon us, the highest and the lowest alike owe this duty. Let it be cheerfully undertaken. He is no man who now, in defense of home and fireside, shirks duty.

"A flag is the emblem of sovereignty—a symbol and guarantee of protection. Ours the 'Star-Spangled Banner'—the sun in heaven never looked down on so proud a banner of beauty and glory. Men of the Black Brigade, rally around it! Assert your manhood, be loyal to duty, be obedient, hopeful, patient. Slavery will soon die; the slaveholders' rebellion, accursed of God and man, will shortly and miserably perish. There will then be, through all the coming ages, in very truth, a land of the free—one country, one flag, one destiny. I charge you, men of the Black Brigade of Cincinnati, remember that for you, and for me, and for your children, and your children's children, there is but one flag, as there is but one Bible, and one God, the Father of us all."

Jebediah was near the front as the Black Brigade's Stars and Stripes led the regiment across the pontoon bridge. In the torchlight, Jebediah counted four rows of eight stars, with one between the top two rows and one between the bottom two rows, thirty-four, remembering then that Kansas had recently joined the Union. He was struck that the eleven stars of the southern states attempting to secede were visibly, emphatically still on the flag, still in the Union of the United States of America. Jebediah called, "That's a lotta stars on our flag, thirty-four of 'em. Count 'em. That's one big Union we're workin' to keep whole. Our flag! One big Union! Our flag! One big Union!"

The call started to catch on around Jebediah, spreading through the regiment. "Our flag! One big Union!" He knew the members of the Black Brigade did not always feel part of that one big Union in Cincinnati. But this morning, marching behind their own flag, he did. They did. And it spread to the second regiment crossing the pontoon bridge, who took up the call as well. The sky lightened over Fort Thomas. The yellow disc crested. The river sheened gold.

The Black Brigade received no uniforms, no guns, no pay; but now, in addition to their tools, they did receive food, drink, shelter, and respect. They enjoyed the right to visit their families.

Up the bluffs anew, it was back to work but not as usual— it felt forward. As they marched up the hills behind Newport, some members of the units improvised band music on sticks, kazoos, Jew's harps, harmonicas, and spoons. Newport ladies, men, and children, and then various local militia units, cheered The Black Brigade as they passed.

Jebediah realized that he, and probably most of his fellow

brigade members, had never been cheered by "others." Except maybe by the young Wulsins on that trip up the river from New Orleans eleven years ago.

The Black Brigade joined seventy-six thousand "squirrel hunters" and worked especially up behind Newport, between Alexandria Road and the Licking River along Cemetery Ridge and Threemile Creek. At the Evergreen Cemetery, each company of each regiment was assigned its tasks. The Black Brigade had started as two regiments of three hundred each, but over the days colored men from all over southern Ohio and parts of Indiana kept pouring in. Some even snuck in from Kentucky. Eventually they numbered slightly more than seven hundred. Presiding Captain Lupton reassigned Marshall P. H. Jones, Powhatan Beatty, and Jebediah Makely to Captain Simon Shepherd's Company 1 in the Third Regiment, to help pull the newcomers together into efficient Fatigue Duty units.

One day, as Jebediah was digging at the trench lines, a nearby green infantry recruit's musket went off, the bullet going through the handle of Jebediah's shovel. Unfazed, Jebediah kept digging. The engineers guiding construction of powder magazines and fortifications reported that the Black Brigade had the most efficient working men in the services.

CHAPTER 47:

THE BLACK BRIGADE II, 1862

Saturday, still in the predawn dark, Lucien and his mule Shadrach boarded the wagon onto the ferry, the Simon Kenton 2. Although he had heard of the approaching rebels, Lucien was stunned to behold the Ohio River suddenly bridged, flat-planked, on floating pontoons. He understood why that new bridge was devoted exclusively to defense efforts. During the day at Findlay Market, he learned more of the story behind both the bridge-building and the Black Brigade.

When Lucien told the news of the pontoon bridge to the family that night, he mentioned the Black Brigade. Eugene wondered if Jebediah might have joined it. He and Lucien showed new interest in joining their mother, Aline, Laure, and the children at mass in Newport the next morning. Papa stayed home to rest. The ladies still wore black in honor of Adhemar. Lucien and Eugene accompanied the carriage on their own horses, Lucien on the young grey gelding, Rocky, and Eugene on the chestnut mare, Flame. Aline drove the carriage's pair of blacks, which, like the other horses, had come with the farm when the Wulsins purchased it.

After mass at All Saints, Aline was visited by the young man who had been especially consoling after Adhemar's funeral. Michael V. Daly, fair, freckled, and ruddy-cheeked, had a large nose like a muffin, ears deep-welled like cupped wings,

hair like tossed hay, and a lyrical voice. She enjoyed his attention, gentle as it was. He had a respectful, beseeching courtesy,
as though he felt privileged in her presence.

Appreciative of his manner in the moment, Aline nevertheless considered Michael little competition for the ultimate
Groom, to whom she had long considered herself betrothed.

As soon as Lucien and Eugene could leave All Saints, they trot-
ted up the bluffs, discovering all kinds of work going on for
defensive barricades, rifle pits, trenches, and bunkers. Various
militia units were drilling, turning volunteers into soldiers—
Lucien couldn't help thinking of Egyptians building pyramids;
he'd never seen such a bustle of tens of thousands of men.

Eugene kept asking here and there for the Black Brigade,
until they found their way up St. John's Hill. They found one
company of the Black Brigade working a whole mile south of
the predominant trench lines, clearing a grove of black locust
trees. There, Eugene spotted a big man swinging his axe,
glistening with sweat, almost dancing in rhythm, chopping
at alternating angles, widening the gap. Lucien and Eugene
watched in silence. When the locust started to lean, the
axeman stepped back, and the tree cracked. Eugene thought
he spotted Esau Makely, realized the axeman was actually his
son, sprang from his horse, wrapped the reins around a tree,
and ran to Jebediah. "Who do you think you are, a runaway, a
secret surviving son of Annie Christmas?"

Jebediah laughed, shouldering his axe, then hugged Eugene
affectionately. "Yeah, that's me, the big black buck, son-of-a-
muck, Jebediah Christmas! Eugene! Lucien!"

Eugene took a smaller downed locust trunk, hand-thick,
laid it on a large fallen trunk, and he and Lucien levered one
end of Jebediah's larger tree up, so men could grab it more easily to carry it to the wagons for bunkers.

Jebediah knew some of the men wondered why Whiteys were helping The Black Brigade turn trees into logs. He knew that some of his cohort could tell these brothers weren't necessarily Whitey. Marshall P. H. Jones and Powhatan Beatty were intrigued by Jebediah's warm connection to Eugene and Lucien.

The white aide with dun skin and a roundish face came over to Lucien, looked closely, and said, "Do I know you?"

"No, Sir, well—actually, yessir. Lucien Wulsin. That is, you've seen me perhaps; I've seen you, at our farm stand at Findlay Market."

"Oh, yes, the paw-paws, the sweet corn, the peaches-and-cream corn. Good corn. Jacob Resor Jr." He offered Lucien, then Eugene, his hand. "You boys want to give us a hand?"

"If we may, Sir, for the afternoon. We won't get in your way, and we just might be good help."

Resor and Jones nodded at each other, then gave Captain Shepherd the nod; he nodded back. Resor called over the other white aide, "This is—"

"Mr. Chatfield, yes, I remember. Lucien Wulsin. Pleased to meet you."

"Will," said Jacob Resor, "We're letting these Wulsins lend a hand today."

After about an hour William Chatfield came over to Lucien, who was chopping a maple. "Good work, Lucien. You and your brother seem to know Jebediah pretty well."

"Oh, yes, well, you see, Mr. Chatfield, he was cook's flunky on our week-long steamboat trip up from New Orleans back in '51. We cottoned to him right away. It was a mighty good week. His daddy Esau Makely was deckhand boss on the Natchez III."

"That's good to know, Lucien. We thank you Wulsin brothers for your good help with the Black Brigade. Call me Will."

"Yes, Sir, I mean, Will. And I want to thank you and Mr. Resor for your help with the Black Brigade."

Chatfield looked at Wulsin, caught a bit by surprise. "You're welcome, Lucien. It's a privilege, and a duty, but a privilege."

After another hour, the workers of the Black Brigade's Third Regiment, Company 1, heard cannon fire. Jebediah, Lucien, Eugene, and others dove down behind felled trees, but—no explosions around them. Eugene looked south; Jebediah knew they had heard it from the north. More deviltry from the likes of the Provost Guards, after all?

Soon several men approached from the north with a white flag. Colonel Taylor's attaché in the 50th Ohio Volunteer Infantry had spotted the brigade a whole mile south and mistakenly assumed them to be enemy. Taylor had ordered artillery to prepare to fire; the leader of the battery, knowing they were the Black Brigade, had put in blanks instead. Informed of the friendly fatigue duty of the Third Regiment of the Black Brigade, Taylor then sent out the white flag. His crew confirmed that some of the Black Brigade was indeed working that far off. The attaché apologized, commended them, and urged them to carry on safely.

Jebediah, Powhatan Beatty, Marshall Jones and the others were not that surprised to realize how close they had come to being under friendly fire. "Damn, who's got our backs?" said Powhatan Beatty.

"Likely they'll jus' up an' shoot us once the work's done," said Jebediah.

"Defenders, yet we're facin' the enemy, with targets on our backsides!" Marshall Jones shook his head.

Eugene asked Jebediah, "Where are your guns?"

"None for us."

"Yet," said Powhatan Beatty. Lucien and Eugene looked at each other, only beginning to grasp some of the complexities of this war between the states.

Captain Shepherd reported to Colonel Dickson, who later had words with Colonel Taylor of the 50th Ohio Volunteer Infantry.

"No guns, and no pay?" asked Lucien.

"Las' week, no wages; this week they'll pay us a dollar a day," declared Jebediah.

Later that afternoon Resor said to Chatfield, "Well, those Wulsin brothers, they look to be doers."

"Yup. They sure trot their logs into place, holdin' their own."

Back at the farm, the Wulsin family was fascinated by details of Eugene and Lucien's day with the Black Brigade. Papa Drausin had heard of the Chasseurs d'Afrique, a brand new black regiment from New Orleans, one of the first in the Union army. Same pay as whites.

But fascinated was not all. After the cacaouettes went to bed, Papa said, "Lucien and Eugene, what you have done this afternoon is dear in relation to Jebediah, and noble helping the Black Brigade."

"Thank you, Papa," they chorused.

Drausin took a breath. His brow furrowed. "However, for Wulsins, your action was brash. In Cincinnati we live on a cliff. We live up high, white. So far. A single slip, we live down below, colored. If one slips, we all slip. For you two to be working with the Black Brigade may raise eyebrows. It's too risky. Do you see?"

"Yes, Papa, I see," said Lucien.

"Eugene?"

Eugene, who had been looking at the floor, raised his eyes. "Yes, I guess, but, Papa, I want to work with Jebediah, and they're helping all of Cincinnati, and I want to help Cincinnati, too."

"Well, join a white fatigue brigade. You may not go back to the Black Brigade."

"Why not? Resor and Chatfield do."

"Eugene, it's fine that they do. But they do not have as

much to lose as we do."

Eugene sat ramrod straight. He said, slowly, "But I want to work with Jebediah helping, and the Black Brigade is—is great. You should see."

"No, Eugene. No."

Eugene's cheeks reddened, eyes wet; he bit his lip to blood. Josephine's eyes moistened, feeling both pain and pride for their fiery son. Her eyes beseeched her rightly concerned husband.

Drausin addressed his impassioned son. "Eugene, do you understand my concern?"

"Yes, I do, Papa, I do. But I told Jebediah I'd work again tomorrow."

Would Drausin want his young son to be passionate with any finer desire? Perhaps not. Perhaps these desires were not just young. Drausin looked into Josephine, who had stood by him through their whole, long, challenging journey. Her green eyes pulled him in, as deep as a well.

"Eugene."

"Yes, Papa."

"One more day." Drausin looked at Lucien, who shook his head slightly. "Just one more day with the Black Brigade. Do you understand?"

"Yessir, thank you, Sir. Yes! Sir!" He stood at attention and saluted his father, cheeks wet, grinning.

"Eugene," said Josephine gently, "see you bring Jebediah back for supper and the night. He deserves it."

"Si, Maman." He ran over and hugged her, then his father too.

The next day Lucien resumed harvesting corn on the farm. Eugene hopped on Flame and led Rocky all the way back to St. John's Hill where the Third Regiment's Company 1 was working, having finished clearing the locust grove. Eugene jumped right in with Jebediah. He noticed Aide Resor conferring with Captain Shepherd, who soon came over to him.

"Wulsin."

"Yessir?"

"If you're so bent on working with us, we'll give you this one more time, no pay, but if you're serious, you ought to consider enlisting."

"Yessir, thank you, Sir. I understand, Sir. Thank you, Sir."

At the end of the afternoon, Eugene and Jebediah rode Flame and Rocky the twelve miles back to the farm in Cold Spring. In recognition of both Jebediah's and Eugene's good work, Captain Shepherd had given Jebediah the night's leave. Eugene had loaded his Springfield rifle, confident he could handle any challenges one way or another. In spite of his sanctioned leave, Jebediah felt more nervous each mile deeper into Kentucky, knowing slavetraders and marauders were possible and unpredictable at any turn. Many courageous and upright men had gone for soldiers in one army or the other. However, the majority of Kentuckian men chose not to go to war, on either side. Nevertheless, Eugene knew some of the leftovers were coyotes, scavengers, some even rabid.

"You're one good worker, Prince Eugene."

"Ha, Lucien's the real worker. You should see him on the farm. 'All day long'!" Jebediah chuckled. "But," Eugene continued, "you, you swing that axe like a song might say—I'm tired. You tired?"

"Yup, I'm tired, but good tired."

"Dollar a day good tired?"

"Yessir, dollar a day tired feels good."

"Axe and pick, but no gun?"

"Yup, no gun, but that'll come."

"Why not now?"

"Ohh, Lordy, Eugene, you tell me. Some prolly think we couldn't shoot straight. Others 'fraid that when we do, we'll shoot 'em all back, for everything." Whipporwills called in the night.

The horses ambled along in the descending dusk, bits jingling, occasionally snorting. Jebediah spoke. "Eugene, are Flame 'n' Rocky havin' their own conversation?"

"Yup, of course."

"Sure seems so." Jebediah went on to tell Eugene of the early days of the Rebel scare, how first they weren't allowed to defend Cincinnati, then came the slave rations, the Provosts making them squat, until Colonel Dickson turned things around and treated them right. They became the Black Brigade, with their own flag, their own officers, and some good white help, like Captain Lupton, Aides Resor and Chatfield, and others.

"Jebediah," Eugene's voice floated in the dark, "why do so many whites treat coloreds so bad?"

"Jesus, Eugene, you're askin' how the worl' got made—I dunno. They think we're thick-skinned, like an ox or mule. But we don't got thicker skins. Fact is, it's like we coloreds had a whole layer of skin already flayed off. White folk don't feel half what we feel. Our skin doesn't protect us. It leaves us raw, to any glance, any slur, any backlash from some sleepy action of ours, any time they don't even see us, like we're a wall, or avoid us like we're a disease, or garbage, or disdain us, like we're jus' plain wrong people, or nonpeople—

"We're thin-skinned, like no coat in a sleet storm. It's hard, it hurts, it's tiring. That's what's tiring us out, most days, so tiring. We're walkin' 'round skinned, ain't got no hide—

"Anything they assume 'bout us is down, not up, is bad, not good, is less, not more. How can we grow in such an all-the-time sleet storm?

"How can I not flinch every time I meet a white? I gotta know what's coming. Why? Why? You tell me, Eugene, livin' white. You tell me—"

"It's not fair, that we get to pass white when we choose, 'n' you don't have that choice. Not fair."

"Would I choose white if I could? I dunno. Seems to me so often their 'I,' that name no one else can call me, the key to who only 'I' am, why a white man's 'I' seems so skinny, so sliver-little, it just hides in that white shell, scared stiff another 'I' will be goin' to up'n' blow it right out. So skinny-little it don't even dare peep out to see the 'I' is livin' inside every colored. I ain't white, black, blue, or green. My I's high, my eye's light, higher'n all colors 'tween white'n' black, white'n' black included.

"Their little I's seem so nearsighted they can't see inside any skin. Little people inside all their big bluster. How's that gonna change? Lordy, they need their schools, their churches, an' their help jus' as much as we do! They were ta go ta Mister Peter Clark's school like me, their I's'd open right up'n' grow."

After long quiet Eugene said, "Jebediah, you know what my mother used to say her mother used to say?"

"Tell me."

"'Bouki the hyena, he's out ridin' the tracks. When you break cover, you watch your back.' I guess what you're saying, Jebediah, is that you always have to watch your back. We Wulsins know, passing white, that once we step off our property 'n' go out in the world, we have to watch our backs, too. But I guess the difference is, you always have to ex-pect Bouki, an' we never know when Bouki might sus-pect us."

"Eugene, I think you're talkin' truth."

CHAPTER 48:

OUR NEW KENTUCKY HOME, 1862

Eugene and Jebediah arrived at the farm unchallenged. After a cleansing swim in the pond, they enjoyed the supper Aline and Caitlin had ready for them: ham, corn, green beans, onions, biscuits, and chokecherry jam.

The younger children, Laure, Clarence, Lillie, and Mary Josephine, kept looking at Jebediah's midnight-black skin. Purple-black, blue-black. Sheen. Sometimes Lillie saw orange and red tinging his hair when a candle glowed behind his head. Some lights reflected yellow on his skin. Lillie, now seven, went up to him, rubbed her hand smoothly along his cheek, and said, "You're all kinds of colors."

Jebediah smiled large, kissed her on the top of her head, and responded, "Yes, dear little Lillie, I sure am, I'm all kinds a colors."

He was struck by the changing colors in the Wulsin family since he had rescued the older four at the Main St. Bridge riots on Election Day, back in '55. Mr. Wulsin was greyer by far, thinner, and yellow. Mrs. Wulsin was also greying, highlighted especially by her black dress. Her eyes, green like summer between the grey hair and the black dress, always seemed to recognize him. Lucien stood quiet and strong now, like a walnut tree. *He's always favored us most*, Jebediah thought. And Eugene, whom he'd hardly looked at in all the work and the dark ride to the farm. *Long, all elbows and angles, high cheekbones, the strongest chin of them all, handsome someday-a-man.*

"Are you the strongest man in the world?" asked Lillie, wide-eyed.

"Oh, no," chuckled Jebediah.

"Lillie, Jebediah just might be stronger than all of us put together," said Eugene.

Lillie and Clarence were looking at everyone in the family, then at Jebediah, trying to figure.

Aline Jebediah watched quietly. On the Natchez III he'd been still a boy, she still a girl, both twelve. By that Election Day seven years back, she was becoming a young woman. Now she was definitely a woman. Aline was fully formed in her mauve dress, poised, with a strong face, brown-black wavy hair, lightly tinted skin, black brows, black eyes, strong shoulders, a doer's mouth.

Aline found herself increasingly touched by the man Jebediah had become. His muscular gait was both relaxed and careful. His mood seemed twofold: joy tempered by pain, pain buoyed by joy. Outward delight; inner sorrow.

"Mr. and Mrs. Wulsin, you sure have a brood to be proud of. What a family. What a family. Look at you all," said the young man who had grown up motherless, mostly alone, except when his father was back in town off the river.

"Jebediah, look at the fine young man you have become," said Papa Drausin, remembering the beloved, savvy, mumbly twelve-year-old boy of the week on the rivers. "Your father—"

"And your mother—" chimed in Josephine, knowing her to have long ago passed, "are proud of you," they declared in unison.

Jebediah, caught by surprise, gulped. He rarely thought of his mother, though he realized he always felt her, even though he'd never known her for memory. His eyes watered and he looked down. Then he raised his eyes back to theirs and said quietly, "Thank you."

After a while Laure asked for the apple song, the one she knew her older siblings used to chant on the riverboat to Cincinnati. "The apple song?"

"Remember, from orange to apple—"

"Ohh, from orange to apple," Eugene took it up, "from clime to clime."

Lucien and Aline joined in—"From palm to pine." Jebediah joined, too. Drausin and Josephine glowed, recalling them as children chanting on the decks of the Natchez III. Clarence, Lillie, and Mary Josephine soon chanted heartily as well; Eugene led them marching it, with the bigs and the littles all forming a line.

"From orange to apple, from clime to clime, from palm to pine—"

"I've never seen an orange tree," realized Lillie.

"But we've sure got good apples," boasted Clarence.

Then, of course:

We're going from Memphis Tennessee
On the Mis-sis-sip-pi River
All the way to Cin-cin-nati
On the O-hi-O.

Jebediah had Lillie on his shoulders. Clarence had Mary Josephine by the hand. Then Eugene stomped his right foot three times, turned around, looked fiercely at all in the room, and stomped off in the opposite direction:

Hey, ho, hey, ho,
Hey, no, hey, no,
We never gonna live in Cai-ro
We ain't never gonna live in Cai-ro.

He slashed his arm down at each "never" and "Cairo," which the others imitated, little Lillie's left hand holding on over Jebediah's eyes.

Any ole place in de whole wide worl'
But Cai-ro,
Never gonna live in Cai-ro.

Then Jebediah unshouldered Lillie, settling into an armchair with her on his lap. The others also sat down, as he
started another song. Father Drausin plucked along with his
mandolin.

Ah bin mos' eberywhere,
Ah've seen mos' eberyting.
Shoot craps wid de president,
An' played kyards wid de king
All—night—long!

Aline joined on the piano and Lucien picked up a violin to
fiddle. Eugene slid onto the bench beside Aline, improvising
melodic embellishments.

Ah've rousted mos' eberywhere,
An' burnt out heaps ob men;
Played kyards wid de cook;
An' shot craps now and den!
All—night—long!

Aline, Lucien, and Eugene joined in on stanzas as some
words resurfaced in their memories; the littles shouted out
each time, waving their arms in a big arc, "All—night—long!"

You wanna know whah we is from?
It suah will make you shivah;
We's from dat dar ol' Ragtown
Un de ol' Cincinnati ribber!
All—night—long!

Now, niggahs, roll yoh cotton,
An' rousters, tote yoh corn!
An' listen for de heavenly trumpet
Ob ol' Gabriel's tootin' horn,
All—night—long!

And, they repeated, of course:

We's from dat dar ol' Ragtown
Un de ol' Cincinnati ribber!
All—night—long!

Then Eugene rose, strode over to Jebediah, and said with a very serious face, "Hello, I am Eugene Wulsin, Prince of Cincinnati. Pleased to meet you." Handshake, slightly deeper bow.

Jebediah stood up straight, shook his hand, and said, giving a slight nod, "Pleased to meet you, Sir."

"Hello, I am Lucien Wulsin, Prince of Cincinnati. Pleased to meet you." Handshake, bow. "Pleased to meet you, Sir."

Jebediah turned to Aline, who rose, blushed, and curtsied with a flourish and big grin, extending her hand. "Hello, I am Aline Adelaïde Wulsin, Princesse of Cincinnatesse. Pleased to meet you, Sir."

"Jebediah Makely," came the pompous tone, "the original Prince of Cincinnati." He kissed her hand. All laughed heartily. Josephine wished young Drausin were with them. And Adhemar. Of course the cacaouettes, Clarence, Lillie, and Mary Josephine, immediately became prince and princesses as well.

Father Drausin began to sing:

'Tis summer, the darkies are gay,
They hunt some more for possum and the coon

On "darkies" Aline and Lucien both glanced at Jebediah, who grinned and nodded them to join him joining Drausin in the song. Jebediah's tender tenor started to weave around Drausin's melody line, harmonizing like a swallow in flying curves, as he had that night on the Natchez III, marooned on the Ohio River above Louisville, eleven years earlier. The others joined in, too:

On the meadow, the hill, and the hay.
The young folks roll on the little cabin floor,

(Clarence, Lillie, and Mary Josephine started rolling on the floor, giggling.)

All merry, all happy and bright:
By'n' by Hard Times comes a knocking at the door,
Then my old Kentucky Home, good night!
Weep no more, my lady, Oh! weep no more to-day!
(Lillie and Mary Josephine mock-wept.)
We will sing one song for the old Kentucky Home

Lillie jumped up, shouted out, arms wide, spinning once all around, "our new Kentucky Home!" And all repeated heartily, the littles shouting with glee:

We will sing one song for our new Kentucky Home
For our new Kentucky home far away.

Later, in their room, Drausin said to Josephine, "I'm impressed with Jebediah's dignity. What an innate gentleman he's become, straight up—literally yes, his height. But inwardly he stands in the light of his right to stand in the light. Humble but present, not obsequious."

Josephine agreed. After putting Clarence, Lillie, and Mary Josephine to bed, Josephine had noticed Aline slip quietly outside, which she refrained from mentioning. "And, Cher, could we have imagined, on the Natchez III, an evening like tonight, eleven years later?"

"Non. How our cup runneth over. We are blessed."

"We are blessed indeed." Josephine, still grieving the loss of Adhemar, seeing her beloved husband thinning, hearing his voice thinning, thought, *How fragile our chalice*. Her fingers touched his cheek and throat, lingering.

After a while Jebediah had said good night to Lucien and Eugene, and had likewise glided outside. Shadows were soft. Aline stood under a persimmon tree, looking south down the valley. The September night air felt like what each of them would like it always to be. He approached. They looked at each other, silent. Finally Jebediah spoke. "Aline Adelaïde, I know there's no way, but I know you need to know, there is always a place for you in my heart."

Aline's onyx eyes were open, her face was open, receiving, as though she'd already read in him the story he'd just told. His scent was strong. Man-scent. Sweet, with an edge, just like before milk might sour. To her it felt like home, the smell of her people. Whom she and her family had been transcending.

For Aline, Jebediah was like the tree of life. She felt something in her altering. Shuddering, she crossed her arms. "Jebediah, Jebediah. I know. I don't know. I've long been given to—" His face stayed straight. "—to our Lord. I don't know that I can be a man's, any man's, woman. But you, dear Jebediah, you always have a place in my heart." He nodded, stepping back from her cinnamon scent. After Aline ascended the "Daughter Stairs," she did not sleep that night. Neither did Jebediah. Both stayed in their rooms.

Well before four in the morning, Eugene and Jebediah rose to fill saddlebags with what Aline had placed on the kitchen table: six loaves of freshly baked bread, two dozen grilled pork sausages, scores of paw-paws, batches of blackberries, and forty green apples, all a treat for the Black Brigade's Company 1 in the Third Regiment.

The two arrived on St. John's Hill in time for Jebediah to begin the day's work with his company, who cheered Eugene and the Wulsins all for the hearty fare. Then Eugene led Rocky back to the farm to help Lucien. Eugene felt troubled the whole way home. *This farm feels like no fit for me.*

Aline Adelaïde Wulsin realized in the ensuing week that she had dreamed she was being pulled in three directions. On one side was the Irishman, Michael V. Daly, on the other side was Jebediah Makely, and up above them both was the Son of God. While Michael and Jebediah were each compelling in different ways, Aline had been spending more and more time at the nearby convent. The One above certainly had the upper hand at present.

In Aline's dream, each of the two living men had one hand pulling her from outside, and each had a spirit hand holding her heart from inside. She realized that Jesus up above was brown, and he had one white spirit-hand and one black spirit-hand, both cradling her heart, which was red. And the spirit hands all blended.

On Wednesday, September 11, Jebediah noticed sunlight flash off field-glasses well south of the razed locust grove. Scouts in grey were surveying the Union trenches. Marshall P. H. Jones grabbed a sheet of tin, rolled it into a cone, and called distinctly to the distant grey scouts, "Black—men—built—these— forts! Black—men—built—these—forts!" The Black Brigade erupted in cheers. Even some union militia, initially skeptical of the Black Brigade, had soon realized the power of the seven hundred men to taunt the Rebs. Brigade after brigade all up and down the miles of barricades. Eventually, seventy-seven thousand Union defenders took up the call.

"Black—men—built—these—forts!"

Two days later, on September 13, sunrise showed the advance Union scouts only green fields and empty forests to the South. The Confederate Army had withdrawn.

The Union fatigue brigades and armed brigades continued their active presence one more week. The Black Brigade now received one and a half dollars per day, the same as other fatigue brigades in the army.

On Saturday afternoon, September 20, the Black Brigade was ordered into line, to formally complete its three weeks of service. Its members had contributed to a gift for their commander, Colonel Dickson. Dickson looked out over the assembled men, trying to see each one of them before speaking to all:

"Soldiers of the Black Brigade! You have finished the work assigned to you upon the fortifications for the defense of the city. You have labored faithfully; you have made miles of military roads, miles of rifle pits, felled hundreds of acres of the largest and loftiest forest trees, built magazines and forts. The hills across yonder river will be a perpetual monument of your labors. You have, in no spirit of bravado, in no defiance of established prejudice, but in submission to it, intimated to me your willingness to defend with your lives the fortifications your hands have built. Organized companies of men of your race have tendered their services to aid in the defense of the city.

"In obedience to the policy of our local Government, the authorities denied you this privilege. A portion of the police, ruffians in character, early learning that your services were accepted, and seeking to deprive you of the honor of voluntary labor, rudely seized you in the streets, in your places of business, in your homes, everywhere, hurried you into filthy pens, thence across the river to the fortifications, not permitting you to make any preparation for camp-life.

"In the department of labor permitted, your zeal has not been dampened by the cruel treatment received. The citizens, of both sexes, have encouraged you with their smiles and words of approbation; the soldiers have welcomed you as co-laborers in the same great cause. When you have received the protection due to a common humanity, you have labored cheerfully and effectively.

"Go to your homes with the consciousness of having performed your duty—of deserving the protection of the law, and bearing with you the gratitude and respect of all honorable men. You have learned to suffer and to wait; but, in your hours of adversity, remember that the same God who has numbered the hairs of our heads, who watches over even the fate of a sparrow, is the God of your race as well as mine. The sweat-blood which the nation is now shedding at every pore is an awful warning of how fearful a thing it is to oppress the humblest being."

Marshall Powhatan Jones had been chosen by the men to present to Colonel Dickson the gift toward which all seven hundred and six members of the Black Brigade had contributed: a sword, to honor his service to them, for enabling their service to the country.

The Black Brigade of Cincinnati was relieved of its valued service. Every man saluted their officers, first Colonel Dickson, and then shook hands with the volunteer aides, including Captain Lupton, Jacob Resor Jr., and William Chatfield. The fatigue soldiers returned to their homes, their families, and their shops, having defended their city and their Union. Jebediah slept better than he could remember in his single boarding house room.

CHAPTER 49:

SOMEONE'S GOT TO GO, 1862

The night before the Black Brigade "retired," Lucien had been whittling by the fireplace as James Gray told his father and the whole Wulsin family about rumors that the Defense of Cincinnati from the Confederate Army would be formally concluded the next day. As he had when he heard about the Ordinance of Succession, Eugene again became strangely still.

He looked at his pale father, his powerful sister Aline mothering their family like a Pouponne herself, his broad-shouldered brother Lucien with calloused hands and dirty nails. Eugene glided over to the piano, letting his fingers brush silently along the black and white keys without sounding a note, something Josephine could not recall Eugene doing before. When he kissed his mother goodnight, he thought she held him extra hard before he turned to his room. But Eugene was not sure.

Lucien could tell something had sparked in his hot-headed brother. And when Lucien went up to bed, he found Eugene hiding a rucksack he was filling.

"Eugene, you can't."

"I have to; no one else can."

"But you're only fifteen."

"Look at me, Lucien; I'm shooting up like bamboo."

Although Lucien had long had the largest hands, Eugene's

forearms and shins were almost stretching right before his eyes, way beyond his cuffs. Lucien had not quite realized.

"I've got to fight this. None of us're going back to New Orleans in chains in one of those copples. I'm going to soldier. Jebediah can't. You can't; you carry the farm. Papa sure can't. Drausin can't, 'cuz of law. I can. I have to. Now's my time, whatever my age."

Lucien looked long into Eugene's orange-brown eyes. Beneath the focused fire, Lucien sensed in his brother roots deep like an oak, a will like Mars. Lucien closed his good eye for a moment, saw fire-orange, and felt his perception confirmed. He went to his room and returned in a minute.

"Brother, I don't know what will happen to any of us, to all of us, and especially to you. You're right. As of now, if any of us can do this, it is only you. All I can give you is my initial silence, and this." Lucien handed Eugene his Bowie knife.

"No, I can't take yours."

"Yes, you can, and you will. James Gray has an extra for me." Eugene paused, then hugged his brother, mindful of the knife. After Eugene slid the sheath onto his belt, Lucien gave him his own personal Bible, received in tenth grade at Hughes High School from Mr. Hinkle. When Eugene read Lucien's name on the inside page, his eyes watered as he realized for the first time the implications of his departure. For a moment he wondered how being shot or stabbed would feel. He clenched, but then his smile beamed wider than the room. He hugged Lucien harder, half-knowing he was feeling the last Wulsin warmth for a long time, maybe ever.

"Oh, my brother."

"Oh, my brother. For brogans, I can't help you; your feet already outgrew mine. Take Drausin's. And, Eugene—those Rebs won't know what hit' em."

❀

The next morning, of course, Eugene was not at breakfast. Lucien had noticed at dawn that Flame was gone. He found a note in the barn saying that Eugene would leave the horse at the Dalys' farm in Newport. Laure, Clarence, Lillie, and Mary Josephine each found a walnut under their pillows. *Sly devil.* Papa and Maman found purple Michaelmas daisies in a cup of water at their bedroom door. A note under the cup read, "Maman and Papa, I'm enlisting. I love you, Eugene." For Lucien he left his greatest treasure—a buffalo horn he'd found in a nearby cave.

Only days later would Aline happen to notice a new entry in her red-leather-bound friendship book.

Dear Sister Aline,

Forget me not! What mixed feeling
These little magic words impart!
Absence and love at once revealing
They sadden while they soothe the heart.

Forget me not! Whatever woes
In Life's precarious paths beset me,
They'll soften, if affliction knows
That those I love will not forget me.

Your Affectionate
Brother,
Eugene

Aline was impressed with the form of Eugene's script. A little wobbly suddenly on "Affectionate."

"Woes." "Life's precarious paths." "Affliction." Her heart tightened. *That dear sly devil.* She felt a little ashamed to realize she was wondering if this fiery third brother of hers might have put some of those well-formed Ps, Fs, Ds, and Ws to work, forging a letter of permission from his father to enlist.

Eugene's siblings weren't the only ones surprised. After Eugene left Flame at the Dalys' around dawn, he discovered an unfamiliar leather envelope as he emptied the contents of the saddlebags into his rucksack. Walking to the Newport ferry to enlist in Cincinnati before heading out to Camp Dennison, Eugene pulled from the envelope a formal note:

> *To Whom It May Concern, September 19, 1862*
> *I, Drausin Wulsin, do hereby give permission for my third son, Eugene Wulsin, age eighteen, to enlist in the Union Army. Signed, Drausin Wulsin, Cold Spring, Kentucky*

Eugene turned around, walked west along the Ohio River shore, then up the Licking River shore, until he found a stand of elms. There he sat down and wept until he was cried out. A year ago he had run away, enlisting in a local Kentucky militia, lying about his age. His father had tracked him down, learned he was injured in a fall, explained to the officer that Eugene was a child, only fourteen years old, and had brought him back to the farm. Now Papa was helping him to leave, to find his place, to serve the just cause.

Eugene felt a hard little shape in the leather envelope. A silver cross on a slender silver chain. When he opened the cross, he smelled earth. He remembered then his mother slipping out the back door for about five minutes last night. She'd probably gone to the garden for that soil. Closing the cross, Eugene placed the chain around his neck. What Eugene did not know was that Maman's own mother, Granmère Josephine, had given that cross to her daughter upon their leaving New Orleans. Then the cross had within it soil from Bayou Rd., which Josephine had worn around her neck for eleven years.

Last night Lucien had indeed not been the only one to notice Eugene's silent fire. Both Josephine and Drausin had intuited his intent. In their bedroom they had agreed to give Eugene their blessing, knowing he would go anyway, even though they were uncomfortable with the lie about his age, heartbroken for him to leave the family, and fearful for him at war. Papa Drausin had written the note and, while Eugene slept, slipped both it and the cross into the envelope and into his saddlebag.

Drausin and Josephine scarcely slept that night, wondering, imagining. "He has the gumption," said Drausin.

"Will he have the sense, though, not to be a fool?" wondered Josephine.

"Who knows? I have not fought, but I know war can temper tempers."

While Eugene wept in Newport, Josephine wept at the farm, though her son was unaware of his mother's tears. *I can't remember ever flooding so, from my own well,* thought Eugene. *Last year Papa brought me back home as a boy. Now, in September, he helps launch me as a man. A confidence. A blessing.* The recognition so touched him that again he was bawling like a baby. *Well, I'd better become a man by the time I get to Camp Dennison.* Eugene washed his streaked face in the Licking and rubbed it hard with his sleeves. On September 20, 1862, Eugene Wulsin, age fifteen, enlisted as Private, "age 18," in the Cincinnati Union Dragoons, to train at Camp Dennison, sixteen miles east of Cincinnati on the Little Miami River.

CHAPTER 50:

BLACK BEAUTY, 1862

Late one afternoon in early October, Lucien returned from helping James Gray cast winter rye in a light drizzle, which surprised into drench. Shadrach had raided the Wulsins' rye seed, feasting on quite a batch. Lucien, who'd forgotten he'd left a bag out, knew the mule could bloat, his intestines blocking, knotting into potentially fatal colic. Lucien walked Shadrach for two hours, until dusk became dark, until he was confident the mule had walked the rye through him.

Returning Shadrach to the paddock, Lucien was hanging up the lead rope when he heard an unfamiliar shift in the mountain of hay in the back of the barn. An unfamiliar scent reached him. Grabbing a pitchfork, he cat-stepped closer, silent. A dark patch several feet above the floor did not fit., too high to be Jezebel. He listened, watched, stood still. Suddenly, two white ovals appeared in the dark. Eyes. Still without moving, he swung the tines forward.

"Please."

A woman? A girl? A decoy for others? Some smudge beneath the whites.

"Please, Sir, help me."

"Who's with you?" Her whites side-to-sided. "Who are you? Step forth, slowly."

"You, your pitchfork, no pitchfork, Sir, please."

Lucien leaned the pitchfork against the wall and lit a lantern. The smudge turned out to be Jezebel, who had brought the stranger a little snip of tin; it sparkled in the lit dark. She took two cautious steps forward, followed by the limping crow.

"Honorée, I am called, Sir." Her voice, rich in timbre, had tenuous strength. She had black hair, tightly curled, rust-red tinge under night-blue turban. Black skin, though dusty from travel; eyes open wide, broad brow, high cheekbones, full lips, strong chin. Upright. Girl? Woman? Certainly woman. She wore a chestnut bodice taut over a cream-colored blouse, along with a blue linsey-woolsey skirt and plain leather shoes, scuffed almost blonde.

Lucien scanned the depths of the barn with his light, returning to her. Confident she was alone he looked at her again, closing his good eye for a moment. The two pictures, outer and inner, fit. Lucien agreed with Jezebel. This stranger became a guest.

"Honorée, I am hardly a Sir. I am Lucien, Lucien Wulsin. And you, you must be hungry, thirsty." She nodded. Lucien fetched her water from the well. She let the cup be. She was reading him as much as he was reading her.

"Rest. You'll be fine here. I'll be right back."

From the kitchen he fetched bread, cheese, and some apples. She was gone, the cup empty.

"Honorée," he whispered. "Honorée, it's alright. Come out. I have food for you." He left the food on a crate and stepped out the front entrance of the barn, standing still to the side. After about ten minutes, he heard rummaging and knew she was eating the bread and cheese. He slowly reentered. To his surprise, Jezebel was delicately taking a piece of cheese Honorée held out on her finger.

"Which way did you come to the barn?"

She pointed out the back door to the north corner of the field. He took the pitchfork and his slingshot up quietly, so no one would hear, and headed to the chicken coop, where he found the skunk, as usual, cleaning up leftover kitchen scraps. "I'm sorry, my friend," Lucien said quietly to the creature who had simply existed, never spraying this trusted human all those nights, months, for two years now. "It's for a higher cause." Lucien stood firm by the black and white scavenger, pulled the slingshot hard close, and popped the stone. It crushed his triangular skull, killing him instantly.

Lucien tied the tail to the pitchfork cross-bar, rested the carcass on the tines, brought it to the barn's back door, sliced the scent gland open, and dragged the skunk along the game trail and horse path, pulling it diagonally across the fields all the way to the edge of the north woods. After burying the skunk with silent thanks, he returned to the barn. The bread, cheese, and apples were gone. The girl was there, in the lamplight. She sniffed, puzzled.

"I figure you're likely to have slavetraders and hounds on your trail. The skunk says you weren't here. You should be safe here tonight, but we've got to move you on tomorrow night."

Honorée seemed relieved, then tense. Lucien felt her beauty could easily bruise. She seemed strong, yet soft.

"Where have you come from?"

"Down below Lexin'ton."

"I was born way down in Louisiana," offered Lucien. "We left'n' came up here as a family."

"Ah was born in Lousiane, mah mammy born in Conga. Famly sold up Kaintucky. Ah's brought up to de house about ten."

"Why'd you run?" Silence. "Were you treated wrong?"

Honorée looked in Lucien's eyes long. His olive skin gleamed in the flickering light. From what she could see, his eyes were likely as brown as hers, his lips almost as full. She felt recognition. She unclenched her jaw, and sighed. "Startin' several months ago, Massa'd come by at night an' take me. Not long 'fore Mistress sniffed it out, an she'd beat me for de liddlest things. He'd take me; she'd beat me. De worse de tobaccy leaves—de less gold leaf, de more he'd take me, de more she'd beat me. De whole plantation 's goin' down, ah could tell. He already sold ma daddy one way, ma mama an' brother two other ways. Ah'd soon end up wit Massa's baby, or sol' down river, back to Lousiane, cuttin' cane to die by. Ain't no way, *no* way ah's goin' back down to Lousiane."

Her voice had rich quality, like moisture in the air; it permeated, even fit the dark, without breaking it. As she spoke, she calmed, her breathing slowing. Lucien was impressed. *This courageous young woman. Though her leather shoes are gouged almost through, her hands are less calloused than my own.*

"Ah chose to run when corn still in de fields, an' nights gettin' longer, to cover more ground. Morgan was fightin' to take Lexin'ton. In the thick o' the confusion, ah took off Satidy night, soaked mah shoes in coal oil with snuff 'n' cayenne pepper, sose hounds cou'n't smell me. Ah had me all Satidy 'n' Sundy nights 'fore anybody knew—been goin' all night, ten nights, holin' up by day in caves, overhangs, even a ole bear den—stunk all ta Tuesdy. Been hungry lots but ah managed. Some corn, mulberries, paw-paws, gooseberries, walnuts, hick'ry nuts, acorns—even cattails, monkey flowers, milk thistle, an' allus more corn—had to gamble on your place, gettin' in outta de rain. Ah watched y'all for a day; ya'll felt like good people. Doin' your own work, hard, too." Honorée was not only courageous, but clearly cleverly crafty.

Lucien fetched the exhausted woman a blanket, then extinguished the light. When he returned to the house, he went to Aline's room and awakened her. "Aline, in the barn I'm hiding someone, a runaway, young woman named Honorée. Don't you think we've got to keep her secret? I'll move her on along to market tomorrow night."

Lucien had remembered how consumed his older sister was seven years ago with Peggy Garner's escape, arrest, murdering her own child, trial, return into slavery, and eventual death by typhoid on a Mississippi plantation. Aline had been a passive witness then. What Lucien did not know was that Aline had actively prayed for the Garner family every night since.

"Yes, of course! Lucien, silence is simplest and safest. Mum's the word. I'll take care of her." The next day, Aline slipped food out to the barn for Honorée. The next night, Lucien was loading the wagon for Findlay Market.

In the dusk, Aline took Honorée down to the pond to bathe. As she helped Honorée off with her layers, she was surprised when the last turned out to be men's worn-out, faded blue pants tied at the knees, to protect her legs. Aline picked peppermint and rosemary for her to brush her cleaned skin with.

After Honorée washed and scrubbed, she just floated. "Ma'am," she called out after a while, "Can a woman ever jus' love a man, jus' love a man, do you think?"

"Why, what a question, Honoreee. 'Just love a man?" Aline was thinking of her recent dream, she being both pulled and held by three different hands, Jebediah's, Michael Daly's, and Christ's. "I certainly do not know for myself. But our mother I think has been able to 'just love her man.' So yes, it's possible."

Aline had prepared a burlap shoulder bag of food. She gave Honorée a fresh shift over white cotton pantalettes, a beige tignon, a bright white apron over a brown linsey-woolsey skirt, and a sky-blue cotton shawl; any runaway notices would describe her previous attire.

"Ma'am, ah tank you."

Aline, putting her hands on Honorée's shoulders, said, "I'm not Ma'am, Honorée, I'm Aline. Please call me that."

"Aline."

Looking her in the eye, Aline said, "Honorée, when you reach your future in Canada, please send us word through the underground grapevine about your well-being. Will you?"

Honorée looked into Aline's black eyes, understood that she meant it, and said, her own eyes tearing up, "I will, Aline."

Aline hugged Honorée, who hugged her back hard. Aline kept thinking of Peggy Garner's thwarted escapes, tearing up as well as she bade the brave young woman—whom she felt was a kindred spirit—goodbye. "You're in good hands."

"Aline," Honorèe called as she was leaving the barn, "your clo'se'll make me feel partly you."

"Yes, Honorèe—and me partly you."

Honorée returned to the barn smelling fresh, feeling grateful, her face shining like a moonlit night.

Tonight there was in fact moonlight. To Lucien, Honorée looked like a lit lamp. She looked at the wagon.

"Will ah hide unner de onions, beets, an' rutabagas?"

"No, you will ride."

She looked perplexed, then scared. "Ah been stayin' outta sight. You showin' me now?"

"You will pass as my slave." He smiled.

These words could be a knife. His tone, though, was blessing. Lucien's olive skin shone; his curls caught all kinds of moonlight. Honorée saw no albino Massa, just a gentle bronze brother.

"You a kine an' courageous man, Lucien, an' hansome too."

Lucien had not heard these words spoken of him before. "Fine young man," yes. Eugene or Drausin were more likely to be called handsome. If any of the Wulsin children were ever teased for their looks, it was likely to be Lucien. He remembered the Irish bully on the playground in first grade, before big brother Drausin snuffed him with a glance.

"Honorée, it hurts me, your master bruising your beauty."

Not just bruise, she thought, looking at Lucien.

Had Lucien beheld such beauty? His Granmère Mathé, maybe. He was inhaling Honorée, while sounding her name inwardly, like new music. He thought of the third wise man, black Caspar, bringing his gift of myrrh from the East. *Does she smell of myrrh?* he wondered. He noticed her shawl rising and falling over her chest and realized she and he were breathing in and out in rhythm.

"Lucien, thank you for your court'sy. You'n fact are de young man ah watcht in de fields." He nodded slightly, not wanting to disturb the image of her in the moonlight. He felt the moon stand still.

Lucien awoke later on the hay, about ten feet from Honorée. On the way to the house to fetch fresh clothes for market, he realized he had dreamed strangely. He was a baby somehow in a double lap, nursing between two brown breasts, one of Granmère Adelaïde, freed slave descendant of Senegal, and one of Granmère Josephine, free, slave-owning descendant of Mali. Nursing from both. And he realized, grinning, that he was an apparently handsome young man, who felt more himself than ever before.

"Cher, you hear?"

"Si, Chérie, I've been listening."

"I noticed some food missing today. I think Aline and Lucien must be tending something in the barn. Should we find out?"

"I think you and I already know, most likely. Do we trust Aline and Lucien?"

"Si, Cher, we would trust Aline and Lucien with our family and our farm."

"Exactly, ma Josie Joe-Jo-Joe; let us sleep."

Honorée gave Jezebel a last snip of cheese.

"Come, Honorée, up into the wagon," called Lucien quietly. He "hop-on-up-nowed" Shadrach's reins. En route in the cool night, Honorée watched the stars.

"'Follow de drinkin' gourd,' de ole one tole me. On clear nights ah foun' de big gourd, followed de line up 'long its two end stars to de North Star at de end o' de liddle gourd, an' follow it all night."

Just before descending into Newport, Lucien stopped so Honorée could shift into the wagon's bed, back beside a hay bale. Pretty much right at dawn, the Simon Kenton II's ferry man nodded to Lucien without a word.

"Halt!" barked a slouch-hatted, grimy man who galloped up and yanked his horse to a stop. "Papers!"

"She's his," called the ferry man. "They're Satidy reg'lars."

"Papers!"

Honorée pulled out a dirty, folded paper and handed it to the slave catcher, who lit a match, read the paper, looked at her, and didn't match her to any warrant descriptions—different garb. The grizzled hunter turned to Lucien, who eyed him levelly. "You?"

"Lucien Wulsin, Cold Spring."

"Alright then," he spat, then grunted, "off ye damn go," wrenching his black horse's neck around, lurch-cantering back up the hill.

Halfway across the river, Lucien asked Honorée what the paper said. "Desirée, property of Drausin Wulsin, Cold Spring." He looked at her. Beaming, she said, "Aline."

"Signature and all?"

"Sinnatcher an' all."

"Dirty?"

"Mud by de pond." Periodically Honorée looked back at the Newport shore, yet neither of them could see unusual activity.

Lucien stepped down from the wagon to thank the ferry man, paying him two dollars for the wagon, forty cents for the two people, and an extra dollar. "Jake Benham, I thank you for always."

The ferry man returned the dollar. "Lucien Wulsin, you're a good young man. Give it to her; she'll need it."

In Yeatman's Cove on the Cincinnati shore a familiar stevedore looked at Honorée and, knowing Lucien had no slaves, nodded to Lucien, who returned the nod. Then the man sent a boy running to Black Boyd's Furniture Shop with a message for Jebediah.

Before starting up the slope, Lucien turned to Honorée, who, shining, touched the mud of the bank as though it were gold. Yet her eyebrows tightened; she knew her story was not yet secure. "Honorée, yes, you have crossed the Mason–Dixon line. I wish I could watch over you all your way. But now, on the way to market, just as soon as I say *go*, you get down off the wagon fast, no matter what. Your next help will be there." Lucien helped her aboard, slipping her the dollar.

Honorée nodded, looked at Lucien, and said, "Thank you, for all. Lucien, you a good man, a handsome man, too." She smiled. "An' you got a quiet eye."

Lucien, having started the wagon up Broadway, cut across Sycamore to Main, approaching the Miami Canal bridge, where he halted for traffic. Out of the side of his eye, Lucien noticed tall Jebediah appear on the sidewalk. "Honorée, go."

Jebediah reached his hand to Honorée's, swinging her down to the sidewalk; she quickly disappeared among the crowd. Black hand to black hand, black bodies merging into mist. Without turning his head Lucien jostled the reins forward, listened for disruption, and heard none.

He smiled across the bridge, imagining that Jebediah and Honorée might make their way discreetly to Schmidt's Brewery, hide down below in the catacombs till dark, then proceed to the woods behind Mr. Strong's house, waiting there until the next leg of the journey. Of course, Lucien also knew that all those places and people most likely had changed by now.

He looked at his long fingers, dirty-nailed, covered with cuts, scraped on the outside, callouses on the palms. "You'll be in good hands," Aline had told Honorée. Strangely, Lucien only now realized, his right hand still tingled, though he had only touched her hand once, helping her into the wagon. He hoped Honorée's journey would go well. He wondered if he might always be looking in the dark for two white ovals.

And Lucien wondered how his young brother Eugene was faring in the 4th Ohio Volunteer Cavalry. Lucien spent that long night with his older brother Drausin, at 22 Carr St.

The next morning, Lucien leaned on the railing of the Simon Kenton 2, watching the muscling waters of the Ohio River. He enjoyed a smoke rolled from some of their own yellow leaf tobacco. He thought of Honorée, whom he'd unlikely ever see again. He felt his young heart seize. The yellow dawn, the white steam from the blind ferry mules' flanks, the grey mist rising from the river, the blue cigar smoke—all was fused and enhanced by some lingering scent of Honorée. *Will I ever see you again?*

Looking toward Newport, then west downriver, Lucien also wondered if he'd ever again see the Ohio enter the Mississippi. Solemnly he declared to himself in a voice so low no passenger could hear, "I am Lucien Wulsin, known somehow by Honorée, my Delta Queen."

Honorée dozed in the Strongs' woods before heading north on the Miami Canal the next night. Several times she said to herself, equally quietly, "He did not take me. He be*held* me. He did not seek 'le clé de mon corps,' mais il a touché mon coeur. In his way, Lucien knew me." She smiled.

CHAPTER 51:

COLD SPRING, 1863

Papa Drausin sometimes could not stop shaking. The new year, 1863, brought much rain and more cold to Cold Spring, Kentucky. Fever and chill tossed Drausin back and forth between fire and ice. Josephine, Aline, and Caitlin took care of him, in turns. Laure was learning, too. Much of what they had done for dying baby Adhemar they did now for Papa Drausin: onions in bone broth; compresses of apple cider vinegar on forehead and feet; minced garlic in water twice a day; peppermint, oregano, and basil teas; and hot peppers in the gumbo, to get him to sweat.

Josephine knew any body needed cleaning, being such an earthly thing. She knew most cleaning was by water, inside and out, drinking and bathing. She also knew some cleansing was by fire. Fevers weren't just the boogie man, Loup Garou the Werewolf. You could wash out, and you could dry out. A good fever was like putting the body in the oven on a low simmer, or hanging it out in the summer wind.

But Josephine also knew that too much fever, too hot or too often, would so dry out the poor body that it would turn brittle, lose its force, and crack like a withered plant. That old life-body would just up and drift away, dried leaves crackling. And she knew that was happening to her beloved, still-beautiful-to-her Drausin. *What Drausin felt almost losing me at Adhemar's birth, I'm starting to feel with him. Will I soon stand alone on the horizon of the cold North? None of our children yet launched? Drausin, I feel like a kite in a too-strong wind, fraying. Will my string break sooner rather than later? Mercy. How strong will our Wulsins turn out to actually be? Stronger than me, I hope.*

One weekend that spring, young Drausin showed up by surprise, with a second surprise. Everyone already knew that although he, now tallest in the family, had been admitted to the Hamilton County Bar last October, he had only recently officially completed law school.

The real surprise was his companion, a short, broad young man who stepped through the door, straw hat in hand, bowing politely with a room-size smile. To Aline and Lucien, he looked vaguely familiar. Papa and Maman recognized him in a flash but remained silent, smiling. The youngsters were baffled. Young Drausin drew himself up, puffed out his chest, and proclaimed like a herald, "Ladies and Gentlemen of the famous, noble, Wulsin farm, I have the honor of presenting to you none other than the illustrious, mysterious, and thoroughly likable Henry—Wulson."

The eyes of the older three recognized more clearly some version of what confused the ears of the whole family. Henri—yes, but "Wulson"? Impossible.

"Yes, dear Wul-sins, this here Wul-son currently resides at 531 Sycamore St., officially employed by George Alces as cigar maker. He showed up last week at 22 Carr St. and introduced himself as our long-lost cousin, Henry Wulson."

"But how is that possible?" asked Laure, who had been too young to remember. "I thought we were the only Wulsins in the world!"

"Yes," echoed Lillie, "that's us, the only Wulsins in the whole wide world!"

"And," said their young guest, "your tribe may have lost its baby Adhemar, I am so sorry to say, but, don't you see? It has gained its Henry! Henri! Moi! And I am indeed your cousin. Me voila!"

Papa now called out, "Yes, you are, Henri, mon cher Henri, oh my boy, what a joy, come here," enveloping him in a large embrace, loving both him and the Bacas blood in his veins. "I saw my brother Joseph in your face the moment you walked in the door." Henry's father, Joseph Valmont Bacas, had died of pneumonia last November, in 1862, at the age of fifty-five. Papa Drausin felt he was holding his own brother again, with nephew Henri in his arms. Josephine stepped forward to give him a long, warm hug as well, drinking in New Orleans through him.

"Henri!" said Aline and ran to kiss him on both cheeks. "Cousin, cousin."

Lucien and Henry were next to exchange a hearty hug, Henry beholding the strong young man in front of him with wonder, trying to fit this new vision to the little boy he knew. "And Eugene is gone to war?" The others all nodded. Henry saw the concern in Josephine, his Nonc Drauzin, and Aline. "Well, God bless him."

As Henry met the rest of the family, young Drausin explained his connection to Laure, Clarence, Lillie, and Mary Josephine. "Who is your oldest brother?"

"You are."

"Will I have children some day?" They slowly nodded, not having until then conceived of such a notion. "Will you have children some day?"

Laure nodded. "I hope so."

The other three couldn't even respond. "Well, Papa's older brother, Nonc Joseph, is the father of Henri, who is my age. He is our cousin, our first to visit us in our twelve years up here."

"And," said Henry, whose smile seemed as large as his light-olive face, "So long as I am in Cincinnati, I am now Henry

Wulsin, part of your family, the only Wulsins in the world. 'Wulson' with an *o* is just what the landlord wrote down."

"Ah," said Lillie, "your papa Joseph, brother to our papa Drausin! Of course, we're cousins! Hey, everybody, finally we have a cousin, our very own, only-one-so-far cousin!" And she climbed up into Henry's lap. "Why do you work in a cigar store?"

"Well, lively Lillie, I arrived back in November and quickly got work packing pork. I wanted to support myself. Then, when pork-packing season ended, I was relieved and fortunate to get the job wrapping cigars. Mr. Alces says that since Cincinnati is the fourth largest cigar-producing city in the whole country, he wants my New Orleans expertise to help it become first." Privately, Papa Drausin was not so sure about Henry's cigar expertise, but it was a good story for Lillie and the littles.

"But you should have joined us for Christmas! How could you not?" demanded Lillie.

"Yes, you are right, little Miss Lillie, I should have joined you for Christmas. I thought my cigar company needed me then. But I made the wrong decision. Ma faute."

"You're really a Bacas?" asked Laure. Henry nodded.

Lillie asked, "what is Bacas, your ghost name?"

"Yes, you could say that. Yours, too."

Lillie looked at their parents, who nodded. Lillie continued, "None of us has Bacas as our name, but we all have it as our ghost name?"

"Yes," Josephine responded, "you could say that, for all of us." Aline, Drausin, and Lucien were recalling when they knew themselves as Bacas. "I like that," said Lillie.

One Sunday in February, Aline handed her Wreaths of Friendship book to a certain persistently gracious gentleman at the Church of All Saints. The previous Sunday, she had requested an entry from him. This Sunday, as he held the book, opened to a blank page, he thought for a moment, bit his lip, glanced at the lovely woman looking at him expectantly, and began writing on his page with deliberation:

To Aline

From one that can only a friendship reveal
For Sweetness and Virtue and goodness so real.
From a Sympathy strong, tho' calm and unseen,
Comes this tribute of words to the worth of Aline.

Oh how modest, how mild, is that innocent face—,
A child in impression, a maiden in grace.
So lofty, so pure, yet so kind in her mien,
That Queen of our hearts is the gentle Aline.

Like the odor of flowerets, her piety is sweet—
Like the rustling of rose leaves is the tread of her feet.
Like the music of music, that voice is, I ween,
But the echoing soul of our Gentle Aline.

Her kindred—how happy around her at home!
Her friends—how glad, when they see she has come!
May friendship and love, this Smile evergreen,
Bloom o'er her path in life, of our sweetest Aline.

M. V. D. (With a flourish and a wild sail trailing the D)
Newport, Ky, 16th Febr. 1863

"That Queen of our hearts—the rustling of rose leaves—the music of music—this Smile evergreen—this path in life, of our sweetest Aline." What freshness of phrase compared to the other three entries so far, from two brothers and her friend Rose. Aline recalled her strange dream last fall of being pulled in three directions by Michael V. Daly, Jebediah Makely, and Jesus Christ. Was Michael feeling pulled to her as well? *"From one that can only a friendship reveal." "Can only reveal." How do I understand that?*

On January 10, 1863, Drausin and Josephine had received their first letter from Eugene, postmarked in Murfreesboro, Tennessee.

> *Dear Maman and Papa,*
>
> *We have been on a raid to capture Murfreesboro from General Bragg of the South. My tent-mate, Lewis Bone, was killed. We of Ohio's Fourth Volunteer Cavalry were 218 going in, 155 coming out.*

Three days later, Eugene wrote a cryptic note to Aline and Lucien: "Short rations; we have delayed moving on after hard fighting for Murfreesboro."

The next day came a note to Lucien again: "Hard fighting near Murfreesboro." Lucien took the note to his room and sat on his bed, staring at the thin paper. Then he crumpled it up and threw it on the plank floor, resting his head in his hands. Slowly, he shut his eyes. Lucien couldn't stop imagining the worst—determined little brother Eugene advancing toward the slavers. Lucien ground his teeth, his big hands clenching, unclenching.

The whole family was starved from and by these frustrating fragments. *Like feeding a waif crumbs*, thought Aline. Papa had Lucien stand a piece of slate by the fireplace, against the wall. Taking a piece of chalk, Papa drew a rough map of Tennessee, which oddly resembled a piece of slate itself. Near the middle he marked "Nashville." Not far below, he marked "Franklin." A little ways over, due east, he marked "Murfreesboro."

"Murfreesboro is the central fort for General Bragg's Army of the South, encamped for now in Tennessee," Papa explained. He had to sit in his chair to keep his head clear; the persistent fever, even when mild, muddled his thinking—especially after any exertion, including scrawling chalk on slate.

"Is Eugene going to become king of Murfreesboro?" asked Clarence.

"Ah, dear boy, there are no kings in our country. But Eugene is fighting to help Murfreesboro become free of the Rebs." Papa Drausin looked closely at Clarence, Lillie, and Mary Josephine to see if the littles understood. It was clear, at least, that they easily imagined Eugene dashing around on his horse, clearing out the fort. He looked at Lucien, who shrugged and smiled, learning forward on his chair, hands resting on his knees as he listened, as always, to his father. Drausin had to smile, too. *Life, and Eugene did seem so complicated, so strange, yet so simply clear to the youngest folk.*

February 4, Eugene to his parents: "I've been suffering severe fever from January 15 to 29, and then dysentery in the hospital."

"Fourteen days of fever!" exclaimed Josephine to Drausin. "What can possibly be left of our bony boy? Can't you go bring him home?"

"No, Chérie, he has officially enlisted. He is in the hands of Union doctors."

"What hospital? Franklin?"

"I do not know. He does not tell us."

February 14, Eugene to his parents: "Things much better now that I'm recuperating in Nashville, Union Hospital 16."

"I am relieved," said Drausin. "Nashville should offer some of the best Union care."

"I'm glad he says things are better," said Josephine, "but—"
Eugene did not mention, and the family did not know, that the Union Army's Hospital 16 on South College St. in

Nashville specialized in Negroes and contrabands. Eugene did not know whether an officer or a hospital administrator suspected something about him, or whether it was just a coincidence of overflowing hospitals. And he did not dare ask.

February 20: "Dear Papa, Maman, and brothers and sisters, I am sorry Papa is still sick."

March 2: "Dear Parents and Siblings, I may perhaps get discharged next month on account of my disability, or I may rot and die here in the next two or three months. I can never get well in a hospital."

"Our son sounds as though he may be dying, inwardly and outwardly. Dying, our boy, not even a man," said Josephine. "How could we have allowed this folly?"

Drausin had no answer for this question.

On March 16, Eugene, solitarily, secretly, turned sixteen.

March 26, from Eugene to his parents from Nashville's Hospital 16: "I am recovering from disease of lungs; nurse boiled pig hoof until consistency of molasses, then placed a pad on my back and chest."

"Fever, dysentery, lungs—what more could go wrong?" lamented Josephine.

"Maman, take heart. Our son has not actually been injured, thank God. His long legs and arms, skinny as they are, are intact." said Drausin. "And he is now recovering. Have hope, my dear."

"Hope as I might, fear I still must." Josephine did not say that she feared doubly, losing another son and her husband, father of seven still living.

March 26, Eugene to Lucien: "I hope the time is not too far distant when I shall again hear 'Boots and Saddles' blow and remount my charger."

March 27: "Dear Parents, I am sorry Papa is still sick. I am better and hope to rejoin my regiment soon."

March 28, to Aline: "My partner is not dead, but a POW. Getting much better."

Aline was pleased to hear of Eugene's improvement, but she felt increasingly haunted by his inscription in her Wreaths of Friendship book:

Forget me not! Whatever woes
In Life's precarious paths beset me,
They'll soften, if affliction knows
That those I love will not forget me.

Aline prayed nightly for her "Affectionate" brother Eugene in his affliction.

April 22, from Louisville's Hospital 7 to brother Drausin: "I am sending money home."

Ironic, thought Drausin, *that our little brother, sick as he's been, is supporting us.*

April 23, from near Murfreesboro, Tennessee: "Dear Folks, I am back on duty, but not yet very tough or hardy."

May 7, from near Murfreesboro: "Dear Parents, I just came off picket duty, seven days. Start on scout in early morning. Too fatigued to write more."

Yes, Maman Josephine could tell, "letters so short, irregular; he's either too sick, or too tired, to send off more than a hasty line, more like a telegram."

Lucien, "I imagine a soldier with a mailbag coming upon an encampement, walking around with mail-bag open as exhausted soldiers dash off a line on a scrap of paper, with some kind of address. We pay the postage upon receipt."

May 9, to Lucien: "On picket near Murfreesboro: banter about romances. PS, my battle cry is now 'Death or the Roll of Honor.' (The former will come first, I am afraid.)"

Lucien thought, *Our first taste of the black humor of soldierly banter? I don't think of Eugene of all people as a fatalist.*

May 15, to Lucien: "In Murfreesboro, traveling light, moving continually."

May 18, from Murfreesboro, to parents: "I'm glad you mean to still live on the farm."

May 26, from Murfreesboro, to parents: "I am now very healthy."

"Four and a half months to become 'very healthy,'" said Josephine to Drausin. "That's a long time sick. Will healthy last as long?"

"Ma Chérie, youth can bounce back strong, unlike its opposite," he smiled wryly.

May 28, from Murfreesboro, to Aline: "—fun as well as hardships, may raid soon into Georgia."

Papa drew on the slate map the Tennessee River heading down from near Knoxville in the east, westward right down through Chattanooga. Just west of the town he drew a line straight down, marking the border between Alabama and Georgia, intersecting Tennessee's lower east-west border. The children wondered where in Georgia Eugene might ride his horse. "Our Eugene, first right through Chatta-chatta-chatta-noogaahh," shouted Lillie, the other peanuts taking up the Chattanooga chant, of course.

June 1, from Murfreesboro, to ten-year-old Clarence: "I play horse and house every day."

June 3, from Murfreesboro, to Lucien: "—instead of raid into Georgia, moved camp five hundred yards. I have scurvy, can hardly eat crackers. Will soon be cured."

Scurvy! Josephine mentioned those Louisiana lemons brother Joseph Bacas had shipped north to help Drausin's health some years ago. "If only—" Papa smiled, picturing Eugene's cavalry galloping around the Tennessee hills with crates of lemons strapped behind their saddles.

June 10, from Murfreesboro, to brother Drausin: "I went with wagon foraging to farm. Nearly driven off by young lady who struck one of our boys with stone, injuring him fatally. Left as guard. Never want to be in that position again. Have scurvy slightly."

June 10, from Murfreesboro, to Lucien: "I am now six feet tall, weighing 133, sunburnt, ride small black gelding and carry a carbine, revolver, and sabre. Glad farm is improving."

Lucien exclaimed to the family, "Six feet tall, one hundred thirty-three pounds! Eugene's long bones alone would weigh more than that!"

"Is Eugene a skeleton on a horse?" asked Lillie.

"Non, chou-chou, but he sure has become a tall drink of water. Dieu de Dieu," assured Josephine. Now Lillie was picturing a tall drink of water in a blue uniform galloping a horse along the Tennessee River, shooting guns galore.

June 20, from Murfreesboro, to Lucien: "Busy days, three-thirty in the morning to eight-thirty at night."

On July 13, General Morgan, who had threatened Cincinnati the previous September, had recently returned to Kentucky and actually entered Ohio through Indiana. Morgan fostered fear north of the Ohio River, the Mason–Dixon line, as his alligator-horsemen galloped east for two weeks, mainly on the run, through Ohio countryside.

"Alligator-horsemen?" asked Lilllie, trying to picture Confederate cavalry galloping on alligators. Lucien smiled, recalling Kaintuck's lesson years ago on the Natchez III.

"Oh, Lillie, the map of Kentucky looks like the head of an alligator. That's one reason Morgan's men are called Alligator Horsemen, but they do ride horses, not alligators." Lillie, who found maps too abstract, only partially understood.

Finally, on July 26, Morgan surrendered with his exhausted cavalry in Lisbon, southeastern Ohio.

July 15, from Huntsville, Georgia, to Lucien: "—short rations."

Papa placed a dot on the slate map for Huntsville, in Georgia.

July 29, from Fayetteville, Tennessee, to family: "Ample rations again at last. Skirmishes." Papa placed a dot for Fayetteville, back in Tennessee.

"How did they get back into Tennessee? Jump the border? Pay at the gate?" asked Lillie.

August 4, from near Winchester, Tennessee, to Lucien: "Rations and supplies plentiful."

Papa placed a dot and wrote in "Winchester."

August 8, from near Winchester, to Lucien: "Men and horses worn out. Half of regiment without horses, have to use mules."

If half their horses are gone, how much of our boy could be left? wondered Josephine.

Sounds grim, Drausin fretted only to himself.

August 16, from near Winchester, to Lucien: "Not all letters getting thru. Some captured? Last summer the Ohio Fourth Volunteer Cavalry could count over seven hundred able-bodied men; now we can count nearer two hundred and three.

Unwell but getting better."

Two hundred three out of seven hundred! Still unwell! Lucien refrained from sharing this latest arithmetic with the family.

August 18, from near Winchester, to Lucien: "Very hot days, chilly nights."

Throughout these eight months of sparse communications from Eugene, Lucien thought more about his brother in urgent danger than about his father, who had been dying for years. Lucien read Eugene's notes with pride for his deeds and concern for his well-being. On one level Eugene's notes tortured him, as though some tendons of Lucien's own being stretched all the way from Cold Spring to Murfreesboro and Winchester, tied to Eugene's saddle. *I, instead of Eugene, should be experiencing all that he has described, as well as all that he would not describe home. How can our younger brother be leading the way into war? Wouldn't you know? Our coon-catcher.*

Lucien felt a heavy ache in his chest, an ache of impossibility. He felt harnessed like Shadrach the mule, not just to a plow but to the whole family farm, pulling it through each day. Yet, like Shadrach perhaps, Lucien muscled in that harness, rejoiced in the strengthening, crucial as he was to this duty only he could do. In fact, all things considered, Lucien accepted his harness—for now. He was glad young brother Eugene was armed with both his Bowie knife and his Bible. *If only I could have sent along a piano in his pouch.*

As he lay under his quilt that night, Papa Drausin reflected, *In our clan, only my Papa and Nonc Drauzin have fought, have gone to war, with Old Hickory and the pirates Lafitte, against the bloody Brits. Now our fifth child, Eugene—six feet, one hundred thirty-three pounds, sixteen, a ridiculous bunch of numbers—leads our way into the debilitating, gory, nonglory of endless days, nights, and months, a war that consumes, consumes both the beasts and the bodies of these good men, these good boys. Why? All to keep us Wulsins from being sold into slavery, that was our boy's notion. May he, protecting us, somehow succeed for every-one in our country. May he somehow not fail as I have failed him—I, too weak and too old to protect my son.* Under the quilt, Drausin shivered, feeling the night chill that permeated his brave son's bones. He reached a hand for the warmth of Josephine, slumbering beside him.

CHAPTER 52:

SEVEN TIMES SEVEN, 1863

These days and nights Drausin felt like some old bullfrog. He did not always know if he lay on land or in water. He felt like some ancient Atlantean, all moist, mist, hardly a hard body, almost no bone. *The opposite of Eugene,* he realized. *Two different death-dancers.* Night hardly cooled him, outside or in. Nothing was crisp; edges blurred.

Sometimes he'd be floating along, quietly at least, when something would trigger the coughing. Then his lungs would reach deep, hauling up whatever they could, like that dredging when the Roeblings started the Ohio River bridge. Yet Drausin felt long emptied; what his lungs were reaching for, he could not tell. His head would snap back, his back curve forward; he felt he was being hollowed out, dry-flushed. During one exhausting bout, he wished his lungs could just come on out, like Josephine's uterus after Adhemar's birth.

Josephine shifted soul, as in the births of each of the ten children, and as around the framing deaths of first baby Barthelemy and last baby Ahdemar. Night and day became blurred, and she hardly knew inside and out, interweaving waking, dreaming, and sleeping, within the zone Papa Drausin had been inhabiting for weeks.

"I am sorry to leave you, to leave you all so soon, ma Chère; I, only forty-nine."

"Si, mon amour, only forty-nine. Mais t'en fais pas, we will be fine. You and I, and now we all, we have woven our basket well. We will hold."

"Forty-nine. Seven times seven, Jacob's Ladder, up to heaven—seven times seven, Jacob's Ladder, up to heaven—" Drausin smiled, eyes closed.

Drausin asked the date. "August 5," replied Josephine, her hand holding his.

"August—our month. When will I die—my wife's birthday, August 11? My son Ahdemar's re-birthday, back to heaven, August 13? My father's birthday, August 15? Clarence's tenth birthday, the 20th? Maybe my father's death day, August 29?—ironic—or all the way to my own birthday, September 6? I wonder."

On August 15, 1863, Lucien wrote to brother Drausin that Eugene had written on August 13 that he himself was again "sick of fever," but that "father is unable to help."

Lawyer Drausin was granted leave from Mr. Goshorn's office to move back to the farm. He made sure Papa's will was in order. Papa said, "Mon cher Drauzin, dear Drausin," holding his eldest son's hands in his, "I leave you my name and our family. Watch for Eugene. And do not let Lucien break."

"Papa, you are well on your way; I am well on mine, making law in Cincinnati. I'm becoming a little Lincoln." Both Drausins smiled, recalling their "Mockingbird" meeting with then-candidate Lincoln, which may have altered young Drausin's course in life. "I will have our family in hand. Eugene I will find. By Lucien I will stand. You can rest."

Son Drausin kissed father Drausin's forehead. And joined Lucien and James Gray in the fields—corn, corn, and more corn. Laure had charge of Lillie and Mary Josephine. Clarence helped the men in the field, back and forth between working with them and playing with the young girls. Aline ran the household so that Maman Josephine could tend Papa Drausin night and day.

One day a buggy pulled up to the farmhouse. A strong, black-bearded monk in a camel-brown cassock stepped down, looking over the valley at the farmed fields, then up at the farmhouse. Aline went to greet him. With the gentlest of smiles he took Aline's hand as they approached the front door. "Laure," she said, "tell Maman a visitor has come to see Papa."

Aline led him in, introducing Brother Augustine, of the Trappist monastery in Gethsemane, Kentucky, over in Nelson County. Josephine could not help feeling protectively resentful of this untimely intrusion, yet she respected of course the Trappist brothers, and she trusted Aline's judgment. As she read Aline's face for clues, the Trappist's face caught her, shining like the dawn's rays. She turned to Drausin, who was glowing like the sun himself, then back to Aline, who nodded. Brother Augustine was beaming even more than Drausin.

Drausin raised his weak arms, "Cher frère!" Brother Augustine strode to the bedside, embracing his ailing older brother. Josephine and Aline wept at the sight. Lucien and his brother Drausin came in from the barn. Lucien and Laure still did not understand. When Brother Augustine stood back, Josephine embraced him long. Brother Augustine turned to the taller young man, whose city hands had clearly been grabbing country earth for a change, and asked, "Ti-Drauzin?"

Young Drausin looked at him and nodded, smiling. "Nonc Leon?"

"Si, mon vieux, si," and they embraced. Turning, the visitor continued, "And you, you must be Lucien; you would not remember me." Brother Augustine recognized Lucien's hands as a fellow earth worker's, scarred, calloused, each a tool, well-used to grip, loose yet firm, splotch-stained, grit-grained all year. And he met Laure, Clarence, Lillie, and Mary Josephine.

Josephine declared, "Cher Leon, you will dine with us and stay the night. Now, would you like tea or wine?"

"Ohh—thank you, no—water, dear Josephine—yes, thanks to Aline, Abbot Berger has granted me my first leave from Gethsemane in fourteen years. In fact, forgive me for my faltering—you are hearing my first words in twelve years."

Lucien and Laure, and certainly Clarence and Lillie, could hardly imagine a dozen years of silence. To Laure it sounded like heaven. To Lillie, the worst circle of Hell.

Reading puzzlement not only in the children but in everyone except Aline, Brother Augustine apologized, deferring to Aline.

"Well," started Aline, looking at each member of her family, first and last her ailing father, "as you know, since my experience of Peggy Garner and her children years ago, I have made periodic visits to the monastery down south at Gethsemane. One day when I was working in the fields with other lay folk, a Brother working nearby heard my voice and my name, as he later wrote me in a note.

"My voice and name rang in him for days and nights until one night in prayer, it came to him: *Might she possibly be his blood brother Drauzin's first-born, Aline Adelaïde Bacas?* In ensuing visits he listened when he could, increasingly convinced of the similarity, in face as well, although both voice and face were no longer a seven-year-old girl's but an eighteen-year-old wom-an's." Aline paused, checking in with Brother Augustine, who nodded encouragingly.

"Finally he asked his Abbott what to do, having given up all family and previous ties for devotion to Christ. Having observed the depth of my—piety," Aline blushed, hardly able to say the word in relation to herself, "my restraint, and my judgment, the Abbott urged Brother Augustine to write his story, to share with me in a note the next time, as long as I would honor his vow to the Trappist monastery by withhold-ing his story from our family."

Here, Aline looked at her father and mother with a shrug of apology, lowering her eyes. "I agreed and have honored my vow, both to Brother Augustine and to Abbott Berger. But last week, with Papa fading fast, I wrote the Abbott, begging per-mission to allow Brother Augustine to visit his brother. Yes, everybody, Brother Augustine was, indeed is, Papa's younger brother Leon Bacas."

She smiled at Leon, who smiled at all. Papa Drausin and Josephine glowed. The young children clapped and beheld him in awe. They had found a new uncle in a strange land where they had none—

Papa said, in a voice like a distant flute, "Children, you are each great gifts in my life. Your mother is the great gift of my life. And this reunion with my brother Leon is a great gift of my life." They retired to the living room as Papa's eyes closed and he dozed.

Leon enjoyed his first jambalaya, and family, in fifteen years. Touched that Josephine remembered his favorite, he savored the many flavors, while putting sausage and chicken aside on his plate.

Later, he revisited his older brother. In a voice like a horse long kept in stall, faltering out in the wild, easily fatigued, Leon told his story. Lucien and Laure listened on the other side of the door, their eyes wide.

"Drauzin, after Papa banished us as bastards, he, he who would not wash off his 'white,' would not claim his roots in Gonaïves, would not marry our mother, would not make us his children legitimate—after we four brothers strode out of his shop singing, I hated him like fire in my heart; I hated him in me, bile in my veins.

"Yes, I hit the streets, I whored whores, sucked muck, sold mold, stole gold. I wrecked ships to sift, to sell wreckage—everything I could do to soil, burn, boil Bacas, to stink Bacas to shit, till I got barred in the prison ship. And still, all my Bacas broken down, I still stunk to hell. It did not work.

"So, I vowed to myself that if I got out alive, I would work the other side. One night I slipped a guard a golden ring I'd hidden under my tongue; on the way to the head I slid like an eel over the side, swam to shore, and hid in warehouses till I stowed away on a freight packet upriver to Louisville. I trekked nights through woods till I stumbled onto monks working fields at Gethsemane. For three days I watched from the trees. And yes, I even prayed. Since I had failed to break Bacas down, to defile it, I would instead go up, give it up, transcend my identity.

"I offered myself to the Abbot. He kept me toiling with the layfolk for a year. Then he accepted me as a postulant; eventually I undertook the vow of silence. Having given up my name, I surrendered my voice as well. Brother Augustine has remained both silent and largely invisible in the world."

"And the bile in your blood?"

"Long gone. Christ and I have long forgiven our father. And I have prayed daily for my brothers and sisters."

Drausin, well familiar with Josephine's and Aline's practice of prayer, was touched. He wondered how much brother Leon's praying may have begotten blessing upon their family's risk-fraught venture in Cincinnati.

"And 'Augustine'?"

"The Abbott chose my new name. As one who had savored

sins and found Christ, Augustine understood Original Sin. Only years later did I read Augustine refer to Apuleius as 'the most notorious of us Africans,' very aware of his own indigenous Berber heritage. I later read in his Confessions, 'Belatedly I loved thee, O Beauty so ancient and so new/Thou didst call and cry aloud, and didst force open my deafness. Thou didst gleam and shine, and didst chase away my blindness/Thou didst touch me, and I burned for thy peace.' Then I knew why the Abbott had named me Augustine. I burn no longer for anger, but for peace."

"My dear brother Leon, dear Brother Augustine, thank you for your story now, your visit here, and for your prayers all these years. They may well have helped Josephine and me to fulfill ours. I am proud of you, as Maman would be, and even, in his better moments, Papa. You have gone down, and up. We Wulsins have gone over, more horizontally, with our own new name. However, maybe we have simply imitated our father, passing white."

"No, no, no, my brother Drauzin. You Wulsins have gone over, but you have gone together, for the sake of each other, for all your children together. You have chosen division from our race for unity for your own family. Our father chose division for all, with his incomplete union with Maman Adelaïde. Clearly no banishing in your brood."

"I pray that may remain so." Drausin, as his strength allowed, shared some details of the riddles of Maman Adelaïde's death and passing, and of his visit with dying Barthelemy. Brother Augustine, brother Leon, fatigued by his own monologue, listened with half-interest, his practiced attentions more on the eternal truths of spirit than on the ephemeral tribulations of soul. Soon, Brother Augustine blessed Drausin. "Bon voyage, mon cher frère; que Dieu te bénisse."

At one moment that night, Drausin whispered over, "Ma Jose."

"Si, mon amour."

"Nephew Henry has recently visited, bringing us all a living slice of my dead brother Joseph. Now brother Leon, long assumed dead, has appeared out of nowhere at my last minute, as Brother Augustine. I wonder how brother Jean-Baptiste fares, Dr. Backus, serving all peoples, not only our kind, out in San Francisco?"

"Chou-chou, I wish we knew. Probably well. What a brothers four you have been!"

"Yes, we brothers four, less or more—" Drausin floated back into sleep.

In the morning Brother Augustine returned to silence in Gethsemane. As Aline, Drausin, and Lucien watched Uncle Leon's buggy head toward Alexandria, Lucien wondered at the forces that had rent their father's family asunder.

"How can we hold our Wulsins together?"

"We already do," said Aline, resting an arm around the hip of each brother, who each laid an arm on her shoulders.

"We do," said brother Drausin, "especially you two. And we three, God willing, will." Drausin followed Lucien out to the cornfields; Aline returned inside.

Maman embraced her eldest, whispering in her ear, "I am heartened now to know, chère Aline, what you have long known, that in Brother Augustine we share a partner in prayer."

CHAPTER 53:
UP TO HEAVEN, 1863

Drausin's breathing shortened, shallowed. He recalled his own haunt-dream, long gone. Valsin slave-whipper, Drauzin slave-whipped, back and forth, the grimace of each mirroring the other, a knife slice. His strange pull down to the slave markets, until he met Josephine. *The grimace curves down, around, and, rising, flowers—hibiscus.*

"Chérie," said Drausin to Josephine one morning, "my granpère, Manuel Jean-Baptiste Bacas, first came as a stranger to this land in New Orleans. If he was indeed from St. Domingue, and served in the New Orleans Negro Militia, when did he discover he could pass white? How? Why? When did he choose to hail from Genoa rather than Gonaïves?

"And my father, Barthelemy, growing up so? Did he know? He had to remember his colored childhood. He *had* to know. So Papa, too, chose to stay white. He gave his beloved Adelaïde the privilege of living with a man living white, by their laws. Though she could not marry her love. Though their nine children could not inherit his property. Oh, the twists. Even when Nonc Drauzin, my dear namesake, showed us the truth, Barthelemy could not choose it, not for the sake of his love, not for the sake of his children. The angry bastard passed as white at all costs, shattered his family, and saddened his beloved to death, dying alone."

"Remember, Cher, when you—Apollo—defeated your brother Jean-Baptiste Bacchus in the musical duel?"

Drausin grinned. "Si, si, and he slinked out the door—everyone chanting, 'Va-t-en Bacchus! Va-t-en Bacas!'" His grin fell. "Was someone always being booted out our door, one way or another? I recall Nonc Dominique Cossé dit Chevalier, banished from our home and even from his own four children, through Granpère Jean-Baptiste's will. Then our father Barthelemy banished his own four sons."

"Mon Cher, if your father held onto white in spite of his family, you and I, at least we have chosen white *for*, not *in spite of*, our family."

"Yes, Cherie, that is true. We two, we do for, not in spite of, our family. Yet now I, we, oh Chèrie, I have brought you into our Bacas curse. Who do we fool? We're cursed. As was Jean-Baptiste Manuel, as was Barthelemy, as am I—following our familial law, fixed like train tracks, our fate. Ha! Did you and I truly choose white? To escape the threat of becoming enslaved, outer maybe yes—but inner—

"At what costs? What prices do we pay, my love? What costs will our children suffer, my love? Will we too shatter, we Wulsins, my love? Disappear like Leon, dear Leon? Will we scatter? Like Jean-Baptiste, long gone to San Francisco, passing like us?

"We Wulsins, at least we enjoy jambalaya chez nous. Will Clarence enjoy jambalaya wherever he makes his home?

"Leon long ago stole; what have you and I stolen, from each of our children, my love? Are they, we, freer to be? Cutting a mule's ears doesn't make him a horse. How much of who they truly are have we cut off, hidden, in each of our dear, promising children? Have we freed them to become? Or have we erased them? Are they more visible now, or less? Are their faces finer, or fading? I do not know, I wish I knew. How much have we in fact enslaved ourselves to passing white? What have we done? What have we undone?"

Josephine stroked his brow, soothing a threatening cough; he'd been pumping up his fever. "Oh, my love, I know, I too don't know. But, however much we do not know, we *do* know at least we are one another's pond, all of us; we bathe ourselves through each other, renewing our source each night, as we go forth by day."

"Yes, you are so right, comme de'habitude. That at least is true. Of course, of course." Drausin slipped back into sleep.

Another day—"May I tell you a secret, chou-chou?" Josephine nodded. Drausin continued. "I am so tired of whites." She chuckled. He smiled.

"Yes, I like them, I respect them, I love them. I'm glad to be considered one of them, by and large, but, Chérie, these white people, they tire me, deeply tire me. Their voices are like paper, shuffling in the wind. They rarely say straight what they mean.

"Give me heart-talk, straight talk. As if they're half-deaf, they always detour into 'should' instead of 'am' and 'do'. White tires me, tires me deeply.

"For our children, at least the younger ones, white's second nature, from Laure on down—Clarence, Lillie Alice, Mary Josephine—but I worry about the strain on our older ones."

"Si, mon Cher, me too," replied Josephine. "I know, I do, but remember, thanks to you, we are making our way, we are. Did we dare so imagine, when we read the dregs in your coffee cup? Did we dare to hope? That it could be so, that it could be this? It is so, and it will be so.

"For us, in our time, our ship is white; white we can sail, here, now. This white boat floats. So long as our crew sails savvy. And you've shown us each how to captain, when our turn comes."

"Oh, my sweet, ever my first mate, our real captain. You keep the ship ship-shape—ma Chère, your mother used to say, the more we fear harm, the more fear harms. We must let our children forget, let them sail this white ship, Chérie. This we have to do."

"I will try, I'll surely try."

Another night—"Ma Chère, Granpère Manuel Jean-Baptiste bought teenage Adelaïde Beaulieu, and others. Barthelemy owned Alfonce, Nelson, Ernestine, Marcelite, and others. Former slave Adelaïde Pouponne owned others, too, though she freed Ernestine, Marcelite, and Chloe, but not Chloe's children, and she sold Rose and Betsy.

"And you and I—we bought Claire, in spite of ourselves, overwhelmed with babies as we were; we finally freed her when we freed ourselves from New Orleans. Not only have you and I perpetuated, but we have perpetrated. We have forged links in that cursed chain—we chose to own another. We are links; are we passing that cursed chain on to our children and theirs, if not outwardly, inwardly? Are we, my companion in love and in liberty? Oh, we juggle the devil's torches, willy nilly."

"Si, mon amour, we are links, I, and mine, mon Cher. Ma granmère Marie-Françoise Lalande, daughter of a slave, and my mother Josephine Tassey Mathé both supported themselves savvily investing in slaves as well as land. And my father Samuel Young, of course—Black Betty and others—and yes, notre chère Claire. All of us, our hands, our souls, are dirty. So many strands form our knot.

"But—Aline and I know, we are not all tied for all time. Neither our ancestors, nor our descendants. Through our prayers today we, like Christ, can harrow Hell, can heal soiled souls, both back in time and forward in time. Prayer can pardon. Prayer can purge, can purge, mon Cher, time past, time forth, je t'assure."

"Oh, Chèrie, pray so. I hope. I so hope."

"Ma Jose, I had a dream—back in the woodshop battle, our father Barthelemy chose true, reclaimed Gonaïve over Genoa, shed white, wed Maman, and we all crafted cabinets in closing circles in New Orleans."

"And—"

"And—there were no Wulsins, anywhere, in the whole world, not a Wulsin white in Cincinnati."

Both pondered that picture long.

Josephine looked into her husband's brown eyes, reflecting her greens. She leaned close, face to face, whispering, "The blessing of a curse?"

Drausin, after silence, nodded with a new smile she'd never seen.

"Grâce à Dieu?" he asked.

"Grâce à Dieu."

"Chérie?"

"Si, mon amour?"

"Do you think that having to clarify, having to spell 'Wulsin' aloud almost daily all their lives might somehow strengthen our children?"

"Si, mon amour, I think it just might strengthen our children."

"And their children?"

"Si, and their children's children's children."

"Chou-chou?"

"Si, Chérie?"

"We age all over, everywhere, except, when I look into your eyes, I see ageless you."

"Ahh," Drausin smiled. "And I see ageless you."

"Chèrie."

"Si, mon Apollo?"

"Is it possible that all our efforts to save our children from shackles, from whip and rape, that feeding them our very own gumbo, that dressing them in white, that all *that*, for better and for worse, may not after all hold a candle to the light of who each child is and will become, whatever the betters and the worses we chose? Is this thought heresy, ma chère Josie?"

"Non, pas de tout, mon Drauzin, my Drausin. When all those layers fall away, the flame of each of us remains. This I know to be true."

One midnight hour: "I did not much make, or find my way—"

"Mon Cher, you made, you found *our* way, our way."

"Yes, that is true, ma chère. My parents, together as two all those years, could not hold us nine together; we scattered, shards—ma pauvre mère—"

"And my parents, white Samuel Young and octaroon Josephine Tassey, could not unite for long. Then we grafted with Simeon Mathé. You, mon Cher, have fathered one mighty tribe, like Jacob."

Drausin chuckled. "And you, my Rachel, water at the well. We have only ten, not thirteen, and now only eight."

"But you, Cher, you and I together, we have held our family whole, for thirty-three years now. And for thirty-three years you have been our glue."

He shook his head. "No, you are the glue. I—maybe our

music." Drausin paused. "I'm sorry the farm was not our answer. No Cincinnatus I."

"Well, it may not have saved you, but it has planted seeds in us all, for generations, for *generations*, mon Cher. We were right to move, to Cincinnati, and to the farm. Cincinnati: We: Oui."

"Ma Chère, I'm like one of those oxbow ports on the old Mississippi; one night the river breaks on through, and I'm already drying up inland. I've been an eye, an ear, but what have I put my hand to? I've long receded to the periphery, almost disappearing, except I will not survive to tell the tale."

"Cher, mon héros, our children and our children's children will write the tale we only began—for them to tell."

Drausin smiled, then frowned. "Chérie, our young Drausin will navigate with his mind. But Lucien, he could give till his heart bursts. You must not let the farm crush Lucien. How long can his young back shoulder two hundred and twenty acres? He's too young to Atlas; fear not—let the farm go, if that's needed to let each go forth."

"Si, chou-chou. Si."

"Jose, ma Jose, remember I told you how as a boy I loved to stir alum into the ollas full of muddy Mississippi River water? Stirring all around one way, then all around the other way, until the alum let the sediment settle, clarifying the upper waters for drinking. Do you think you and I have been clarifying the waters of my life?"

"Si, mon cher Cher, I do indeed think we have been trying, 'clarifying' the muddy waters of your life, of our lives, clarifying our Mississippis, indeed, you and I."

"In these our last days and nights together?"

"Yes, Chou-chou, in these our last days and nights together. When we remeet on the other side, we'll be well beyond days and nights."

"Aline," Drausin called his daughter to him, reaching for her hand. "Ma chère Aline Adelaïde, you are still here with us, thank heavens. Many years I thought you would leave, one direction or another. Have you chosen to remain? Or have you felt you could not go?"

"Cher Papa," she sandwiched his hand in hers. "My heart has reached wide, and it beats close. I trust its way. Yes, its way is here; here I embrace."

"As Maman says, 'Que Dieu te bénisse.' It gives me peace to know you will stand shoulder to shoulder with your mother these coming years. She is strong, but she can strain—and, Aline, do not let Lucien break his back."

Aline started to smile, then saw how deep was her father's concern. "Si, si Papa. T'en fait pas. Tout va bien." Aline kissed him on his brow. Relieved, Drausin slipped back into sleep.

Another evening, after supper, Drausin asked for Lucien, who came in quietly. "Lucien, my moonshine boy, my mightiest man, I am sorry to have moved us all to our farm we have come to love. I am sorry I have become too weak to work alongside you. I see the barn, the farm, the animals, the fields all on your shoulders. I feel I have failed you as a father and as a fellow farmer."

"On the contrary, mon cher Papa, what you have accomplished in our family, with your ear listening, has given us all the best tools possible to make our way in this whole country up here. I know not what I will find, what I will do, but I know I can tune in, can harmonize, can blend, in ways that will work, whatever my work, thanks to you, cher Papa." Lucien kissed his fading father on his brow.

Drausin slept, relieved of some of Lucien's load.

Josephine whispered, stroking his brow, "I have loved being the apron that serves your pants."

"Ha, we all know the apron directs the pants, and the pants serve the apron, which I have loved," Drausin smiled, kissing her hand, "ever since you lavendered into view on the bayou. Do I see you, emerald eyes on bayou?"

"Is that you, my handsomest, brow and jaw, crowned in glints of light?" she responded. "Marie LaVeau knew, the Voodoun Queen knew. When I told her you surprised me shining in glints of light by the waters of Bayou St. Jean, she said, 'Gilded splinters, gilded splinters, he's your one.' She knew you to be my true."

After a cool compress, Josephine held Drausin's hot hand. She sang to him ever so softly some of the lullaby she had sung to babies Barthelemy, Aline, Ti-Drauzin, Lucien—all her ten babies, right through to Adhemar. "Fe dodo, mo fils, crab dans calalou. Go to sleep, my son, crab is in the shell. Papa, li couri la riviere. Papa has gone to the river."

Drausin smiled, eyes closed, hearing a duet with his mother Adelaïde Pouponne Beaulieu and his wife Josephine Young, seeing as well a parade of their own ten babies circling 'round him, hand in hand, singing along in chorus, gilded splinters crowning each.

Another time, Josephine heard Drausin singing low, almost muttering,

> Nègre pas capab marche sans mais,
> Milatte pas capab marche sans corde,
> Blanc pas capa marche sans l'arzan.

> Negro cannot walk without corn,
> Mulatto cannot walk without rope,
> White man cannot walk without money.

Drausin recalled his failing father Barthelemy saying of his departed Adelaïde, parents of nine children together, that though they had become vieux commes les chemins, old like roads, and in spite of his falling apart her final year, they were amoureux comme deux colombes, loving like two doves.

"Ma chère Josephine, nous aussi, nous sommes amoureux comme deux colombes—you are always my Daphne, my laurel tree. Oh-o-oh, Mah Lady, Oh-o-oh, Mah Lady, Oh-o-oh, Mah Lady Jo-o-oe! Or—you, my Orpheus's Eurydice?" Drausin felt himself reaching for her. Who now was fading though, receding, back into black mists?

Drausin asked for his old mandolin. Unable any longer to lift it, he rested it on his chest, letting his fingers walk the neck, then skip, pluck, finding the song his ears longed to hear.

> Ma Creole Belle,
> I love you well,
> My Darlin' ba-by
> Ma Creole Belle.

Our stars do shine,
You're ever mine,
My darlin' Jo-o-osie
Ma Creole Belle.

Josephine lifted the mandolin from under his limp arm, leaned over his closed eye-lids, paper-brittle, and whispered into his cool ear, "Mo coeur tâcher dans to chaîne comme boskoyo dans cypière." My heart is linked in your chain like cypress knees.

Drausin remembered first hearing these words as young Josephine whispered in his ear outside Cathedral St. Louis. They had eased his agony after her stepfather, Simeon Mathé, forbade them from seeing each other, much less marrying. Josephine's whispered words then gave Drauzin hope to persist in his pursuit—and now they eased his letting go.

Drausin dreams—An apple tree—Lightning strikes the tree; eight apples survive, seeding.

Drausin to Josephine: "Sleeping, I find how I die."

Late-summer thunder sounds through the window.

Drausin: "Some say Bon Dieu rolls his stones—
others say Devil drives his two black horses and char-
iot across the sky—

"Josephine, I see no more shadows. Where do shadows go?"

Josephine gave the nod to Aline; brother Drausin headed off in the buggy to fetch Father Patrick from Newport to administer last rites, the Commendation of the Dying.

James Gray helped the boys build a pine box, which Papa Drausin, former cabinetmaker, could have done alone one afternoon.

The Wulsins gathered around. Papa Drausin, smile slight, gazed at each: Josephine, Aline, Drausin, Lucien, Laure, Clarence, Lillie, Mary Josephine. "Eugene?"

Lucien: "Eugene rides his horse in Georgia, Papa."

Drausin nodded. "I wish him long life. Adhemar?"

Aline: "Adhemar lies in his box beneath the catalpa tree, Papa."

Drausin nodded, looked at Josephine again, and closed his eyes. They knew their father had practiced dying for years. *It's time to reap*, thought Lucien, eyes moist. As they turned to let him rest, a weak whisper held them another moment.

"Mes enfants—" eyes still closed.

"Si, Papa."

"Take care of each other, each sister, each brother. Cast no one out."

"Si, Papa," replied each.

"Always," added Aline, who had already been including those on the other side in her attentions.

Understanding, Papa smiled.

Although his father had taught Lucien to plow two years ago, he of course had been little help since. Lucien felt he was looking at the shell of the man. As he himself swelled with muscle, his father became an egg leaking out of a hole in its shell. Not having seen him walk for weeks, Lucien realized he missed his father's stride. Not that it was striking. Quite the opposite. But he remembered his mother speaking of loving to dance with his father because he led, not her, not with his arms or feet, but *around* her, through the music; he let the music lead them together, that was it.

Lucien also remembered his Granpère Barthelemy dominating rooms like a storm, a flood. *Our father's movement was not like someone barging into a room. Not like someone shouting. More like someone listening, with his whole being.* Lucien had taken for granted all his life but had not realized until now that *our father's very presence was like a tuning fork, bringing everyone into tune with themselves and with each other. Even enabling Kaintuck to become Declan with us back on the Natchez III.* As Papa waned fast, Lucien newly appreciated their father's lifelong new-moon gesture, allowing room for each one's presence.

Drausin, from what Josephine could figure from fragments, was conversing—with Maman Adelaïde, Granpère Manuel Jean-Baptiste, Père Barthelemy, Nonc Drauzin, brother Joseph Valmont, nephew Adhemar, baby Barthelemy, baby Adhemar—

In his last hours Josephine sang for him, ever so softly.

I'm coming, I'm coming, and my head is hanging low,
I hear their gentle voices calling,
Old Black Joe.
I hear their gentle voices calling,
Old Black Joe.

At eight-thirty in the morning of August 25, 1863, Drausin Wulsin's final breath glided over gasps.

At two-thirty that afternoon, the family Wulsin, along with James, Margaret, and little Lucien Gray, buried Papa

Drausin Wulsin in his fresh pine box next to Adhemar, up the ridge beneath the catalpa tree's heart-shaped leaves, about halfway between the farmhouse and the yellow former slave house. Lucien's shoulders ached. He knew the farm's two hundred twenty acres now weighed on him alone.

A rooster crowed. Mourning doves coo-whooed low and long.

The New Orleans *Picayune* printed news of the death in Cincinnati of Drauzin Valsin Bacas, age forty-nine. That city knew who was who.

- FIN -

Lucien:
I Too Shall Pass

TWELVE YEARS AFTER THE DEATH
OF DRAUSIN I

Lucien Wulsin returned to the upstate New York Adirondacks wilderness in the summer of 1874. Chase Davis had told Lucien to meet him in Albany. Surprise. A lady on each of Davis's arms joined them for the journey, all the way to Bisby Lake. Audrey and Madeleine, cheery, soft, hardly hardy. Equally spooked by mouse and moose. Hardly the atmosphere of the previous summer. When, after several days, the ladies were shipped, miffed, back to Albany, Maurice and Wilkinson made clear that the presence of the feminine persuasion did not fit at Bisby Lake: "No room for Eve in our Eden." Davis and Wulsin acknowledged and apologized.

When Lucien returned to Bisby Lake in '75, the main lodge felt like the icehouse, not the hearth of the camp. When he closed his good eye, he saw brown waters roiling above the floor. After supper, Lucien asked. Silence. Wilkinson, eyes and mouth angling up to the right under tousled hair, and melancholy

Maurice looked at each other. Wilkinson then said, "Wulsin, this last week, before you arrived, we formed a legal entity, the Bisby Club, owning this lake and its surrounding land."

This seemed like a wise development, though its timing struck Lucien as strange.

"We?" Silence.

"Yes, we three, Maurice, Wilkinson, and Davis," said Wilkinson.

"Why, if I may ask?" Lucien had not seen this exclusion coming.

"Why, the ladies last summer. That broke our code."

"I see," said Lucien, looking over at Chase Davis, whose eyes were fixed on the fire. This news shocked Lucien, though it certainly explained the ice. Yet it did not explain Davis, whose initiative those ladies of the night had been.

"I see, I certainly see." Lucien looked into Wilkinson's eyes, which were a wall, then into Maurice's eyes, which were fog. Davis stuck to the fire.

"Well, gentlemen, in that case, although I have enjoyed our adventures at Bisby Lake, you shall not see me here again."

"Wulsin, you are not welcome here again," said Wilkinson.

As Lucien packed his backpack in his room, he overheard Davis complain. Wilkinson asserted, "Look, Davis, Wulsin himself is okay, but we can't have a nigger in the woodpile." Lucien shouldered his pack and slipped into the black night's back country.

He trekked for hours, up along Lower Sylvan, then along Upper Sylvan. Part of Lucien wanted to bash branches, hurl rocks, and howl. "Complot plis fort passé orange," he recalled his Granmère Josephine saying when he was too young to have a clue as to its meaning. "Conspiracy is stronger than witchcraft." Those Bisby boys sure spooked him out of his place in the place.

But in time Lucien settled into his rhythm, quiet as a buck, placing each footstep carefully, his soft moccasins feeling the contour of the land beneath him before releasing his weight onto it. Sometimes he felt almost a mattress of rich humus from ancient leaves, sometimes smooth granite shelves. Sometimes his feet felt an animal path opening up the woods for him. He listened keenly to every sound—the night-talk, the chuck-chuck of a lynx, the short-short-long of the whippoorwills. The dark began to reveal itself, allowing him to read the forest terrain increasingly accurately. He felt the wild move more and more through him, less and less at him. After half the night, Lucien's blood felt purged of the bile enough for him to rest, which he did beneath a curving cedar by a stream. He tied a line to the cedar, threading it through his light tube-tarp, tying the other end low on a nearby birch. He crawled inside the baglike shelter and pulled his slouch-hat's cheesecloth mosquito netting over his face and neck to his shoulders.

In my thirty years, colored young, white the rest of my life, I have largely slipped through the strains, pains, and conflicts of most of my folk. I remember my parents had occasional doubts about their decision to pass. Occasional? Must have been constant. When I was just six, Kaintuck's hostility toward us turned into tales and affection on the Natchez III's trip north from New Orleans up the Mississippi. Those first days of school in Cincinnati, Irish boys teased me to tears till brother Drausin silenced them. I became a Findlay Market fixture. Cincinnati seemed to acquire a taste for me as one of its own. The habit has become mine as much as Cincinnati's. The war certainly leveled us all. The Invincibles have chosen me as their secretary. Mr. Baldwin promoted me to partner. Pathways of promise.

And now, my friends at Bisby Lake have turned out to be black bears. Are we always, in fact, blind? Chase Davis of Grandin Road, cousin of my dear canoe camarado Nick Longworth. Will Nick turn out to be a black bear, too? I can't imagine that. But I did not imagine this. Is this the beginning of the end? Possibly. Will my banishment from Bisby Lake affect brother Drausin's future in law back in Cincinnati? Will the Baldwin Piano Company drop me? Have I turned out to actually be just the nigger I joked to Drausin about having as his valet at Fort McHenry? Will we Wulsins be moving from 349 Richmond over to Bucktown? Who knows? My life right now feels as fragile as a birchbark canoe. What will I do?

As Lucien finally slipped into sleep, another ancestral proverb surfaced, in his father's voice. "Ça ou pédi nen fè ou va trouvé nen sann; what you lose in the fire, you'll find in the ashes."

Lucien forgot it the next day.

ABOUT ATMOSPHERE PRESS

Founded in 2015, Atmosphere Press was built on the principles of Honesty, Transparency, Professionalism, Kindness, and Making Your Book Awesome. As an ethical and author-friendly hybrid press, we stay true to that founding mission today.

If you're a reader, enter our giveaway for a free book here:

SCAN TO ENTER
BOOK GIVEAWAY

If you're a writer, submit your manuscript for consideration here:

SCAN TO SUBMIT
MANUSCRIPT

And always feel free to visit Atmosphere Press and our authors online at atmospherepress.com. See you there soon!

ABOUT THE AUTHOR

JOHN WULSIN taught high school English for forty years, mostly at Green Meadow Waldorf School in Spring Valley, New York. With degrees in English and American Language and Literature from Harvard (A.B.) and Columbia (M.A.), he also taught numerous adult courses in the History of English Poetry. He participated in frequent writer's workshops on poetry, especially with poets Dan Masterson and Suzanne Cleary. He took numerous workshops sponsored by the Texas Writer's League. He edited *The Riddle of America* and coedited *Books for the Journey*. He also authored *The Spirit of the English Language*.

John is currently revising his second novel, *Lucien: I Too Shall Pass*, with Austin's Atmosphere Press (2025).

9 798891 324978